Still Pickled After All These Years

A Comic Collection by Brian Crane

Andrews McMeel
Publishing

Kansas City

Pickles is syndicated by the Washington Post Writers Group.

Still Pickled After All These Years copyright © 2004 by Brian Crane. All rights reserved. Printed in the United States of America. No part of this book may be used or reproduced in any manner whatsoever without written permission except in the case of reprints in the context of reviews. For information, write Andrews McMeel Publishing, an Andrews McMeel Universal company, 4520 Main Street, Kansas City, Missouri 64111.

04 05 06 07 08 BBG 10 9 8 7 6 5 4 3 2 1

ISBN: 0-7407-4340-6

Library of Congress Control Number: 2003113250

For my wonderful children, Matthew, Emily, Sarah, Amy, Jonathan, Christina, and Laura. I'm dedicating this book to you instead of buying birthday presents this year.

Love,
Dad

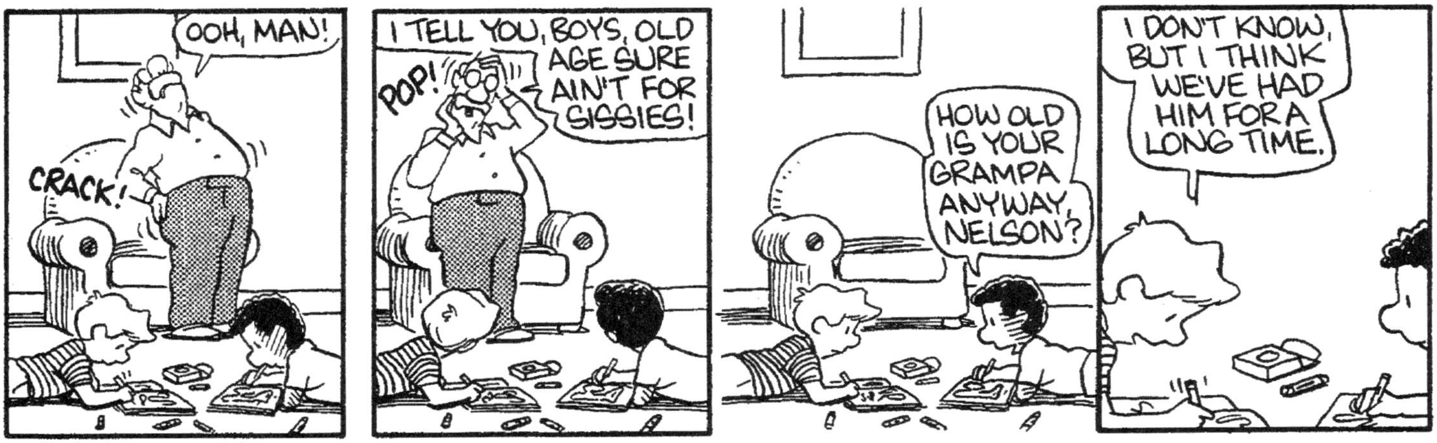
OOH, MAN!
CRACK!
I TELL YOU, BOYS, OLD AGE SURE AIN'T FOR SISSIES!
POP!
HOW OLD IS YOUR GRAMPA ANYWAY, NELSON?
I DON'T KNOW, BUT I THINK WE'VE HAD HIM FOR A LONG TIME.

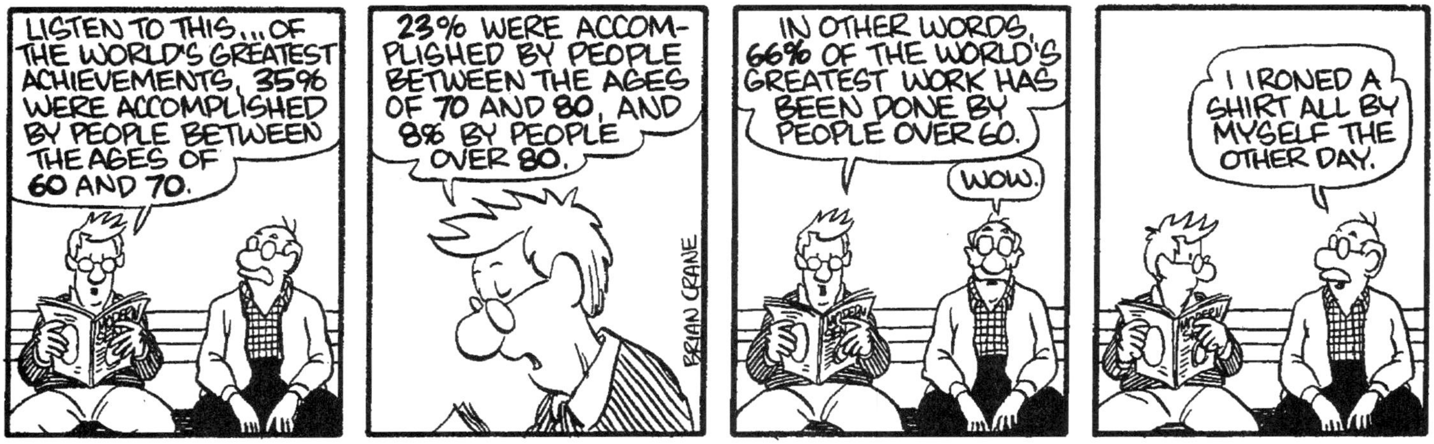
LISTEN TO THIS... OF THE WORLD'S GREATEST ACHIEVEMENTS, 35% WERE ACCOMPLISHED BY PEOPLE BETWEEN THE AGES OF 60 AND 70.
23% WERE ACCOMPLISHED BY PEOPLE BETWEEN THE AGES OF 70 AND 80, AND 8% BY PEOPLE OVER 80.
BRIAN CRANE
IN OTHER WORDS, 66% OF THE WORLD'S GREATEST WORK HAS BEEN DONE BY PEOPLE OVER 60.
WOW.
I IRONED A SHIRT ALL BY MYSELF THE OTHER DAY.

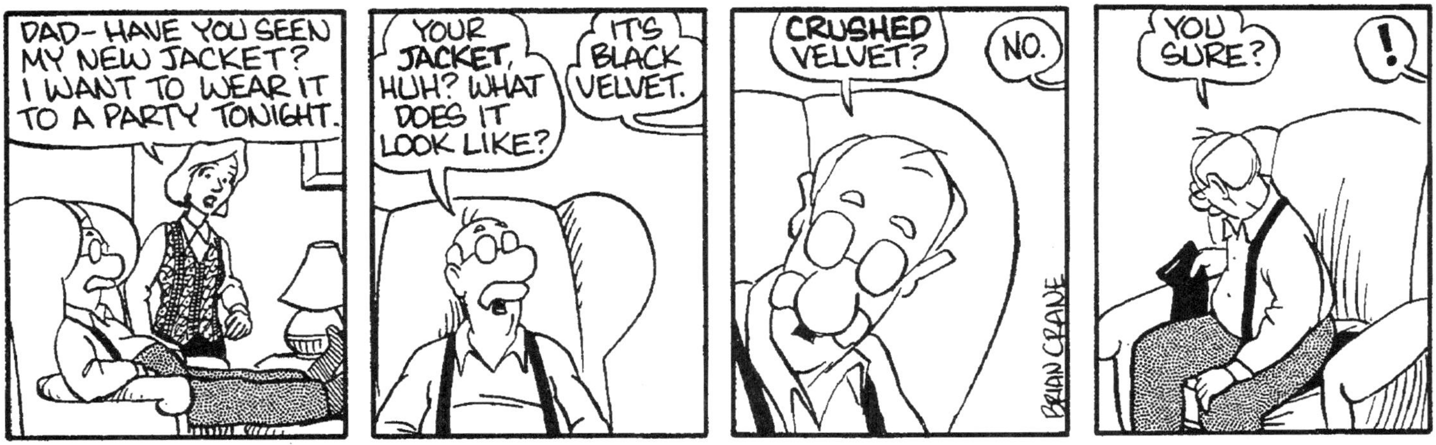
DAD- HAVE YOU SEEN MY NEW JACKET? I WANT TO WEAR IT TO A PARTY TONIGHT.
YOUR JACKET, HUH? WHAT DOES IT LOOK LIKE?
IT'S BLACK VELVET.
CRUSHED VELVET?
NO.
BRIAN CRANE
YOU SURE?
!

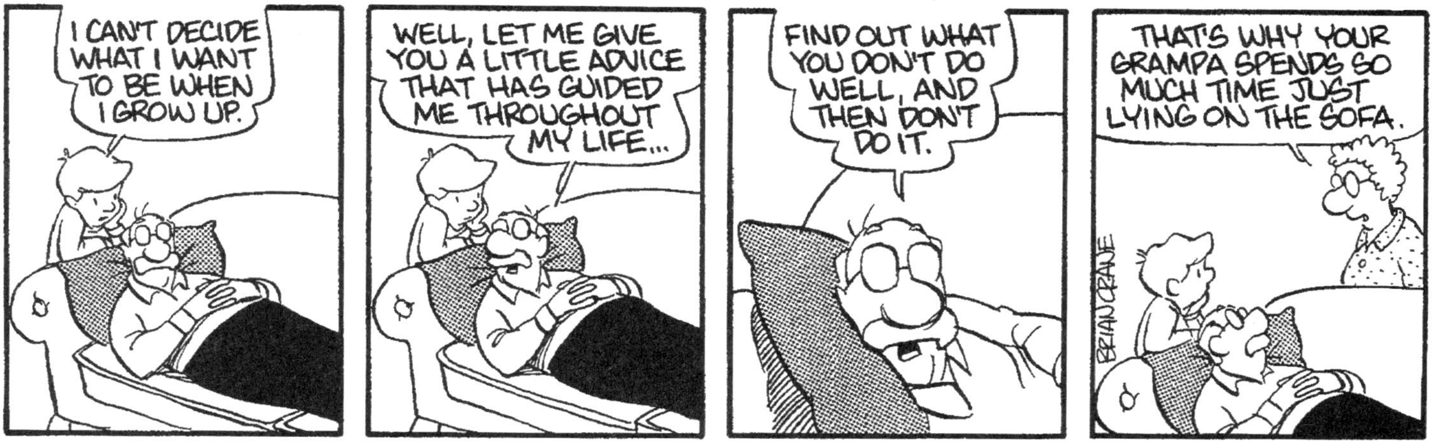
I CAN'T DECIDE WHAT I WANT TO BE WHEN I GROW UP.
WELL, LET ME GIVE YOU A LITTLE ADVICE THAT HAS GUIDED ME THROUGHOUT MY LIFE...
FIND OUT WHAT YOU DON'T DO WELL, AND THEN DON'T DO IT.
THAT'S WHY YOUR GRAMPA SPENDS SO MUCH TIME JUST LYING ON THE SOFA.
BRIAN CRANE

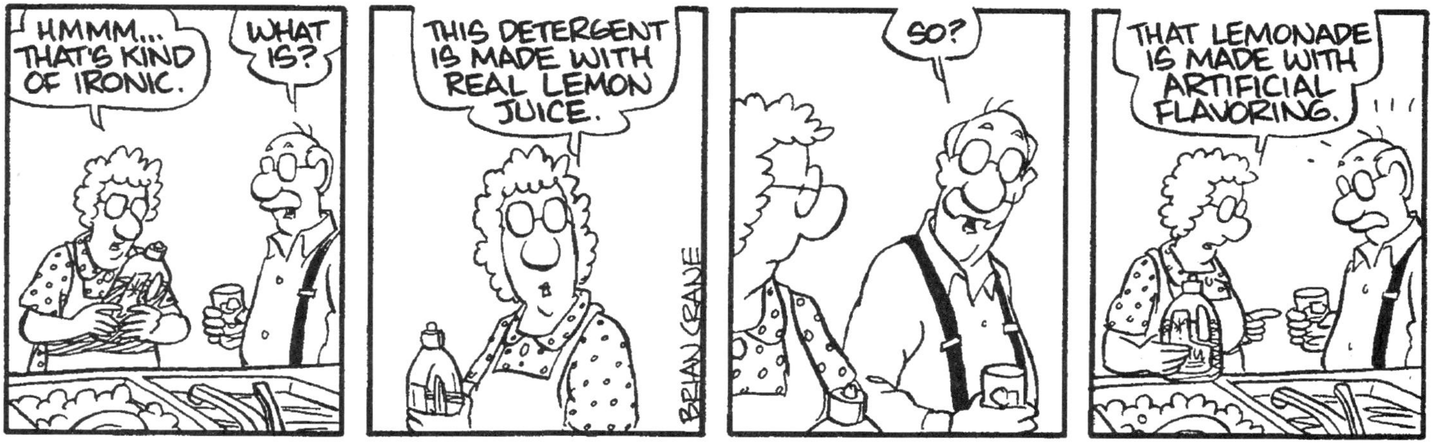
HMMM... THAT'S KIND OF IRONIC.
WHAT IS?
THIS DETERGENT IS MADE WITH REAL LEMON JUICE.
BRIAN CRANE
SO?
THAT LEMONADE IS MADE WITH ARTIFICIAL FLAVORING.

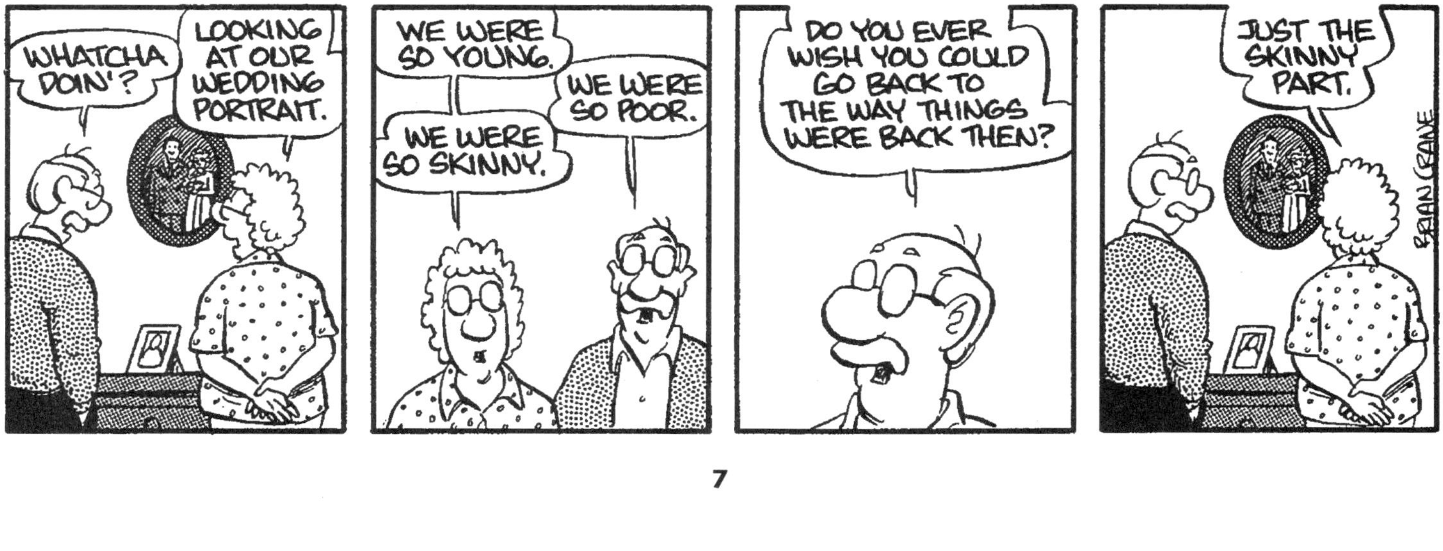
WHATCHA DOIN'?
LOOKING AT OUR WEDDING PORTRAIT.
WE WERE SO YOUNG.
WE WERE SO SKINNY.
WE WERE SO POOR.
DO YOU EVER WISH YOU COULD GO BACK TO THE WAY THINGS WERE BACK THEN?
JUST THE SKINNY PART.
BRIAN CRANE

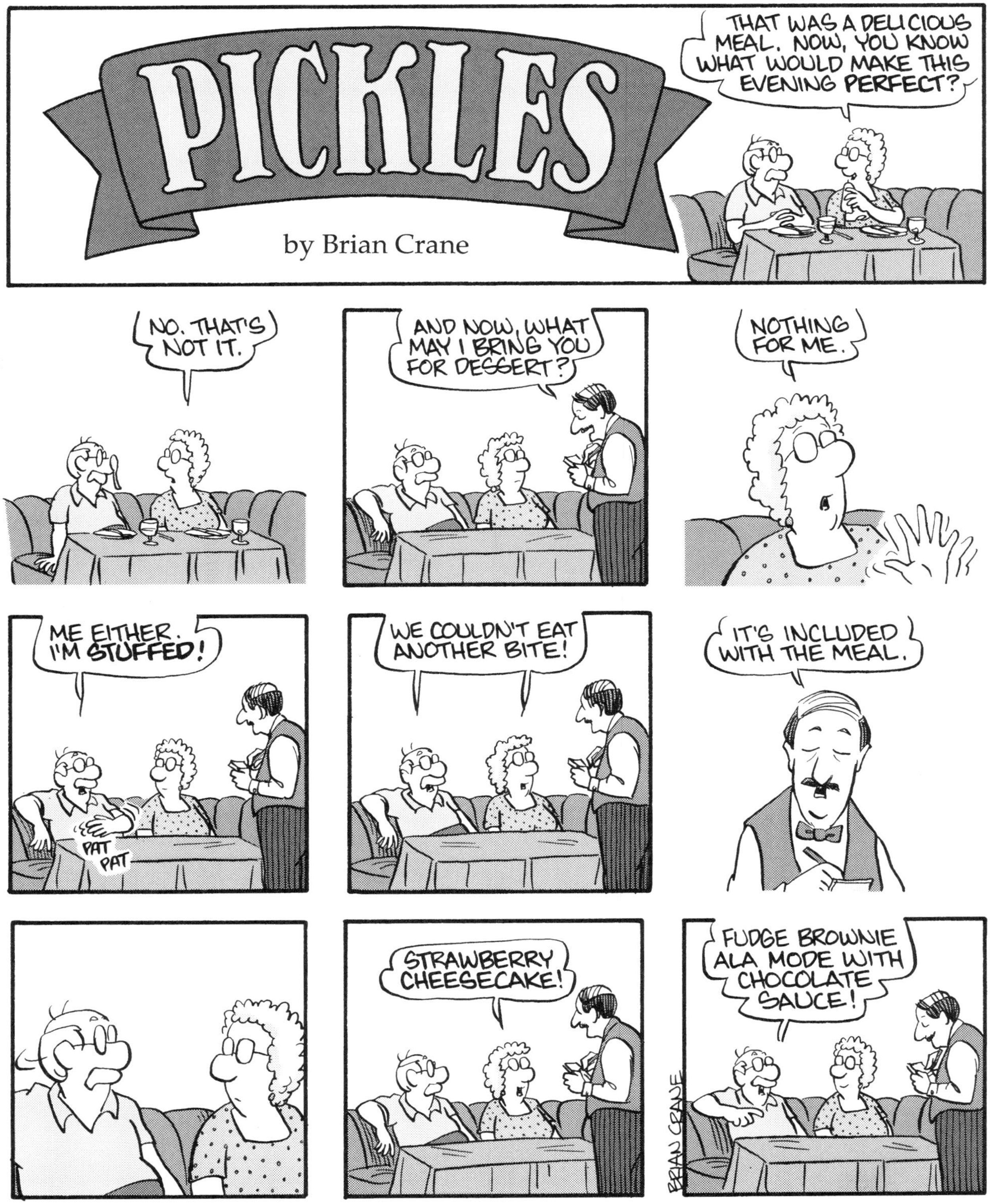
PICKLES
by Brian Crane
THAT WAS A DELICIOUS MEAL. NOW, YOU KNOW WHAT WOULD MAKE THIS EVENING PERFECT?
NO. THAT'S NOT IT.
AND NOW, WHAT MAY I BRING YOU FOR DESSERT?
NOTHING FOR ME.
ME EITHER. I'M STUFFED!
PAT PAT
WE COULDN'T EAT ANOTHER BITE!
IT'S INCLUDED WITH THE MEAL.
STRAWBERRY CHEESECAKE!
FUDGE BROWNIE ALA MODE WITH CHOCOLATE SAUCE!
BRIAN CRANE

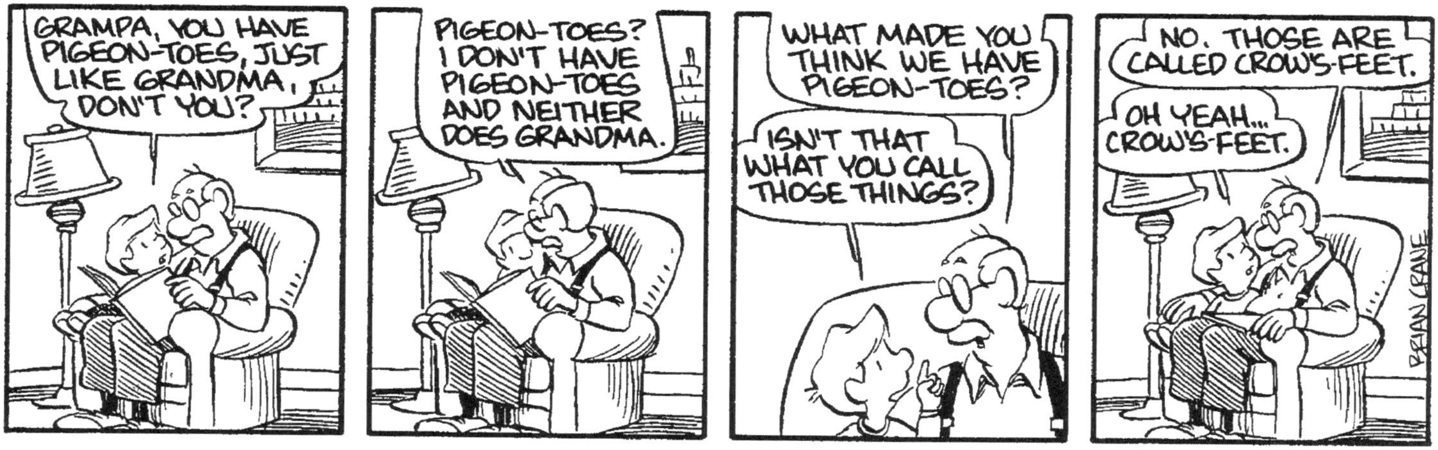
GRAMPA, YOU HAVE PIGEON-TOES, JUST LIKE GRANDMA, DON'T YOU?
PIGEON-TOES? I DON'T HAVE PIGEON-TOES AND NEITHER DOES GRANDMA.
WHAT MADE YOU THINK WE HAVE PIGEON-TOES?
ISN'T THAT WHAT YOU CALL THOSE THINGS?
NO. THOSE ARE CALLED CROW'S-FEET.
OH YEAH... CROW'S-FEET.
BRIAN CRANE

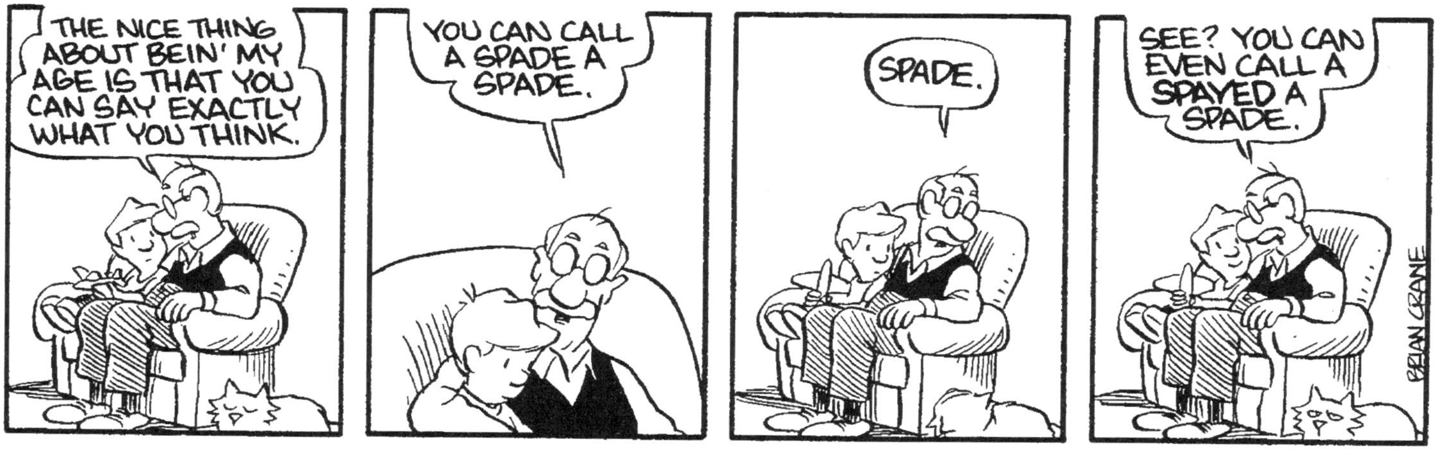
THE NICE THING ABOUT BEIN' MY AGE IS THAT YOU CAN SAY EXACTLY WHAT YOU THINK.
YOU CAN CALL A SPADE A SPADE.
SPADE.
SEE? YOU CAN EVEN CALL A SPAYED A SPADE.
BRIAN CRANE

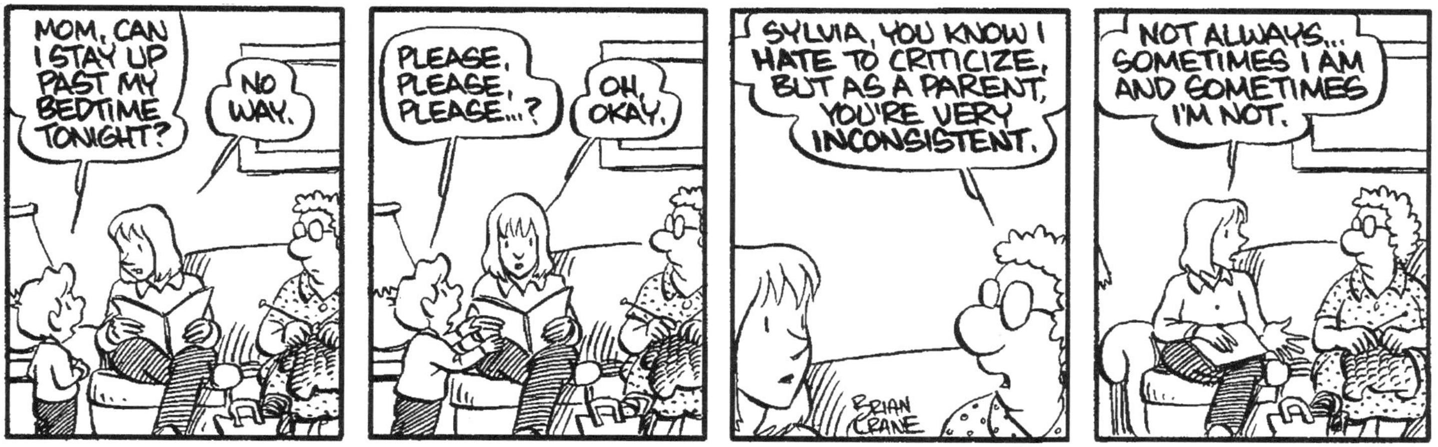
MOM, CAN I STAY UP PAST MY BEDTIME TONIGHT?
NO WAY.
PLEASE, PLEASE, PLEASE...?
OH, OKAY.
SYLVIA, YOU KNOW I HATE TO CRITICIZE, BUT AS A PARENT, YOU'RE VERY INCONSISTENT.
BRIAN CRANE
NOT ALWAYS... SOMETIMES I AM AND SOMETIMES I'M NOT.

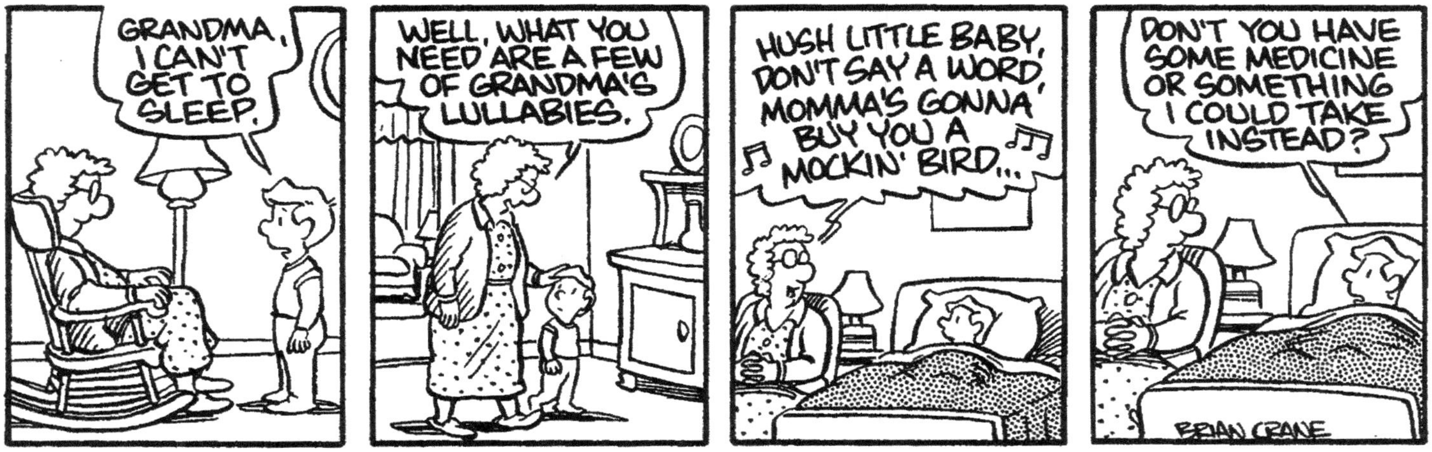
GRANDMA, I CAN'T GET TO SLEEP.
WELL, WHAT YOU NEED ARE A FEW OF GRANDMA'S LULLABIES.
HUSH LITTLE BABY, DON'T SAY A WORD, MOMMA'S GONNA BUY YOU A MOCKIN' BIRD...
DON'T YOU HAVE SOME MEDICINE OR SOMETHING I COULD TAKE INSTEAD?
BRIAN CRANE

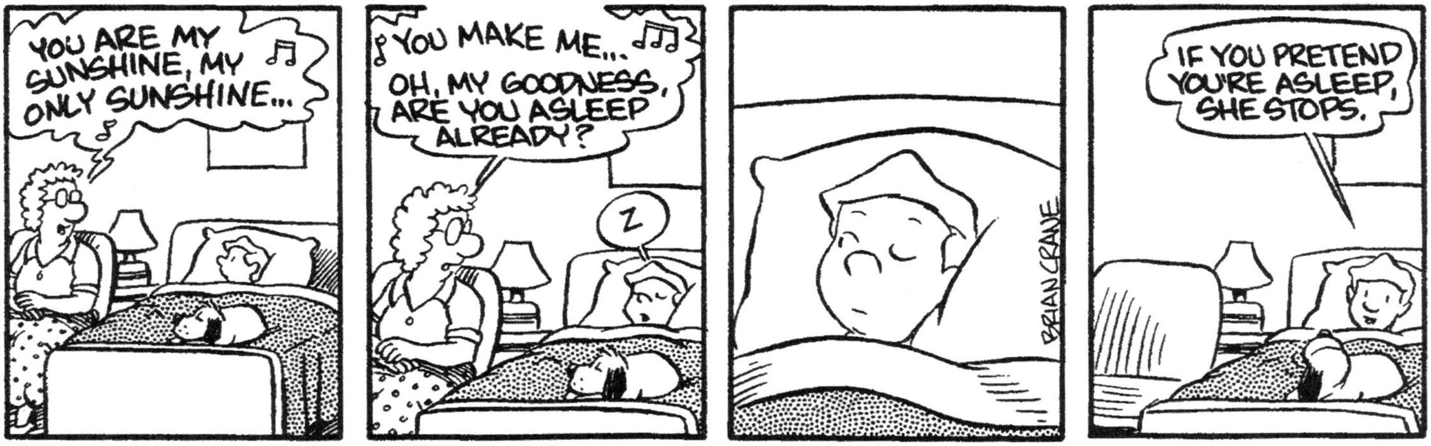
YOU ARE MY SUNSHINE, MY ONLY SUNSHINE...
YOU MAKE ME...
OH, MY GOODNESS, ARE YOU ASLEEP ALREADY?
Z
BRIAN CRANE
IF YOU PRETEND YOU'RE ASLEEP, SHE STOPS.

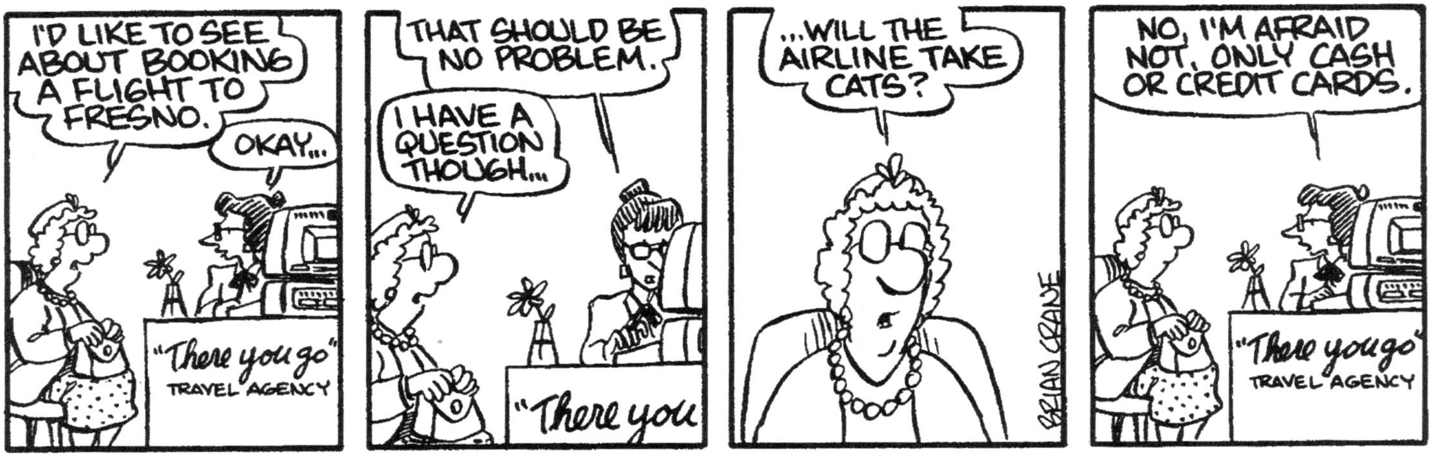
I'D LIKE TO SEE ABOUT BOOKING A FLIGHT TO FRESNO.
OKAY...
"There you go" TRAVEL AGENCY
THAT SHOULD BE NO PROBLEM.
I HAVE A QUESTION THOUGH...
"There you
...WILL THE AIRLINE TAKE CATS?
BRIAN CRANE
NO, I'M AFRAID NOT. ONLY CASH OR CREDIT CARDS.
"There you go" TRAVEL AGENCY

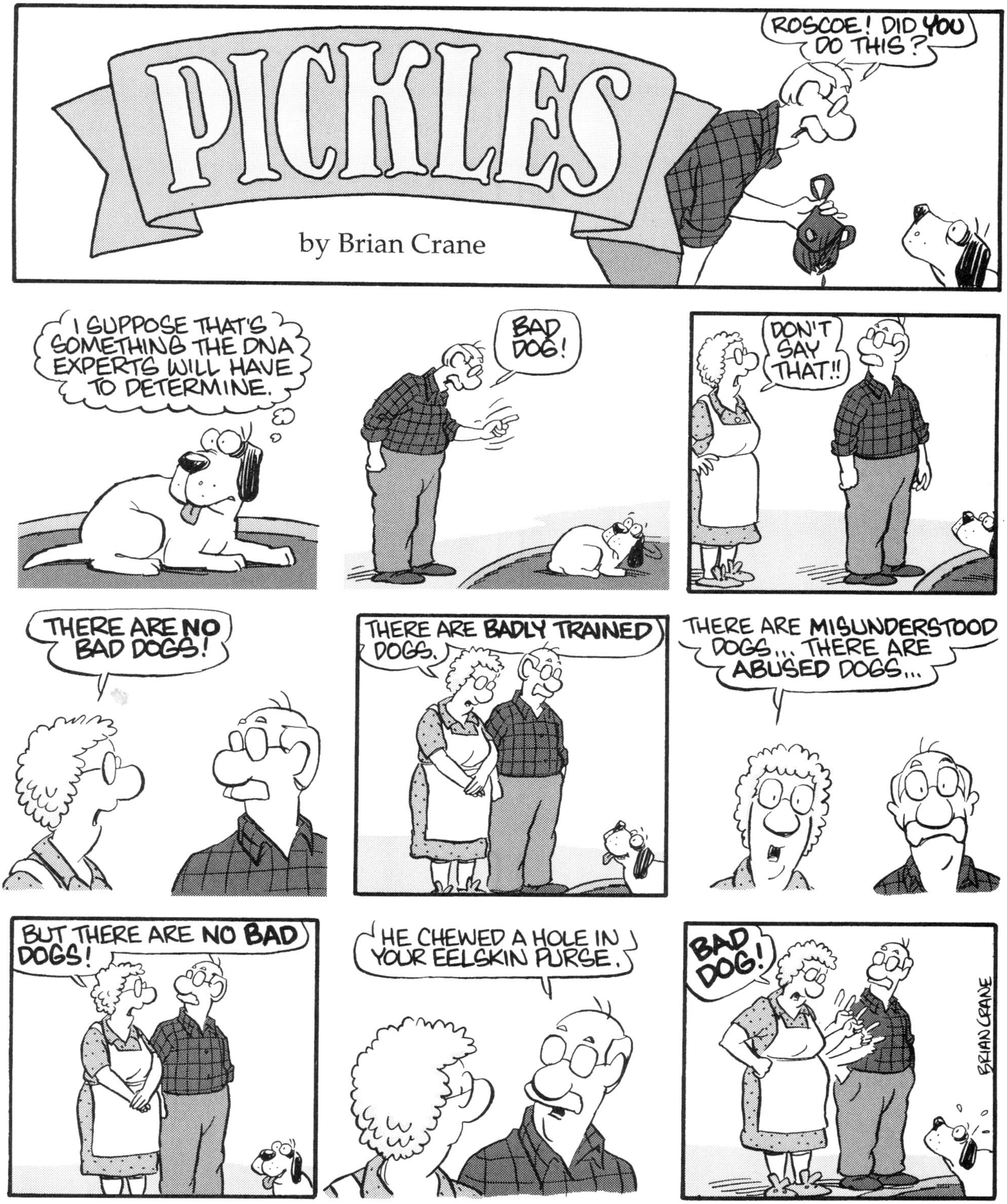
PICKLES
by Brian Crane
ROSCOE! DID YOU DO THIS?
I SUPPOSE THAT'S SOMETHING THE DNA EXPERTS WILL HAVE TO DETERMINE.
BAD DOG!
DON'T SAY THAT!!
THERE ARE NO BAD DOGS!
THERE ARE BADLY TRAINED DOGS.
THERE ARE MISUNDERSTOOD DOGS... THERE ARE ABUSED DOGS...
BUT THERE ARE NO BAD DOGS!
HE CHEWED A HOLE IN YOUR EELSKIN PURSE.
BAD DOG!
BRIAN CRANE

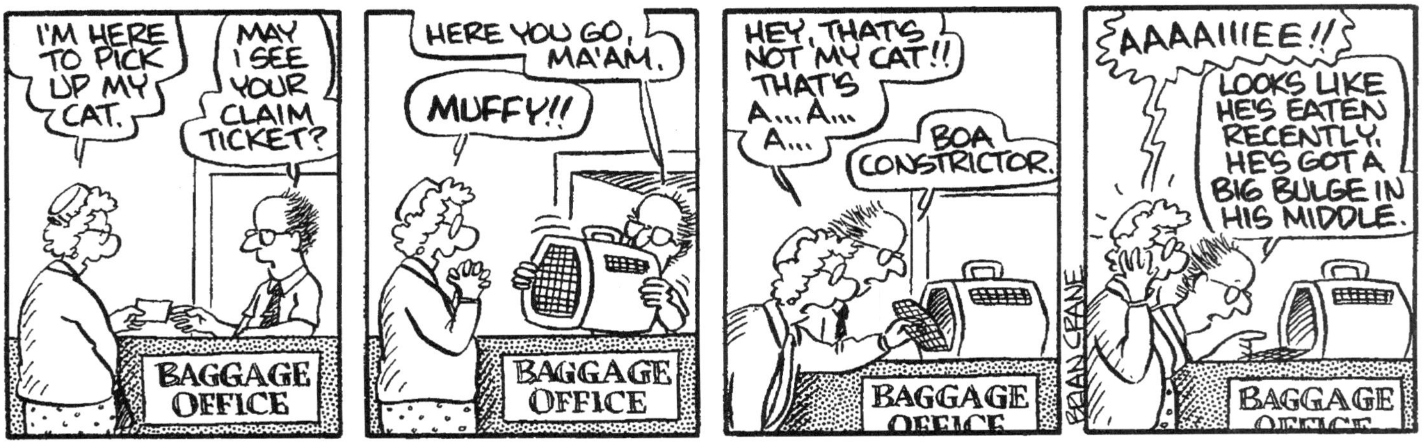
I'M HERE TO PICK UP MY CAT.
MAY I SEE YOUR CLAIM TICKET?
BAGGAGE OFFICE
HERE YOU GO, MA'AM.
MUFFY!!
BAGGAGE OFFICE
HEY, THAT'S NOT MY CAT!! THAT'S A... A... A...
BOA CONSTRICTOR.
BAGGAGE OFFICE
BRIAN CRANE
AAAAIIIEE!!
LOOKS LIKE HE'S EATEN RECENTLY. HE'S GOT A BIG BULGE IN HIS MIDDLE.
BAGGAGE

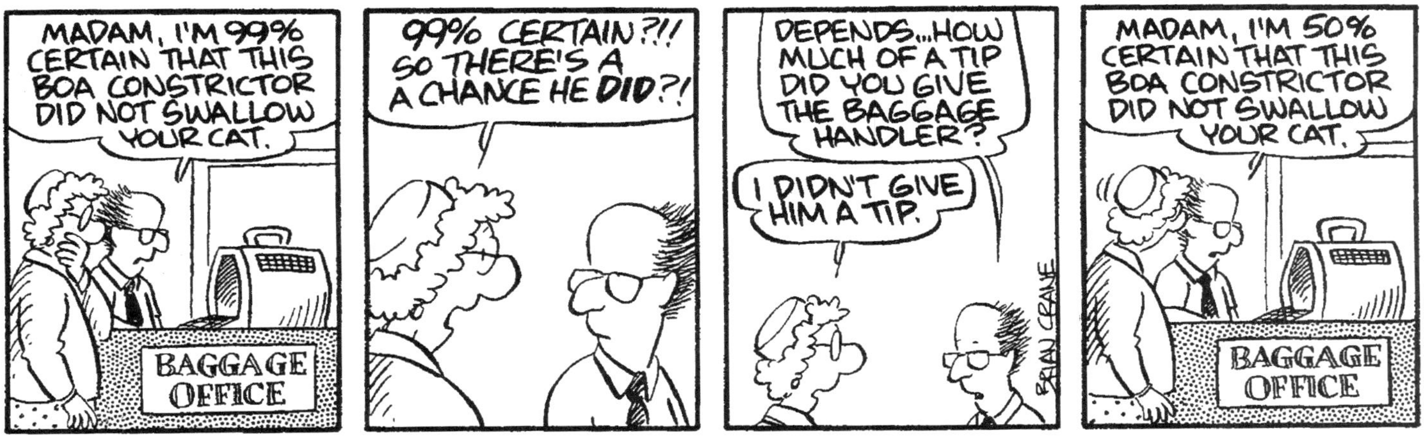
MADAM, I'M 99% CERTAIN THAT THIS BOA CONSTRICTOR DID NOT SWALLOW YOUR CAT.
BAGGAGE OFFICE
99% CERTAIN?!! SO THERE'S A CHANCE HE **DID**?!
DEPENDS... HOW MUCH OF A TIP DID YOU GIVE THE BAGGAGE HANDLER?
I DIDN'T GIVE HIM A TIP.
BRIAN CRANE
MADAM, I'M 50% CERTAIN THAT THIS BOA CONSTRICTOR DID NOT SWALLOW YOUR CAT.
BAGGAGE OFFICE

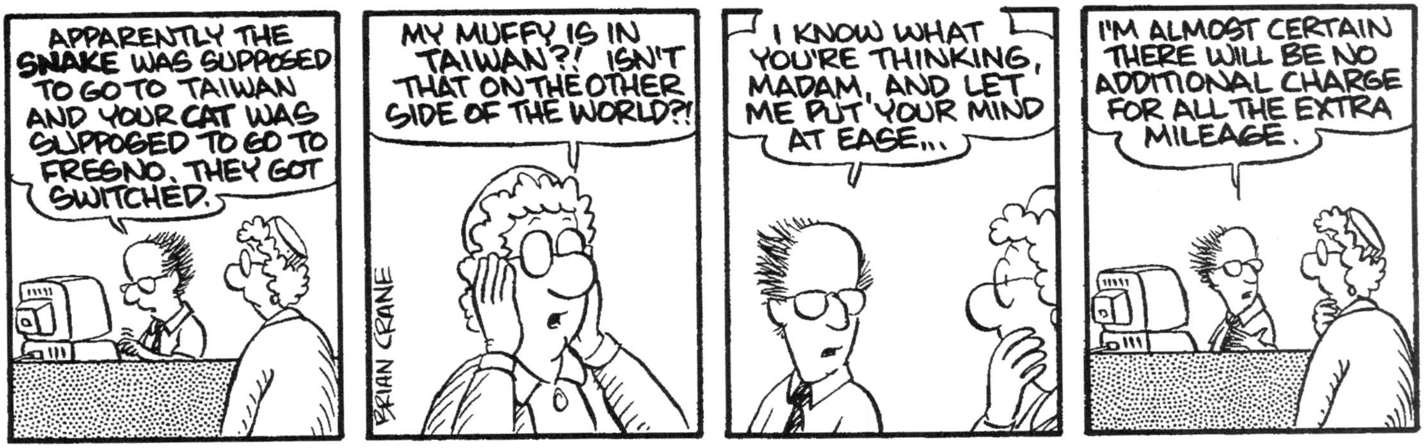
APPARENTLY THE **SNAKE** WAS SUPPOSED TO GO TO TAIWAN AND YOUR **CAT** WAS SUPPOSED TO GO TO FRESNO. THEY GOT SWITCHED.
MY MUFFY IS IN TAIWAN?! ISN'T THAT ON THE OTHER SIDE OF THE WORLD?!
BRIAN CRANE
I KNOW WHAT YOU'RE THINKING, MADAM, AND LET ME PUT YOUR MIND AT EASE...
I'M ALMOST CERTAIN THERE WILL BE NO ADDITIONAL CHARGE FOR ALL THE EXTRA MILEAGE.

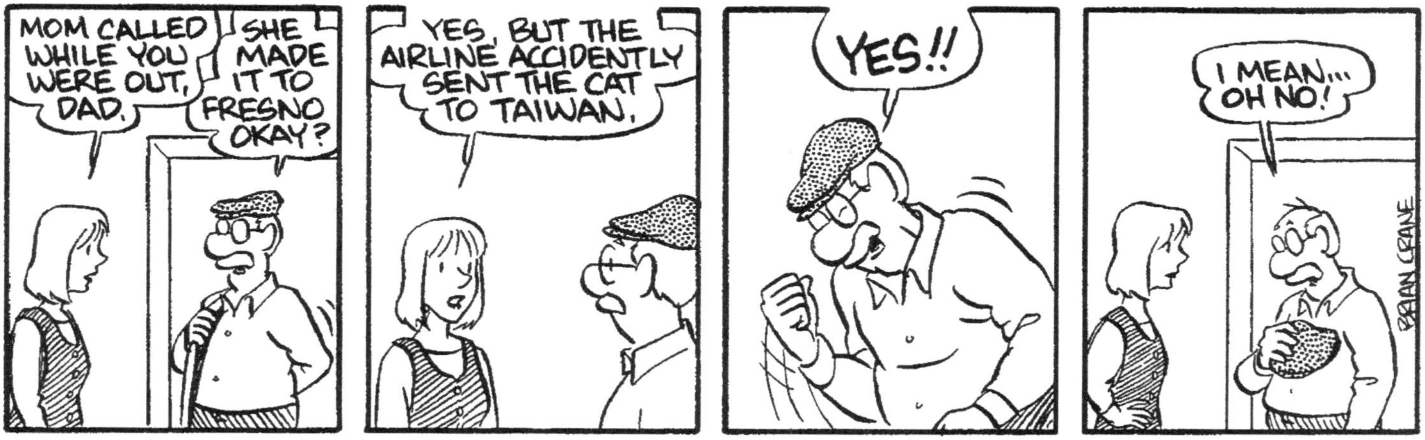
MOM CALLED WHILE YOU WERE OUT, DAD.
SHE MADE IT TO FRESNO OKAY?
YES, BUT THE AIRLINE ACCIDENTLY SENT THE CAT TO TAIWAN.
YES!!
I MEAN... OH NO!
BRIAN CRANE

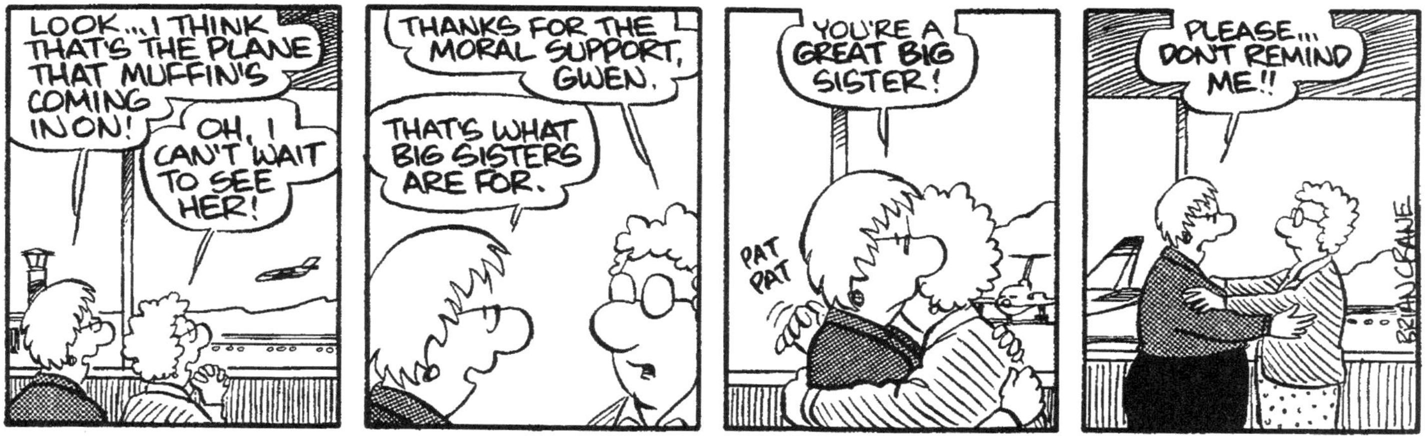
LOOK... I THINK THAT'S THE PLANE THAT MUFFIN'S COMING IN ON!
OH, I CAN'T WAIT TO SEE HER!
THANKS FOR THE MORAL SUPPORT, GWEN.
THAT'S WHAT BIG SISTERS ARE FOR.
YOU'RE A GREAT BIG SISTER!
PAT PAT
PLEASE... DON'T REMIND ME!!
BRIAN CRANE

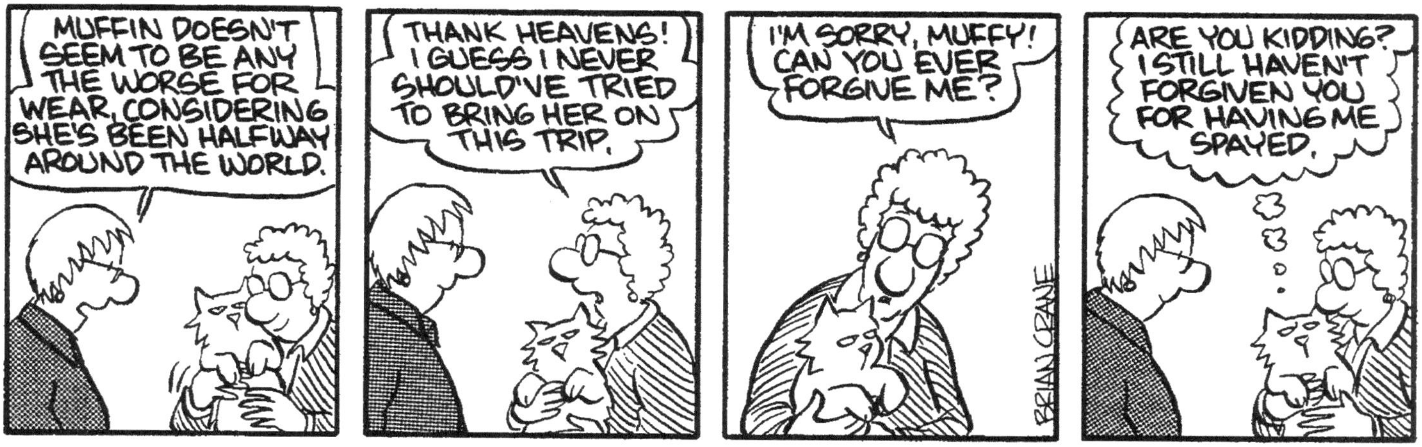
MUFFIN DOESN'T SEEM TO BE ANY THE WORSE FOR WEAR, CONSIDERING SHE'S BEEN HALFWAY AROUND THE WORLD.
THANK HEAVENS! I GUESS I NEVER SHOULD'VE TRIED TO BRING HER ON THIS TRIP.
I'M SORRY, MUFFY! CAN YOU EVER FORGIVE ME?
BRIAN CRANE
ARE YOU KIDDING? I STILL HAVEN'T FORGIVEN YOU FOR HAVING ME SPAYED.

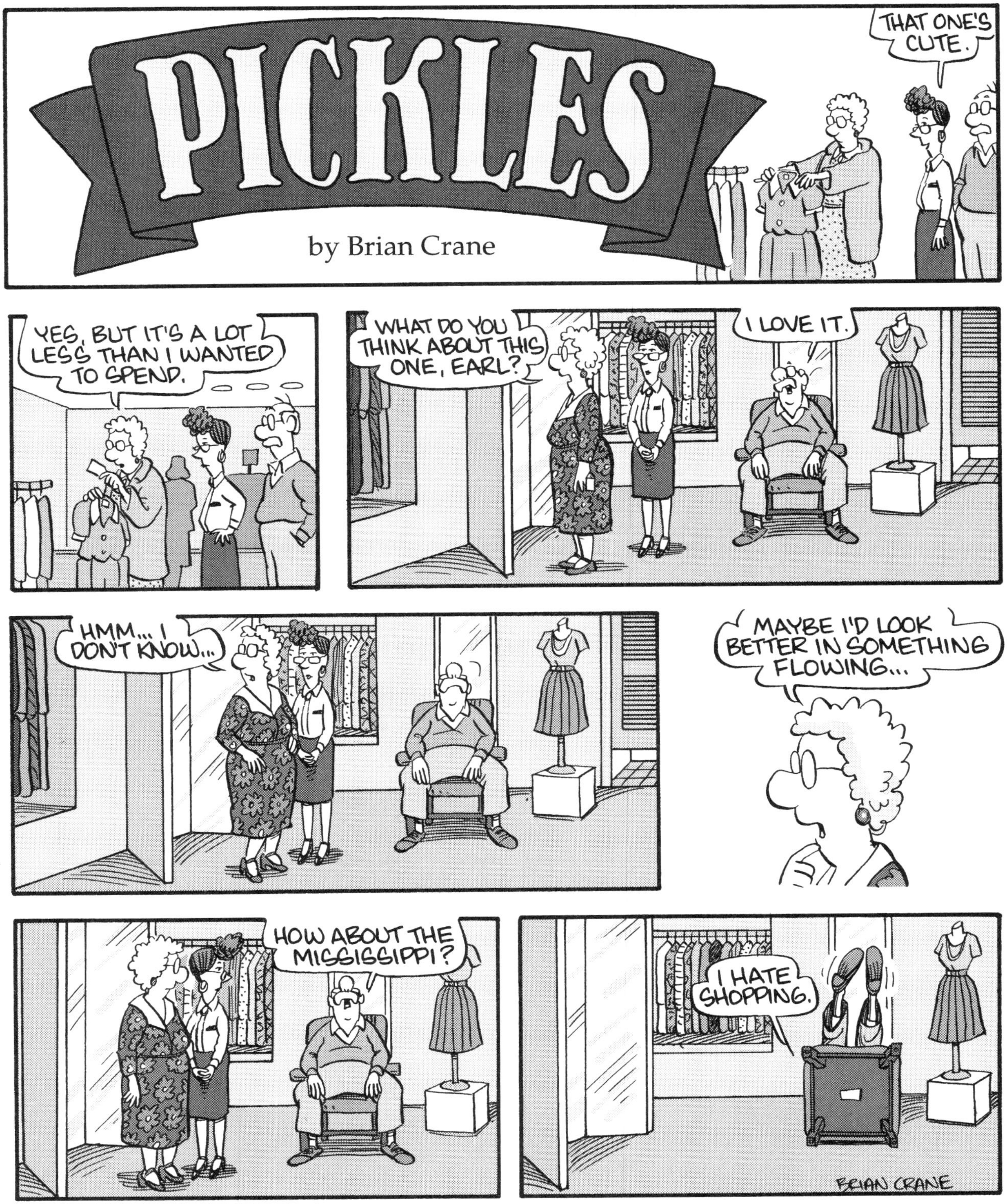
PICKLES
by Brian Crane
THAT ONE'S CUTE.
YES, BUT IT'S A LOT LESS THAN I WANTED TO SPEND.
WHAT DO YOU THINK ABOUT THIS ONE, EARL?
I LOVE IT.
HMM... I DON'T KNOW...
MAYBE I'D LOOK BETTER IN SOMETHING FLOWING...
HOW ABOUT THE MISSISSIPPI?
I HATE SHOPPING.
BRIAN CRANE

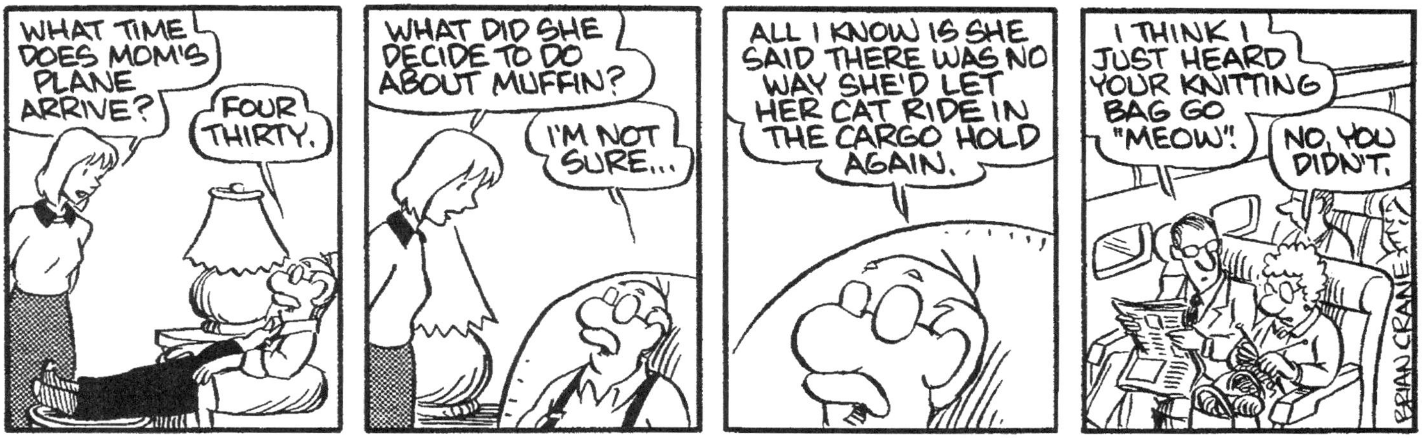
WHAT TIME DOES MOM'S PLANE ARRIVE?
FOUR THIRTY.
WHAT DID SHE DECIDE TO DO ABOUT MUFFIN?
I'M NOT SURE...
ALL I KNOW IS SHE SAID THERE WAS NO WAY SHE'D LET HER CAT RIDE IN THE CARGO HOLD AGAIN.
I THINK I JUST HEARD YOUR KNITTING BAG GO "MEOW".
NO, YOU DIDN'T.
BRIAN CRANE

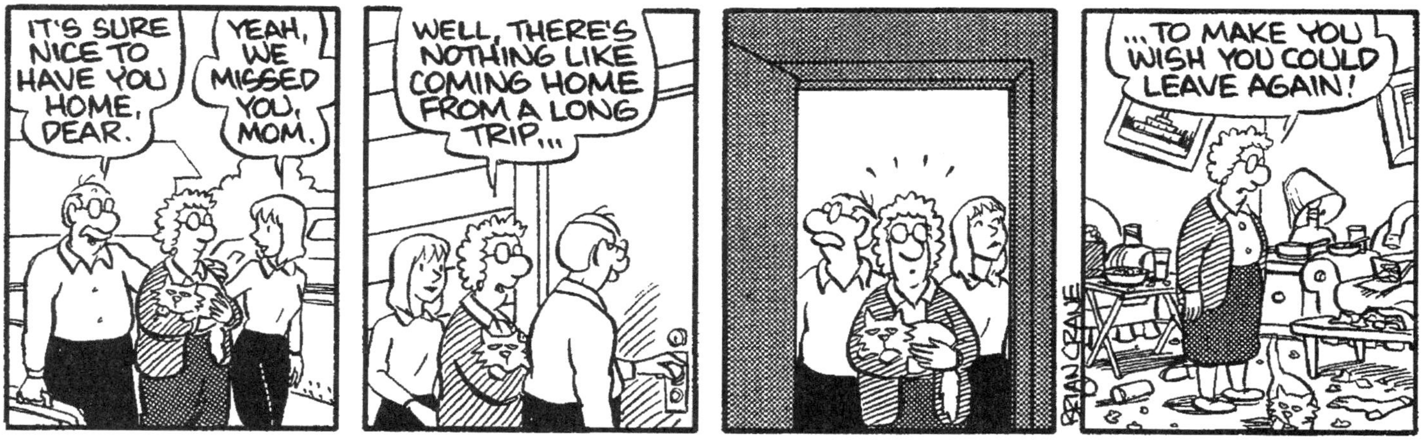
IT'S SURE NICE TO HAVE YOU HOME, DEAR.
YEAH, WE MISSED YOU, MOM.
WELL, THERE'S NOTHING LIKE COMING HOME FROM A LONG TRIP...
BRIAN CRANE
...TO MAKE YOU WISH YOU COULD LEAVE AGAIN!

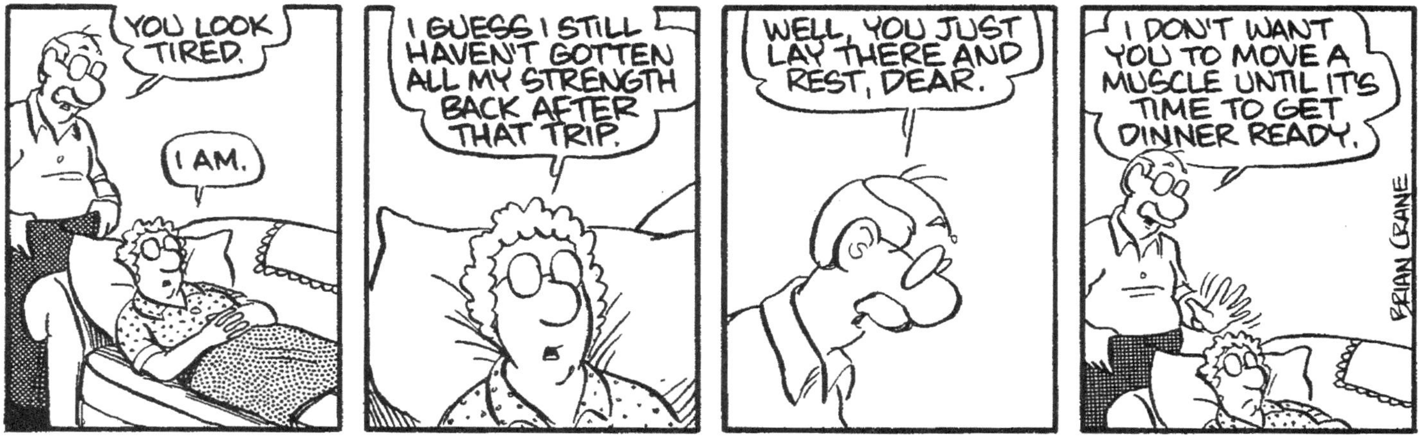
YOU LOOK TIRED.
I AM.
I GUESS I STILL HAVEN'T GOTTEN ALL MY STRENGTH BACK AFTER THAT TRIP.
WELL, YOU JUST LAY THERE AND REST, DEAR.
I DON'T WANT YOU TO MOVE A MUSCLE UNTIL IT'S TIME TO GET DINNER READY.
BRIAN CRANE

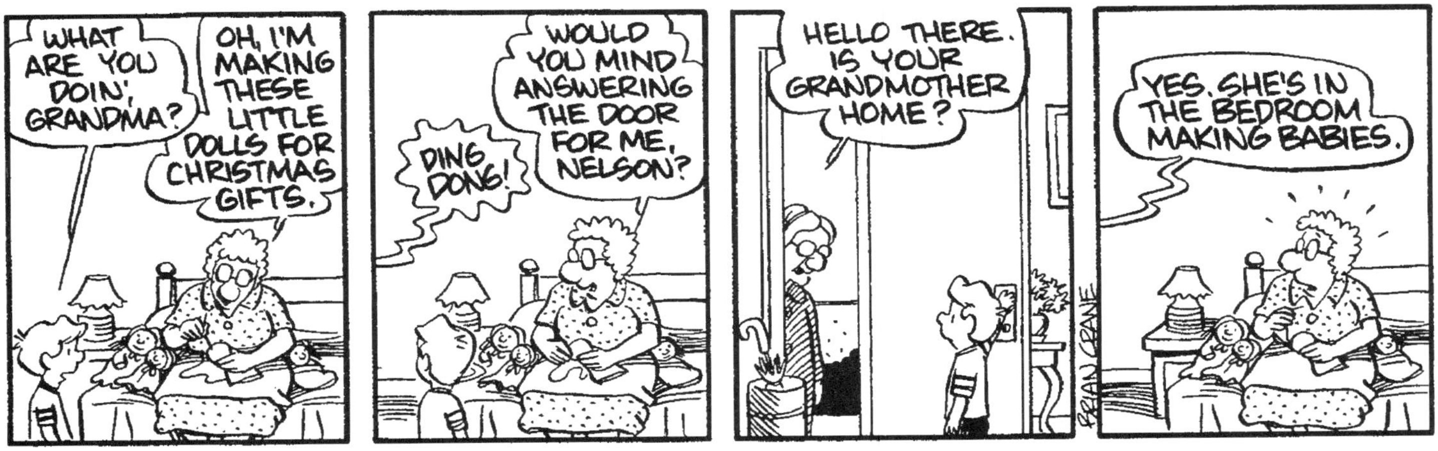
WHAT ARE YOU DOIN', GRANDMA?
OH, I'M MAKING THESE LITTLE DOLLS FOR CHRISTMAS GIFTS.
DING DONG!
WOULD YOU MIND ANSWERING THE DOOR FOR ME, NELSON?
HELLO THERE. IS YOUR GRANDMOTHER HOME?
BRIAN CRANE
YES. SHE'S IN THE BEDROOM MAKING BABIES.

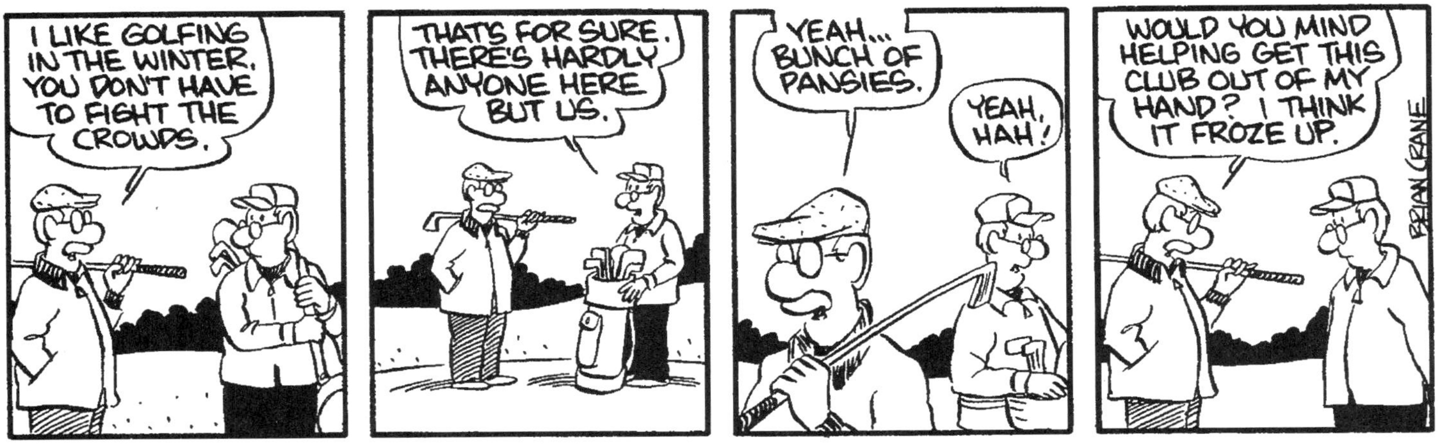
I LIKE GOLFING IN THE WINTER. YOU DON'T HAVE TO FIGHT THE CROWDS.
THAT'S FOR SURE. THERE'S HARDLY ANYONE HERE BUT US.
YEAH... BUNCH OF PANSIES.
YEAH, HAH!
WOULD YOU MIND HELPING GET THIS CLUB OUT OF MY HAND? I THINK IT FROZE UP.
BRIAN CRANE

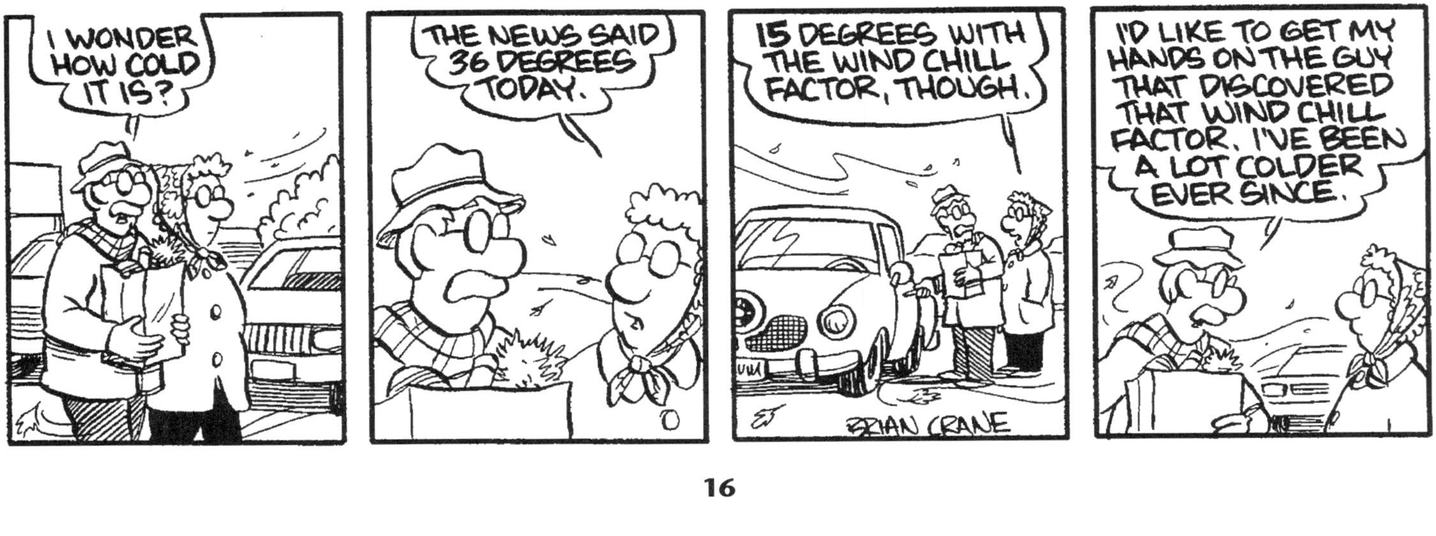
I WONDER HOW COLD IT IS?
THE NEWS SAID 36 DEGREES TODAY.
15 DEGREES WITH THE WIND CHILL FACTOR, THOUGH.
BRIAN CRANE
I'D LIKE TO GET MY HANDS ON THE GUY THAT DISCOVERED THAT WIND CHILL FACTOR. I'VE BEEN A LOT COLDER EVER SINCE.

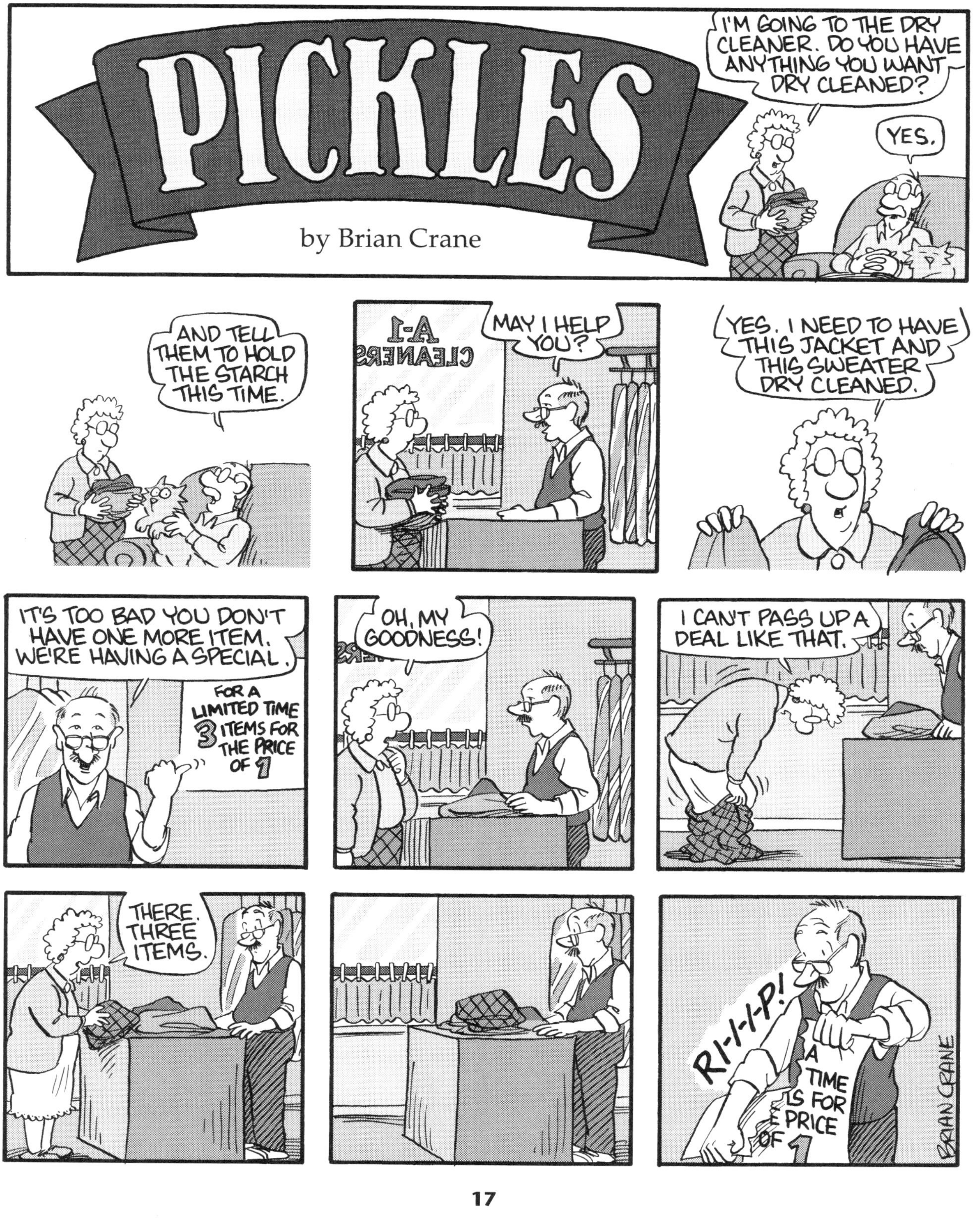
PICKLES
by Brian Crane
I'M GOING TO THE DRY CLEANER. DO YOU HAVE ANYTHING YOU WANT DRY CLEANED?
YES.
AND TELL THEM TO HOLD THE STARCH THIS TIME.
A-1 CLEANERS
MAY I HELP YOU?
YES. I NEED TO HAVE THIS JACKET AND THIS SWEATER DRY CLEANED.
IT'S TOO BAD YOU DON'T HAVE ONE MORE ITEM. WE'RE HAVING A SPECIAL.
FOR A LIMITED TIME 3 ITEMS FOR THE PRICE OF 1
OH, MY GOODNESS!
I CAN'T PASS UP A DEAL LIKE THAT.
THERE. THREE ITEMS.
RI-I-I-P!
A TIME IS FOR E PRICE OF 1
BRIAN CRANE

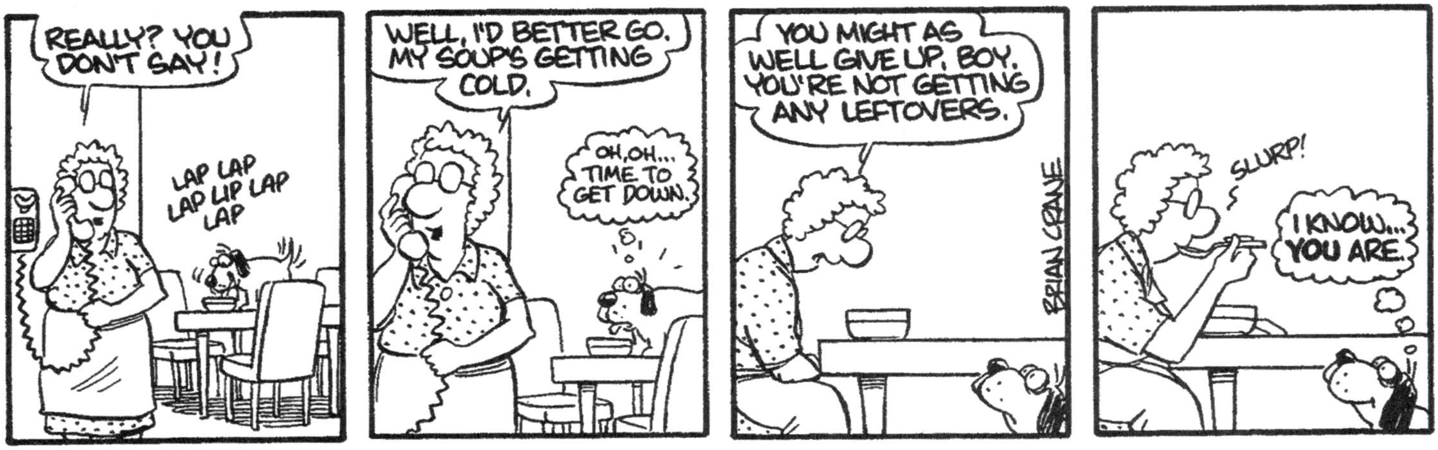
REALLY? YOU DON'T SAY!
LAP LAP LAP LIP LAP LAP
WELL, I'D BETTER GO. MY SOUP'S GETTING COLD.
OH, OH... TIME TO GET DOWN.
YOU MIGHT AS WELL GIVE UP, BOY. YOU'RE NOT GETTING ANY LEFTOVERS.
BRIAN CRANE
SLURP!
I KNOW... YOU ARE.

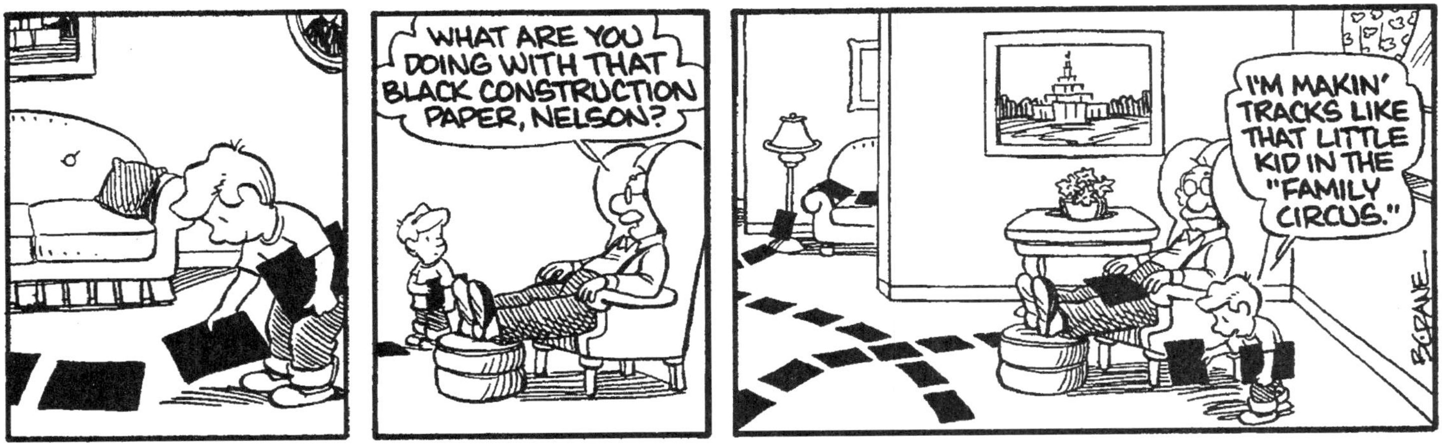
WHAT ARE YOU DOING WITH THAT BLACK CONSTRUCTION PAPER, NELSON?
I'M MAKIN' TRACKS LIKE THAT LITTLE KID IN THE "FAMILY CIRCUS."
B. CRANE

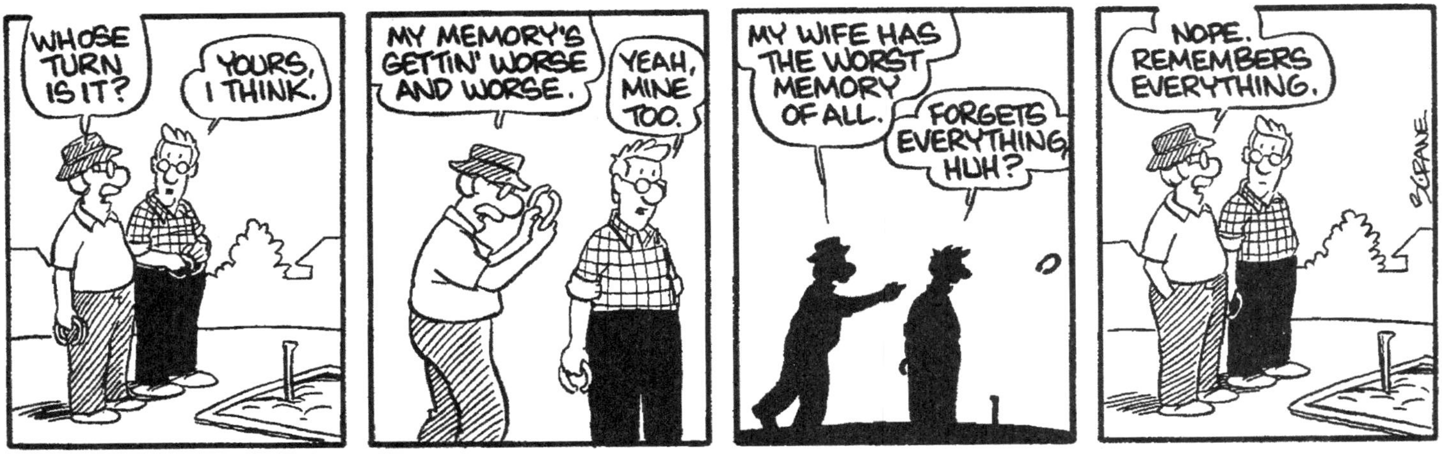
WHOSE TURN IS IT?
YOURS, I THINK.
MY MEMORY'S GETTIN' WORSE AND WORSE.
YEAH, MINE TOO.
MY WIFE HAS THE WORST MEMORY OF ALL.
FORGETS EVERYTHING, HUH?
NOPE. REMEMBERS EVERYTHING.
B. CRANE

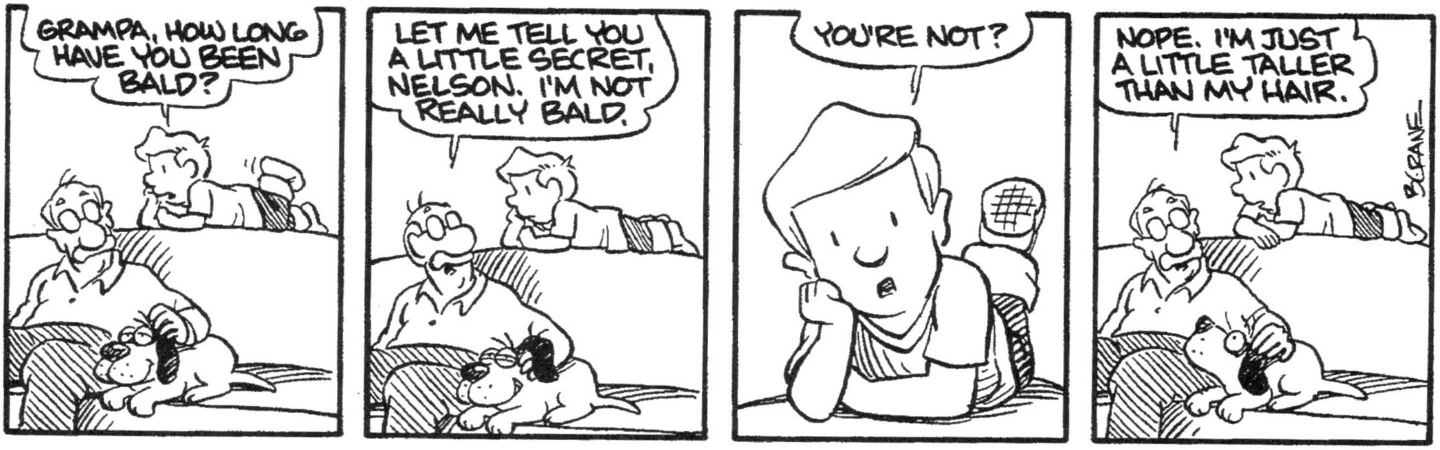
GRAMPA, HOW LONG HAVE YOU BEEN BALD?
LET ME TELL YOU A LITTLE SECRET, NELSON. I'M NOT REALLY BALD.
YOU'RE NOT?
NOPE. I'M JUST A LITTLE TALLER THAN MY HAIR.
B.CRANE

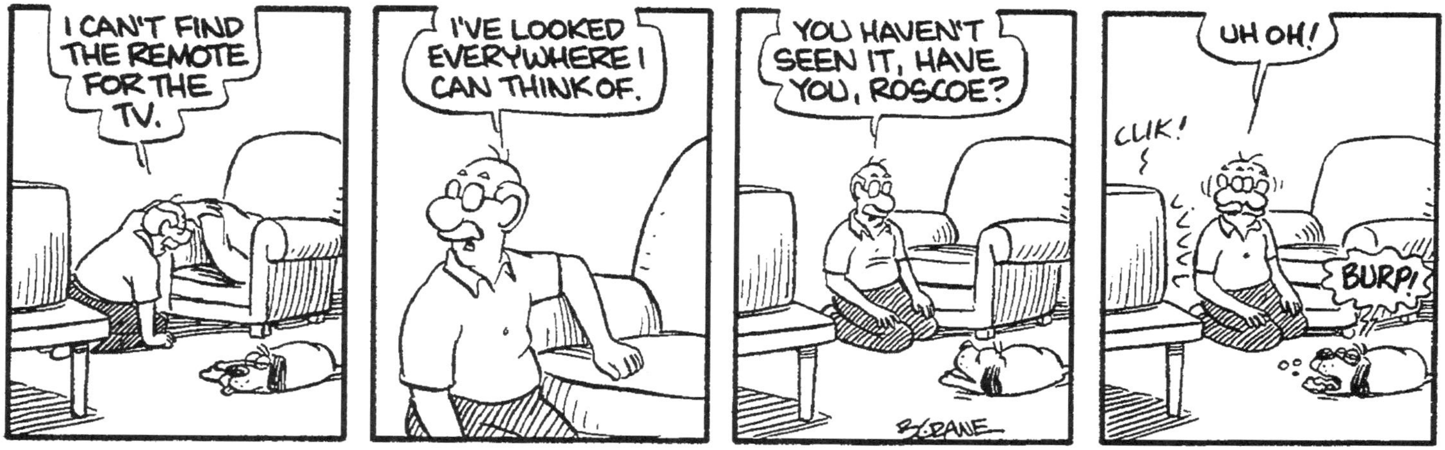
I CAN'T FIND THE REMOTE FOR THE TV.
I'VE LOOKED EVERYWHERE I CAN THINK OF.
YOU HAVEN'T SEEN IT, HAVE YOU, ROSCOE?
B.CRANE
CLIK!
BURP!
UH OH!

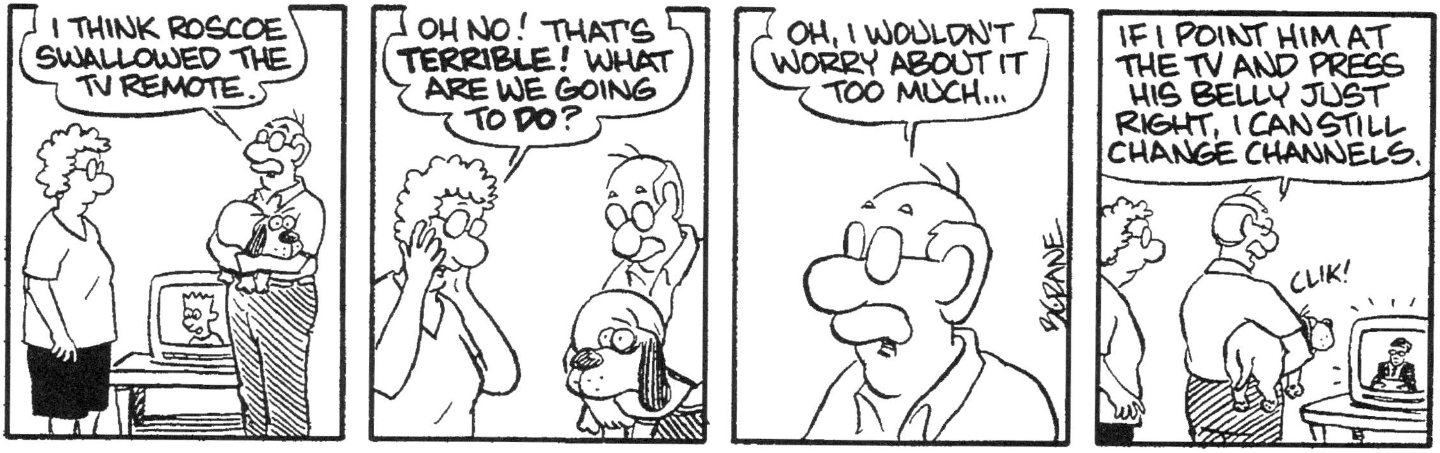
I THINK ROSCOE SWALLOWED THE TV REMOTE.
OH NO! THAT'S TERRIBLE! WHAT ARE WE GOING TO DO?
OH, I WOULDN'T WORRY ABOUT IT TOO MUCH...
B.CRANE
IF I POINT HIM AT THE TV AND PRESS HIS BELLY JUST RIGHT, I CAN STILL CHANGE CHANNELS.
CLIK!

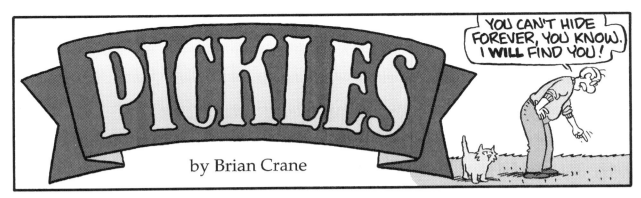

PICKLES

by Brian Crane

YOU CAN'T HIDE FOREVER, YOU KNOW. I **WILL** FIND YOU!

TALKING TO THE LAWN CAN'T BE A SIGN OF GOOD MENTAL HEALTH.

STILL LOOKING FOR THAT SILVER DOLLAR, HUH, DAD?

YER DARN TOOTIN'.

TICK TICK TICK

IT'S AN 1892 LIBERTY HEAD. IT'S PROBABLY WORTH SOMETHING.

I LOST IT HERE IN THE BACKYARD SEVENTEEN YEARS AGO.

I'VE BEEN LOOKIN' FOR IT EVER SINCE.

I KNOW. YOU'VE TOLD ME ABOUT IT MANY TIMES.

SOME DAY I'M GOING TO FIND IT, TOO.

I'M SURE YOU WILL, DAD. GOOD LUCK!

TICK TICK

MOM, ARE YOU EVER GOING TO TELL DAD YOU FOUND HIS SILVER DOLLAR SIXTEEN YEARS AGO?

OH, I DOUBT IT. I LIKE HAVING HIM OUT OF THE HOUSE.

20

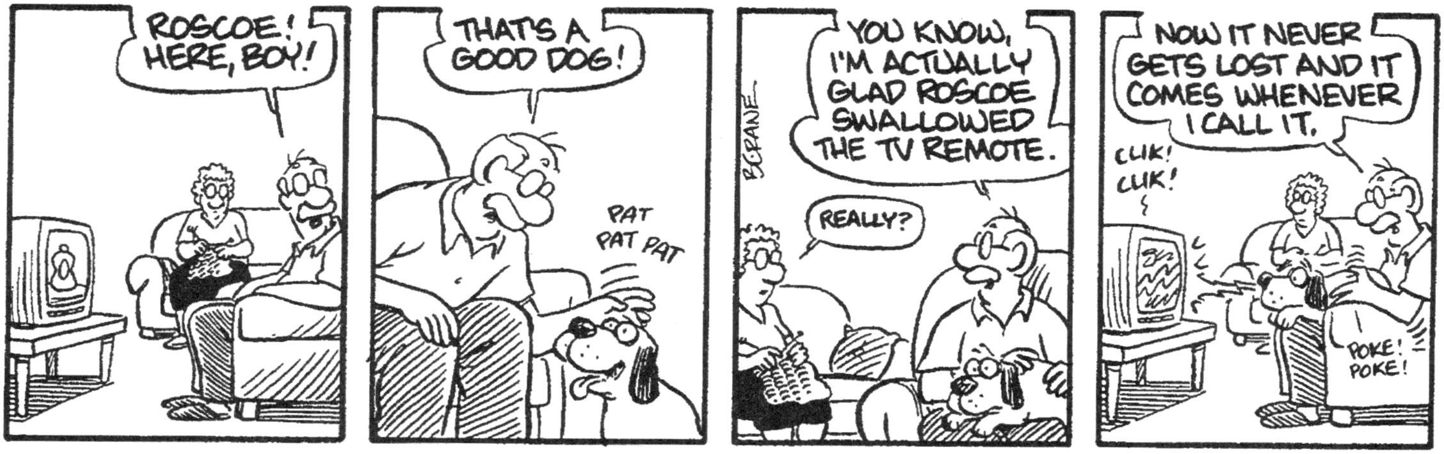
ROSCOE! HERE, BOY!
THAT'S A GOOD DOG!
PAT PAT PAT
YOU KNOW, I'M ACTUALLY GLAD ROSCOE SWALLOWED THE TV REMOTE.
REALLY?
NOW IT NEVER GETS LOST AND IT COMES WHENEVER I CALL IT.
CLIK! CLIK!
POKE! POKE!

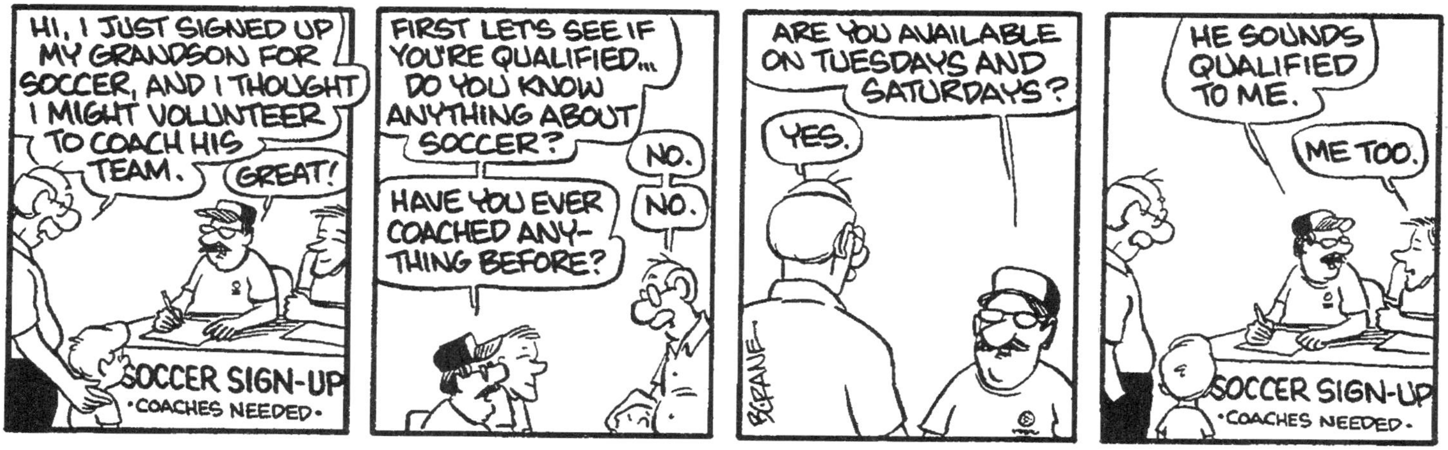
HI, I JUST SIGNED UP MY GRANDSON FOR SOCCER, AND I THOUGHT I MIGHT VOLUNTEER TO COACH HIS TEAM.
GREAT!
SOCCER SIGN-UP
•COACHES NEEDED•
FIRST LET'S SEE IF YOU'RE QUALIFIED... DO YOU KNOW ANYTHING ABOUT SOCCER?
NO.
HAVE YOU EVER COACHED ANYTHING BEFORE?
NO.
ARE YOU AVAILABLE ON TUESDAYS AND SATURDAYS?
YES.
HE SOUNDS QUALIFIED TO ME.
ME TOO.
SOCCER SIGN-UP
•COACHES NEEDED•

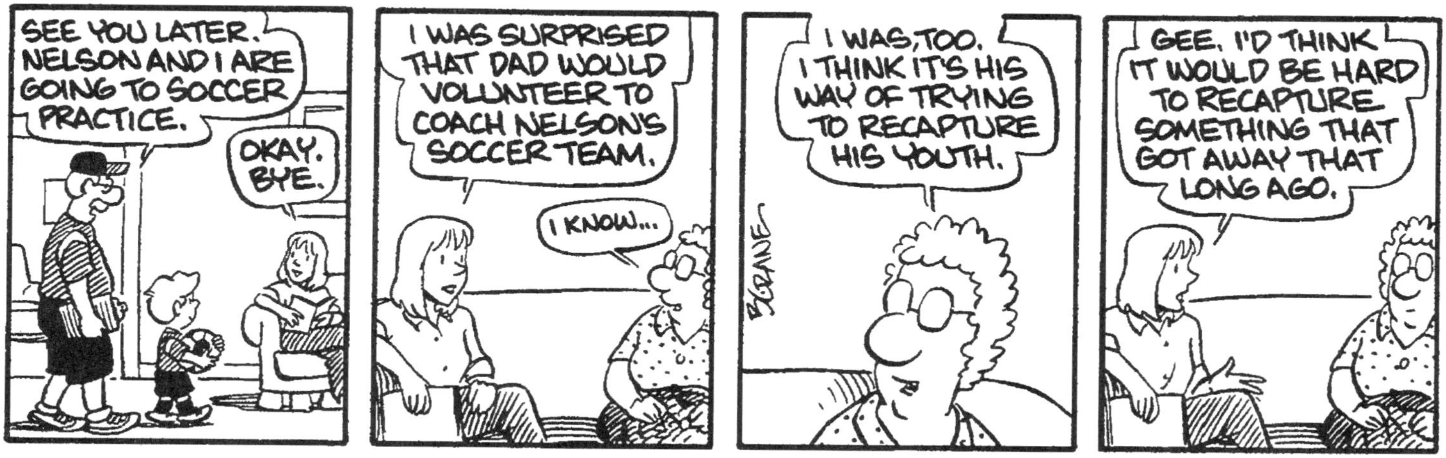
SEE YOU LATER. NELSON AND I ARE GOING TO SOCCER PRACTICE.
OKAY. BYE.
I WAS SURPRISED THAT DAD WOULD VOLUNTEER TO COACH NELSON'S SOCCER TEAM.
I KNOW...
I WAS, TOO. I THINK IT'S HIS WAY OF TRYING TO RECAPTURE HIS YOUTH.
GEE. I'D THINK IT WOULD BE HARD TO RECAPTURE SOMETHING THAT GOT AWAY THAT LONG AGO.

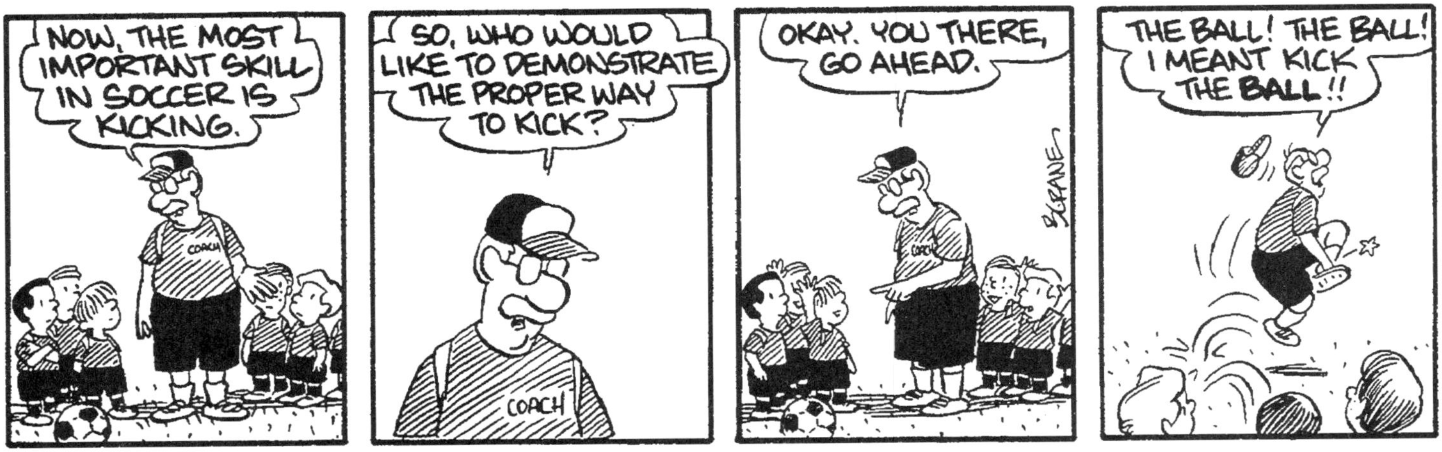
NOW, THE MOST IMPORTANT SKILL IN SOCCER IS KICKING.
SO, WHO WOULD LIKE TO DEMONSTRATE THE PROPER WAY TO KICK?
OKAY. YOU THERE, GO AHEAD.
THE BALL! THE BALL! I MEANT KICK THE **BALL**!!

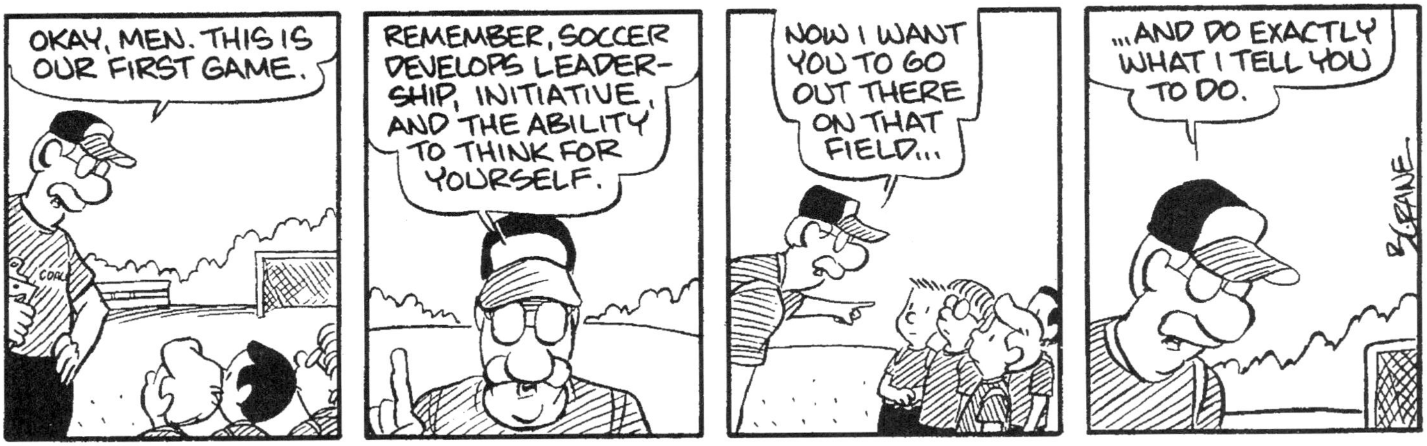
OKAY, MEN. THIS IS OUR FIRST GAME.
REMEMBER, SOCCER DEVELOPS LEADER-SHIP, INITIATIVE, AND THE ABILITY TO THINK FOR YOURSELF.
NOW I WANT YOU TO GO OUT THERE ON THAT FIELD...
...AND DO EXACTLY WHAT I TELL YOU TO DO.

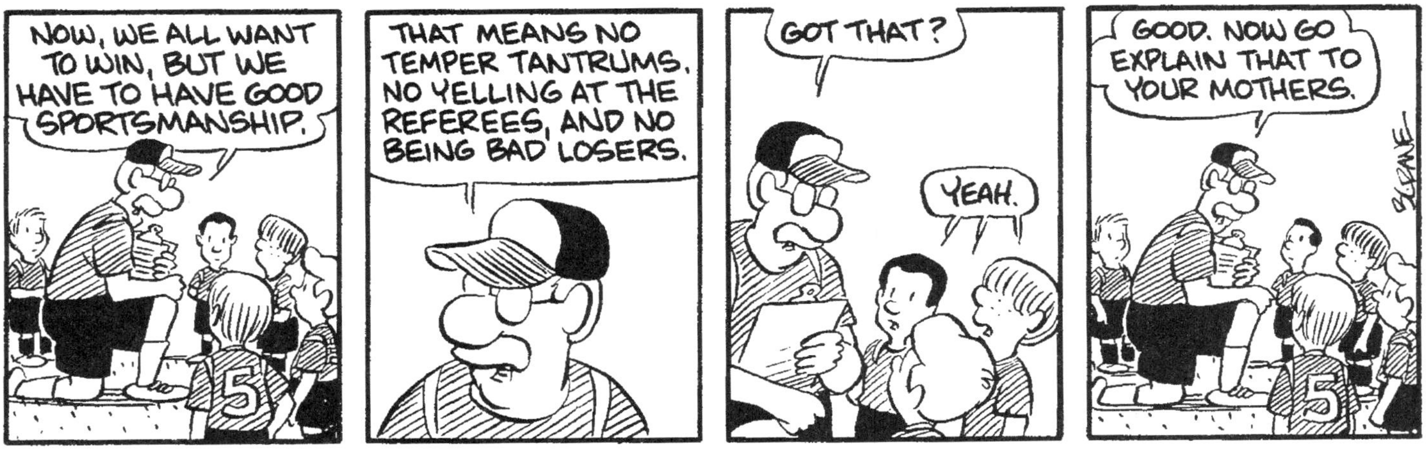
NOW, WE ALL WANT TO WIN, BUT WE HAVE TO HAVE GOOD SPORTSMANSHIP.
THAT MEANS NO TEMPER TANTRUMS, NO YELLING AT THE REFEREES, AND NO BEING BAD LOSERS.
GOT THAT?
YEAH.
GOOD. NOW GO EXPLAIN THAT TO YOUR MOTHERS.

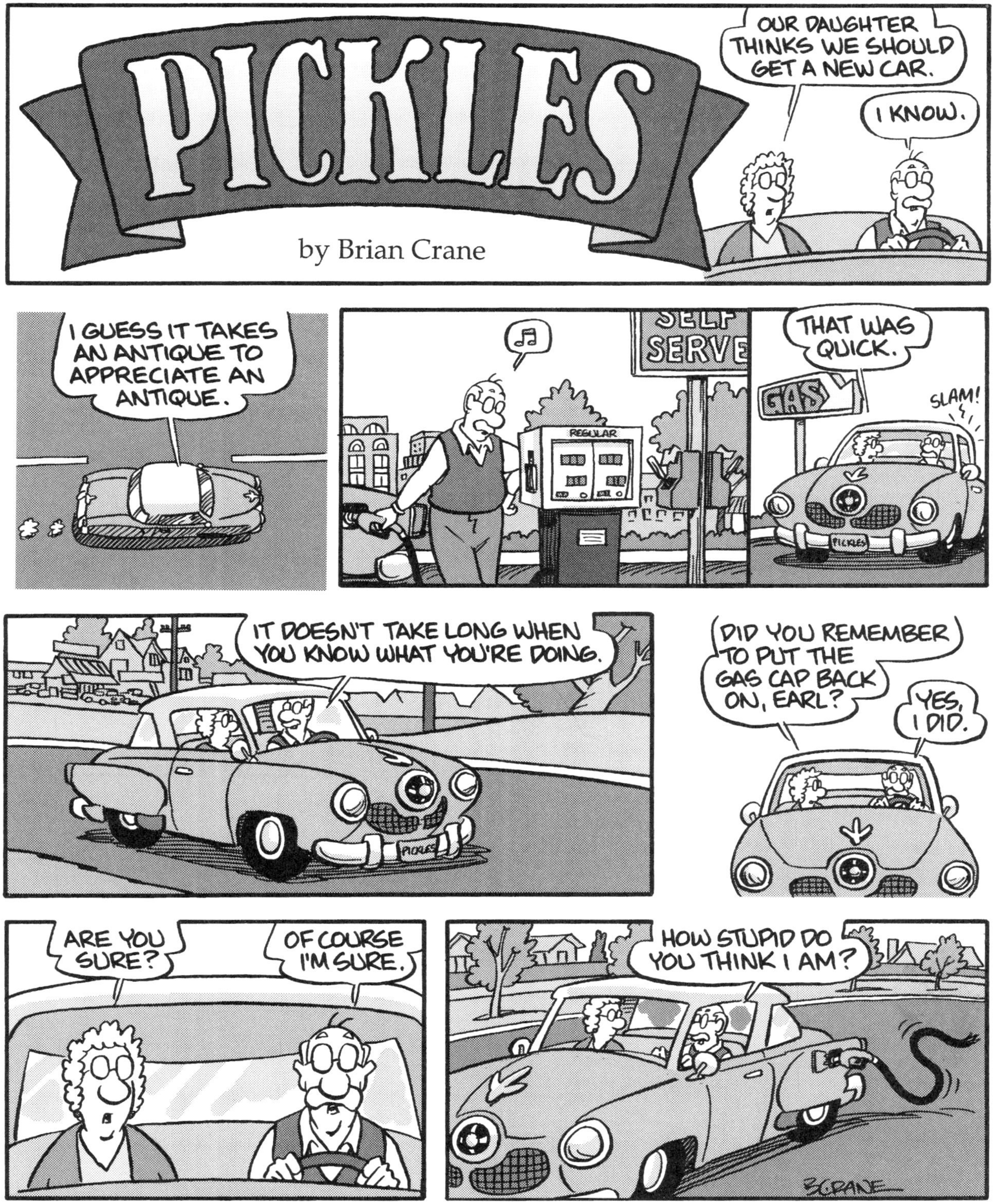
PICKLES
by Brian Crane
OUR DAUGHTER THINKS WE SHOULD GET A NEW CAR.
I KNOW.
I GUESS IT TAKES AN ANTIQUE TO APPRECIATE AN ANTIQUE.
SELF SERVE
REGULAR
GAS
THAT WAS QUICK.
SLAM!
PICKLES
IT DOESN'T TAKE LONG WHEN YOU KNOW WHAT YOU'RE DOING.
PICKLES
DID YOU REMEMBER TO PUT THE GAS CAP BACK ON, EARL?
YES, I DID.
ARE YOU SURE?
OF COURSE I'M SURE.
HOW STUPID DO YOU THINK I AM?
B CRANE

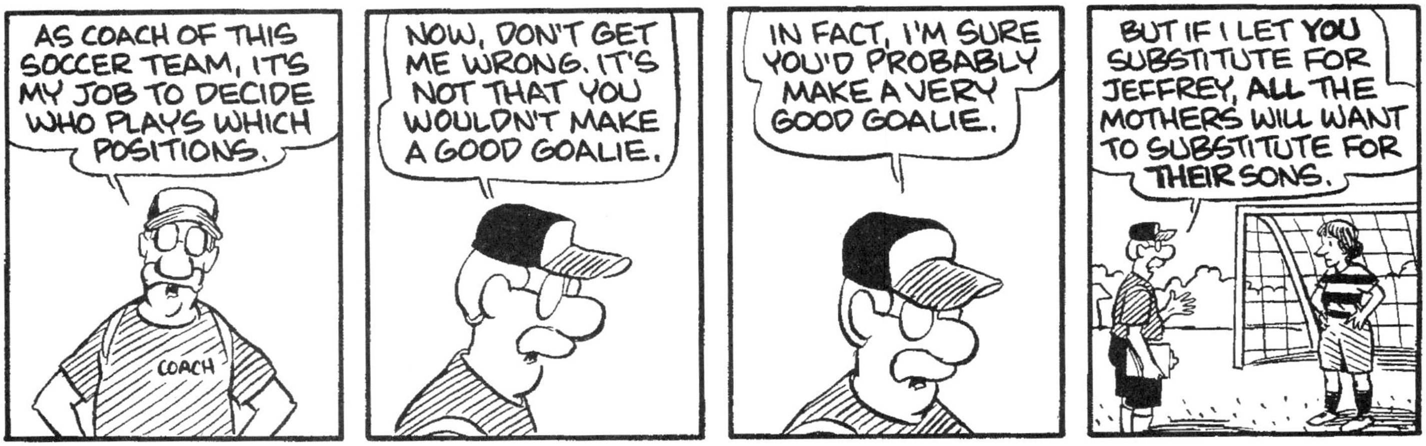
AS COACH OF THIS SOCCER TEAM, IT'S MY JOB TO DECIDE WHO PLAYS WHICH POSITIONS.
COACH
NOW, DON'T GET ME WRONG. IT'S NOT THAT YOU WOULDN'T MAKE A GOOD GOALIE.
IN FACT, I'M SURE YOU'D PROBABLY MAKE A VERY GOOD GOALIE.
BUT IF I LET **YOU** SUBSTITUTE FOR JEFFREY, **ALL** THE MOTHERS WILL WANT TO SUBSTITUTE FOR **THEIR** SONS.

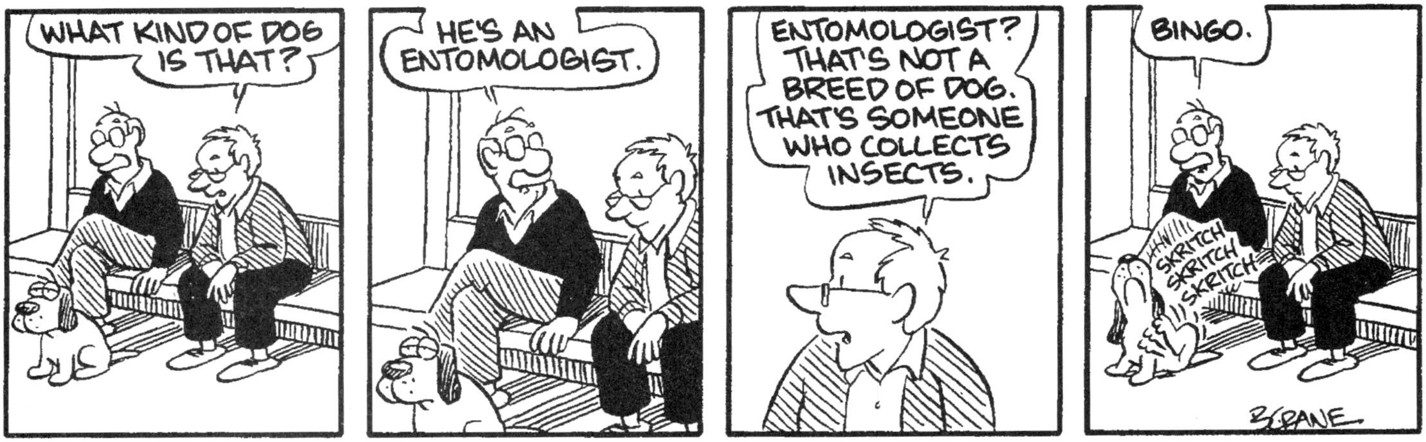
WHAT KIND OF DOG IS THAT?
HE'S AN ENTOMOLOGIST.
ENTOMOLOGIST? THAT'S NOT A BREED OF DOG. THAT'S SOMEONE WHO COLLECTS INSECTS.
BINGO.
SKRITCH SKRITCH SKRITCH

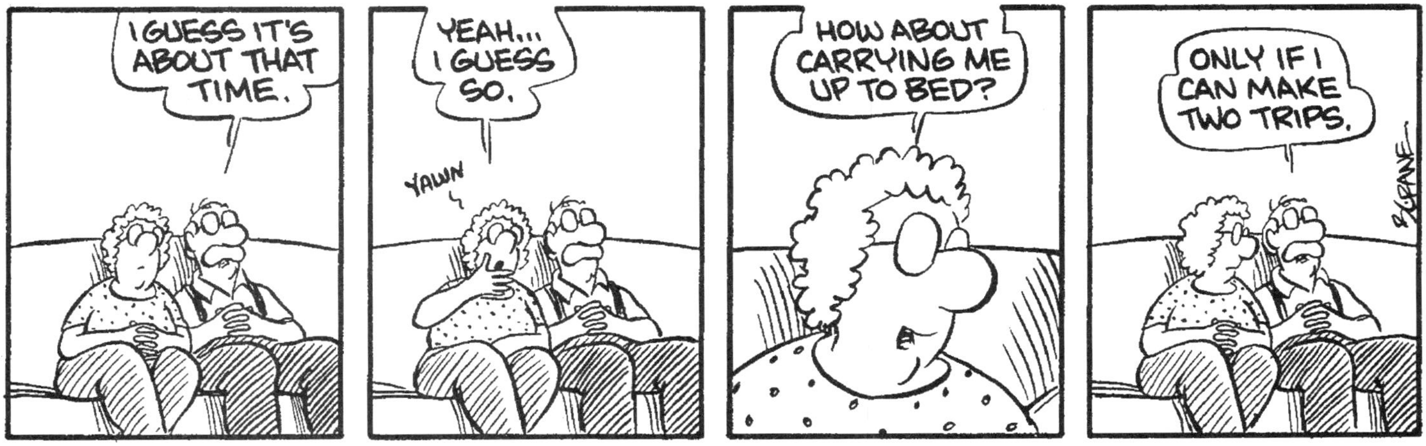
I GUESS IT'S ABOUT THAT TIME.
YEAH... I GUESS SO.
YAWN
HOW ABOUT CARRYING ME UP TO BED?
ONLY IF I CAN MAKE TWO TRIPS.

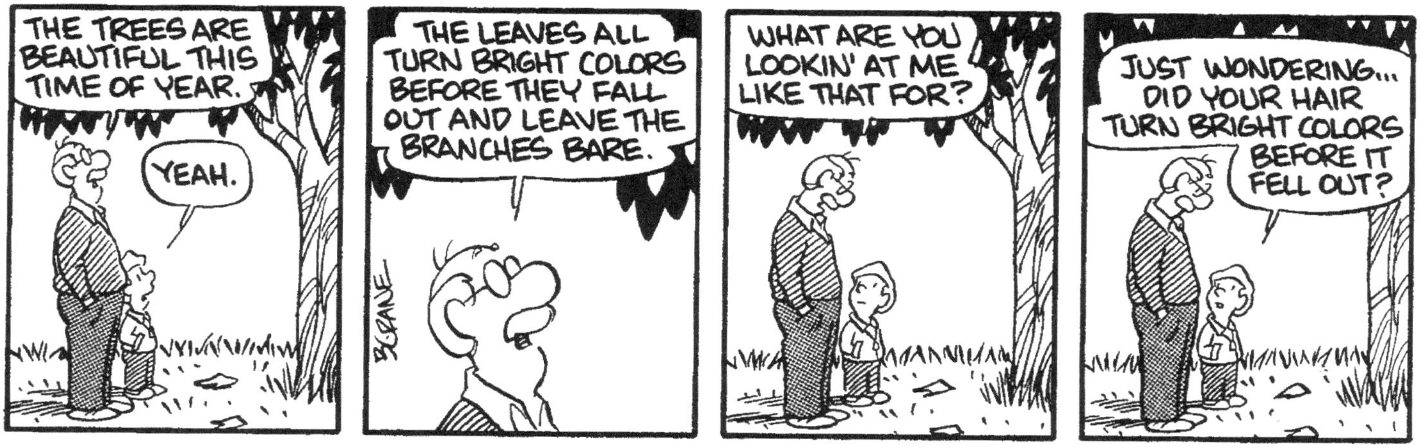
THE TREES ARE BEAUTIFUL THIS TIME OF YEAR.
YEAH.
THE LEAVES ALL TURN BRIGHT COLORS BEFORE THEY FALL OUT AND LEAVE THE BRANCHES BARE.
WHAT ARE YOU LOOKIN' AT ME LIKE THAT FOR?
JUST WONDERING... DID YOUR HAIR TURN BRIGHT COLORS BEFORE IT FELL OUT?

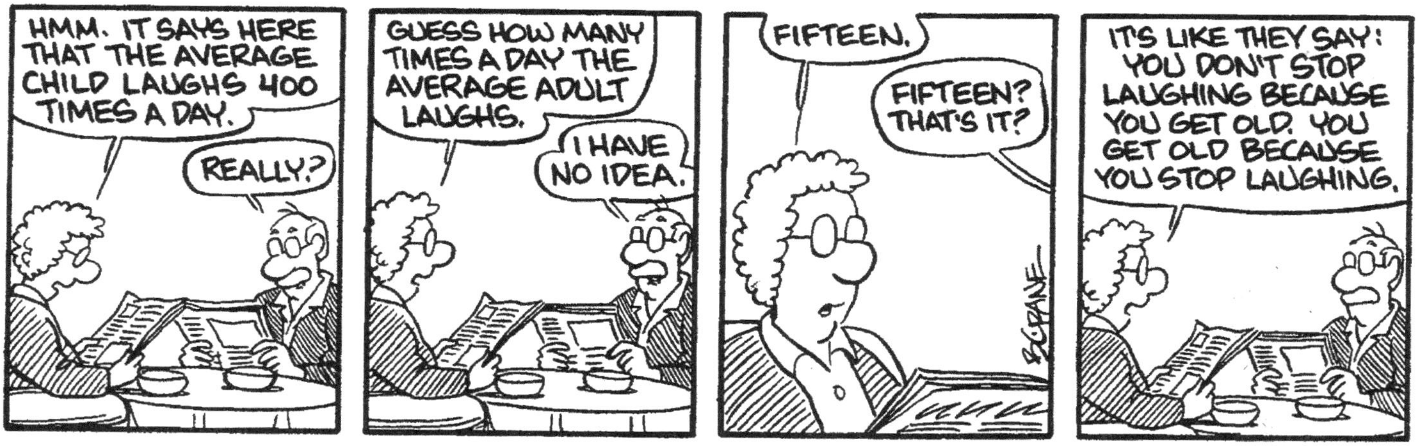
HMM. IT SAYS HERE THAT THE AVERAGE CHILD LAUGHS 400 TIMES A DAY.
REALLY?
GUESS HOW MANY TIMES A DAY THE AVERAGE ADULT LAUGHS.
I HAVE NO IDEA.
FIFTEEN.
FIFTEEN? THAT'S IT?
IT'S LIKE THEY SAY: YOU DON'T STOP LAUGHING BECAUSE YOU GET OLD. YOU GET OLD BECAUSE YOU STOP LAUGHING.

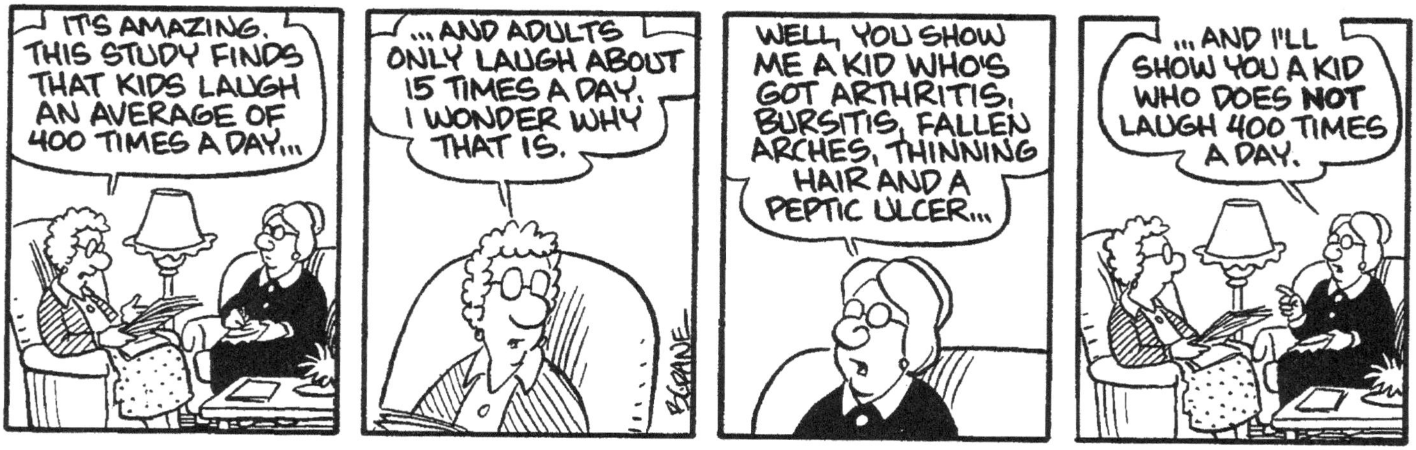
IT'S AMAZING. THIS STUDY FINDS THAT KIDS LAUGH AN AVERAGE OF 400 TIMES A DAY...
...AND ADULTS ONLY LAUGH ABOUT 15 TIMES A DAY. I WONDER WHY THAT IS.
WELL, YOU SHOW ME A KID WHO'S GOT ARTHRITIS, BURSITIS, FALLEN ARCHES, THINNING HAIR AND A PEPTIC ULCER...
...AND I'LL SHOW YOU A KID WHO DOES NOT LAUGH 400 TIMES A DAY.

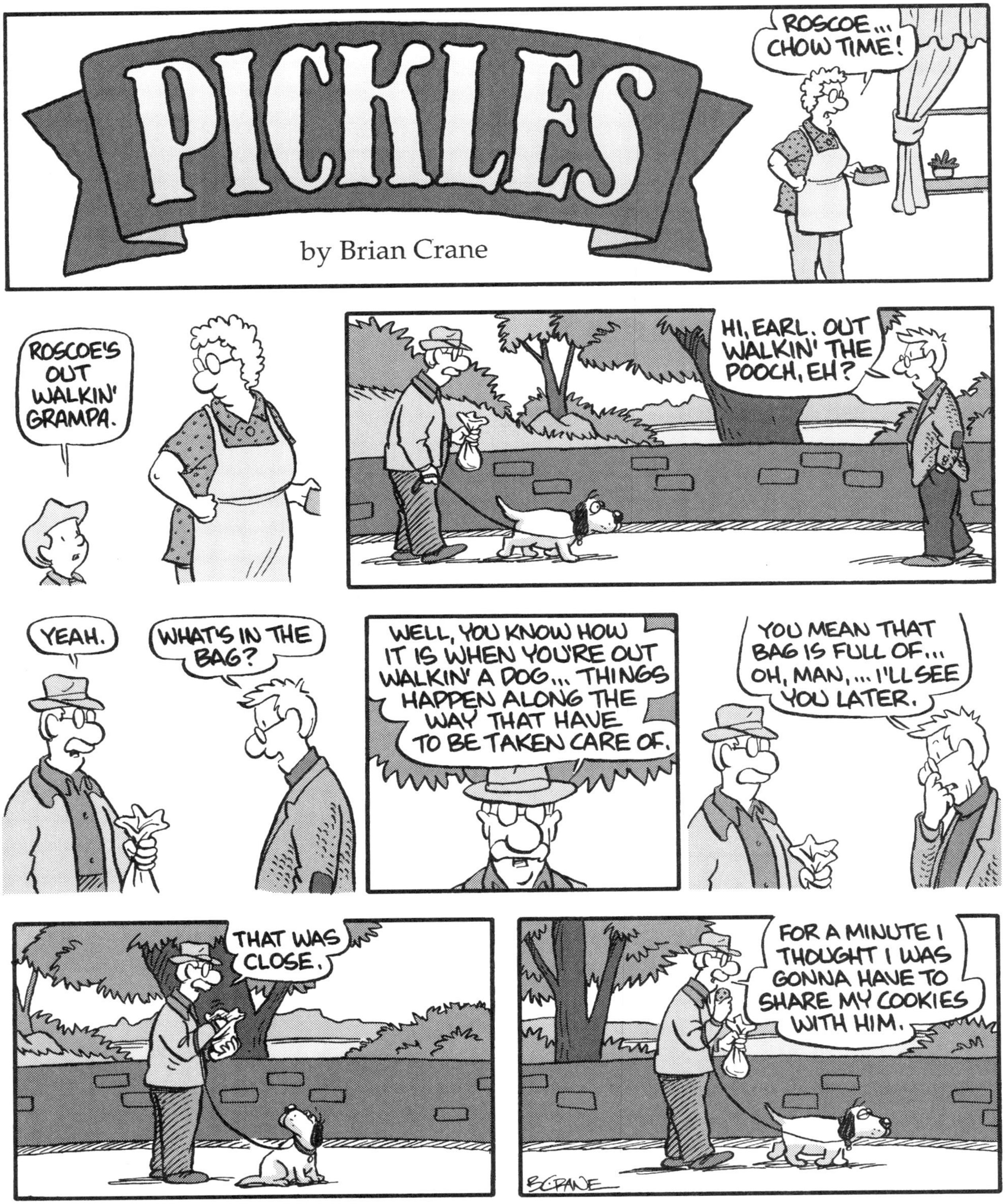
PICKLES
by Brian Crane
ROSCOE... CHOW TIME!
ROSCOE'S OUT WALKIN' GRAMPA.
HI, EARL. OUT WALKIN' THE POOCH, EH?
YEAH.
WHAT'S IN THE BAG?
WELL, YOU KNOW HOW IT IS WHEN YOU'RE OUT WALKIN' A DOG... THINGS HAPPEN ALONG THE WAY THAT HAVE TO BE TAKEN CARE OF.
YOU MEAN THAT BAG IS FULL OF... OH, MAN,... I'LL SEE YOU LATER.
THAT WAS CLOSE.
FOR A MINUTE I THOUGHT I WAS GONNA HAVE TO SHARE MY COOKIES WITH HIM.
B. CRANE

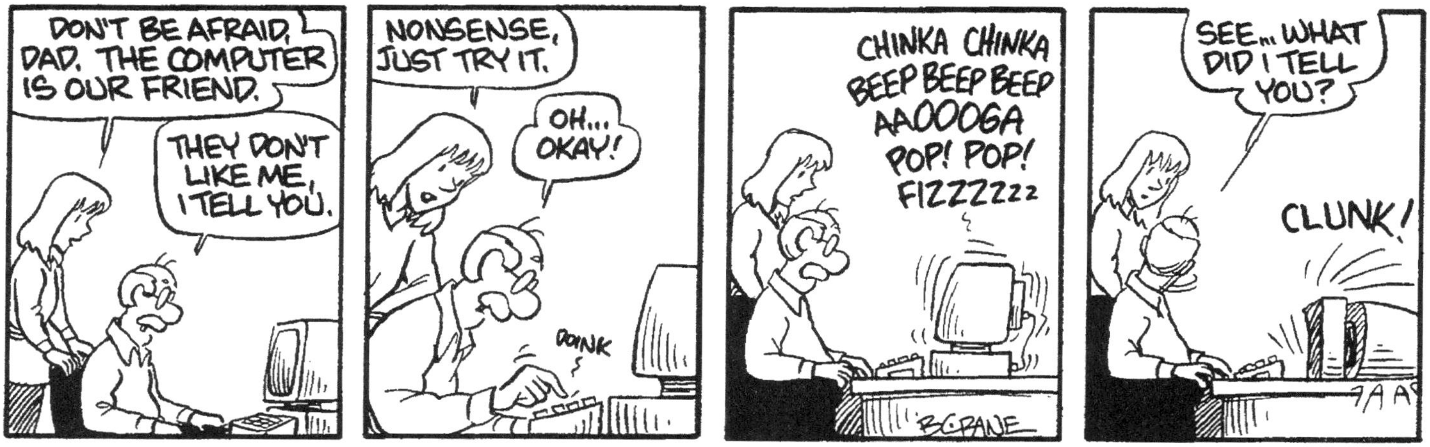
DON'T BE AFRAID, DAD. THE COMPUTER IS OUR FRIEND.
THEY DON'T LIKE ME, I TELL YOU.
NONSENSE, JUST TRY IT.
OH... OKAY!
DOINK
CHINKA CHINKA
BEEP BEEP BEEP
AAOOOGA
POP! POP!
FIZZZzzz
B.CRANE
SEE... WHAT DID I TELL YOU?
CLUNK!

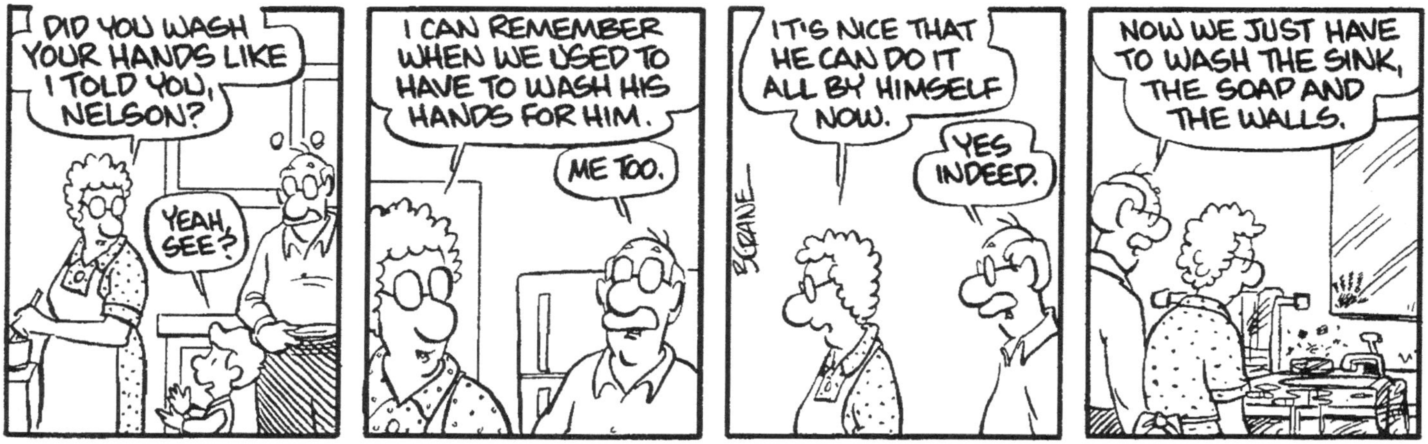
DID YOU WASH YOUR HANDS LIKE I TOLD YOU, NELSON?
YEAH, SEE?
I CAN REMEMBER WHEN WE USED TO HAVE TO WASH HIS HANDS FOR HIM.
ME TOO.
B.CRANE
IT'S NICE THAT HE CAN DO IT ALL BY HIMSELF NOW.
YES INDEED.
NOW WE JUST HAVE TO WASH THE SINK, THE SOAP AND THE WALLS.

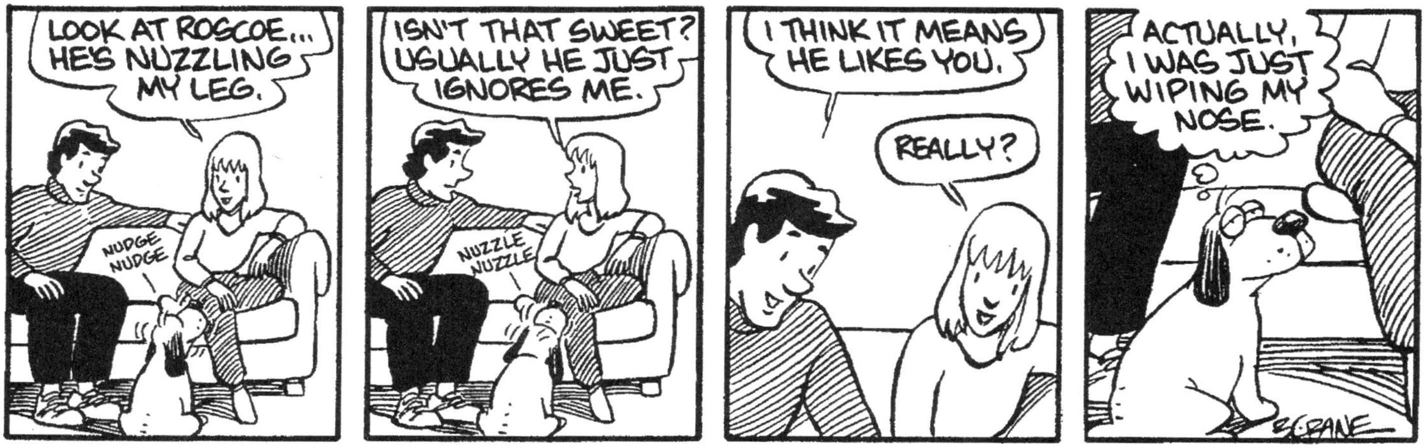
LOOK AT ROSCOE... HE'S NUZZLING MY LEG.
NUDGE NUDGE
ISN'T THAT SWEET? USUALLY HE JUST IGNORES ME.
NUZZLE NUZZLE
I THINK IT MEANS HE LIKES YOU.
REALLY?
ACTUALLY, I WAS JUST WIPING MY NOSE.
B.CRANE

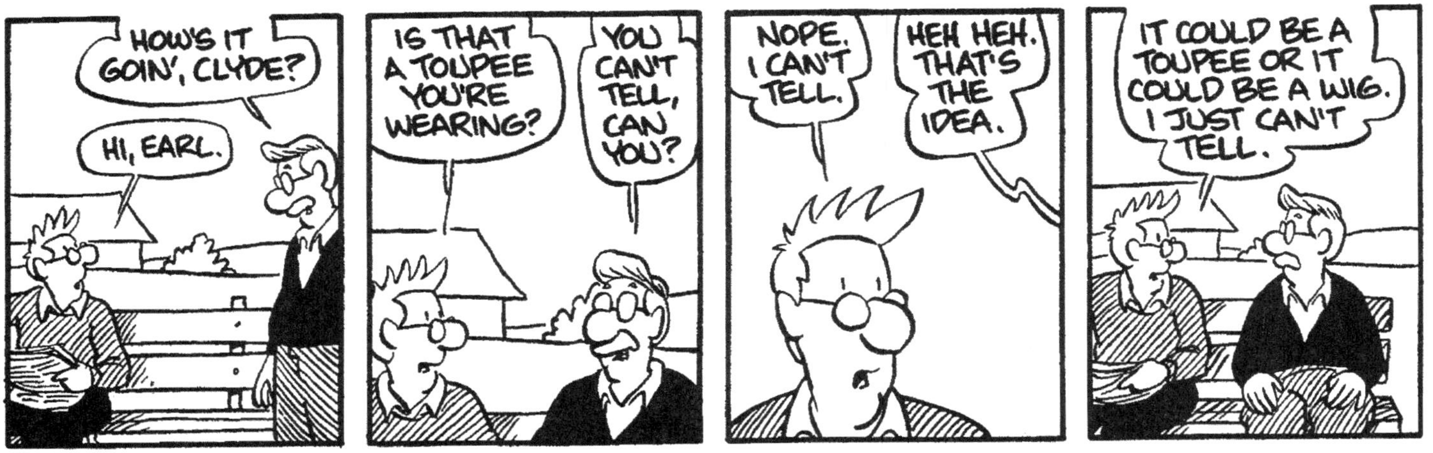
HOW'S IT GOIN', CLYDE?
HI, EARL.
IS THAT A TOUPEE YOU'RE WEARING?
YOU CAN'T TELL, CAN YOU?
NOPE. I CAN'T TELL.
HEH HEH. THAT'S THE IDEA.
IT COULD BE A TOUPEE OR IT COULD BE A WIG. I JUST CAN'T TELL.

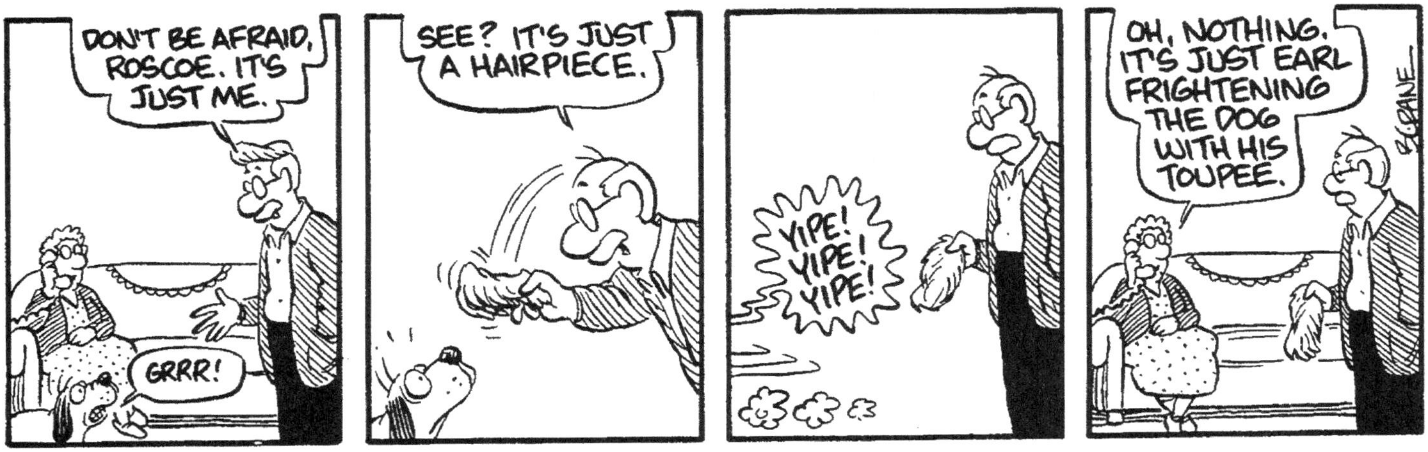
DON'T BE AFRAID, ROSCOE. IT'S JUST ME.
GRRR!
SEE? IT'S JUST A HAIRPIECE.
YIPE! YIPE! YIPE!
OH, NOTHING. IT'S JUST EARL FRIGHTENING THE DOG WITH HIS TOUPEE.

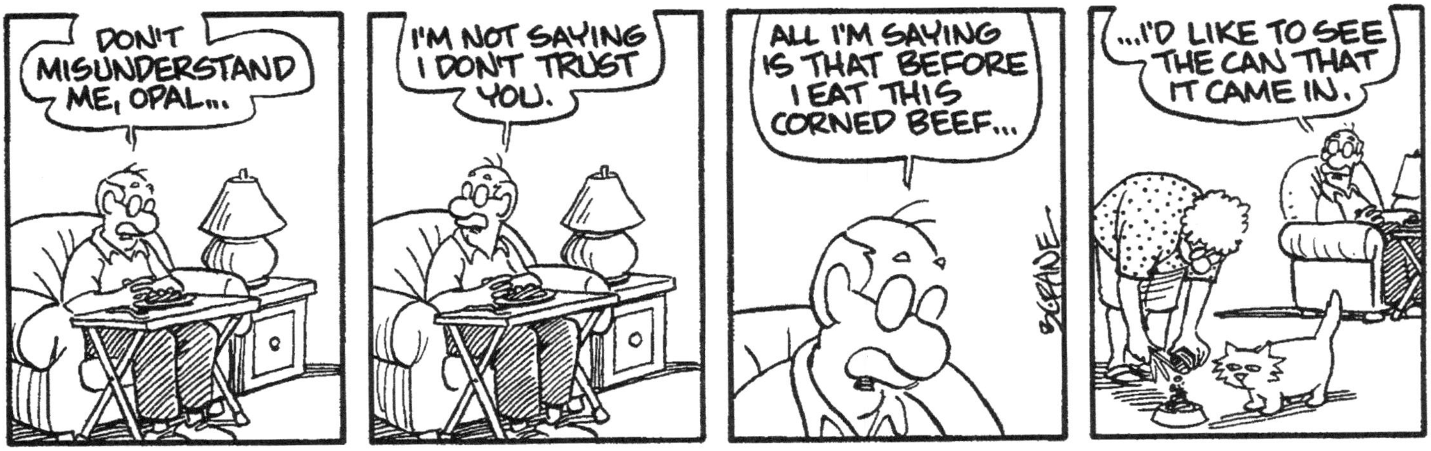
DON'T MISUNDERSTAND ME, OPAL...
I'M NOT SAYING I DON'T TRUST YOU.
ALL I'M SAYING IS THAT BEFORE I EAT THIS CORNED BEEF...
...I'D LIKE TO SEE THE CAN THAT IT CAME IN.

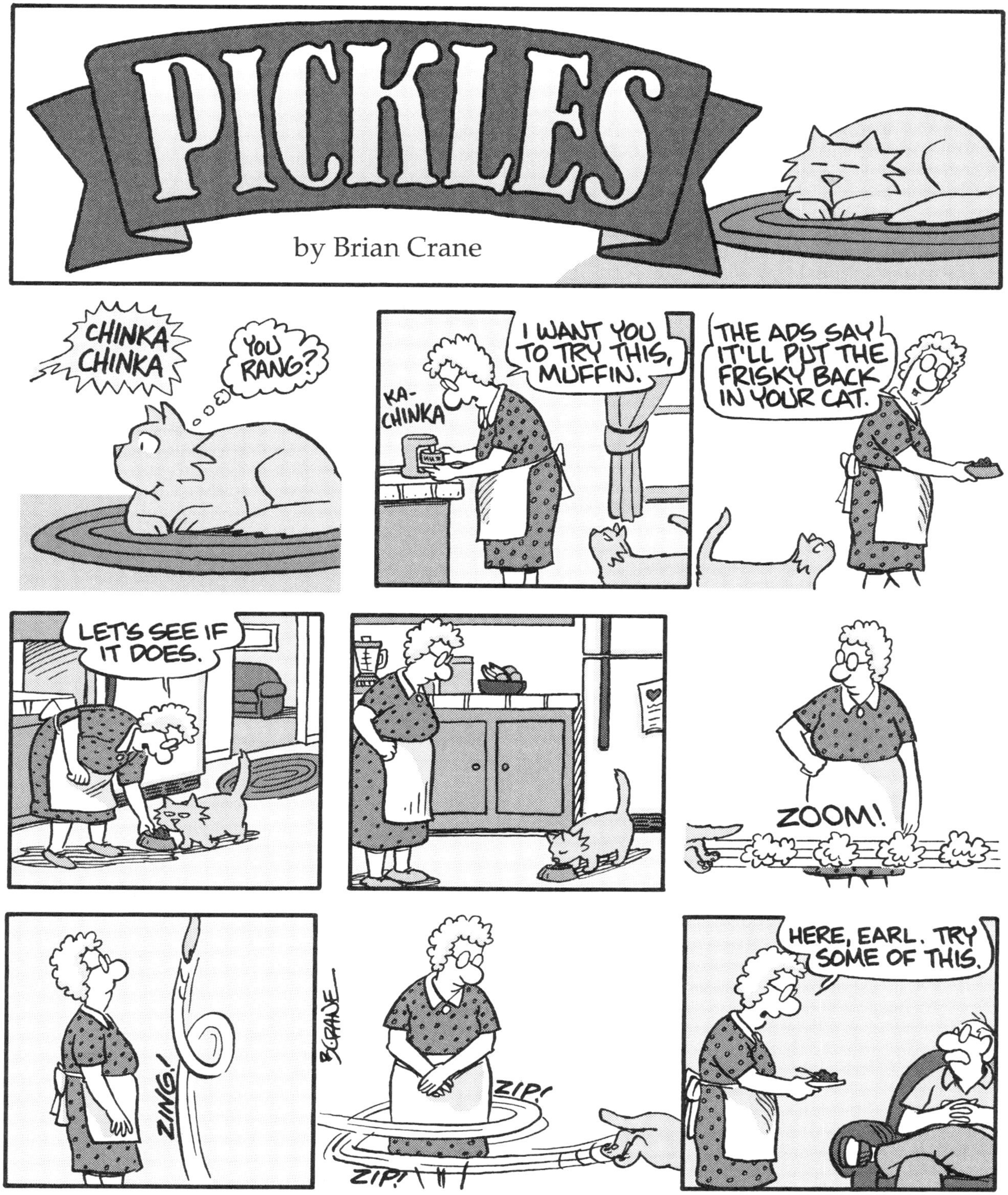
PICKLES
by Brian Crane
CHINKA CHINKA
YOU RANG?
KA-CHINKA
I WANT YOU TO TRY THIS, MUFFIN.
THE ADS SAY IT'LL PUT THE FRISKY BACK IN YOUR CAT.
LET'S SEE IF IT DOES.
ZOOM!
ZING!
ZIP!
ZIP!
B. CRANE
HERE, EARL. TRY SOME OF THIS.

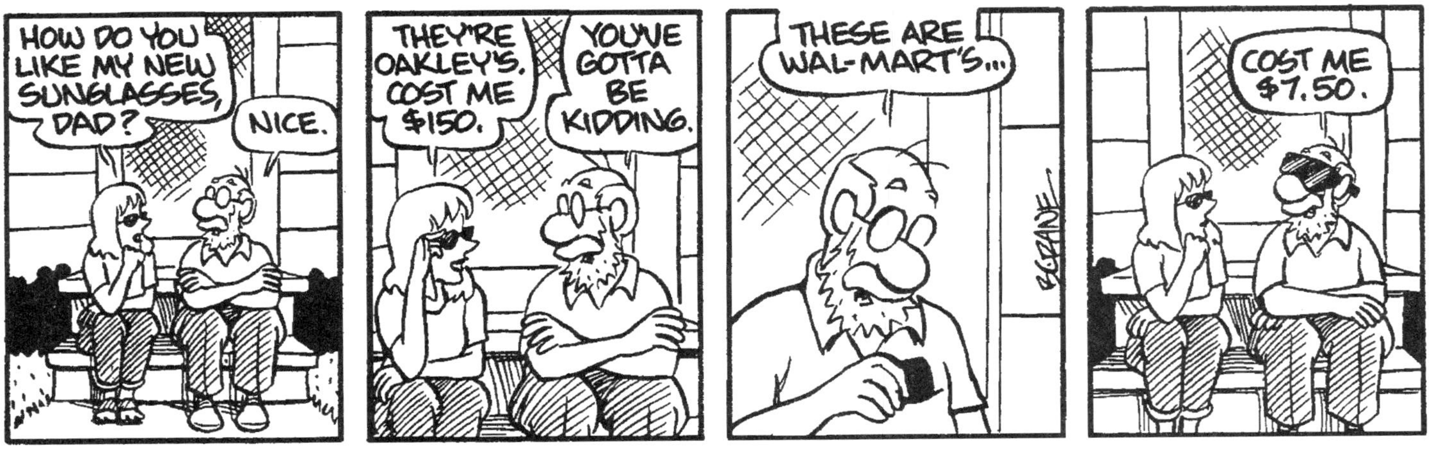
HOW DO YOU LIKE MY NEW SUNGLASSES, DAD?
NICE.
THEY'RE OAKLEY'S. COST ME $150.
YOU'VE GOTTA BE KIDDING.
THESE ARE WAL-MART'S...
COST ME $7.50.

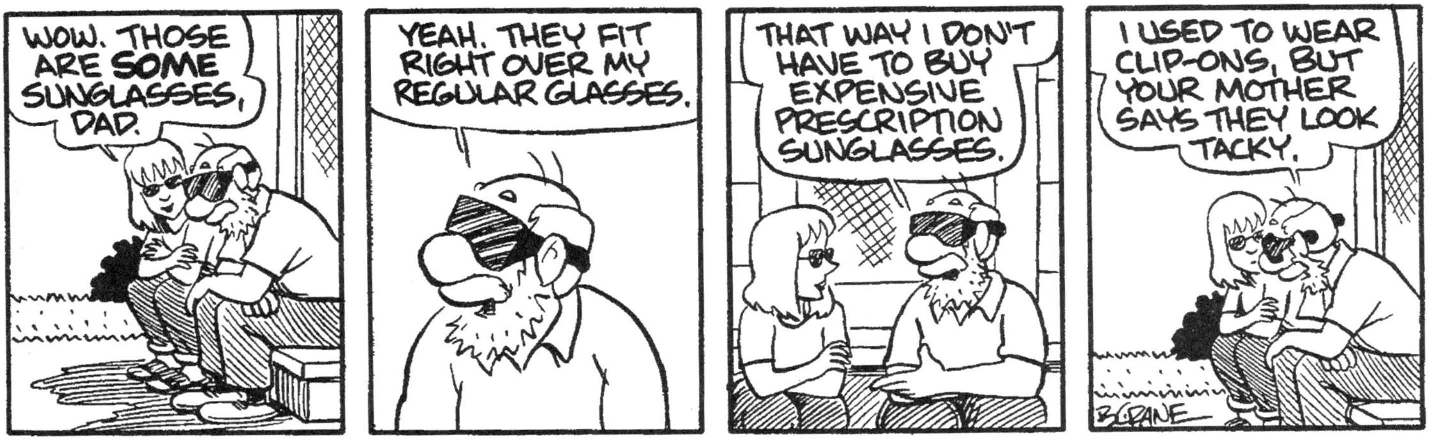
WOW. THOSE ARE **SOME** SUNGLASSES, DAD.
YEAH. THEY FIT RIGHT OVER MY REGULAR GLASSES.
THAT WAY I DON'T HAVE TO BUY EXPENSIVE PRESCRIPTION SUNGLASSES.
I USED TO WEAR CLIP-ONS, BUT YOUR MOTHER SAYS THEY LOOK TACKY.

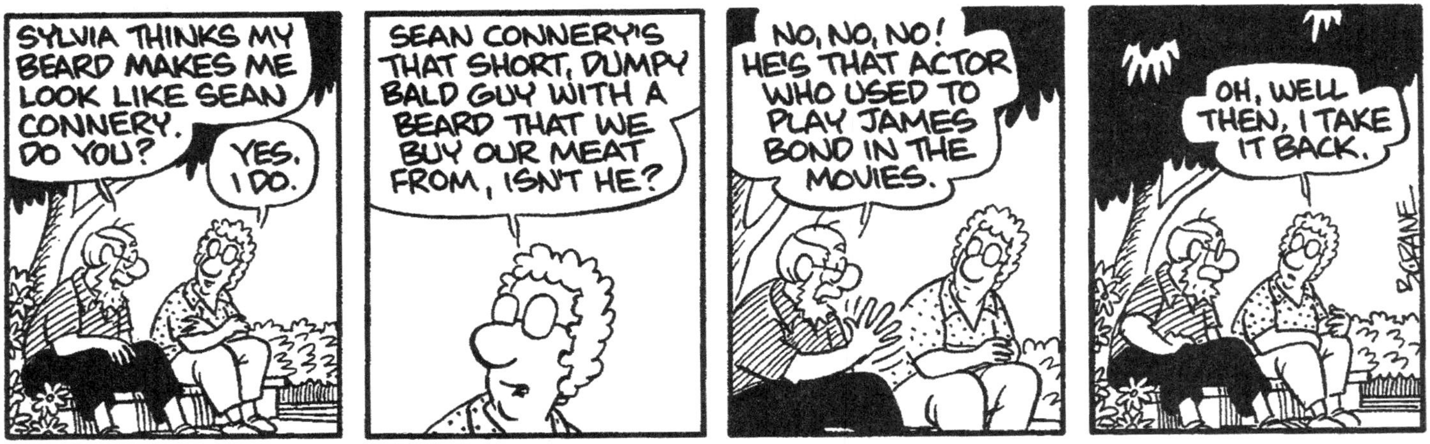
SYLVIA THINKS MY BEARD MAKES ME LOOK LIKE SEAN CONNERY. DO YOU?
YES. I DO.
SEAN CONNERY'S THAT SHORT, DUMPY BALD GUY WITH A BEARD THAT WE BUY OUR MEAT FROM, ISN'T HE?
NO, NO, NO! HE'S THAT ACTOR WHO USED TO PLAY JAMES BOND IN THE MOVIES.
OH, WELL THEN, I TAKE IT BACK.

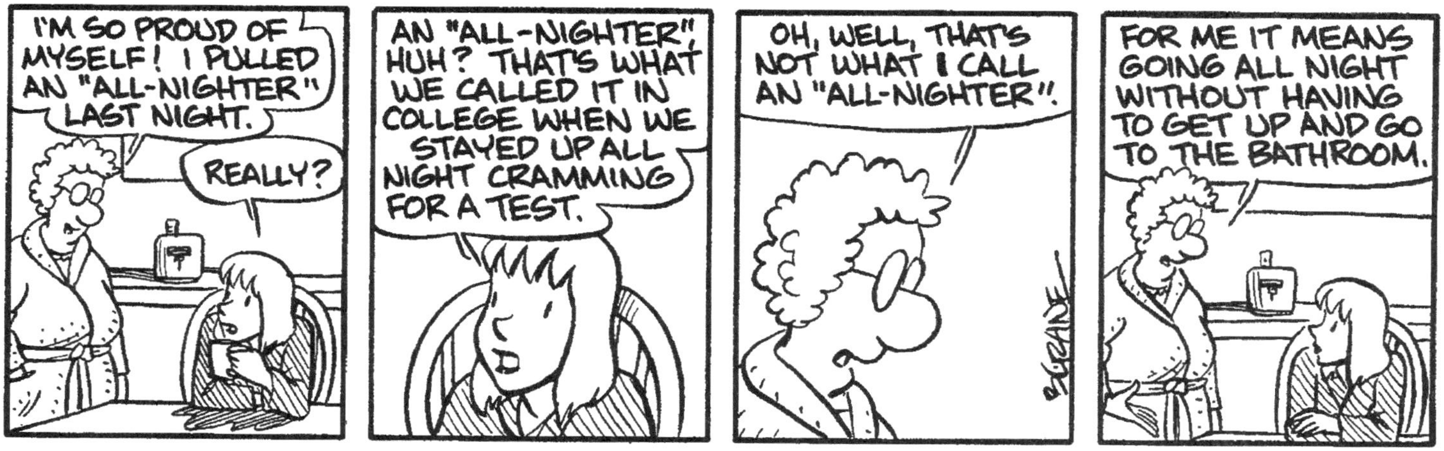
I'M SO PROUD OF MYSELF! I PULLED AN "ALL-NIGHTER" LAST NIGHT.
REALLY?
AN "ALL-NIGHTER", HUH? THAT'S WHAT WE CALLED IT IN COLLEGE WHEN WE STAYED UP ALL NIGHT CRAMMING FOR A TEST.
OH, WELL, THAT'S NOT WHAT I CALL AN "ALL-NIGHTER".
FOR ME IT MEANS GOING ALL NIGHT WITHOUT HAVING TO GET UP AND GO TO THE BATHROOM.

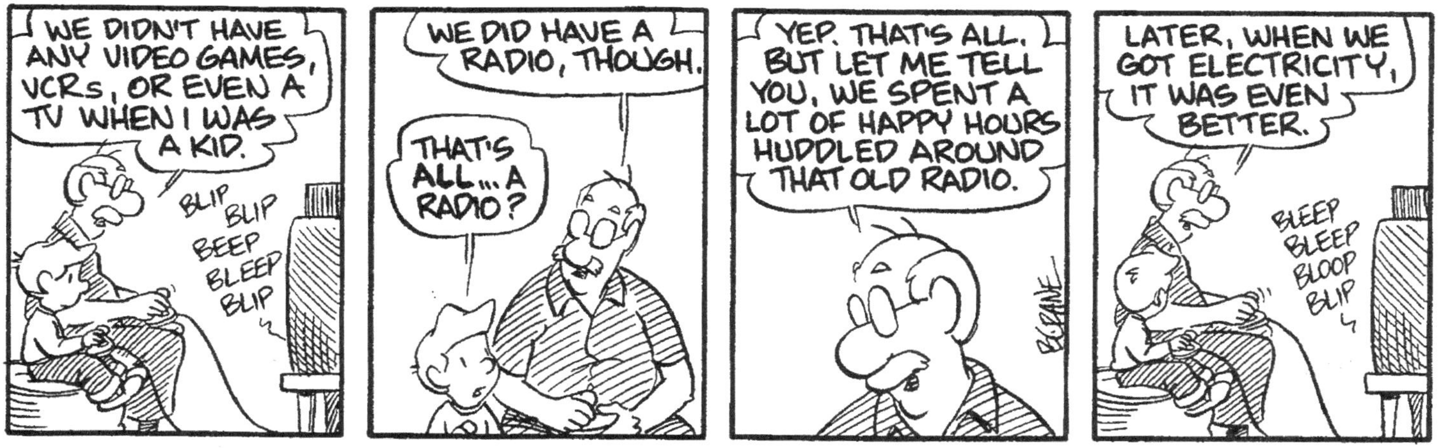
WE DIDN'T HAVE ANY VIDEO GAMES, VCRs, OR EVEN A TV WHEN I WAS A KID.
BLIP BLIP BEEP BLEEP BLIP
WE DID HAVE A RADIO, THOUGH.
THAT'S ALL... A RADIO?
YEP. THAT'S ALL. BUT LET ME TELL YOU, WE SPENT A LOT OF HAPPY HOURS HUDDLED AROUND THAT OLD RADIO.
LATER, WHEN WE GOT ELECTRICITY, IT WAS EVEN BETTER.
BLEEP BLEEP BLOOP BLIP

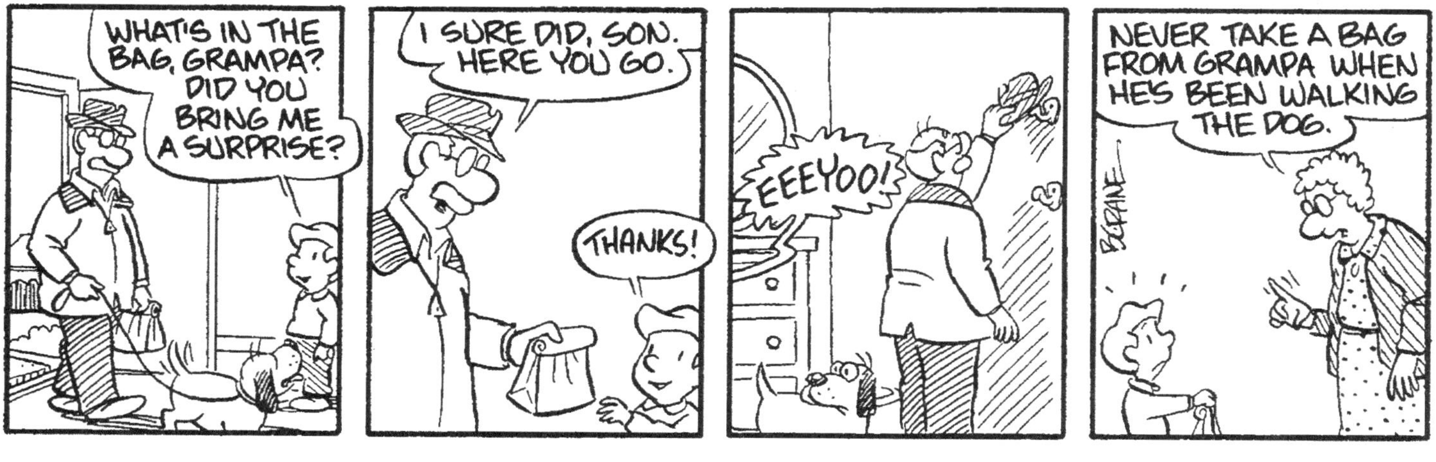
WHAT'S IN THE BAG, GRAMPA? DID YOU BRING ME A SURPRISE?
I SURE DID, SON. HERE YOU GO.
THANKS!
EEEYOO!
NEVER TAKE A BAG FROM GRAMPA WHEN HE'S BEEN WALKING THE DOG.

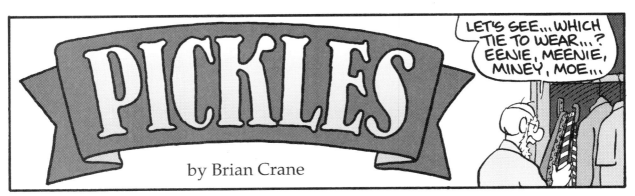

PICKLES

by Brian Crane

LET'S SEE... WHICH TIE TO WEAR...? EENIE, MEENIE, MINEY, MOE...

AAH... GOOD OLD MOE!

SHALL WE GO?

YOU'RE NOT GOING TO CHURCH LOOKING LIKE **THAT**, ARE YOU?

WHAT'S WRONG WITH THE WAY I LOOK?

WELL, ASIDE FROM THAT UGLY BEARD, YOUR TIE HAS THE THREE STOOGES ON IT.

I'M NOT SHAVIN' OFF THE BEARD.

THEN AT LEAST GO CHANGE THAT TIE. PICK OUT ONE THAT MATCHES YOUR SOCKS.

OKAY, IF YOU INSIST...

I'VE NEVER BEEN SO EMBARRASSED IN MY LIFE!

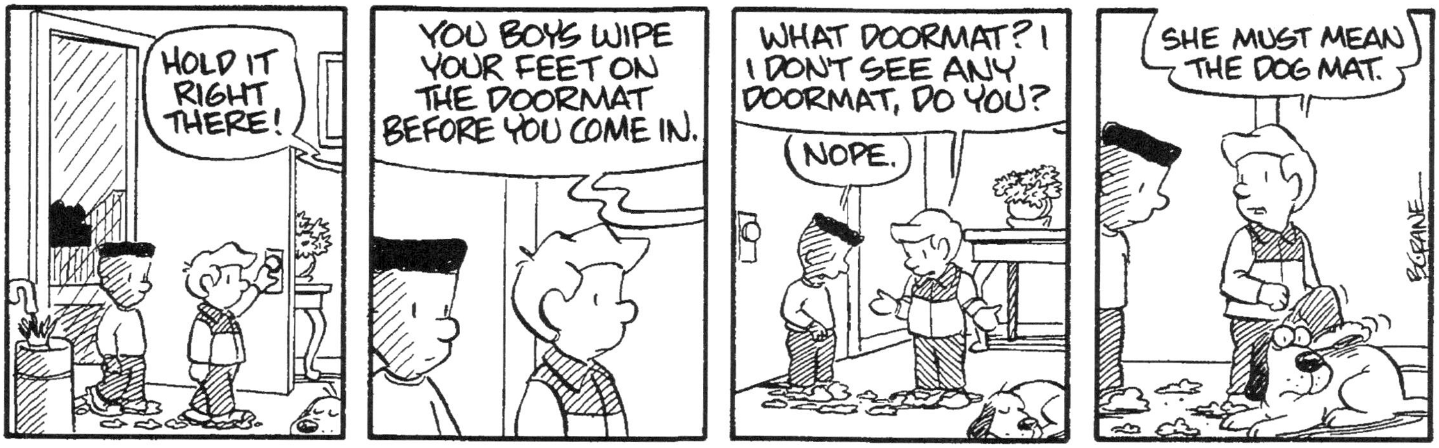
HOLD IT RIGHT THERE!
YOU BOYS WIPE YOUR FEET ON THE DOORMAT BEFORE YOU COME IN.
WHAT DOORMAT? I DON'T SEE ANY DOORMAT, DO YOU?
NOPE.
SHE MUST MEAN THE DOG MAT.

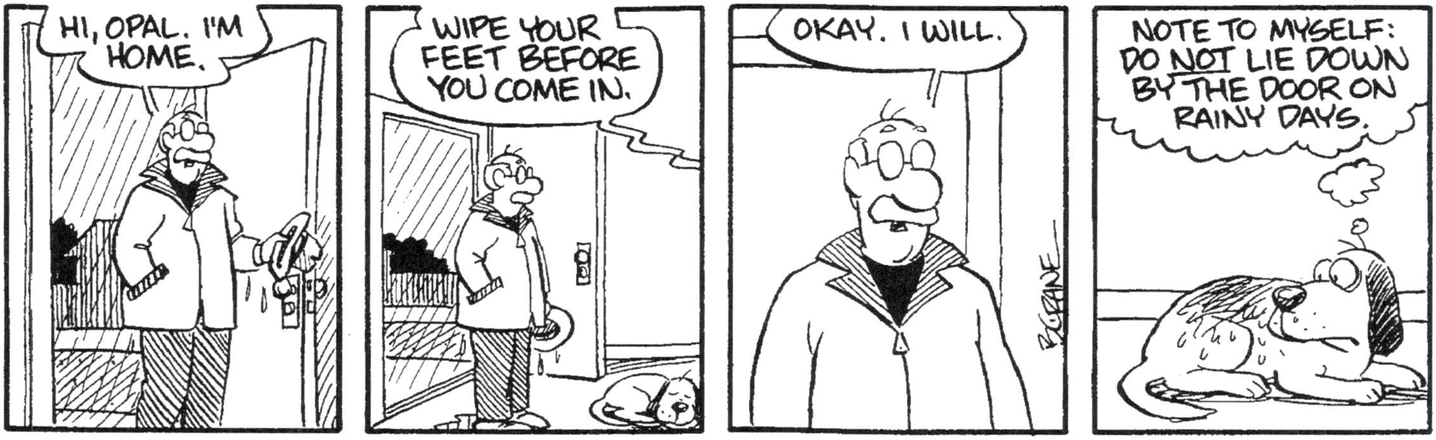
HI, OPAL. I'M HOME.
WIPE YOUR FEET BEFORE YOU COME IN.
OKAY. I WILL.
NOTE TO MYSELF: DO NOT LIE DOWN BY THE DOOR ON RAINY DAYS.

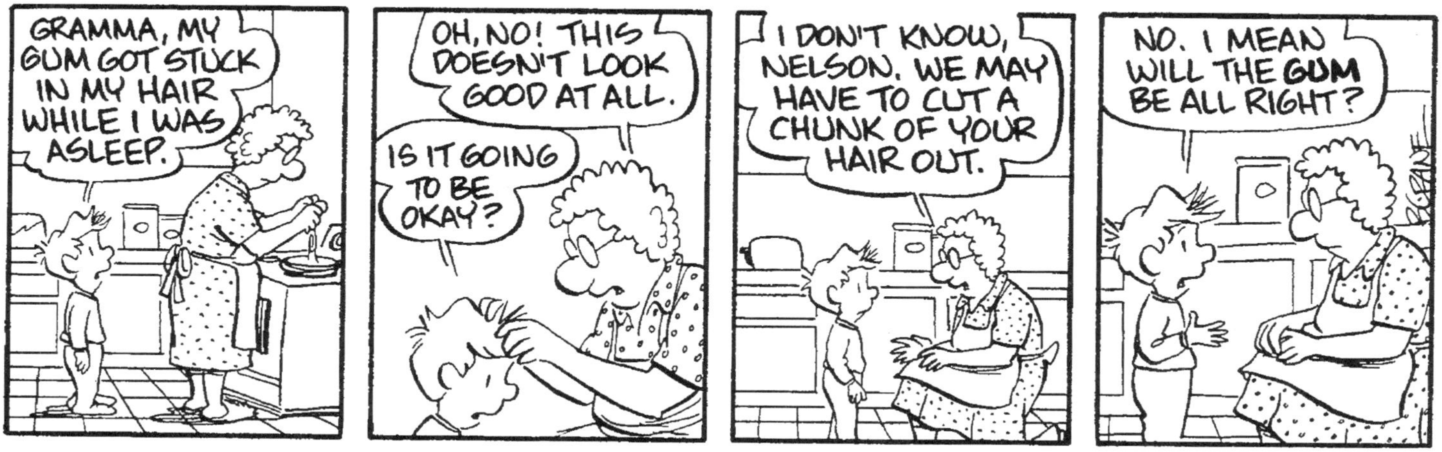
GRAMMA, MY GUM GOT STUCK IN MY HAIR WHILE I WAS ASLEEP.
OH, NO! THIS DOESN'T LOOK GOOD AT ALL.
IS IT GOING TO BE OKAY?
I DON'T KNOW, NELSON. WE MAY HAVE TO CUT A CHUNK OF YOUR HAIR OUT.
NO. I MEAN WILL THE GUM BE ALL RIGHT?

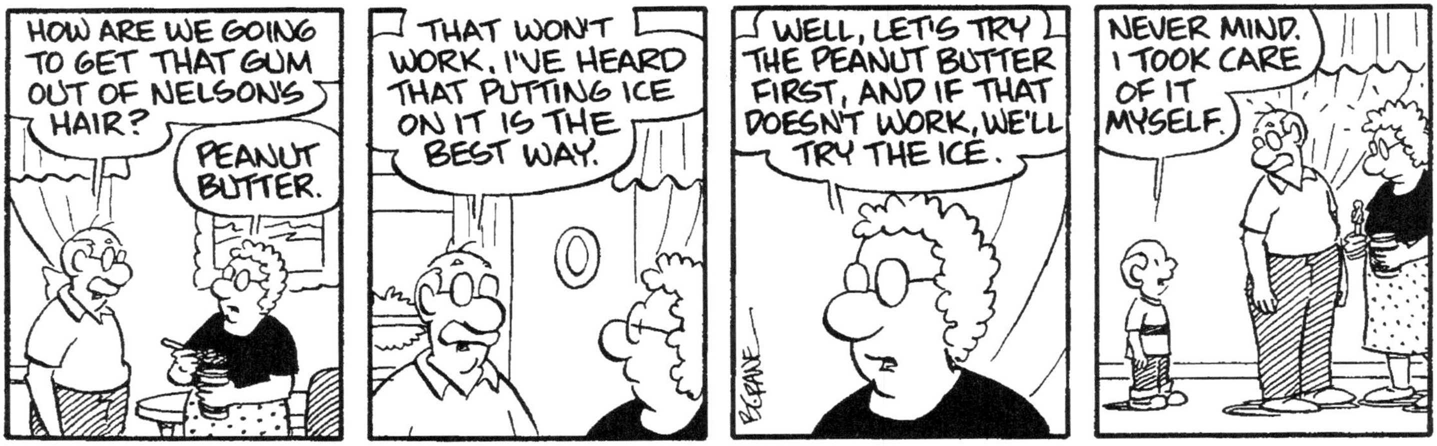
HOW ARE WE GOING TO GET THAT GUM OUT OF NELSON'S HAIR?
PEANUT BUTTER.
THAT WON'T WORK. I'VE HEARD THAT PUTTING ICE ON IT IS THE BEST WAY.
WELL, LET'S TRY THE PEANUT BUTTER FIRST, AND IF THAT DOESN'T WORK, WE'LL TRY THE ICE.
NEVER MIND. I TOOK CARE OF IT MYSELF.

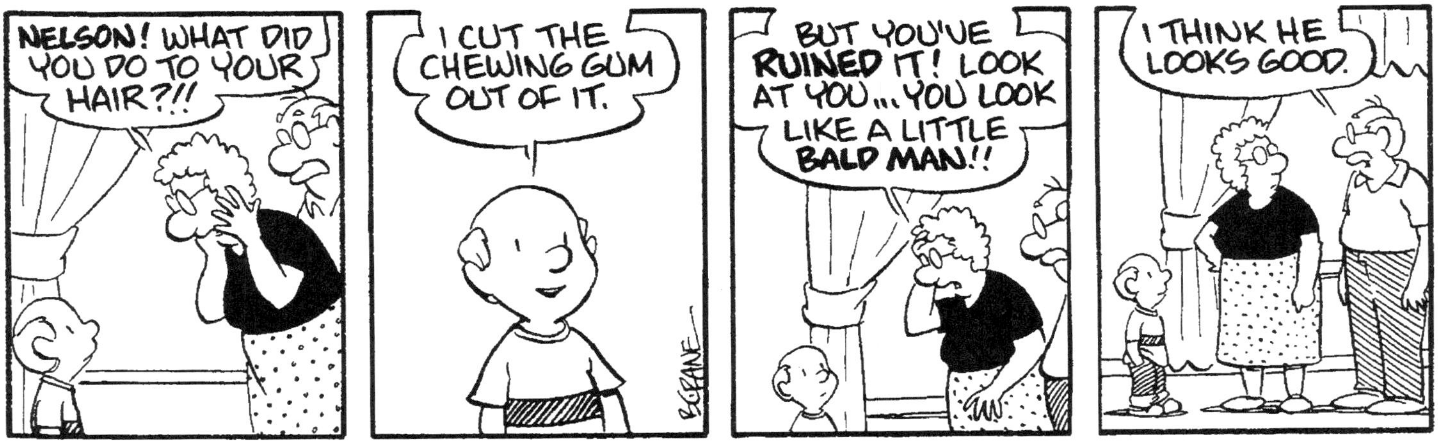
NELSON! WHAT DID YOU DO TO YOUR HAIR?!!
I CUT THE CHEWING GUM OUT OF IT.
BUT YOU'VE RUINED IT! LOOK AT YOU... YOU LOOK LIKE A LITTLE BALD MAN!!
I THINK HE LOOKS GOOD.

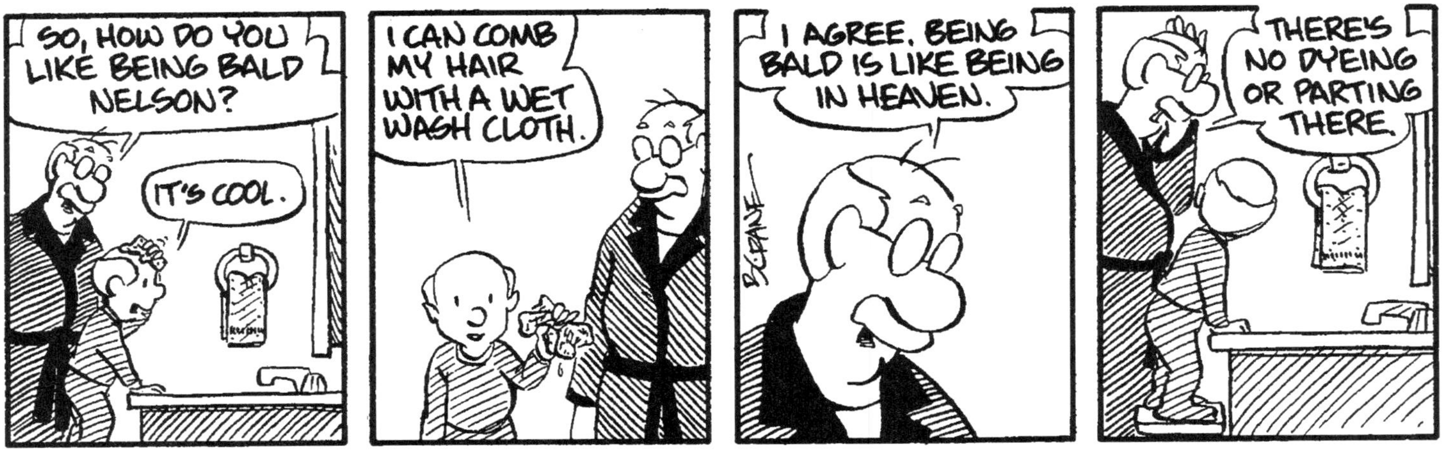
SO, HOW DO YOU LIKE BEING BALD NELSON?
IT'S COOL.
I CAN COMB MY HAIR WITH A WET WASH CLOTH.
I AGREE. BEING BALD IS LIKE BEING IN HEAVEN.
THERE'S NO DYEING OR PARTING THERE.

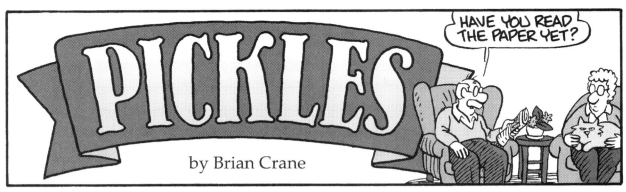

PICKLES

by Brian Crane

HAVE YOU READ THE PAPER YET?

NO. IF I WANT BAD NEWS I'LL READ MY BANK BOOK.

HMM... HERE'S SOME GOOD NEWS FOR YOU.

WHAT IS IT?

SOME SCIENTISTS AT A UNIVERSITY DID A STUDY...

UH HUH...

IT TURNS OUT THAT WOMEN WITH LARGE REAR ENDS TEND TO LIVE LONGER.

THEY'RE NOT SURE WHY.

SOME PEOPLE DON'T HANDLE GOOD NEWS VERY WELL.

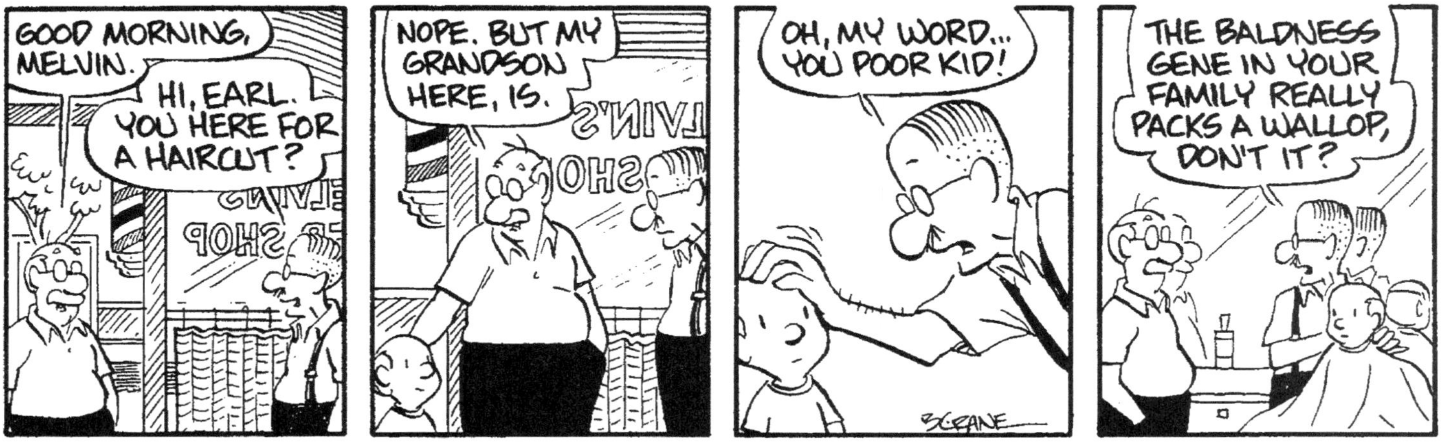
GOOD MORNING, MELVIN.
HI, EARL. YOU HERE FOR A HAIRCUT?
NOPE. BUT MY GRANDSON HERE, IS.
OH, MY WORD... YOU POOR KID!
THE BALDNESS GENE IN YOUR FAMILY REALLY PACKS A WALLOP, DON'T IT?

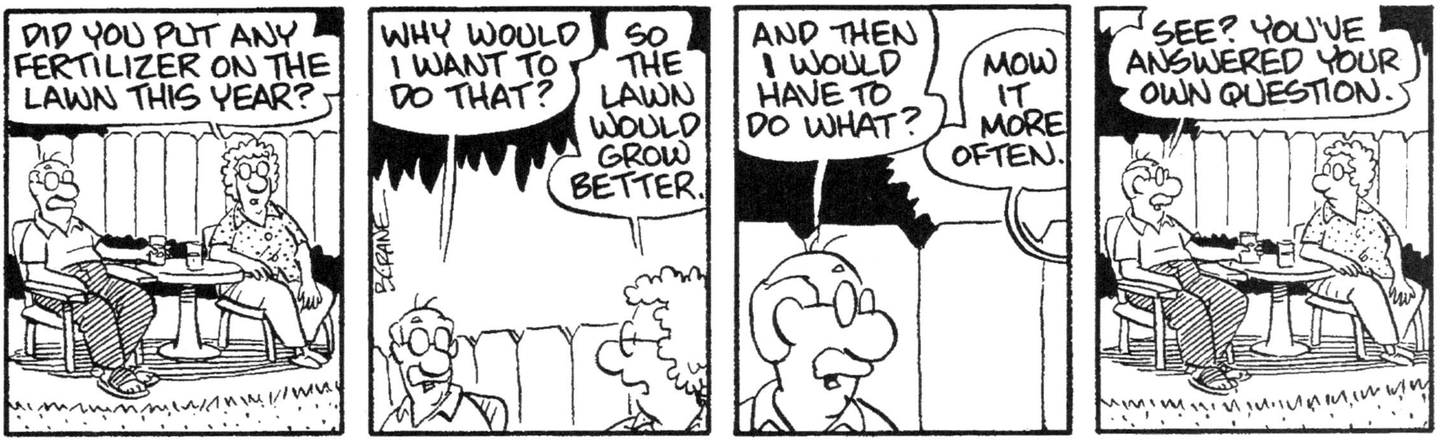
DID YOU PUT ANY FERTILIZER ON THE LAWN THIS YEAR?
WHY WOULD I WANT TO DO THAT?
SO THE LAWN WOULD GROW BETTER.
AND THEN I WOULD HAVE TO DO WHAT?
MOW IT MORE OFTEN.
SEE? YOU'VE ANSWERED YOUR OWN QUESTION.

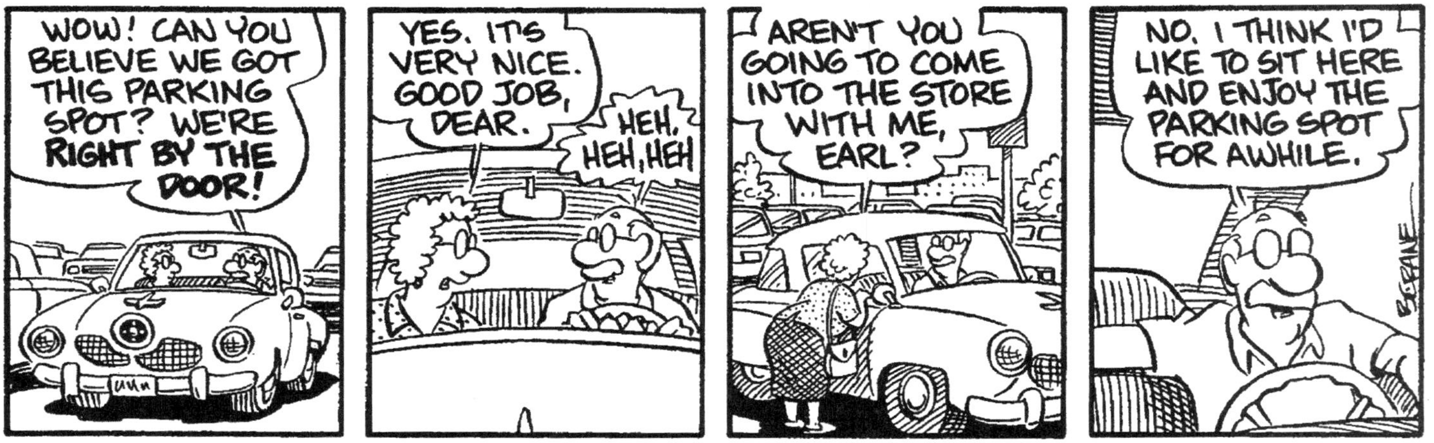
WOW! CAN YOU BELIEVE WE GOT THIS PARKING SPOT? WE'RE RIGHT BY THE DOOR!
YES. IT'S VERY NICE. GOOD JOB, DEAR.
HEH, HEH, HEH
AREN'T YOU GOING TO COME INTO THE STORE WITH ME, EARL?
NO. I THINK I'D LIKE TO SIT HERE AND ENJOY THE PARKING SPOT FOR AWHILE.

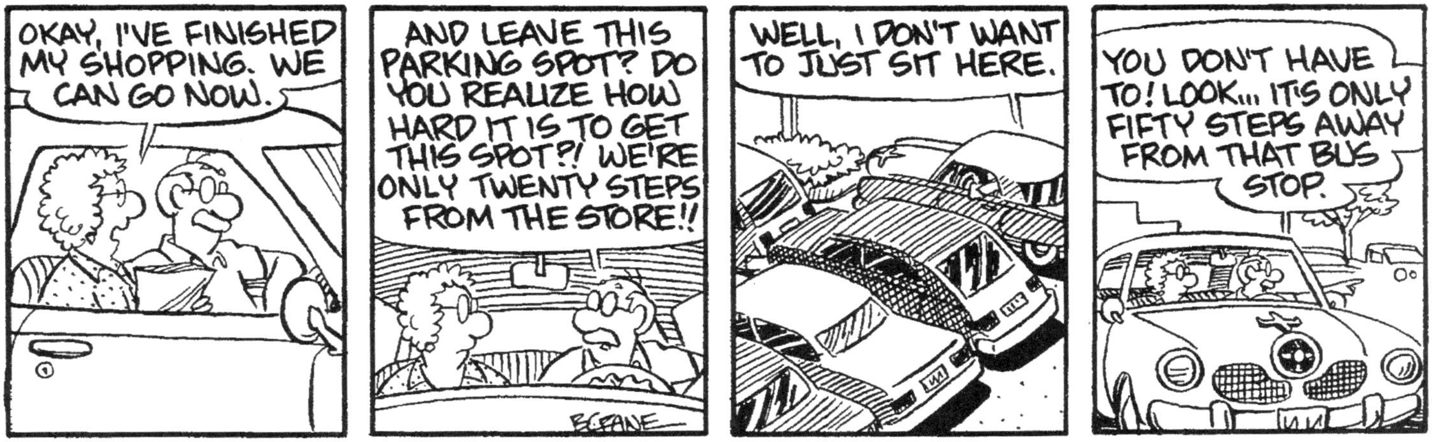
OKAY, I'VE FINISHED MY SHOPPING. WE CAN GO NOW.
AND LEAVE THIS PARKING SPOT? DO YOU REALIZE HOW HARD IT IS TO GET THIS SPOT?! WE'RE ONLY TWENTY STEPS FROM THE STORE!!
WELL, I DON'T WANT TO JUST SIT HERE.
YOU DON'T HAVE TO! LOOK... IT'S ONLY FIFTY STEPS AWAY FROM THAT BUS STOP.

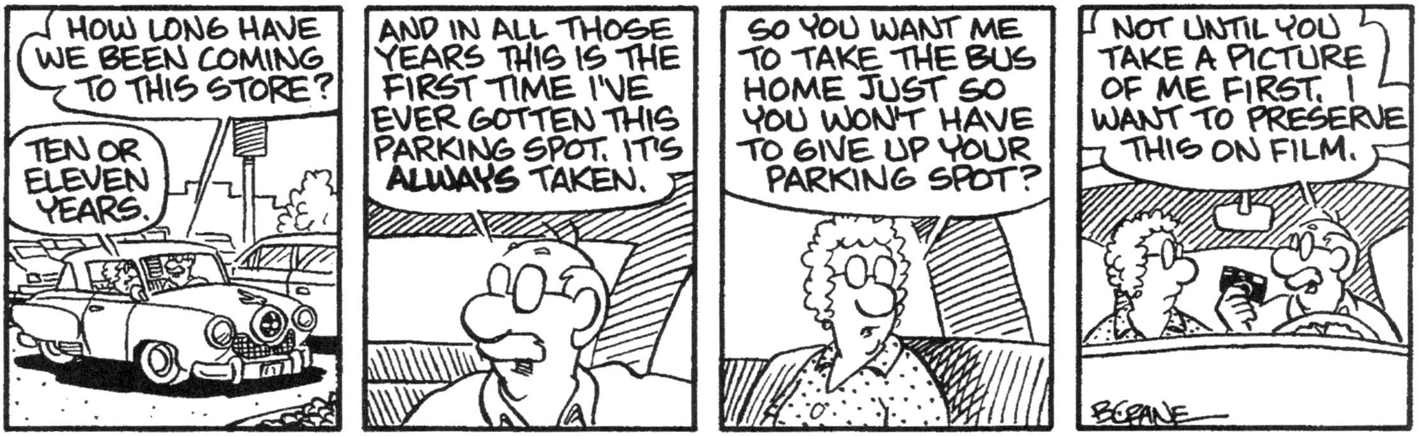
HOW LONG HAVE WE BEEN COMING TO THIS STORE?
TEN OR ELEVEN YEARS.
AND IN ALL THOSE YEARS THIS IS THE FIRST TIME I'VE EVER GOTTEN THIS PARKING SPOT. IT'S **ALWAYS** TAKEN.
SO YOU WANT ME TO TAKE THE BUS HOME JUST SO YOU WON'T HAVE TO GIVE UP YOUR PARKING SPOT?
NOT UNTIL YOU TAKE A PICTURE OF ME FIRST. I WANT TO PRESERVE THIS ON FILM.

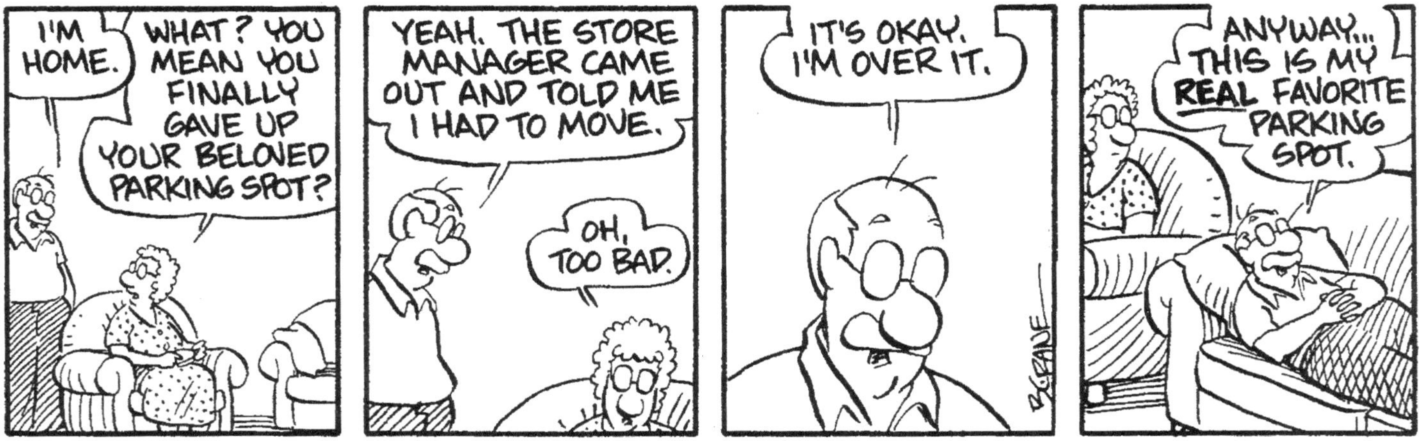
I'M HOME.
WHAT? YOU MEAN YOU FINALLY GAVE UP YOUR BELOVED PARKING SPOT?
YEAH. THE STORE MANAGER CAME OUT AND TOLD ME I HAD TO MOVE.
OH, TOO BAD.
IT'S OKAY. I'M OVER IT.
ANYWAY... THIS IS MY **REAL** FAVORITE PARKING SPOT.

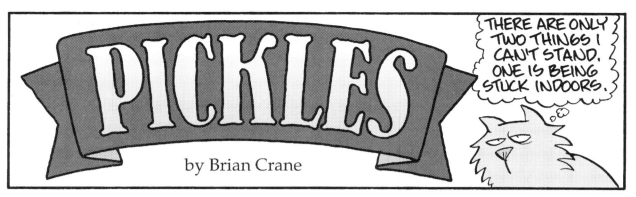

PICKLES

by Brian Crane

THERE ARE ONLY TWO THINGS I CAN'T STAND. ONE IS BEING STUCK INDOORS.

THE OTHER IS BEING STUCK OUTDOORS.

I THINK MUFFIN WANTS OUT.

LOOKS LIKE ROSCOE WANTS OUT NOW.

UH OH. SOUNDS LIKE HE WANTS BACK IN NOW.

SCRATCH. SCRATCH.

OOPS. GUESS WHO WANTS IN AGAIN.

MEOW

AND TO THINK I WAS WORRIED I'D HAVE NOTHING TO DO AFTER I RETIRED.

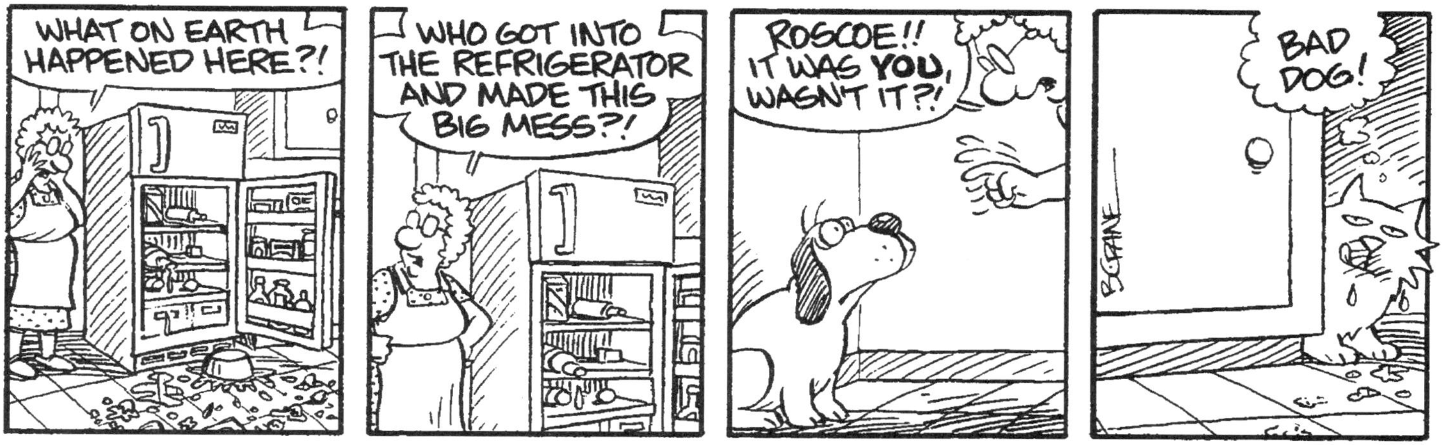
WHAT ON EARTH HAPPENED HERE?!
WHO GOT INTO THE REFRIGERATOR AND MADE THIS BIG MESS?!
ROSCOE!! IT WAS **YOU**, WASN'T IT?!
BAD DOG!

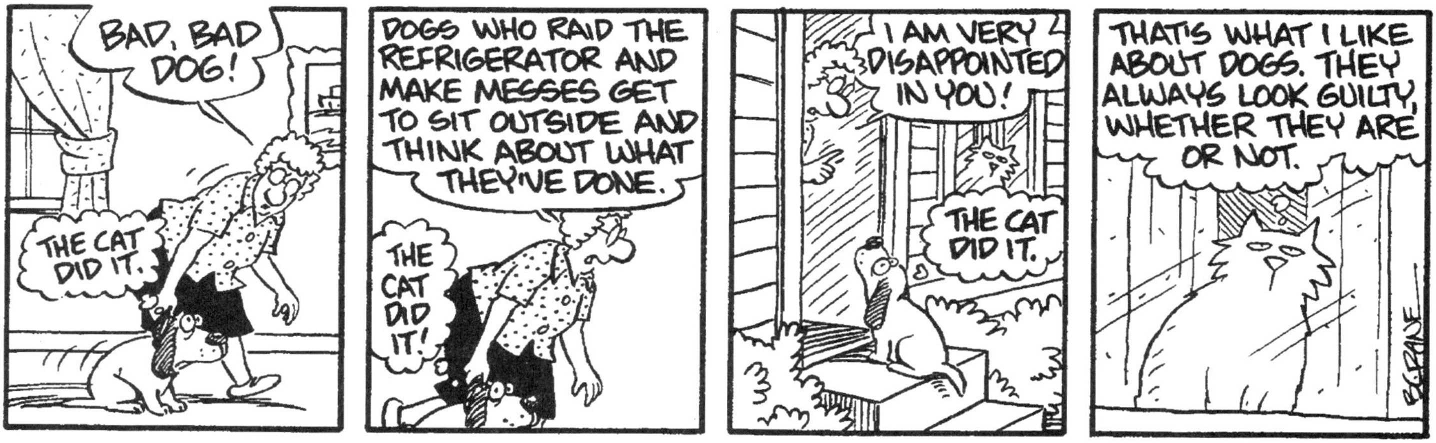
BAD, BAD DOG!
THE CAT DID IT.
DOGS WHO RAID THE REFRIGERATOR AND MAKE MESSES GET TO SIT OUTSIDE AND THINK ABOUT WHAT THEY'VE DONE.
THE CAT DID IT!
I AM VERY DISAPPOINTED IN YOU!
THE CAT DID IT.
THAT'S WHAT I LIKE ABOUT DOGS. THEY ALWAYS LOOK GUILTY, WHETHER THEY ARE OR NOT.

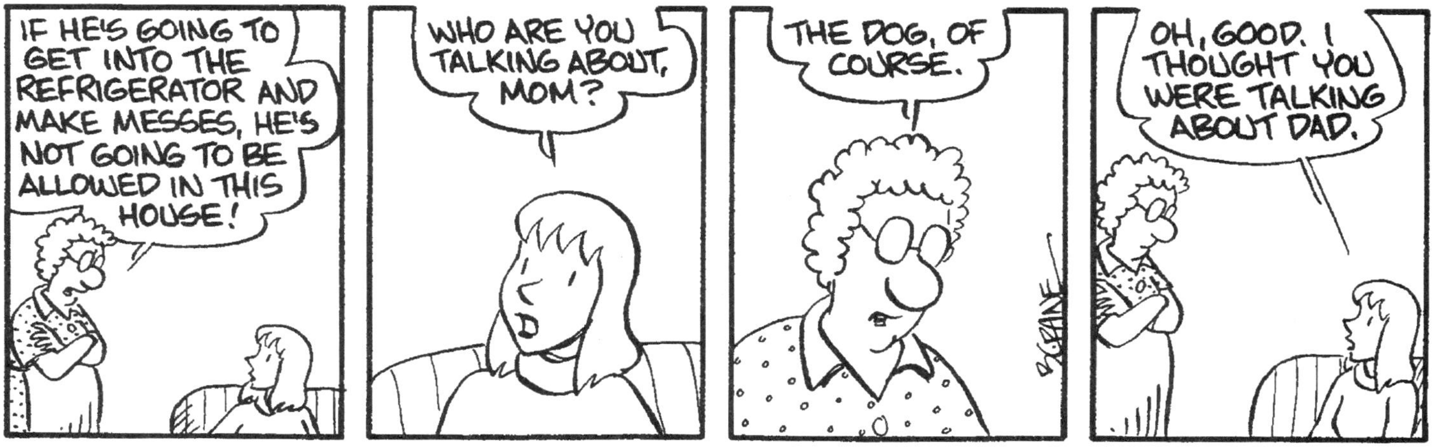
IF HE'S GOING TO GET INTO THE REFRIGERATOR AND MAKE MESSES, HE'S NOT GOING TO BE ALLOWED IN THIS HOUSE!
WHO ARE YOU TALKING ABOUT, MOM?
THE DOG, OF COURSE.
OH, GOOD. I THOUGHT YOU WERE TALKING ABOUT DAD.

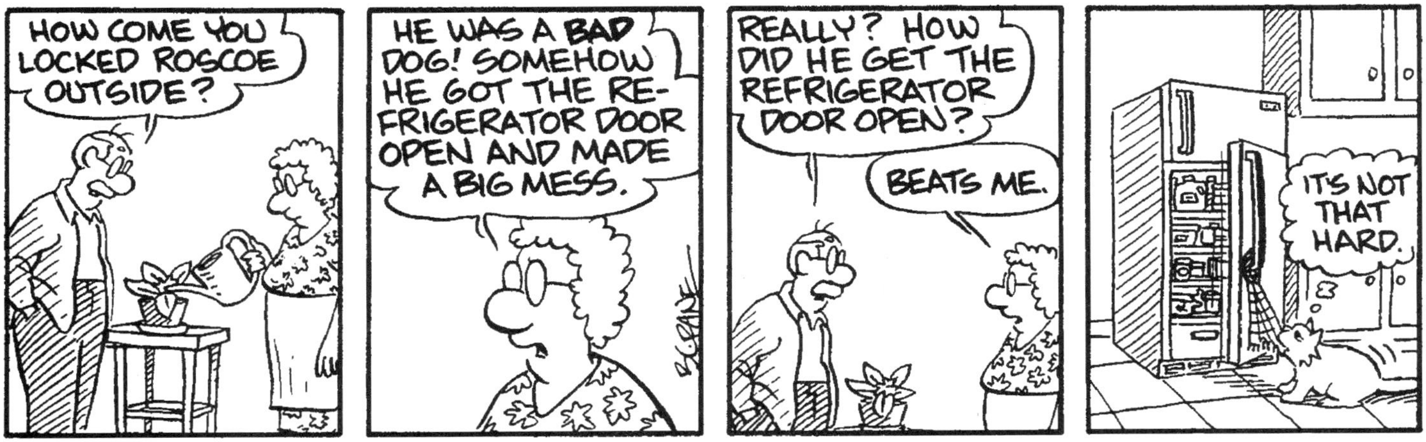
HOW COME YOU LOCKED ROSCOE OUTSIDE?
HE WAS A BAD DOG! SOMEHOW HE GOT THE RE-FRIGERATOR DOOR OPEN AND MADE A BIG MESS.
REALLY? HOW DID HE GET THE REFRIGERATOR DOOR OPEN?
BEATS ME.
IT'S NOT THAT HARD.

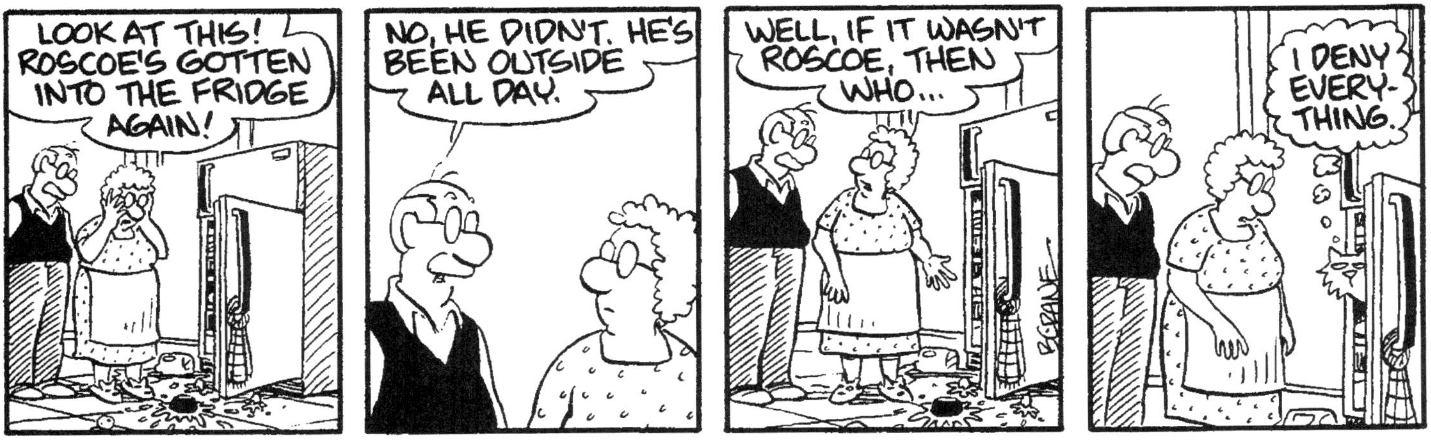
LOOK AT THIS! ROSCOE'S GOTTEN INTO THE FRIDGE AGAIN!
NO, HE DIDN'T. HE'S BEEN OUTSIDE ALL DAY.
WELL, IF IT WASN'T ROSCOE, THEN WHO...
I DENY EVERY-THING.

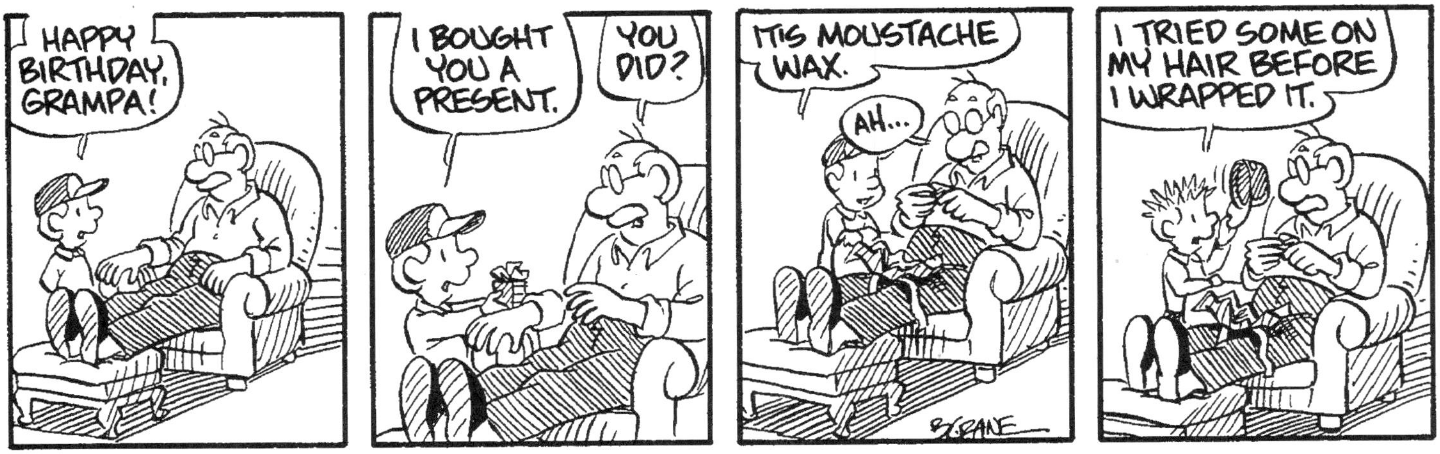
HAPPY BIRTHDAY, GRAMPA!
I BOUGHT YOU A PRESENT.
YOU DID?
IT'S MOUSTACHE WAX.
AH...
I TRIED SOME ON MY HAIR BEFORE I WRAPPED IT.

PICKLES

by Brian Crane

THIS OLD SWING SURE IS GETTING CREAKY.

CREAK!! SQUEAK!

THAT'S NOT THE SWING. IT'S MY KNEES.

WELL, OUR DAUGHTER'S GETTING MARRIED. LET'S HOPE HER MARRIAGE LASTS AS LONG AS OURS.

WE'VE BEEN TOGETHER A LONG TIME, HAVEN'T WE?

YES, INDEED. AND WE'VE BEEN THROUGH A LOT OF TRIALS AND TRIBULATIONS.

REMEMBER WHEN I LOST MY JOB? YOU WERE RIGHT THERE BY MY SIDE.

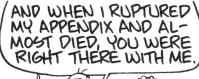

AND WHEN I RUPTURED MY APPENDIX AND ALMOST DIED, YOU WERE RIGHT THERE WITH ME.

AND WHEN THAT HOUSE FIRE DESTROYED EVERYTHING WE HAD, YOU WERE THERE TOO.

NO MATTER WHAT WENT WRONG, YOU WERE ALWAYS THERE. YOU KNOW WHAT THAT MEANS, DON'T YOU?

WHAT?

YOU'RE BAD LUCK.

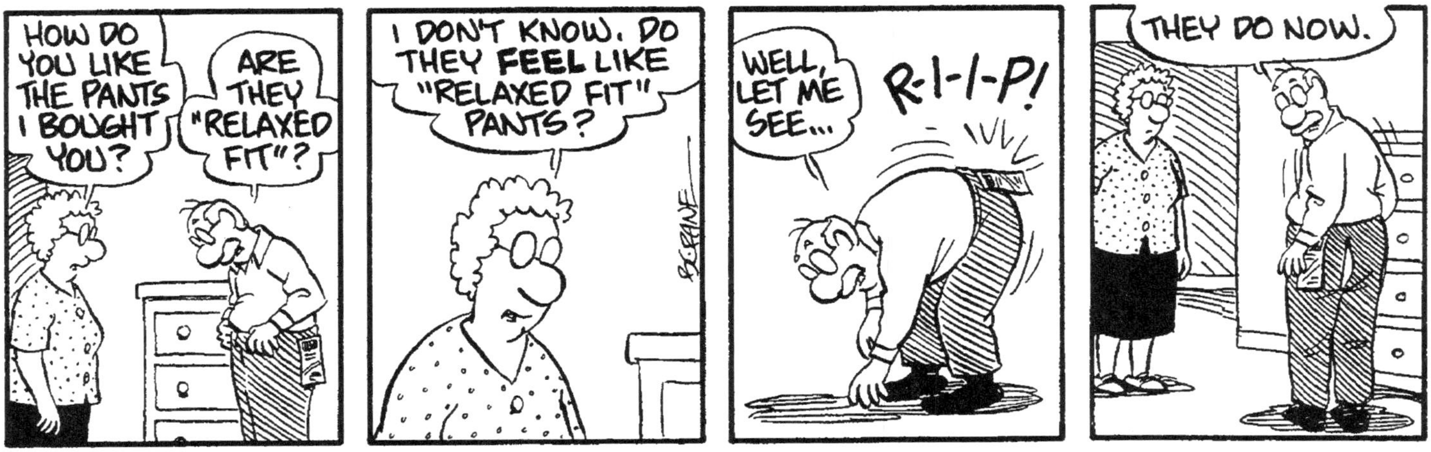
HOW DO YOU LIKE THE PANTS I BOUGHT YOU?
ARE THEY "RELAXED FIT"?
I DON'T KNOW. DO THEY **FEEL** LIKE "RELAXED FIT" PANTS?
WELL, LET ME SEE...
R-I-I-P!
THEY DO NOW.

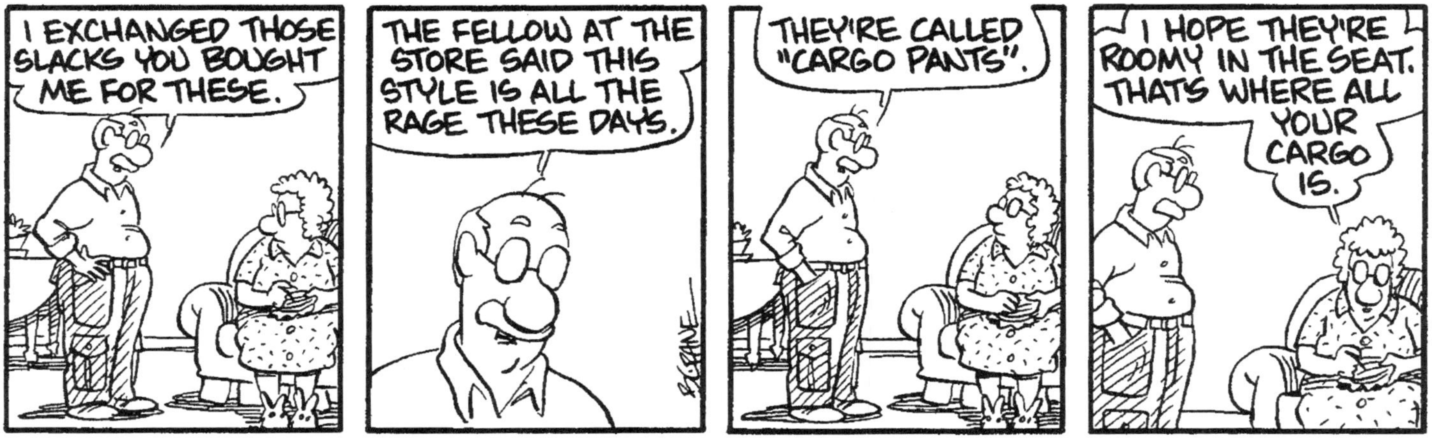
I EXCHANGED THOSE SLACKS YOU BOUGHT ME FOR THESE.
THE FELLOW AT THE STORE SAID THIS STYLE IS ALL THE RAGE THESE DAYS.
THEY'RE CALLED "CARGO PANTS".
I HOPE THEY'RE ROOMY IN THE SEAT. THAT'S WHERE ALL YOUR CARGO IS.

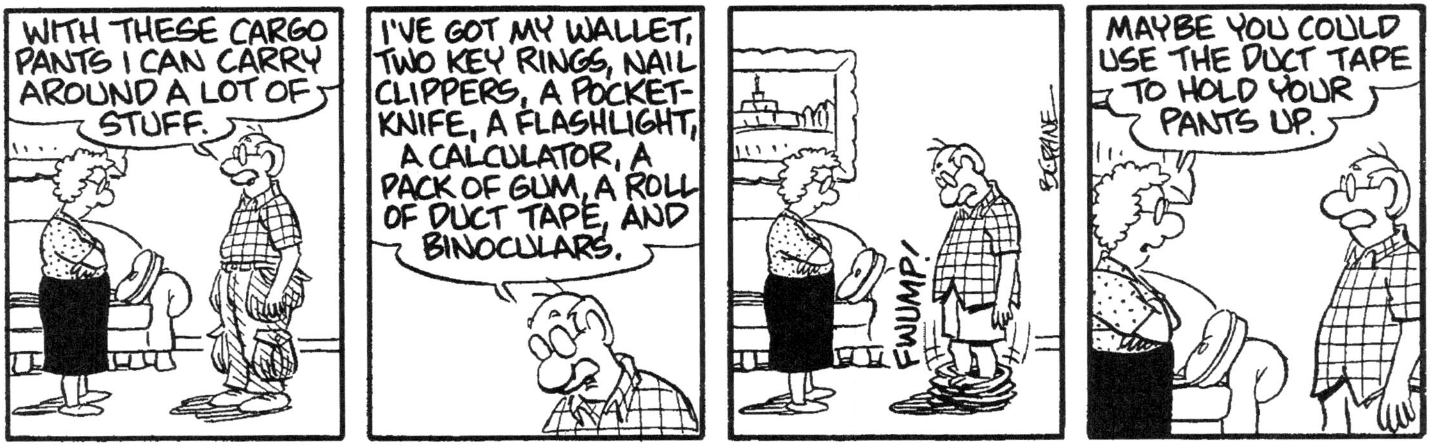
WITH THESE CARGO PANTS I CAN CARRY AROUND A LOT OF STUFF.
I'VE GOT MY WALLET, TWO KEY RINGS, NAIL CLIPPERS, A POCKET-KNIFE, A FLASHLIGHT, A CALCULATOR, A PACK OF GUM, A ROLL OF DUCT TAPE, AND BINOCULARS.
FWUMP!
MAYBE YOU COULD USE THE DUCT TAPE TO HOLD YOUR PANTS UP.

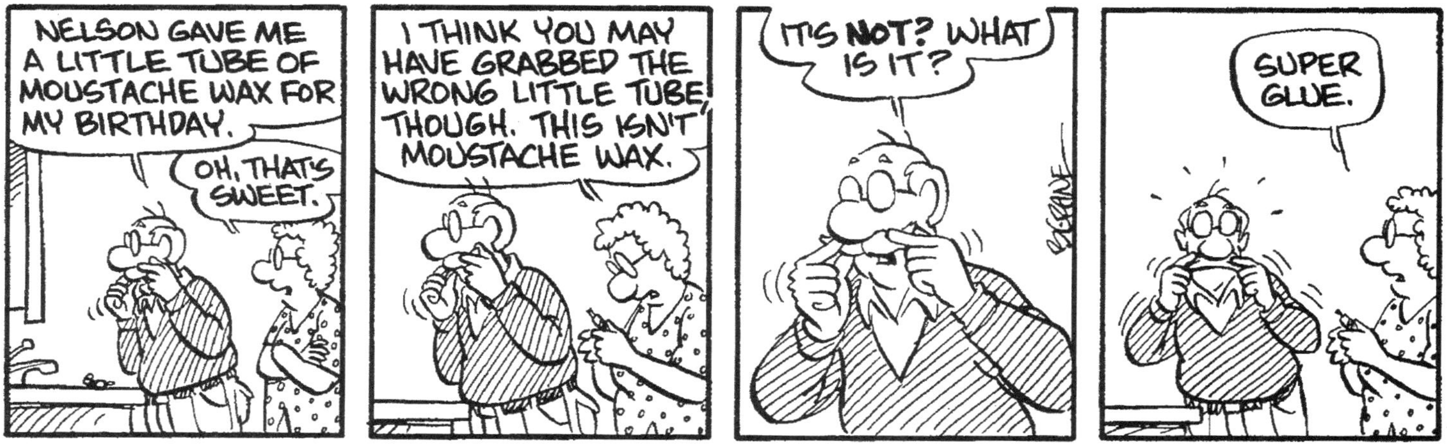
NELSON GAVE ME A LITTLE TUBE OF MOUSTACHE WAX FOR MY BIRTHDAY.
OH, THAT'S SWEET.
I THINK YOU MAY HAVE GRABBED THE WRONG LITTLE TUBE, THOUGH. THIS ISN'T MOUSTACHE WAX.
IT'S **NOT**? WHAT IS IT?
B.CRANE
SUPER GLUE.

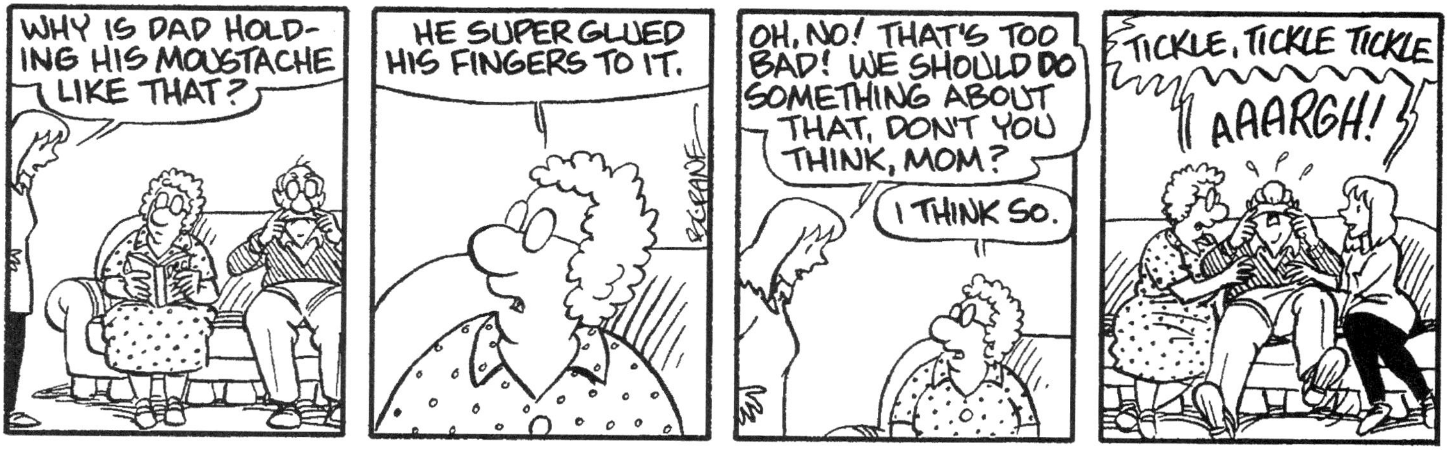
WHY IS DAD HOLDING HIS MOUSTACHE LIKE THAT?
HE SUPER GLUED HIS FINGERS TO IT.
B.CRANE
OH, NO! THAT'S TOO BAD! WE SHOULD **DO** SOMETHING ABOUT THAT, DON'T YOU THINK, MOM?
I THINK SO.
TICKLE, TICKLE TICKLE
AAARGH!

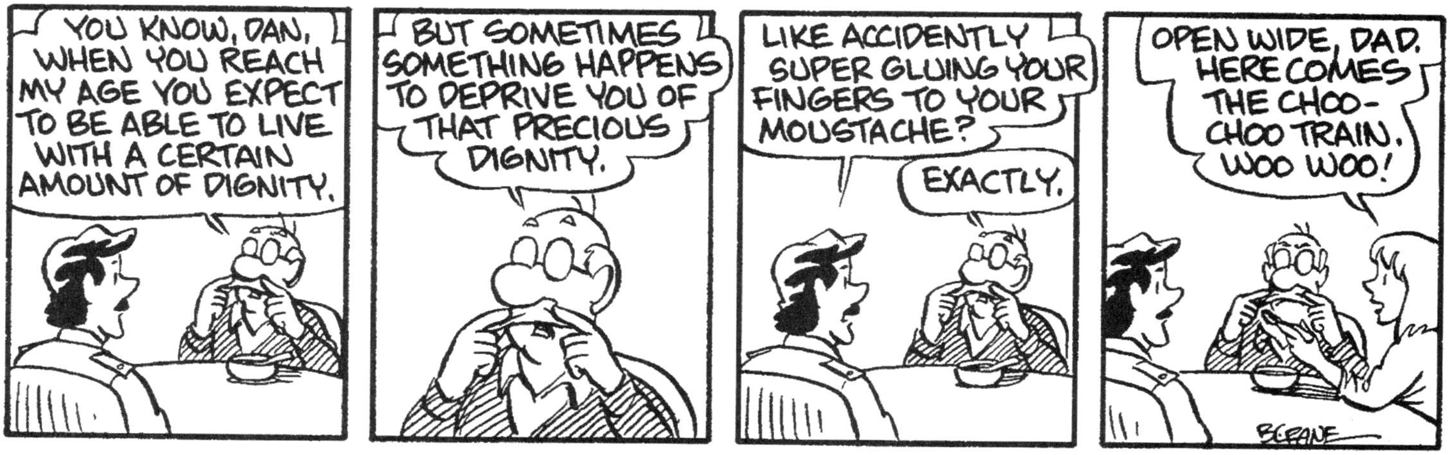
YOU KNOW, DAN, WHEN YOU REACH MY AGE YOU EXPECT TO BE ABLE TO LIVE WITH A CERTAIN AMOUNT OF DIGNITY.
BUT SOMETIMES SOMETHING HAPPENS TO DEPRIVE YOU OF THAT PRECIOUS DIGNITY.
LIKE ACCIDENTLY SUPER GLUING YOUR FINGERS TO YOUR MOUSTACHE?
EXACTLY.
OPEN WIDE, DAD. HERE COMES THE CHOO-CHOO TRAIN. WOO WOO!
B.CRANE

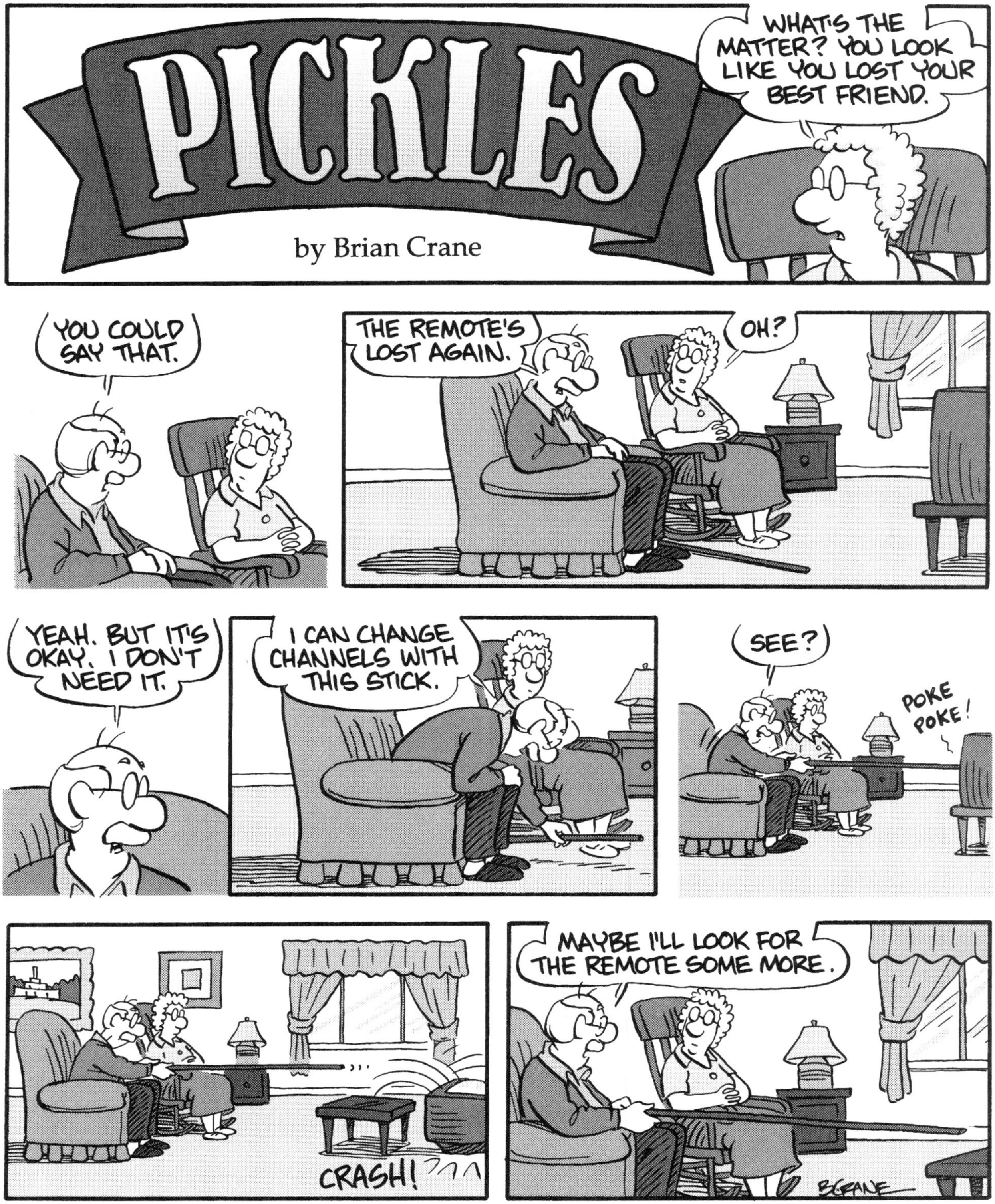
PICKLES
by Brian Crane
WHAT'S THE MATTER? YOU LOOK LIKE YOU LOST YOUR BEST FRIEND.
YOU COULD SAY THAT.
THE REMOTE'S LOST AGAIN.
OH?
YEAH. BUT IT'S OKAY. I DON'T NEED IT.
I CAN CHANGE CHANNELS WITH THIS STICK.
SEE?
POKE POKE!
CRASH!
MAYBE I'LL LOOK FOR THE REMOTE SOME MORE.
B.CRANE

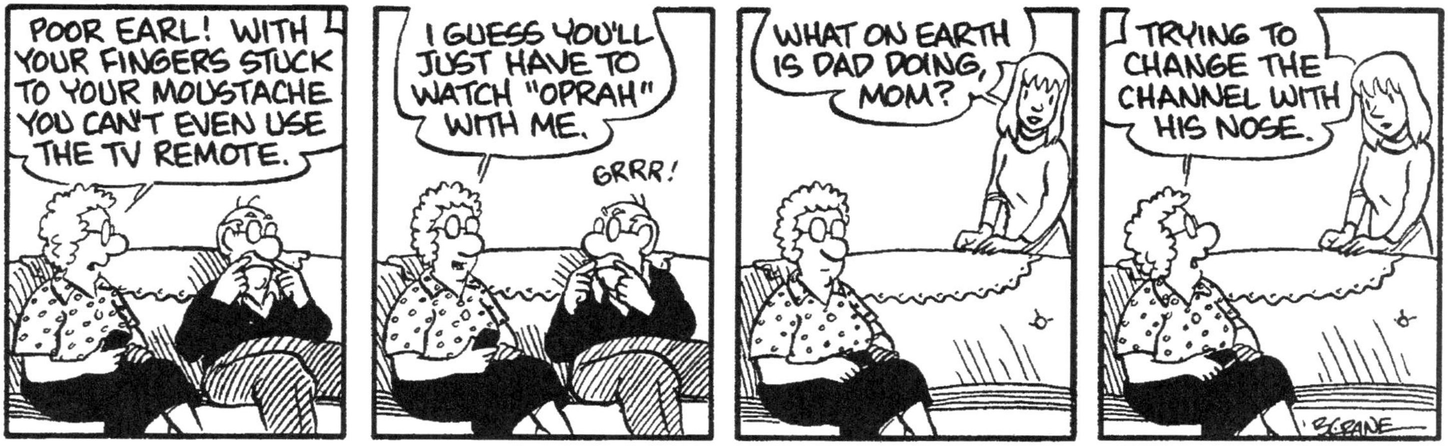
POOR EARL! WITH YOUR FINGERS STUCK TO YOUR MOUSTACHE YOU CAN'T EVEN USE THE TV REMOTE.
I GUESS YOU'LL JUST HAVE TO WATCH "OPRAH" WITH ME.
GRRR!
WHAT ON EARTH IS DAD DOING, MOM?
TRYING TO CHANGE THE CHANNEL WITH HIS NOSE.
B.CRANE

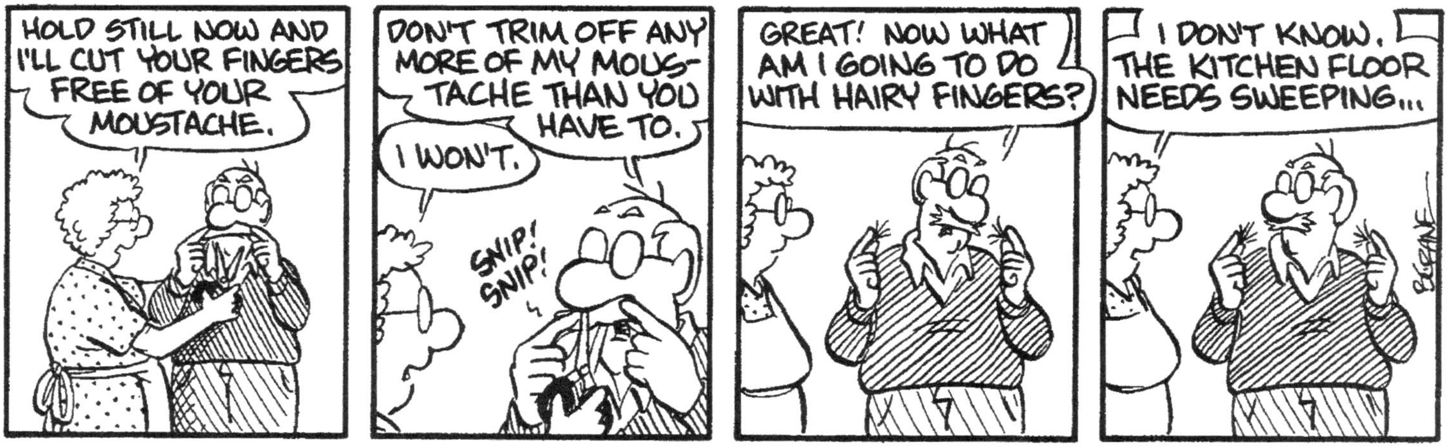
HOLD STILL NOW AND I'LL CUT YOUR FINGERS FREE OF YOUR MOUSTACHE.
DON'T TRIM OFF ANY MORE OF MY MOUS-TACHE THAN YOU HAVE TO.
I WON'T.
SNIP! SNIP!
GREAT! NOW WHAT AM I GOING TO DO WITH HAIRY FINGERS?
I DON'T KNOW. THE KITCHEN FLOOR NEEDS SWEEPING...
B.CRANE

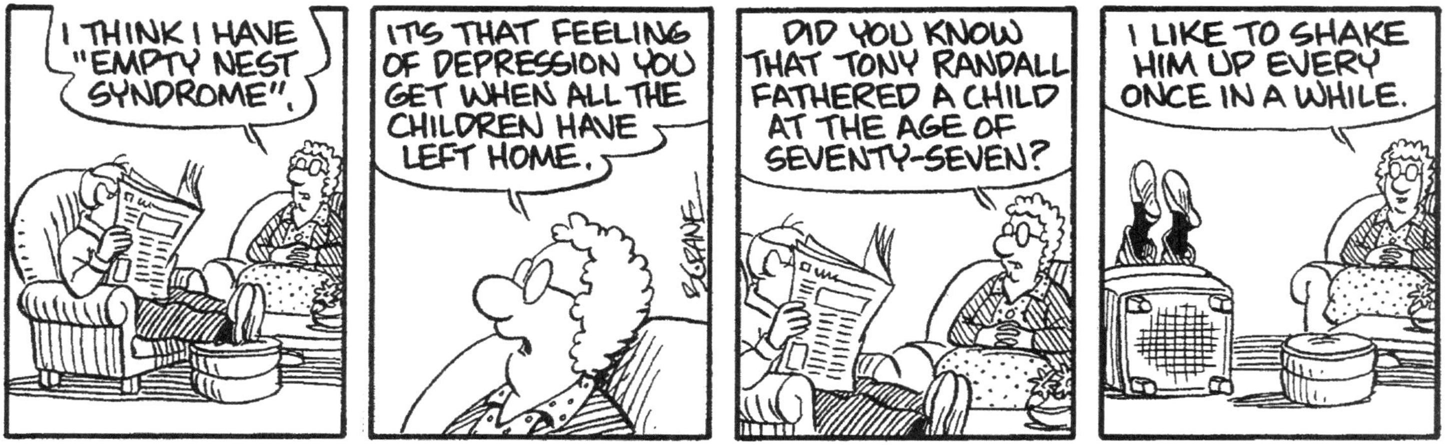
I THINK I HAVE "EMPTY NEST SYNDROME".
IT'S THAT FEELING OF DEPRESSION YOU GET WHEN ALL THE CHILDREN HAVE LEFT HOME.
B.CRANE
DID YOU KNOW THAT TONY RANDALL FATHERED A CHILD AT THE AGE OF SEVENTY-SEVEN?
I LIKE TO SHAKE HIM UP EVERY ONCE IN A WHILE.

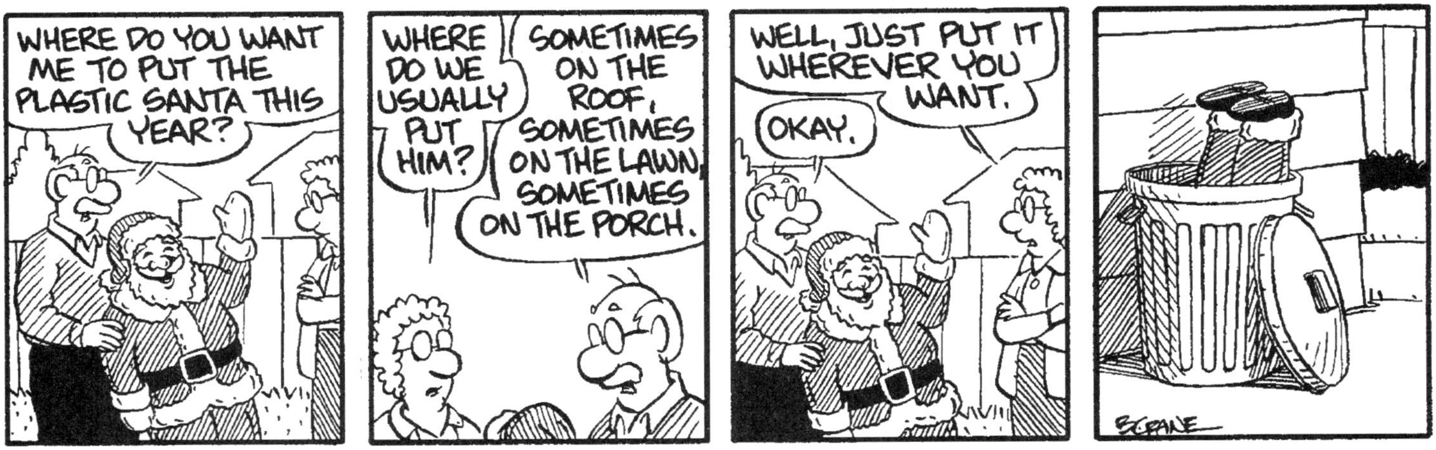
WHERE DO YOU WANT ME TO PUT THE PLASTIC SANTA THIS YEAR?
WHERE DO WE USUALLY PUT HIM?
SOMETIMES ON THE ROOF, SOMETIMES ON THE LAWN, SOMETIMES ON THE PORCH.
WELL, JUST PUT IT WHEREVER YOU WANT.
OKAY.

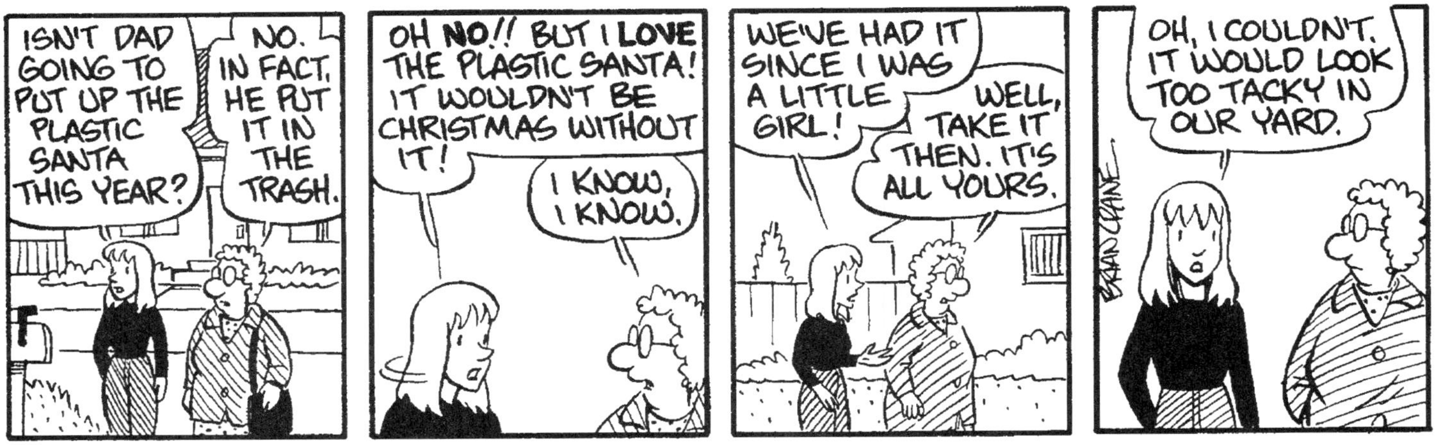
ISN'T DAD GOING TO PUT UP THE PLASTIC SANTA THIS YEAR?
NO. IN FACT, HE PUT IT IN THE TRASH.
OH **NO**!! BUT I **LOVE** THE PLASTIC SANTA! IT WOULDN'T BE CHRISTMAS WITHOUT IT!
I KNOW, I KNOW.
WE'VE HAD IT SINCE I WAS A LITTLE GIRL!
WELL, TAKE IT THEN. IT'S ALL YOURS.
OH, I COULDN'T. IT WOULD LOOK TOO TACKY IN OUR YARD.

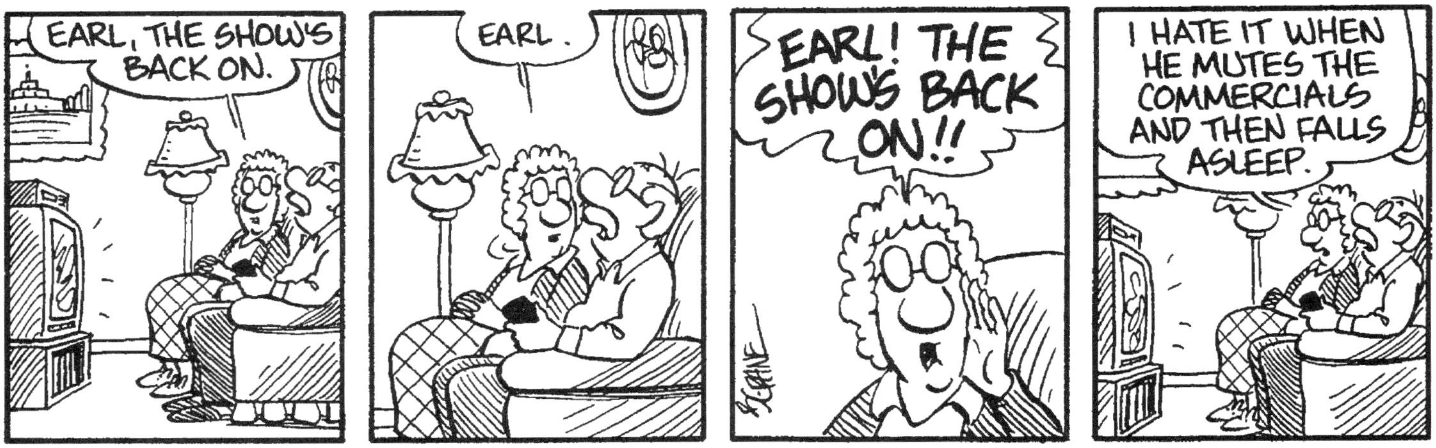
EARL, THE SHOW'S BACK ON.
EARL.
EARL! THE SHOW'S BACK ON!!
I HATE IT WHEN HE MUTES THE COMMERCIALS AND THEN FALLS ASLEEP.

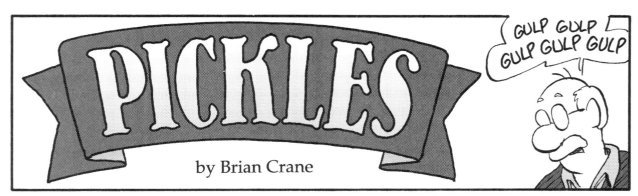

PICKLES

by Brian Crane

GULP GULP GULP GULP GULP

I CAN DO WITHOUT THE SOUND EFFECTS, THANK YOU VERY MUCH.

DON'T YOU HAVE SOMETHING BETTER TO DO THAN FOLLOW ME AROUND ALL DAY?

NO. NOT REALLY.

I LOST A GOLD EARRING ON THE FRONT LAWN YESTERDAY. WHY DON'T YOU GO SEE IF YOU CAN FIND IT FOR ME?

OKAY.

IT WAS RIGHT AROUND HERE. OR MAYBE OVER THERE. I'M NOT SURE. YOU'D BETTER SEARCH THE WHOLE YARD.

I HOPE DAD FINDS YOUR EARRING, MOM.

HE WON'T. IT'S IN MY JEWELRY BOX.

47

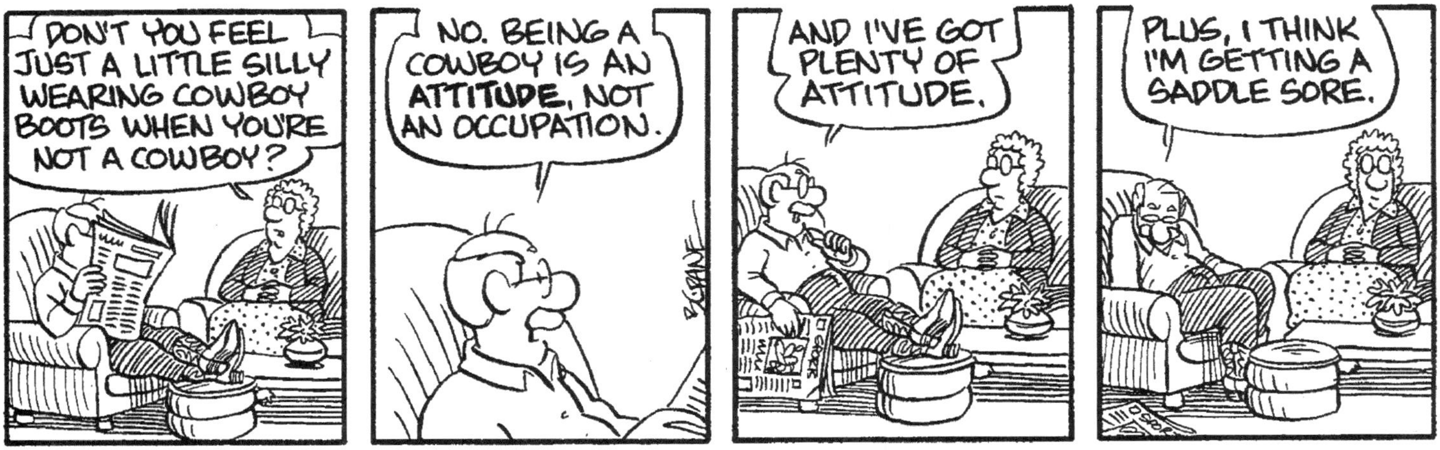
DON'T YOU FEEL JUST A LITTLE SILLY WEARING COWBOY BOOTS WHEN YOU'RE NOT A COWBOY?
NO. BEING A COWBOY IS AN **ATTITUDE**, NOT AN OCCUPATION.
AND I'VE GOT PLENTY OF ATTITUDE.
PLUS, I THINK I'M GETTING A SADDLE SORE.

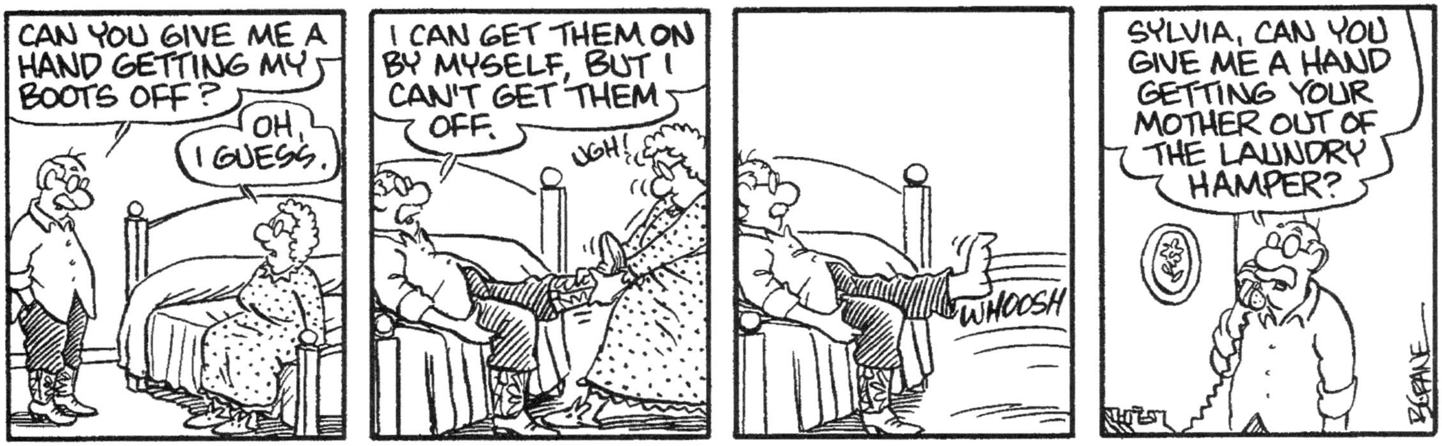
CAN YOU GIVE ME A HAND GETTING MY BOOTS OFF?
OH, I GUESS.
I CAN GET THEM ON BY MYSELF, BUT I CAN'T GET THEM OFF.
UGH!
WHOOSH
SYLVIA, CAN YOU GIVE ME A HAND GETTING YOUR MOTHER OUT OF THE LAUNDRY HAMPER?

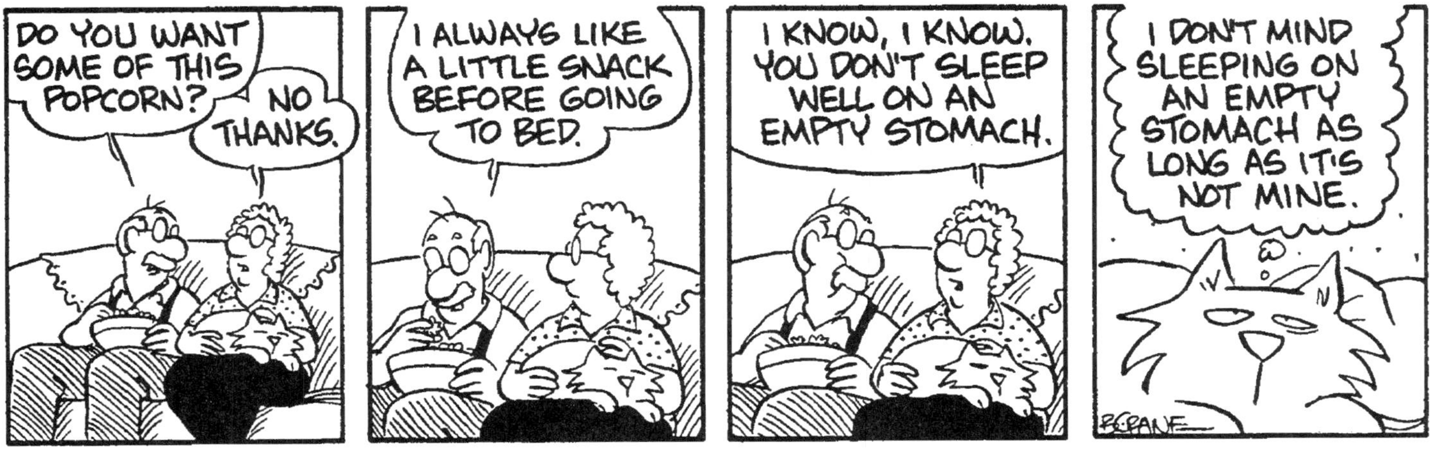
DO YOU WANT SOME OF THIS POPCORN?
NO THANKS.
I ALWAYS LIKE A LITTLE SNACK BEFORE GOING TO BED.
I KNOW, I KNOW. YOU DON'T SLEEP WELL ON AN EMPTY STOMACH.
I DON'T MIND SLEEPING ON AN EMPTY STOMACH AS LONG AS IT'S NOT MINE.

Panel 1: I INSTALLED THE NEW PADDED TOILET SEAT. / GOOD.

Panel 2: IT LOOKS PRETTY FANCY.

Panel 3: IT'S KIND OF A SHAME NO ONE WILL SEE IT BUT US.

Panel 4: MAYBE WE COULD INVITE SOME FRIENDS OVER.

Panel 5: IT WAS NICE OF YOU TO INVITE US OVER. WHAT'S THE BIG OCCASION?

Panel 6: EARL INSTALLED A NEW PADDED TOILET SEAT IN OUR BATHROOM. HE'S VERY PROUD OF IT.

Panel 7: OKAY... WHO'S READY FOR THE RIBBON CUTTING?

Panel 8: YOU KNOW, THE SAD THING IS, THIS IS THE MOST EXCITEMENT I'VE HAD IN A MONTH.

Panel 9: WHAT HAVE YOU GOT IN THE BAG? / A ROLL OF DUCT TAPE.

Panel 10: OH, DUCT TAPE'S GREAT. I USE IT INSIDE MY CAR TO KEEP IT QUIET.

Panel 11: IT KEEPS THE INSIDE OF YOUR CAR QUIET?

Panel 12: YEAH. I JUST PUT A LITTLE PIECE OVER HER MOUTH.

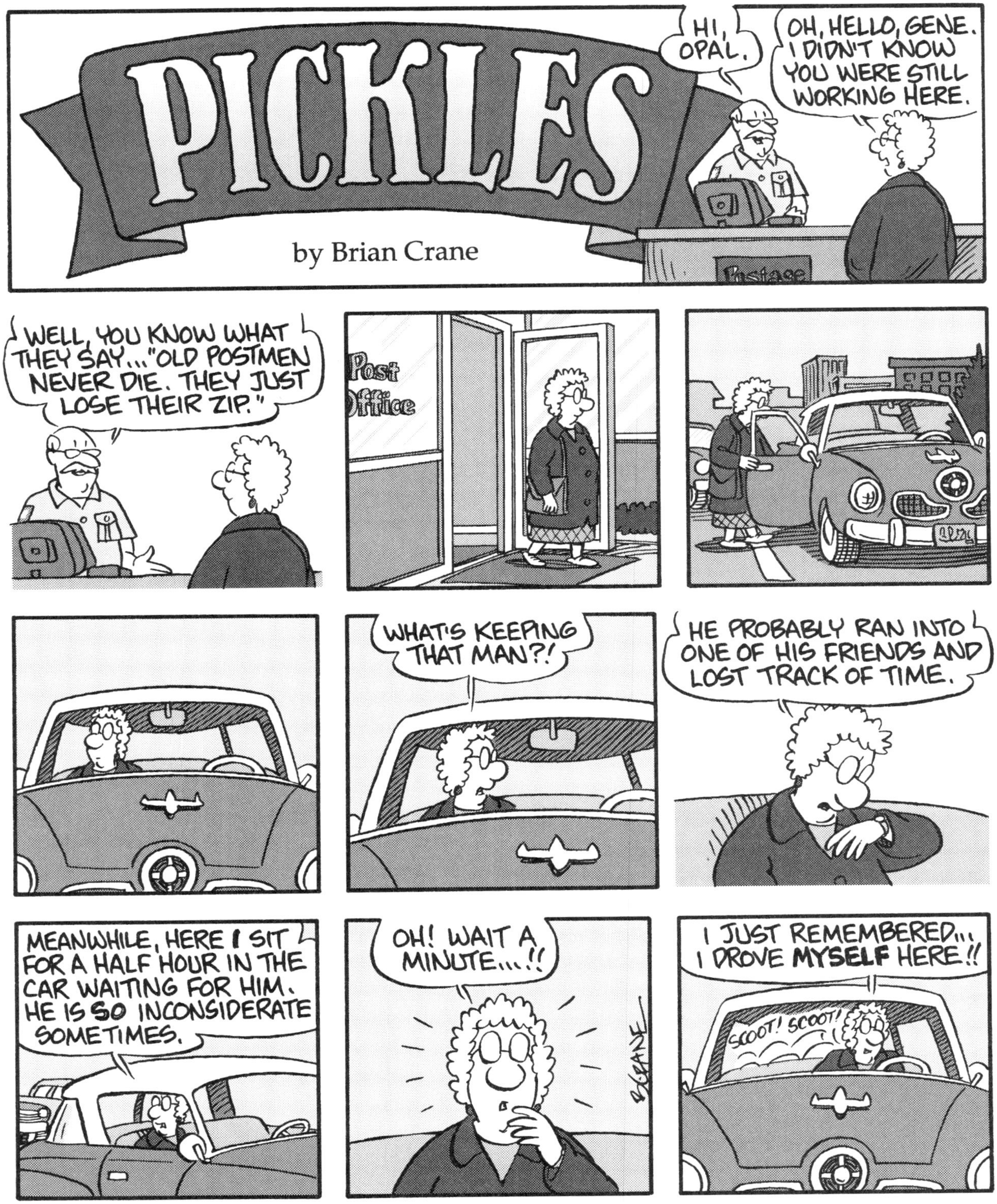
PICKLES
by Brian Crane
HI, OPAL.
OH, HELLO, GENE. I DIDN'T KNOW YOU WERE STILL WORKING HERE.
Postage
WELL, YOU KNOW WHAT THEY SAY..."OLD POSTMEN NEVER DIE. THEY JUST LOSE THEIR ZIP."
Post Office
WHAT'S KEEPING THAT MAN?!
HE PROBABLY RAN INTO ONE OF HIS FRIENDS AND LOST TRACK OF TIME.
MEANWHILE, HERE I SIT FOR A HALF HOUR IN THE CAR WAITING FOR HIM. HE IS SO INCONSIDERATE SOMETIMES.
OH! WAIT A MINUTE...!!
B. CRANE
I JUST REMEMBERED... I DROVE MYSELF HERE!!
SCOOT! SCOOT!

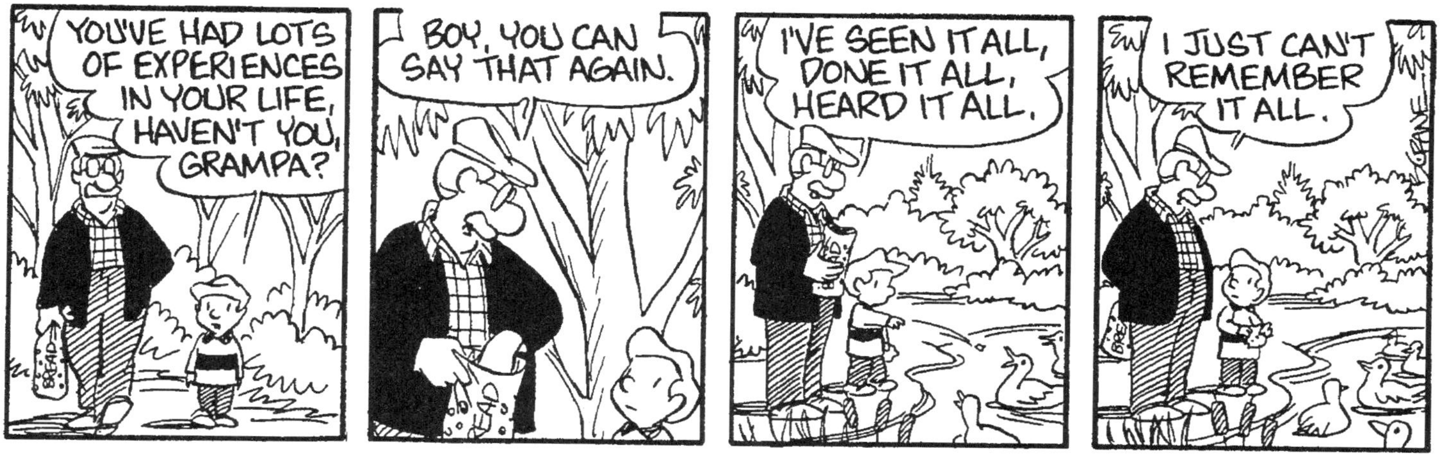
YOU'VE HAD LOTS OF EXPERIENCES IN YOUR LIFE, HAVEN'T YOU, GRAMPA?
BOY, YOU CAN SAY THAT AGAIN.
I'VE SEEN IT ALL, DONE IT ALL, HEARD IT ALL.
I JUST CAN'T REMEMBER IT ALL.

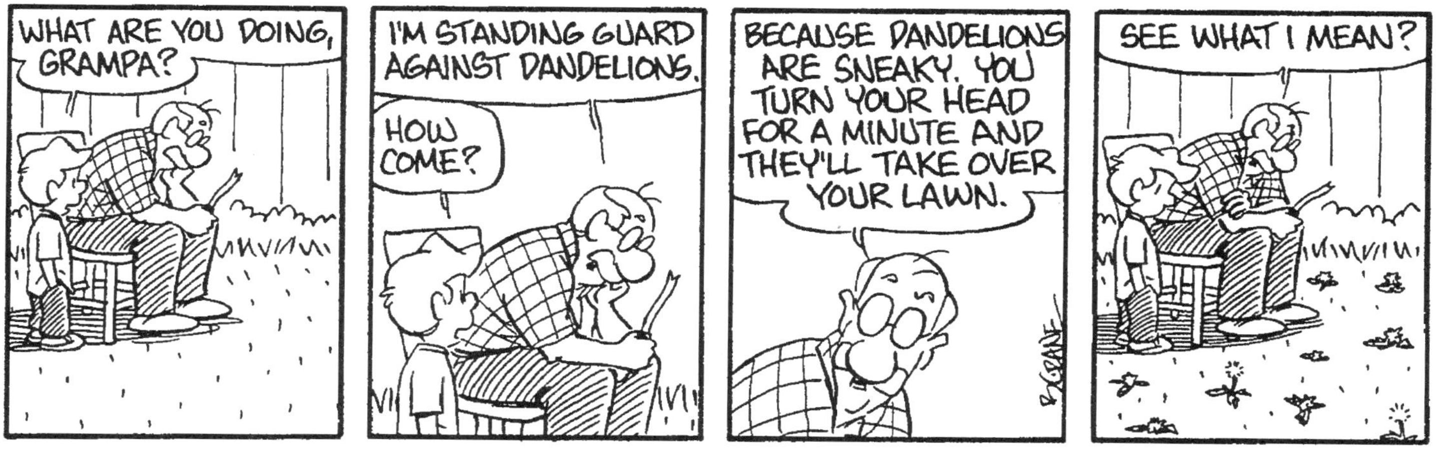
WHAT ARE YOU DOING, GRAMPA?
I'M STANDING GUARD AGAINST DANDELIONS.
HOW COME?
BECAUSE DANDELIONS ARE SNEAKY. YOU TURN YOUR HEAD FOR A MINUTE AND THEY'LL TAKE OVER YOUR LAWN.
SEE WHAT I MEAN?

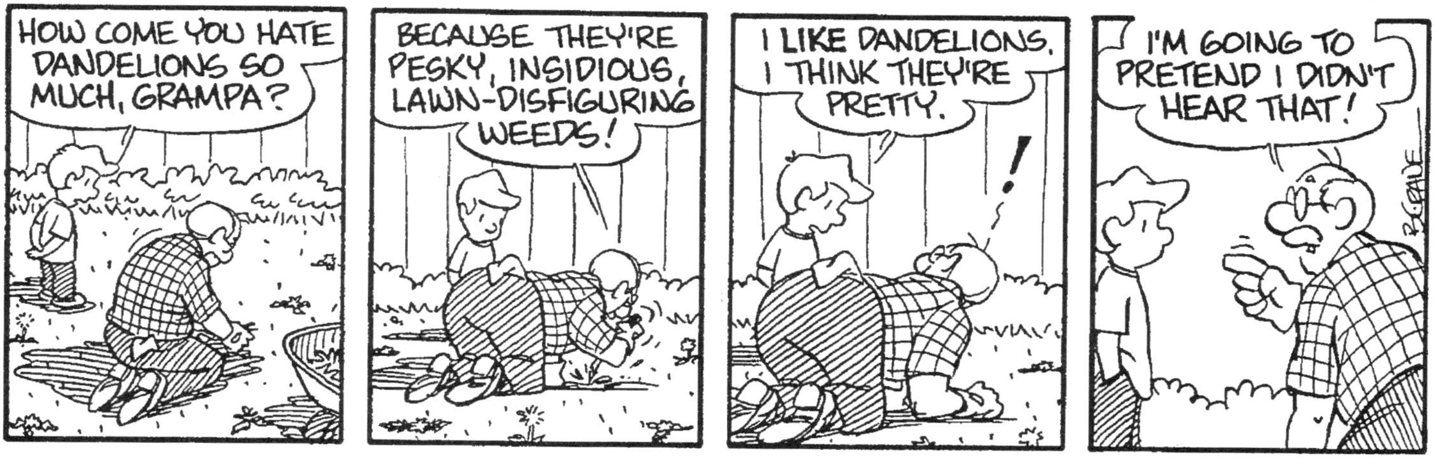
HOW COME YOU HATE DANDELIONS SO MUCH, GRAMPA?
BECAUSE THEY'RE PESKY, INSIDIOUS, LAWN-DISFIGURING WEEDS!
I LIKE DANDELIONS. I THINK THEY'RE PRETTY.
!
I'M GOING TO PRETEND I DIDN'T HEAR THAT!

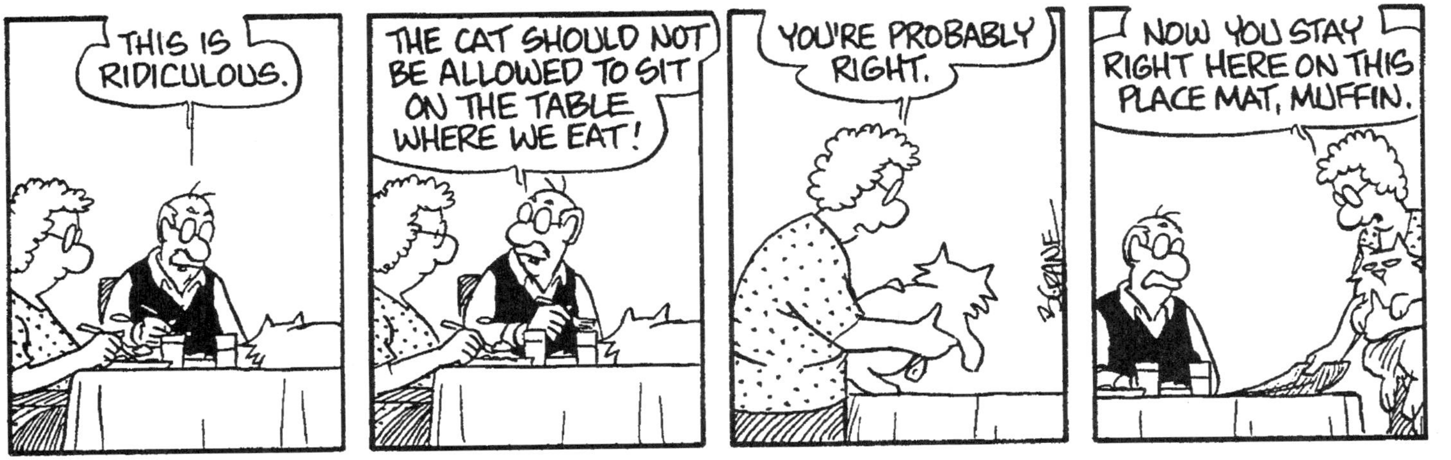
THIS IS RIDICULOUS.
THE CAT SHOULD NOT BE ALLOWED TO SIT ON THE TABLE WHERE WE EAT!
YOU'RE PROBABLY RIGHT.
NOW YOU STAY RIGHT HERE ON THIS PLACE MAT, MUFFIN.

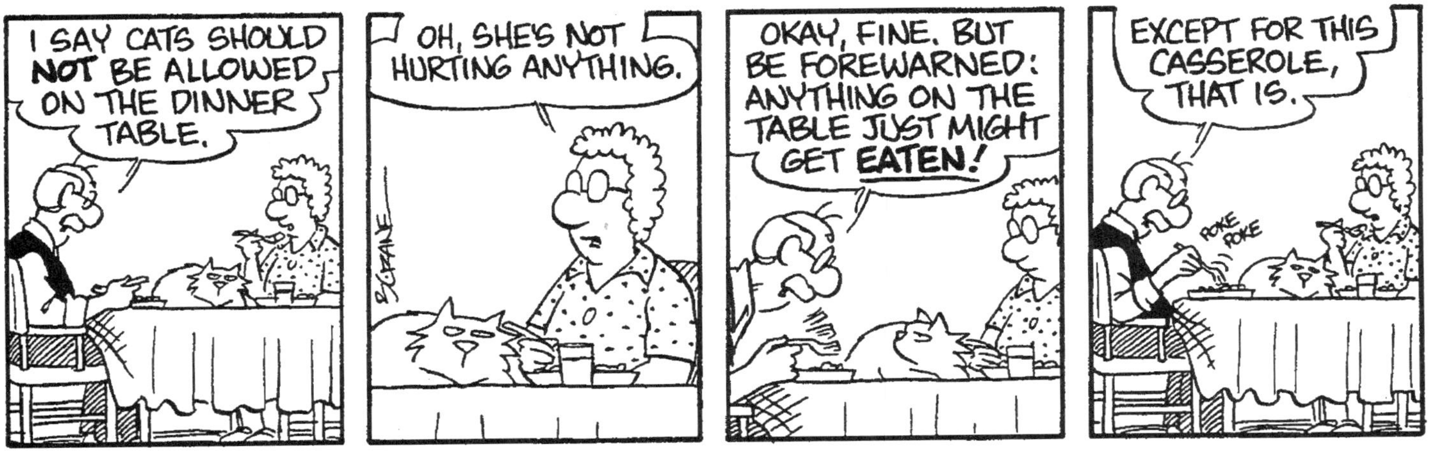
I SAY CATS SHOULD **NOT** BE ALLOWED ON THE DINNER TABLE.
OH, SHE'S NOT HURTING ANYTHING.
OKAY, FINE. BUT BE FOREWARNED: ANYTHING ON THE TABLE JUST MIGHT GET **EATEN!**
EXCEPT FOR THIS CASSEROLE, THAT IS.
POKE POKE

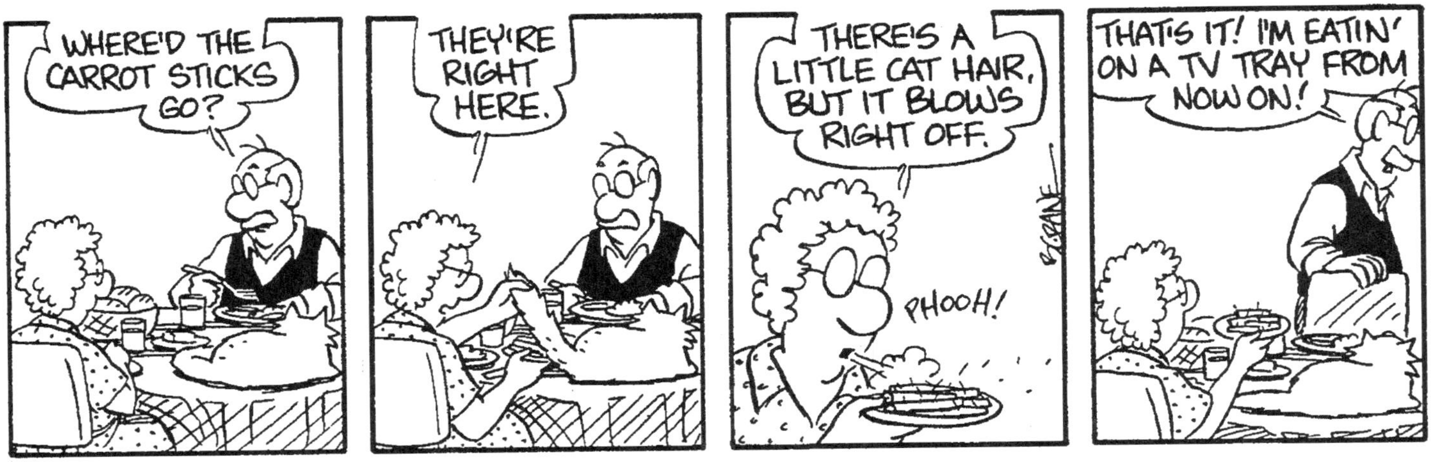
WHERE'D THE CARROT STICKS GO?
THEY'RE RIGHT HERE.
THERE'S A LITTLE CAT HAIR, BUT IT BLOWS RIGHT OFF.
PHOOH!
THAT'S IT! I'M EATIN' ON A TV TRAY FROM NOW ON!

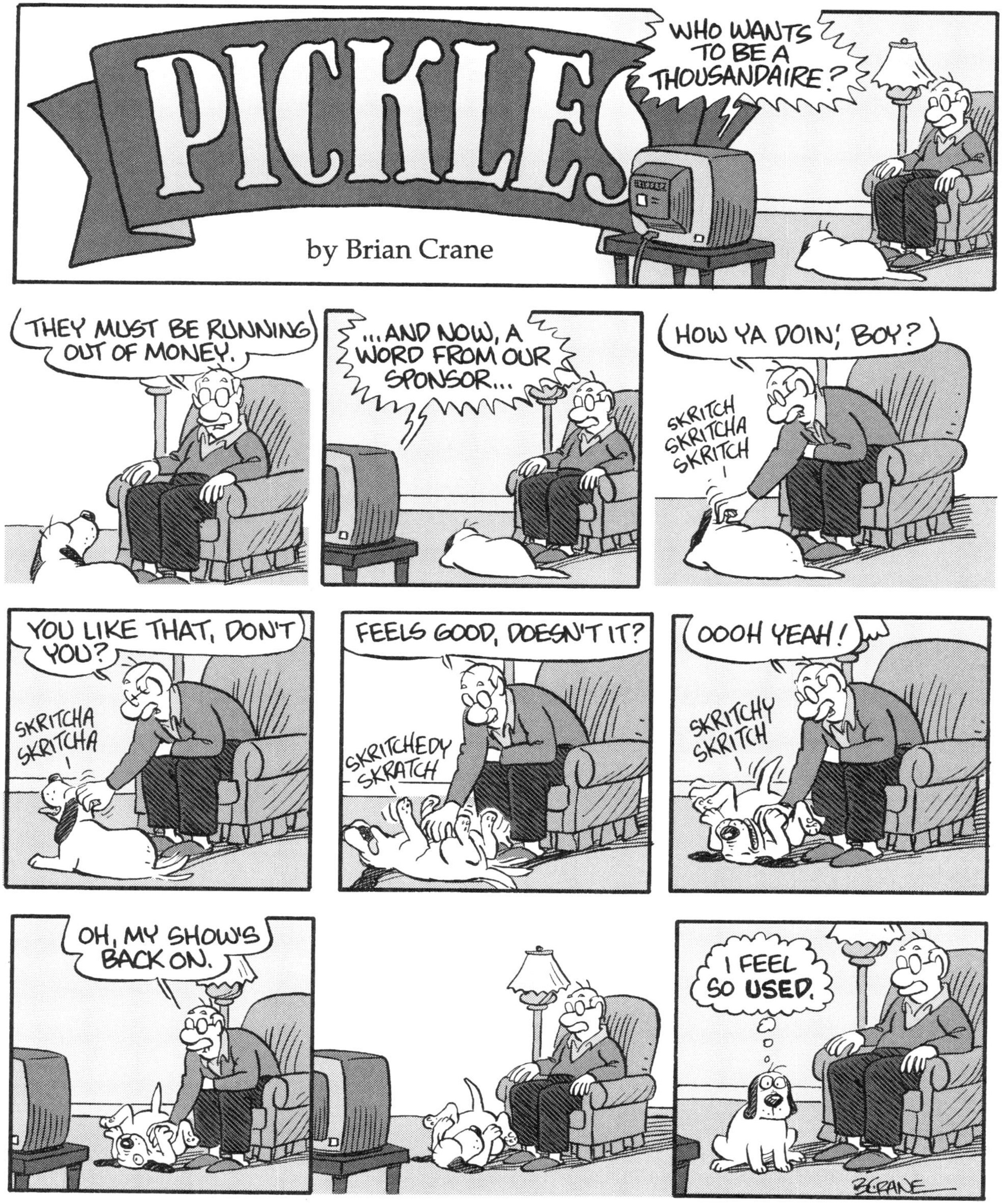
PICKLES
by Brian Crane
WHO WANTS TO BE A THOUSANDAIRE?
THEY MUST BE RUNNING OUT OF MONEY.
...AND NOW, A WORD FROM OUR SPONSOR...
HOW YA DOIN', BOY?
SKRITCH SKRITCHA SKRITCH
YOU LIKE THAT, DON'T YOU?
SKRITCHA SKRITCHA
FEELS GOOD, DOESN'T IT?
SKRITCHEDY SKRATCH
OOOH YEAH!
SKRITCHY SKRITCH
OH, MY SHOW'S BACK ON.
I FEEL SO USED.
B. CRANE

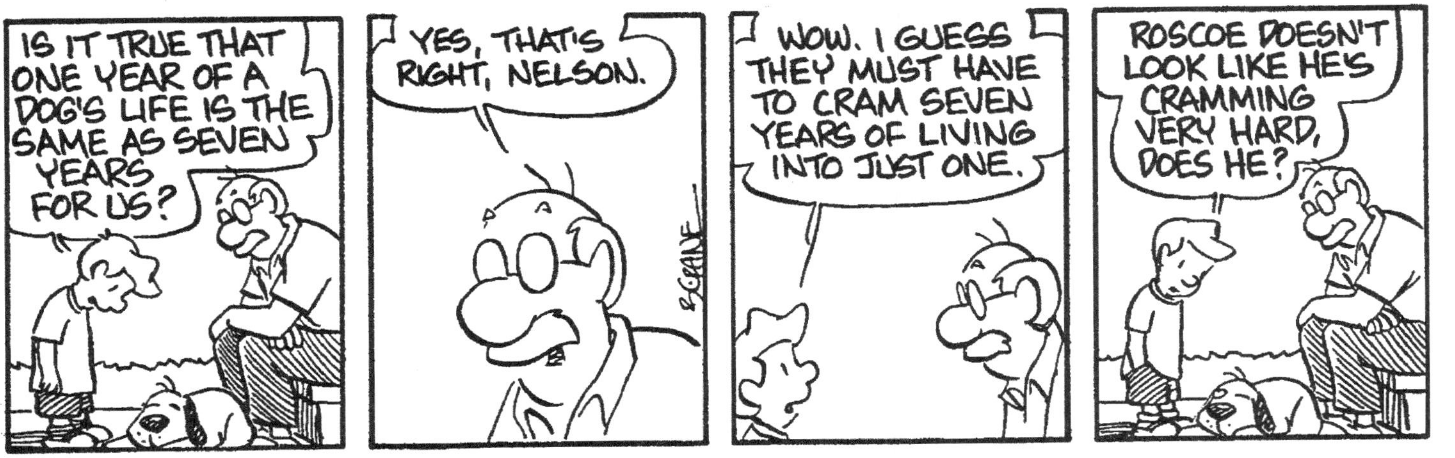
IS IT TRUE THAT ONE YEAR OF A DOG'S LIFE IS THE SAME AS SEVEN YEARS FOR US?
YES, THAT'S RIGHT, NELSON.
WOW. I GUESS THEY MUST HAVE TO CRAM SEVEN YEARS OF LIVING INTO JUST ONE.
ROSCOE DOESN'T LOOK LIKE HE'S CRAMMING VERY HARD, DOES HE?

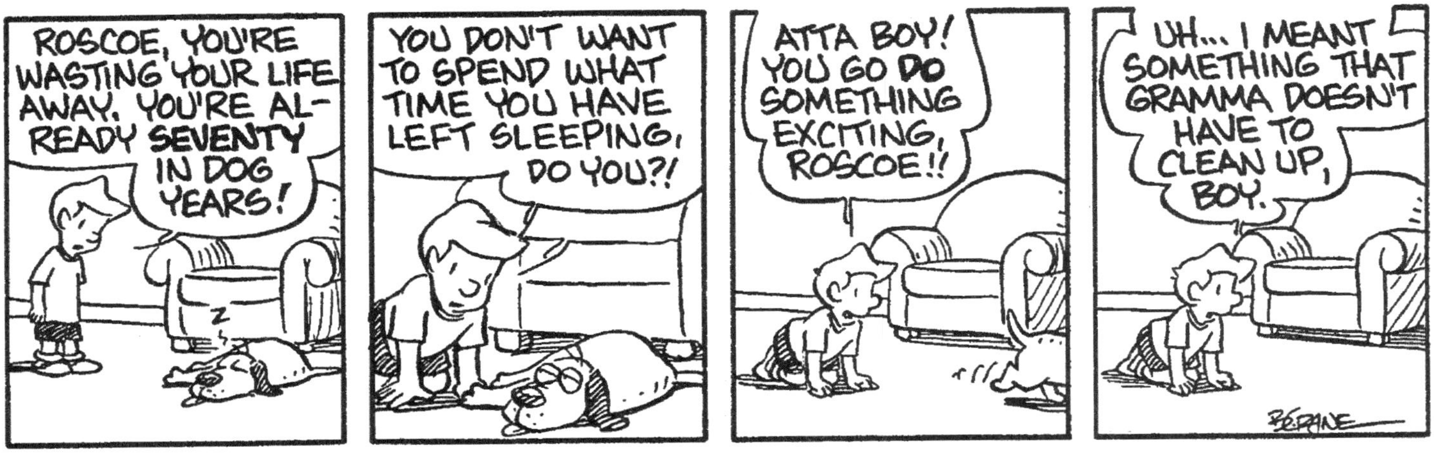
ROSCOE, YOU'RE WASTING YOUR LIFE AWAY. YOU'RE AL-READY SEVENTY IN DOG YEARS!
Z
YOU DON'T WANT TO SPEND WHAT TIME YOU HAVE LEFT SLEEPING, DO YOU?!
ATTA BOY! YOU GO DO SOMETHING EXCITING, ROSCOE!!
UH... I MEANT SOMETHING THAT GRAMMA DOESN'T HAVE TO CLEAN UP, BOY.

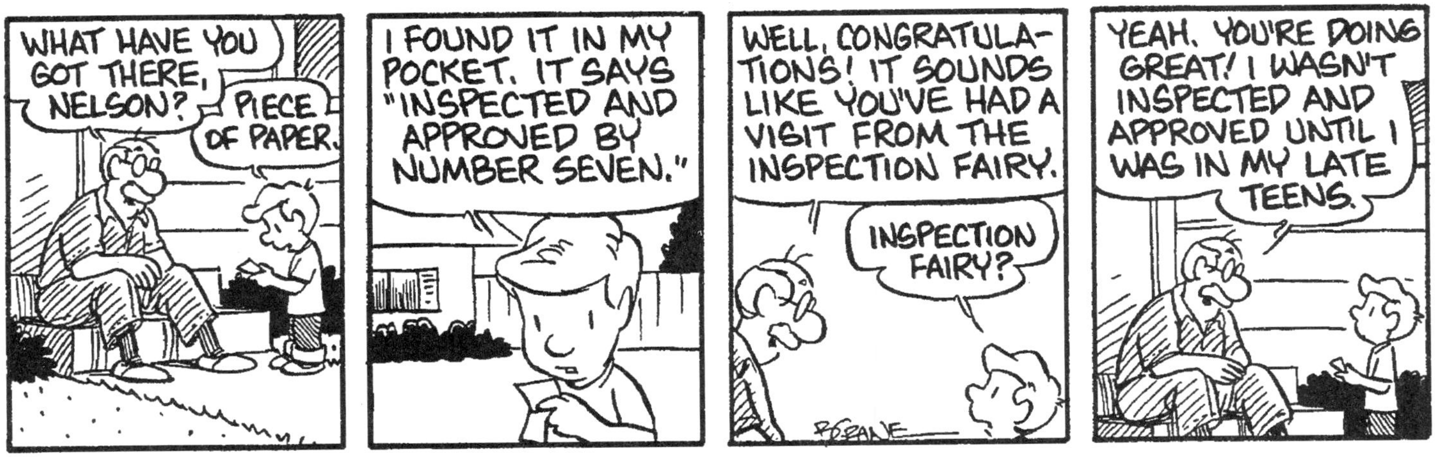
WHAT HAVE YOU GOT THERE, NELSON?
PIECE OF PAPER.
I FOUND IT IN MY POCKET. IT SAYS "INSPECTED AND APPROVED BY NUMBER SEVEN."
WELL, CONGRATULA-TIONS! IT SOUNDS LIKE YOU'VE HAD A VISIT FROM THE INSPECTION FAIRY.
INSPECTION FAIRY?
YEAH. YOU'RE DOING GREAT! I WASN'T INSPECTED AND APPROVED UNTIL I WAS IN MY LATE TEENS.

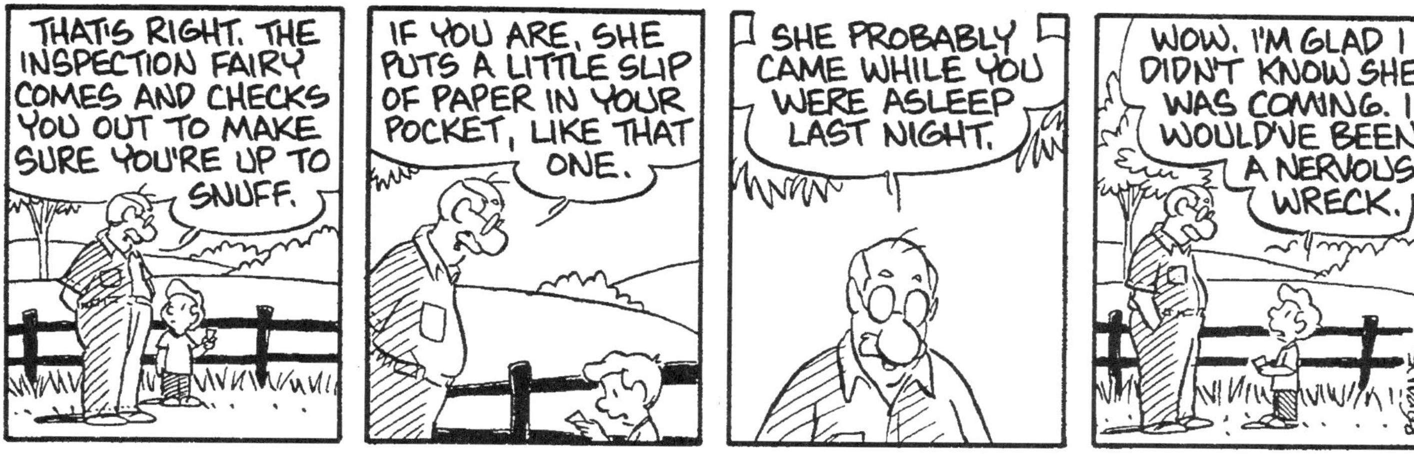
THAT'S RIGHT. THE INSPECTION FAIRY COMES AND CHECKS YOU OUT TO MAKE SURE YOU'RE UP TO SNUFF.
IF YOU ARE, SHE PUTS A LITTLE SLIP OF PAPER IN YOUR POCKET, LIKE THAT ONE.
SHE PROBABLY CAME WHILE YOU WERE ASLEEP LAST NIGHT.
WOW. I'M GLAD I DIDN'T KNOW SHE WAS COMING. I WOULD'VE BEEN A NERVOUS WRECK.

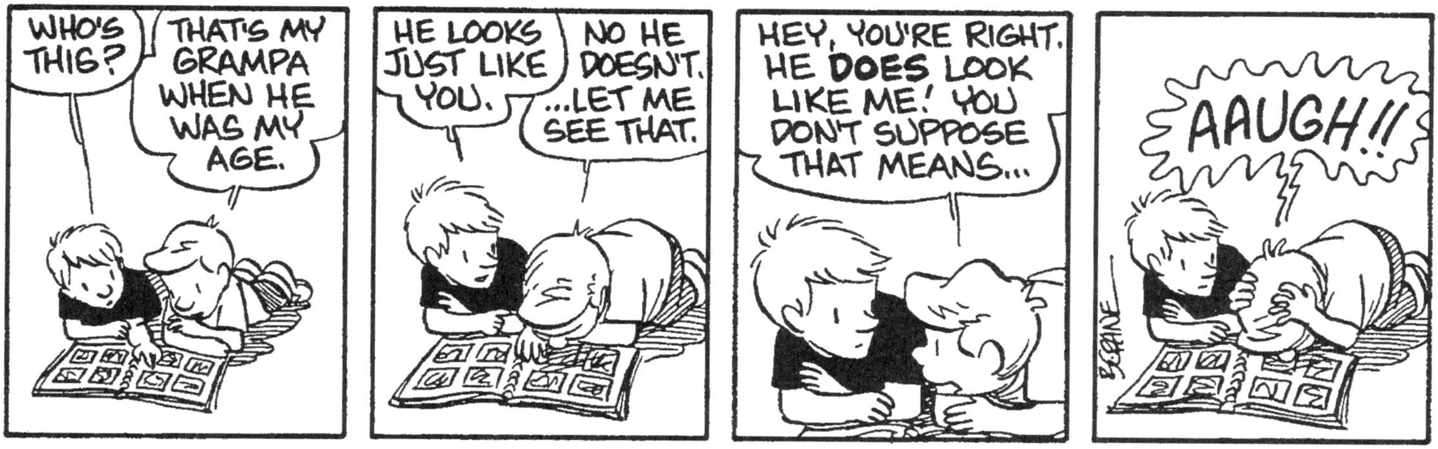
WHO'S THIS?
THAT'S MY GRAMPA WHEN HE WAS MY AGE.
HE LOOKS JUST LIKE YOU.
NO HE DOESN'T. ...LET ME SEE THAT.
HEY, YOU'RE RIGHT. HE **DOES** LOOK LIKE ME! YOU DON'T SUPPOSE THAT MEANS...
AAUGH!!

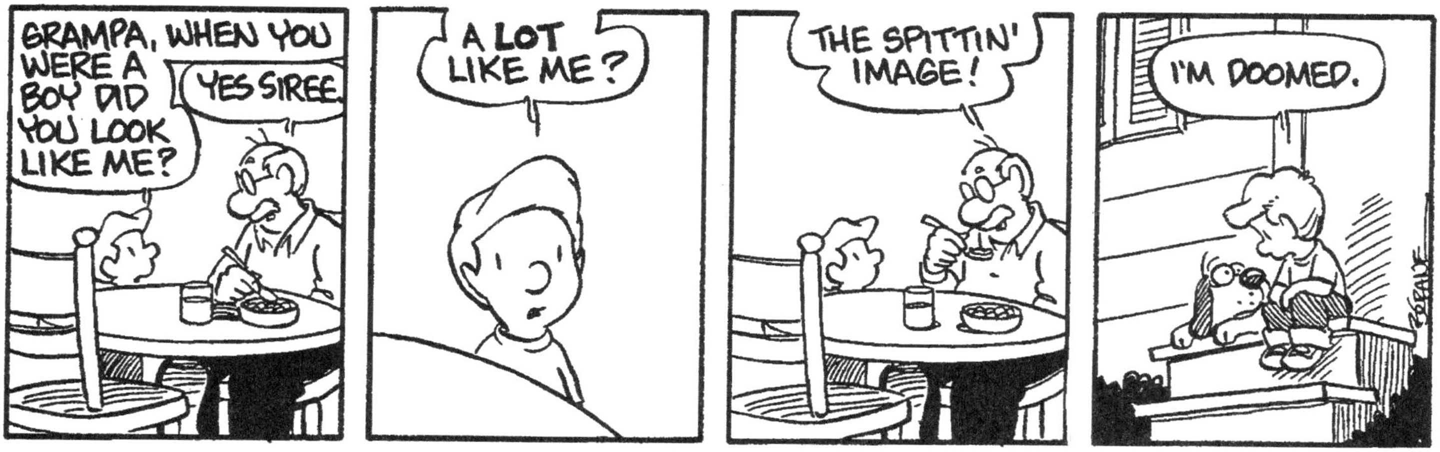
GRAMPA, WHEN YOU WERE A BOY DID YOU LOOK LIKE ME?
YES SIREE.
A **LOT** LIKE ME?
THE SPITTIN' IMAGE!
I'M DOOMED.

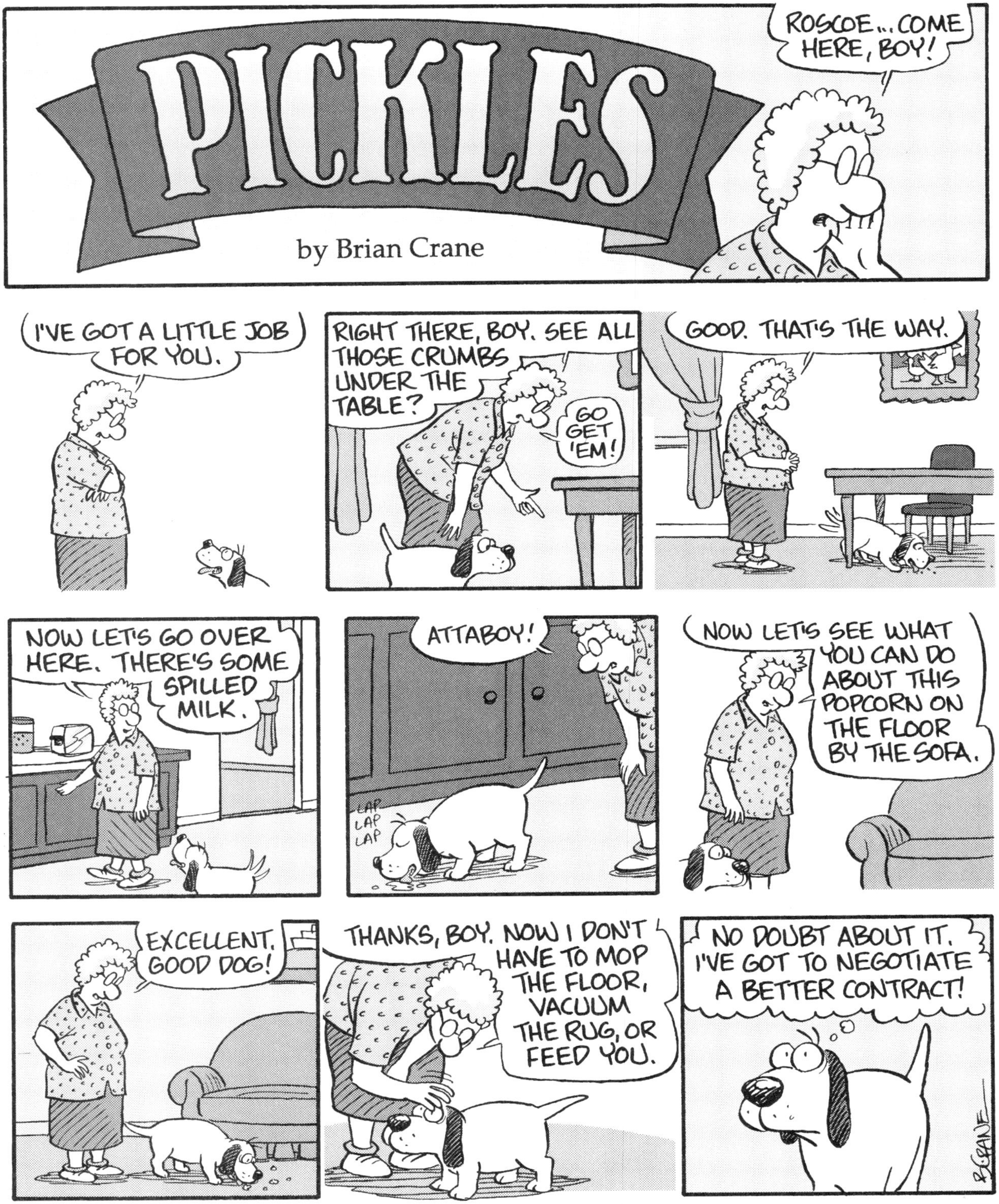
PICKLES
by Brian Crane
ROSCOE... COME HERE, BOY!
I'VE GOT A LITTLE JOB FOR YOU.
RIGHT THERE, BOY. SEE ALL THOSE CRUMBS UNDER THE TABLE?
GO GET 'EM!
GOOD. THAT'S THE WAY.
NOW LET'S GO OVER HERE. THERE'S SOME SPILLED MILK.
ATTABOY!
LAP LAP LAP
NOW LET'S SEE WHAT YOU CAN DO ABOUT THIS POPCORN ON THE FLOOR BY THE SOFA.
EXCELLENT. GOOD DOG!
THANKS, BOY. NOW I DON'T HAVE TO MOP THE FLOOR, VACUUM THE RUG, OR FEED YOU.
NO DOUBT ABOUT IT. I'VE GOT TO NEGOTIATE A BETTER CONTRACT!

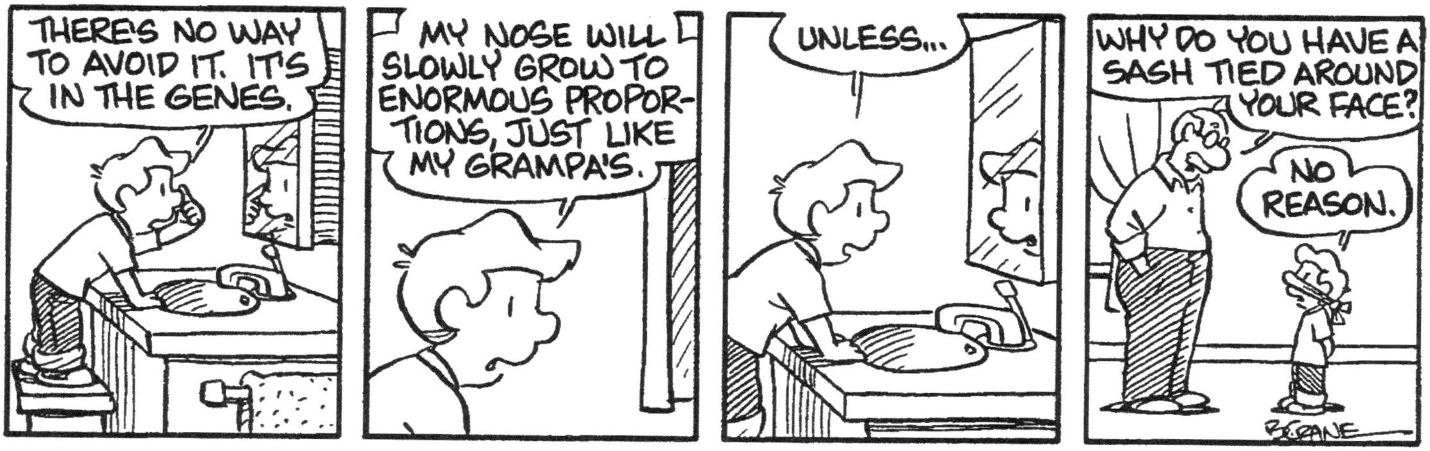
THERE'S NO WAY TO AVOID IT. IT'S IN THE GENES.
MY NOSE WILL SLOWLY GROW TO ENORMOUS PROPORTIONS, JUST LIKE MY GRAMPA'S.
UNLESS...
WHY DO YOU HAVE A SASH TIED AROUND YOUR FACE?
NO REASON.

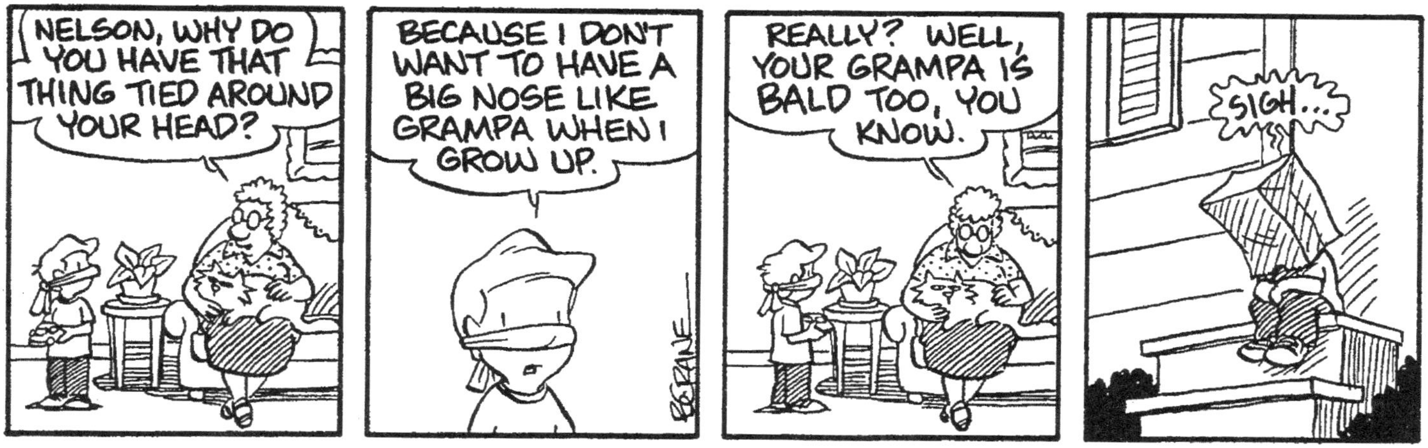
NELSON, WHY DO YOU HAVE THAT THING TIED AROUND YOUR HEAD?
BECAUSE I DON'T WANT TO HAVE A BIG NOSE LIKE GRAMPA WHEN I GROW UP.
REALLY? WELL, YOUR GRAMPA IS BALD TOO, YOU KNOW.
SIGH...

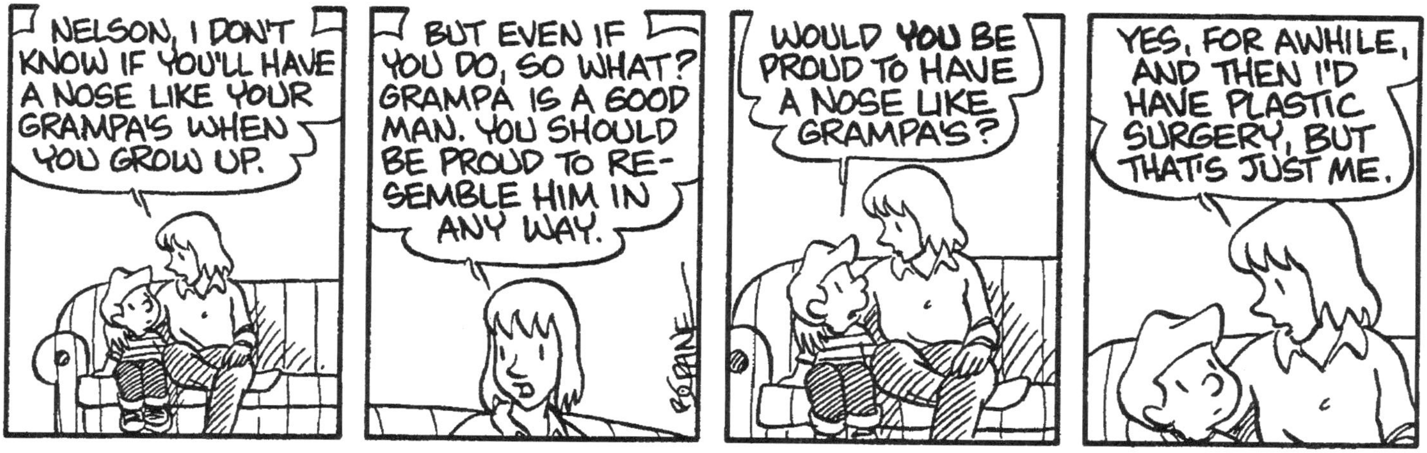
NELSON, I DON'T KNOW IF YOU'LL HAVE A NOSE LIKE YOUR GRAMPA'S WHEN YOU GROW UP.
BUT EVEN IF YOU DO, SO WHAT? GRAMPA IS A GOOD MAN. YOU SHOULD BE PROUD TO RESEMBLE HIM IN ANY WAY.
WOULD **YOU** BE PROUD TO HAVE A NOSE LIKE GRAMPA'S?
YES, FOR AWHILE, AND THEN I'D HAVE PLASTIC SURGERY, BUT THAT'S JUST ME.

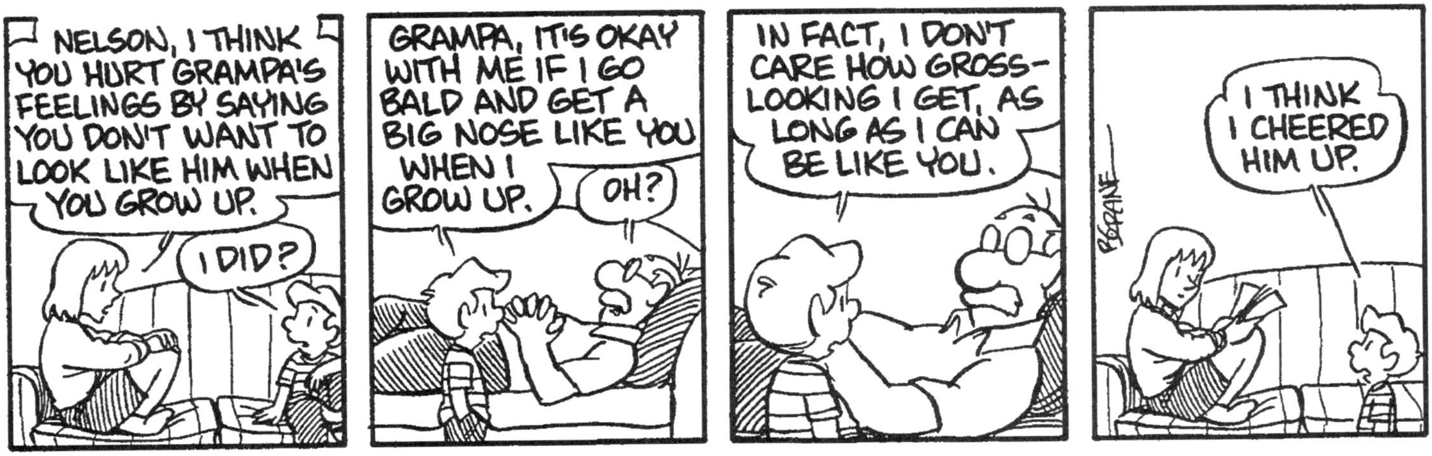
NELSON, I THINK YOU HURT GRAMPA'S FEELINGS BY SAYING YOU DON'T WANT TO LOOK LIKE HIM WHEN YOU GROW UP.
I DID?
GRAMPA, IT'S OKAY WITH ME IF I GO BALD AND GET A BIG NOSE LIKE YOU WHEN I GROW UP.
OH?
IN FACT, I DON'T CARE HOW GROSS-LOOKING I GET, AS LONG AS I CAN BE LIKE YOU.
I THINK I CHEERED HIM UP.

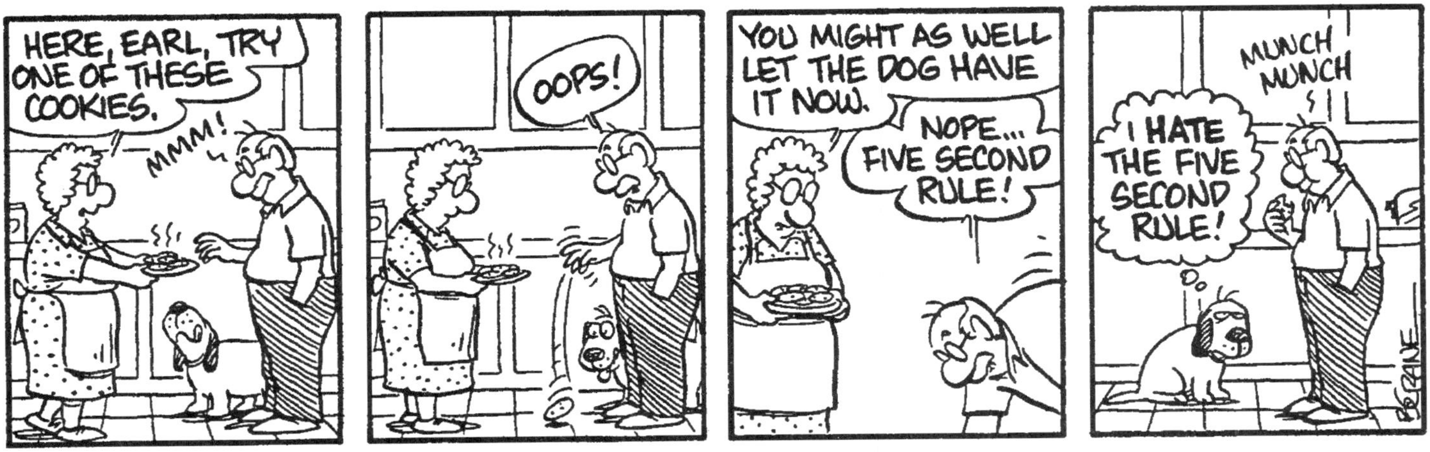
HERE, EARL, TRY ONE OF THESE COOKIES.
MMM!
OOPS!
YOU MIGHT AS WELL LET THE DOG HAVE IT NOW.
NOPE... FIVE SECOND RULE!
MUNCH MUNCH
I HATE THE FIVE SECOND RULE!

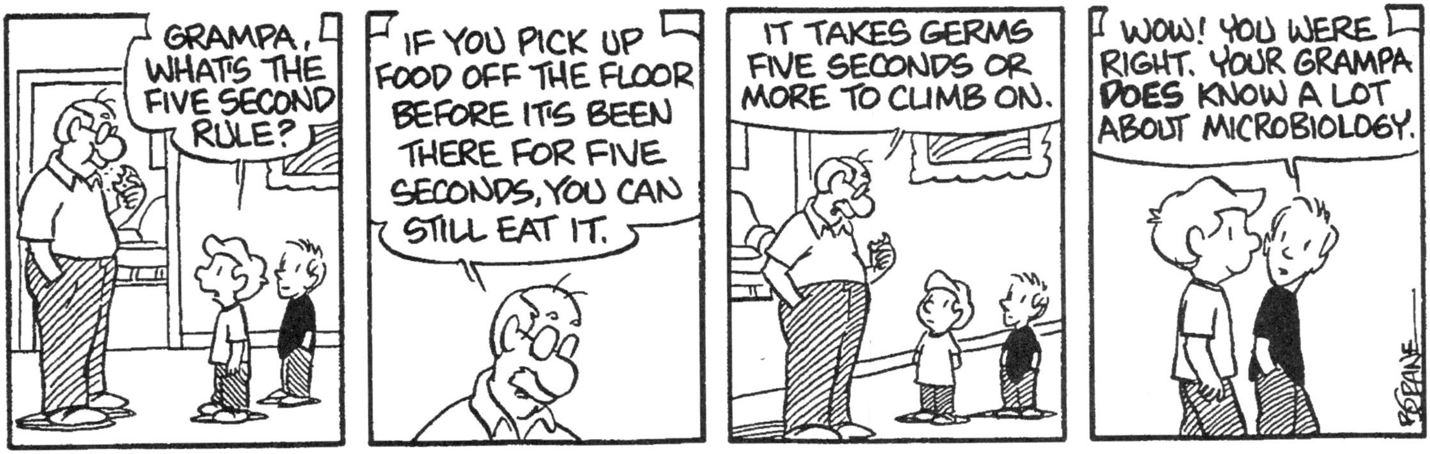
GRAMPA, WHAT'S THE FIVE SECOND RULE?
IF YOU PICK UP FOOD OFF THE FLOOR BEFORE IT'S BEEN THERE FOR FIVE SECONDS, YOU CAN STILL EAT IT.
IT TAKES GERMS FIVE SECONDS OR MORE TO CLIMB ON.
WOW! YOU WERE RIGHT. YOUR GRAMPA DOES KNOW A LOT ABOUT MICROBIOLOGY.

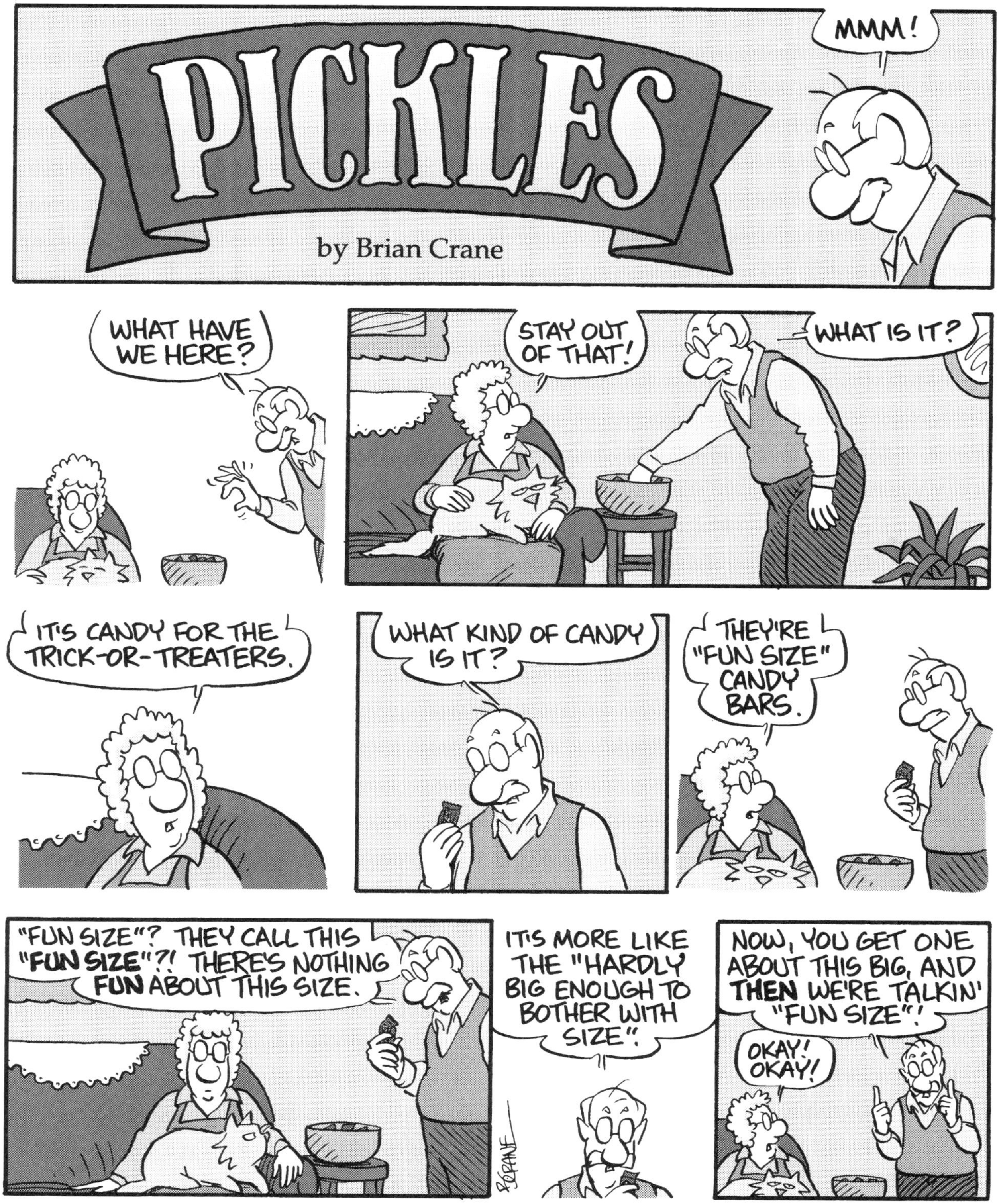
PICKLES
by Brian Crane
MMM!
WHAT HAVE WE HERE?
STAY OUT OF THAT!
WHAT IS IT?
IT'S CANDY FOR THE TRICK-OR-TREATERS.
WHAT KIND OF CANDY IS IT?
THEY'RE "FUN SIZE" CANDY BARS.
"FUN SIZE"? THEY CALL THIS "FUN SIZE"?! THERE'S NOTHING FUN ABOUT THIS SIZE.
IT'S MORE LIKE THE "HARDLY BIG ENOUGH TO BOTHER WITH SIZE".
NOW, YOU GET ONE ABOUT THIS BIG, AND THEN WE'RE TALKIN' "FUN SIZE"!
OKAY! OKAY!

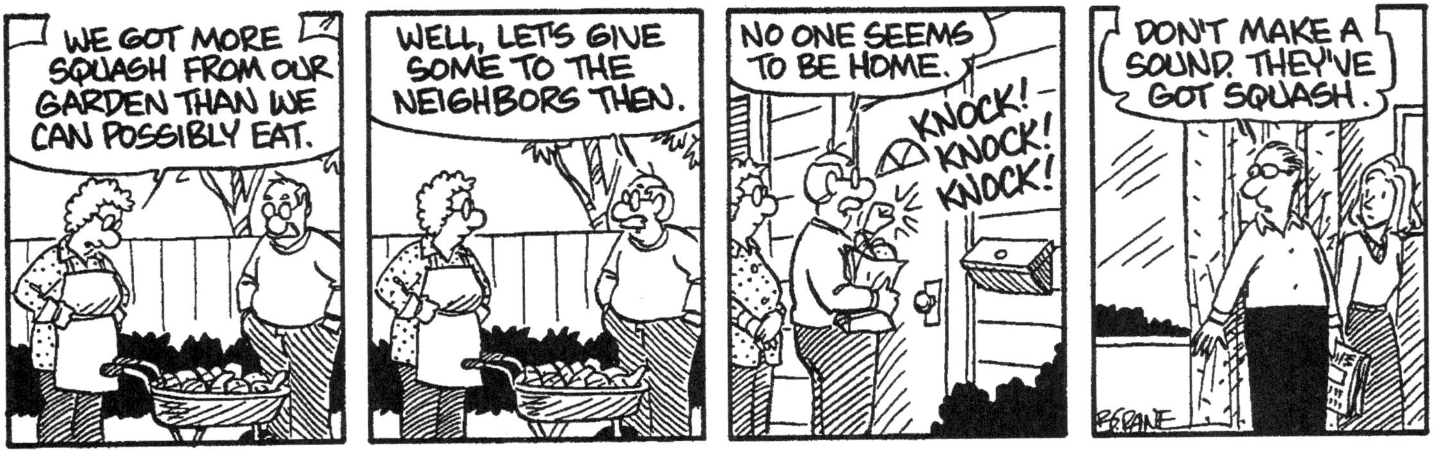
WE GOT MORE SQUASH FROM OUR GARDEN THAN WE CAN POSSIBLY EAT.
WELL, LET'S GIVE SOME TO THE NEIGHBORS THEN.
NO ONE SEEMS TO BE HOME.
KNOCK! KNOCK! KNOCK!
DON'T MAKE A SOUND. THEY'VE GOT SQUASH.

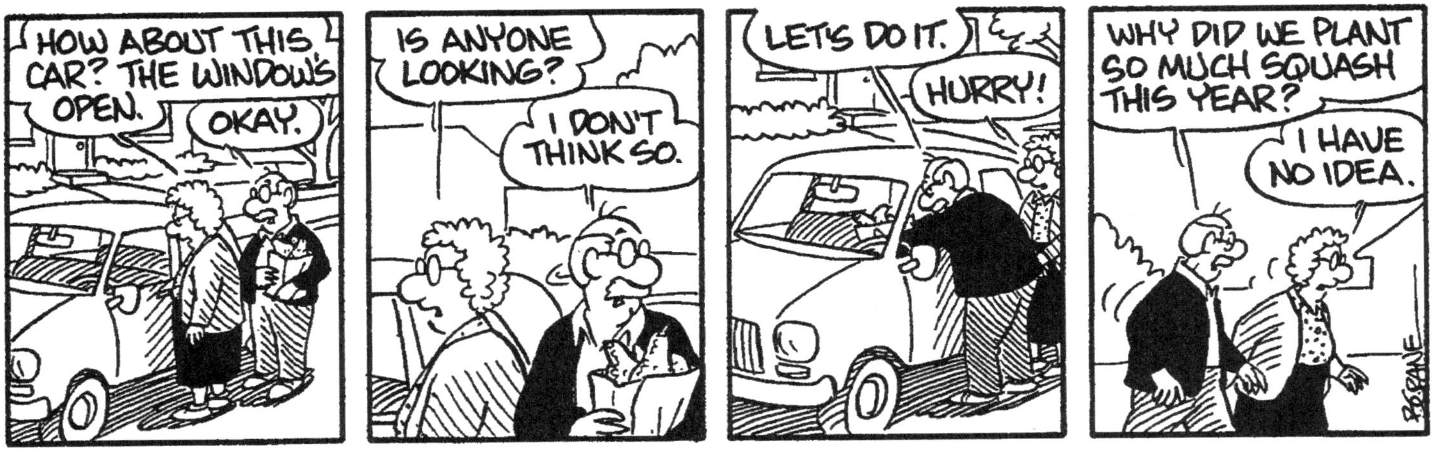
HOW ABOUT THIS CAR? THE WINDOW'S OPEN.
OKAY.
IS ANYONE LOOKING?
I DON'T THINK SO.
LET'S DO IT.
HURRY!
WHY DID WE PLANT SO MUCH SQUASH THIS YEAR?
I HAVE NO IDEA.

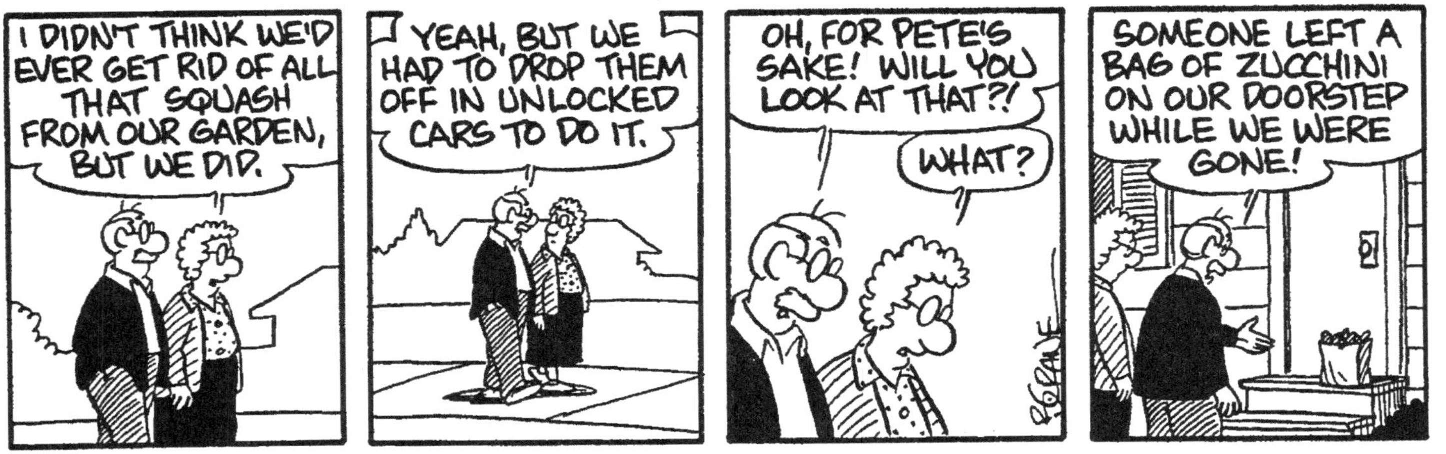
I DIDN'T THINK WE'D EVER GET RID OF ALL THAT SQUASH FROM OUR GARDEN, BUT WE DID.
YEAH, BUT WE HAD TO DROP THEM OFF IN UNLOCKED CARS TO DO IT.
OH, FOR PETE'S SAKE! WILL YOU LOOK AT THAT?!
WHAT?
SOMEONE LEFT A BAG OF ZUCCHINI ON OUR DOORSTEP WHILE WE WERE GONE!

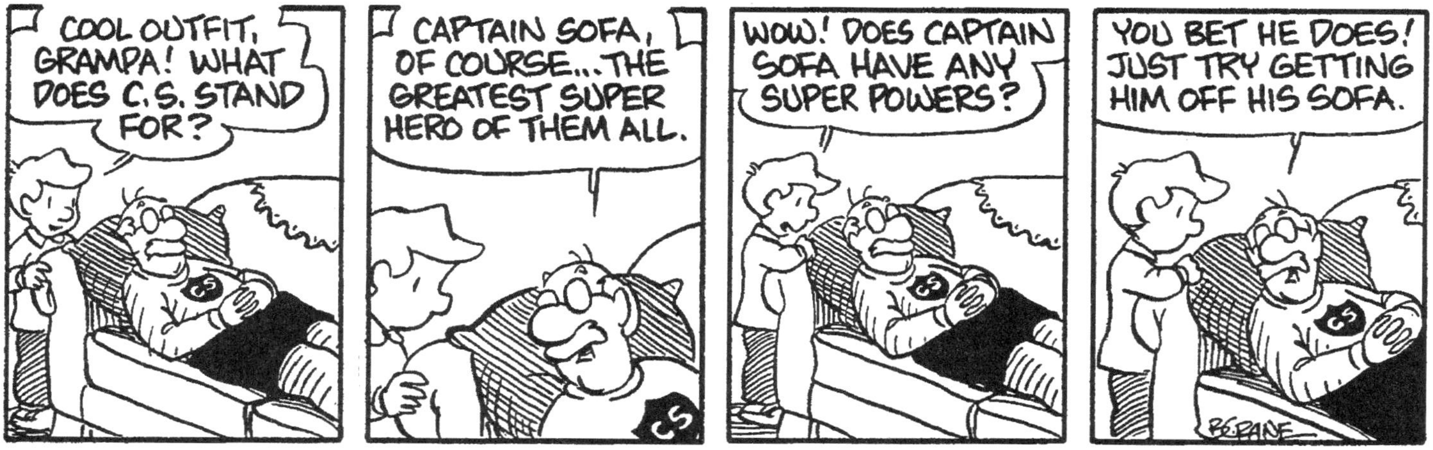
COOL OUTFIT, GRAMPA! WHAT DOES C.S. STAND FOR?
CAPTAIN SOFA, OF COURSE... THE GREATEST SUPER HERO OF THEM ALL.
WOW! DOES CAPTAIN SOFA HAVE ANY SUPER POWERS?
YOU BET HE DOES! JUST TRY GETTING HIM OFF HIS SOFA.

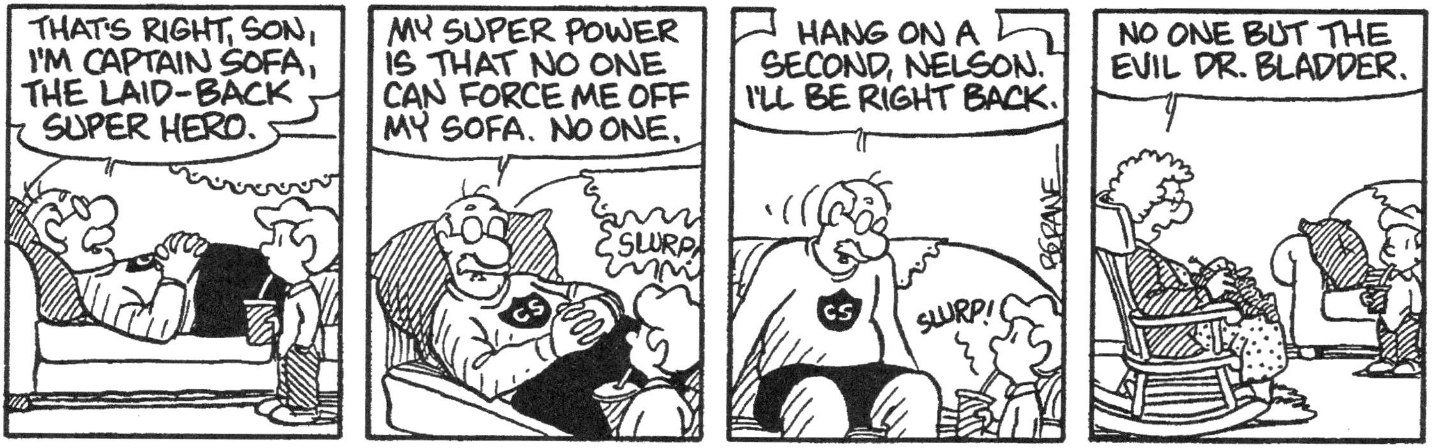
THAT'S RIGHT, SON, I'M CAPTAIN SOFA, THE LAID-BACK SUPER HERO.
MY SUPER POWER IS THAT NO ONE CAN FORCE ME OFF MY SOFA. NO ONE.
SLURP
HANG ON A SECOND, NELSON. I'LL BE RIGHT BACK.
SLURP!
NO ONE BUT THE EVIL DR. BLADDER.

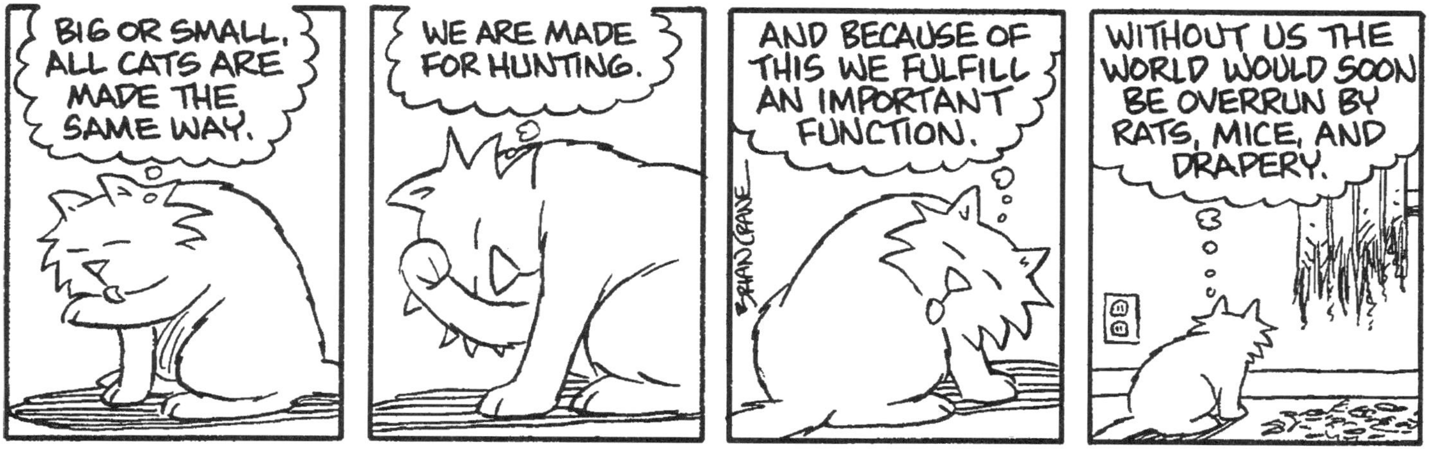
BIG OR SMALL, ALL CATS ARE MADE THE SAME WAY.
WE ARE MADE FOR HUNTING.
AND BECAUSE OF THIS WE FULFILL AN IMPORTANT FUNCTION.
WITHOUT US THE WORLD WOULD SOON BE OVERRUN BY RATS, MICE, AND DRAPERY.

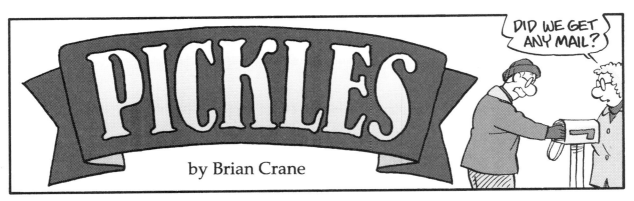

PICKLES

by Brian Crane

DID WE GET ANY MAIL?

A COUPLE OF CHRISTMAS CARDS FOR ME AND A BILL FOR YOU.

EARL, DID YOU NOTICE OUR NEIGHBOR'S YARD ACROSS THE STREET?

THEY MUST HAVE ABOUT A MILLION CHRISTMAS LIGHTS!

NOT TO MENTION THE LIFE-SIZE NATIVITY SCENE.

AND LOOK AT THE ROOF. THEY'VE GOT SANTA WITH HIS SLEIGH AND EIGHT REINDEER.

AREN'T YOU GOING TO PUT UP ANYTHING IN OUR YARD FOR CHRISTMAS?

I SUPPOSE I SHOULD.

SEE OUR DISPLAY ACROSS THE STREET

HEY, WHERE'D YOU GET THE PEACHY SCOOTER, NELSON?

IT BELONGS TO MY FRIEND. I WANT TO GET ONE OF MY OWN, BUT MY MOM WON'T BUY ME ONE.

WELL, THAT'S WHAT GRAMPA'S ARE FOR. HOW MUCH DOES IT COST?

A HUNDRED DOLLARS.

A HUNDRED DOLLARS?

BERNE

OKAY. IF I EVER SEE YOUR OTHER GRAMPA, I'LL TELL HIM.

WELL, BOY, I CAN'T SEE SPENDING A HUNDRED BUCKS ON A SCOOTER LIKE THAT.

BUT I'LL TELL YOU WHAT I'LL DO. I'LL **BUILD** YOU ONE IF YOU WANT.

YOU CAN BUILD ONE OF THESE?

BERNE

OH, SURE! I MADE SEVERAL OF THEM WHEN I WAS YOUNGER.

NOW, LET'S SEE... WHERE CAN I FIND AN ORANGE CRATE AND SOME OLD ROLLER SKATES?

TA-DA! I FINISHED YOUR SCOOTER, SON. ISN'T SHE A BEAUTY?

BUT, GRAMPA, I WANTED A SHINY ALUMINUM ONE LIKE ALL MY FRIENDS HAVE.

BERNE

NELSON... **ANYONE** CAN RIDE A STORE-BOUGHT SCOOTER. IT TAKES A REAL **INDIVIDUAL** TO DRIVE ONE OF THESE BABIES.

IT ALSO TAKES SOMEONE WHO DOESN'T MIND SPLINTERS.

OW!!

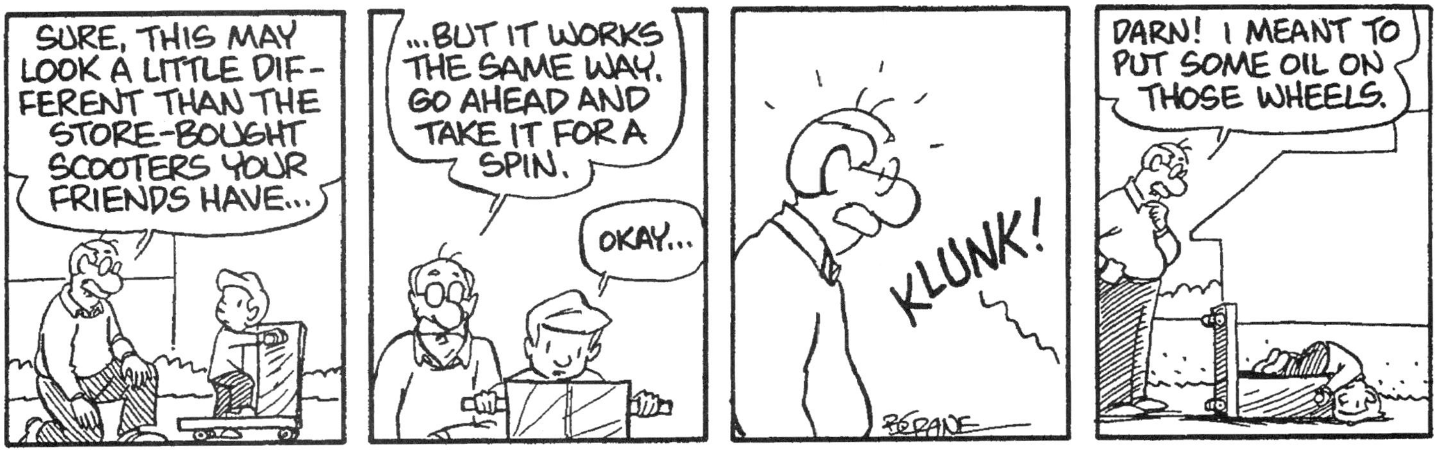
SURE, THIS MAY LOOK A LITTLE DIF-FERENT THAN THE STORE-BOUGHT SCOOTERS YOUR FRIENDS HAVE...
...BUT IT WORKS THE SAME WAY. GO AHEAD AND TAKE IT FOR A SPIN.
OKAY...
KLUNK!
B. CRANE
DARN! I MEANT TO PUT SOME OIL ON THOSE WHEELS.

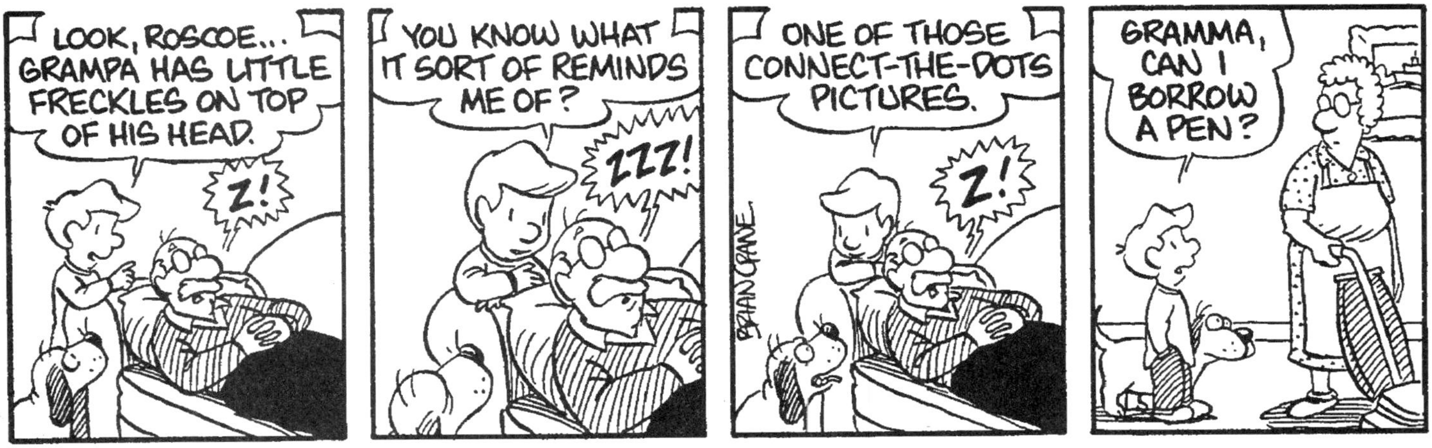
LOOK, ROSCOE... GRAMPA HAS LITTLE FRECKLES ON TOP OF HIS HEAD.
Z!
YOU KNOW WHAT IT SORT OF REMINDS ME OF?
ZZZ!
ONE OF THOSE CONNECT-THE-DOTS PICTURES.
Z!
BRIAN CRANE
GRAMMA, CAN I BORROW A PEN?

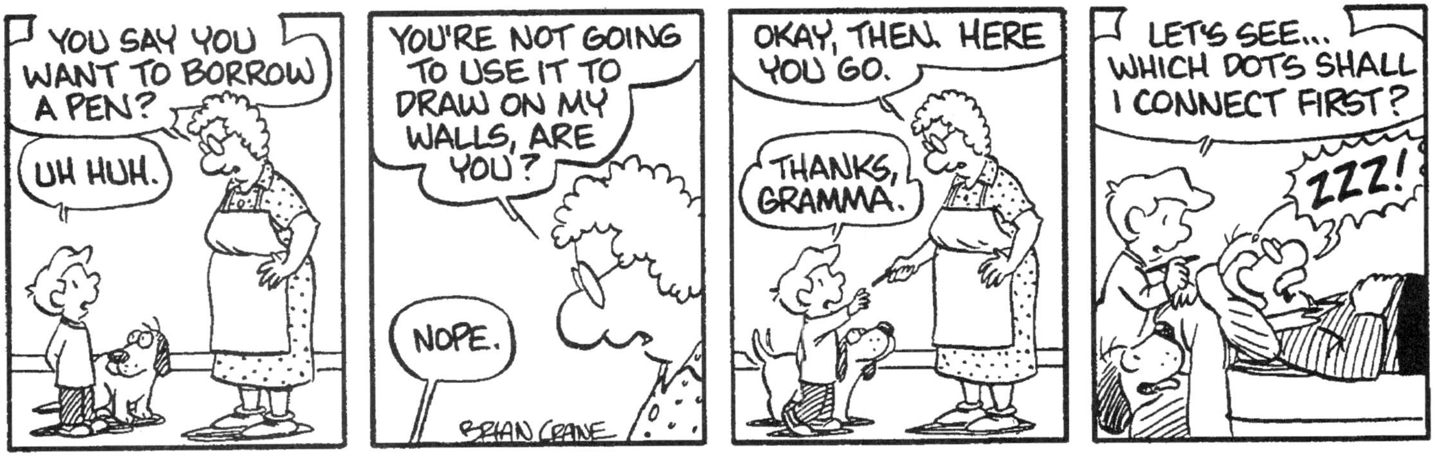
YOU SAY YOU WANT TO BORROW A PEN?
UH HUH.
YOU'RE NOT GOING TO USE IT TO DRAW ON MY WALLS, ARE YOU?
NOPE.
BRIAN CRANE
OKAY, THEN. HERE YOU GO.
THANKS, GRAMMA.
LET'S SEE... WHICH DOTS SHALL I CONNECT FIRST?
ZZZ!

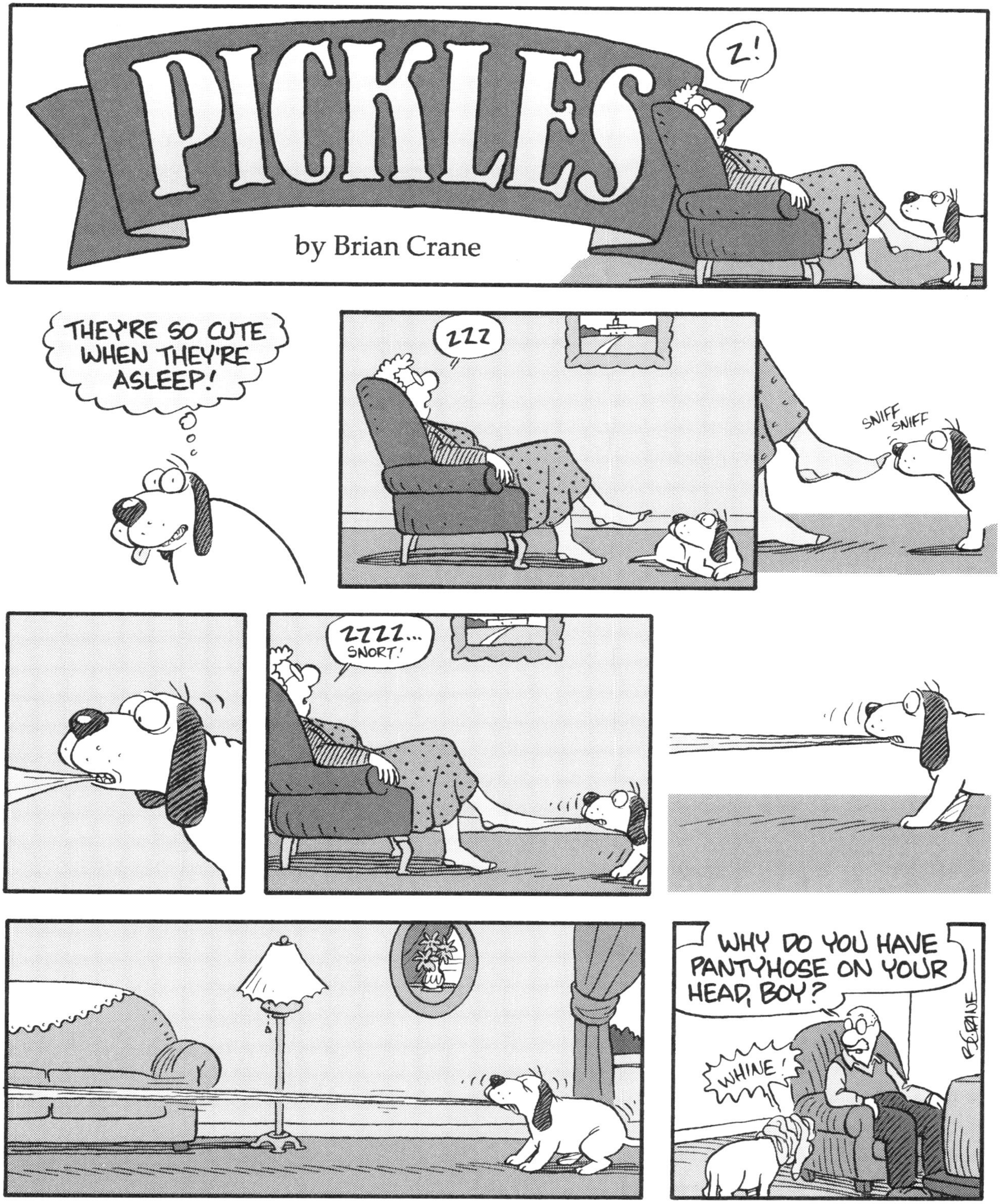
PICKLES
by Brian Crane
Z!
THEY'RE SO CUTE WHEN THEY'RE ASLEEP!
ZZZ
SNIFF SNIFF
ZZZZ... SNORT!
WHY DO YOU HAVE PANTYHOSE ON YOUR HEAD, BOY?
WHINE!
B. CRANE

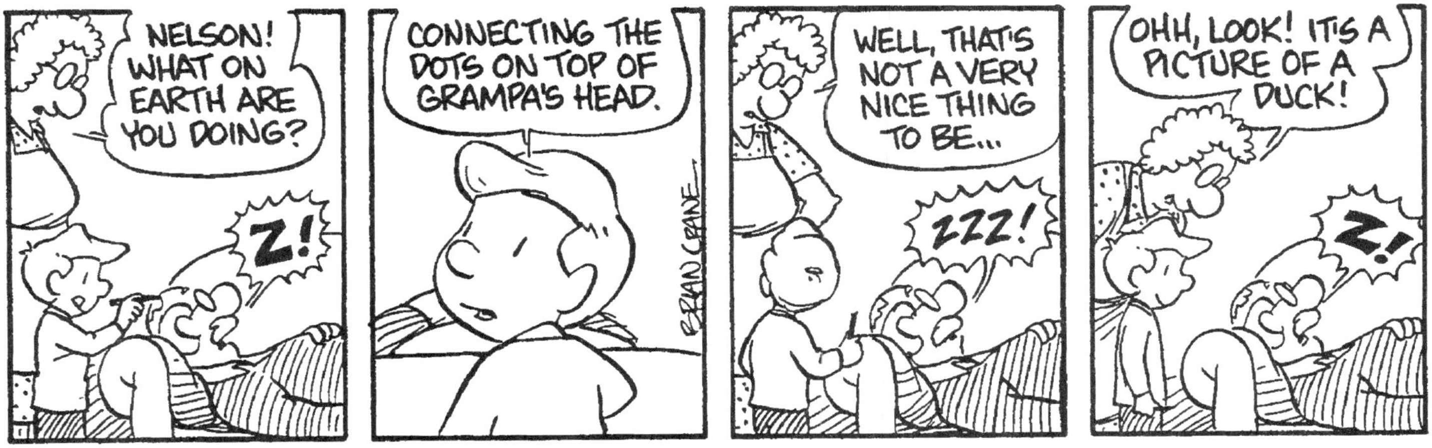
NELSON! WHAT ON EARTH ARE YOU DOING?
Z!
CONNECTING THE DOTS ON TOP OF GRAMPA'S HEAD.
BRIAN CRANE
WELL, THAT'S NOT A VERY NICE THING TO BE...
ZZZ!
OHH, LOOK! IT'S A PICTURE OF A DUCK!
Z!

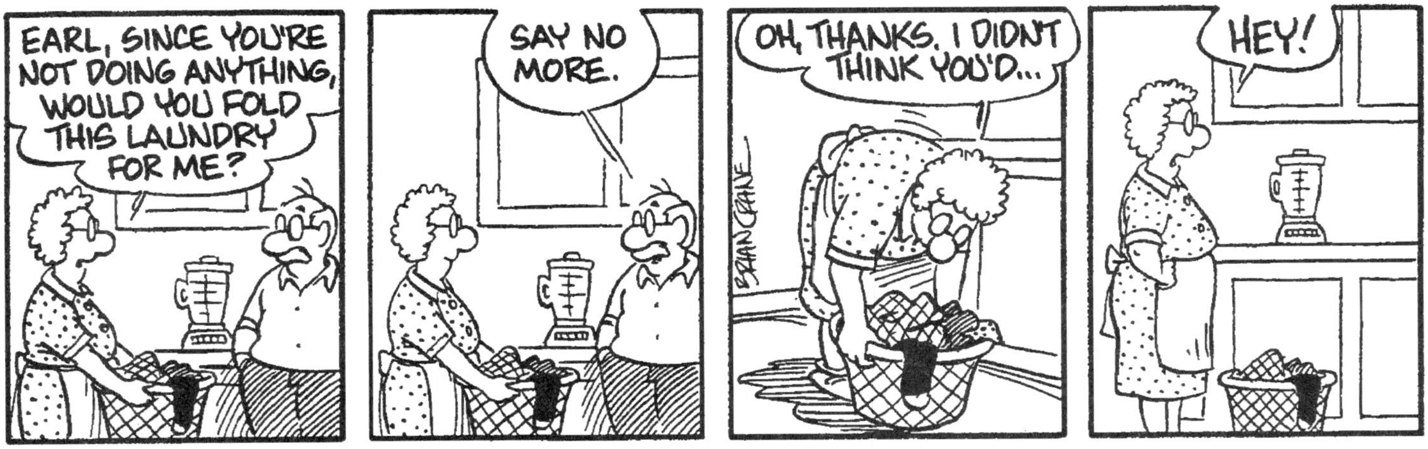
EARL, SINCE YOU'RE NOT DOING ANYTHING, WOULD YOU FOLD THIS LAUNDRY FOR ME?
SAY NO MORE.
BRIAN CRANE
OH, THANKS. I DIDN'T THINK YOU'D...
HEY!

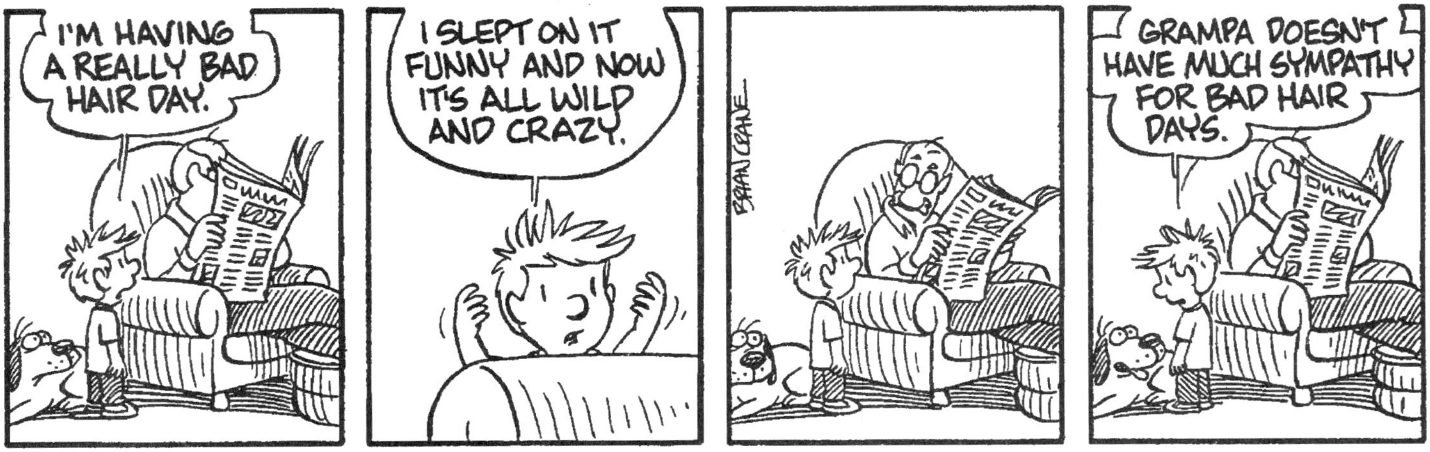
I'M HAVING A REALLY BAD HAIR DAY.
I SLEPT ON IT FUNNY AND NOW IT'S ALL WILD AND CRAZY.
BRIAN CRANE
GRAMPA DOESN'T HAVE MUCH SYMPATHY FOR BAD HAIR DAYS.

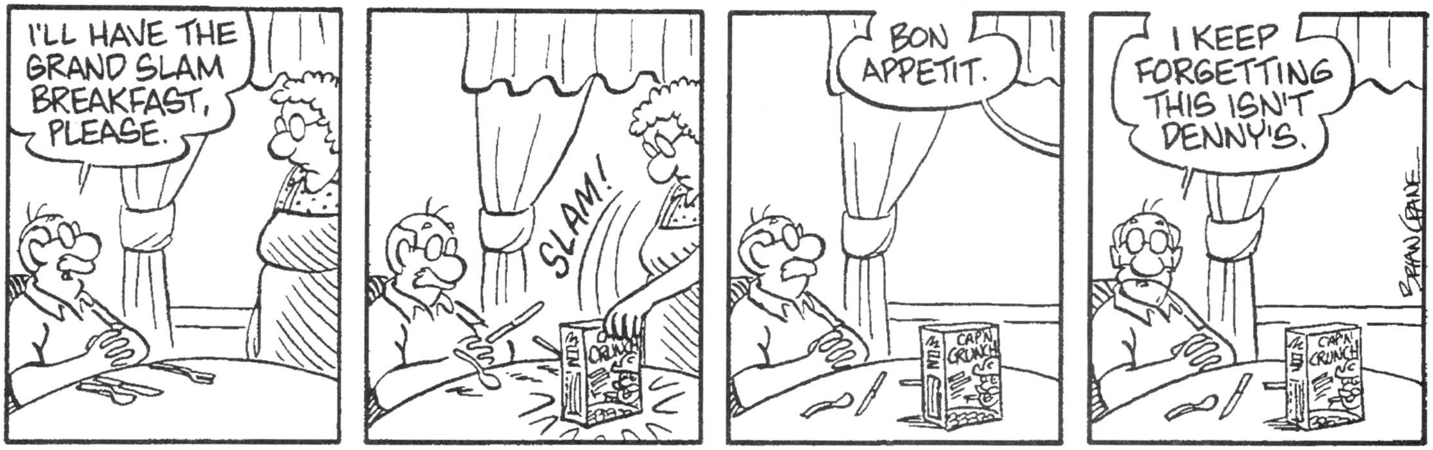
I'LL HAVE THE GRAND SLAM BREAKFAST, PLEASE.
SLAM!
BON APPETIT.
I KEEP FORGETTING THIS ISN'T DENNY'S.
BRIAN CRANE

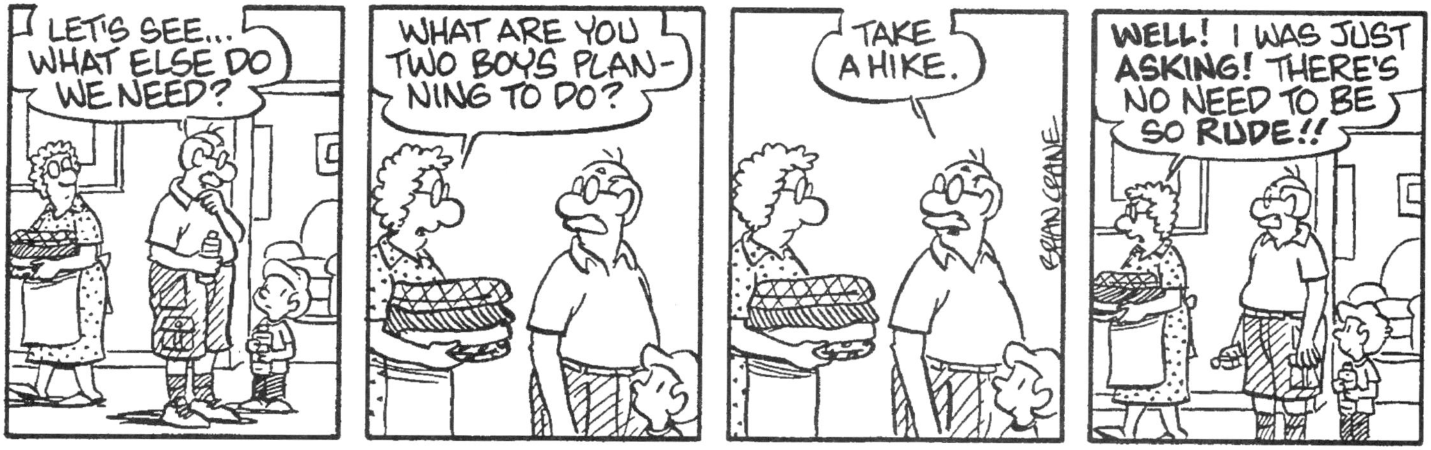
LET'S SEE... WHAT ELSE DO WE NEED?
WHAT ARE YOU TWO BOYS PLAN-NING TO DO?
TAKE A HIKE.
BRIAN CRANE
WELL! I WAS JUST **ASKING!** THERE'S NO NEED TO BE SO **RUDE!!**

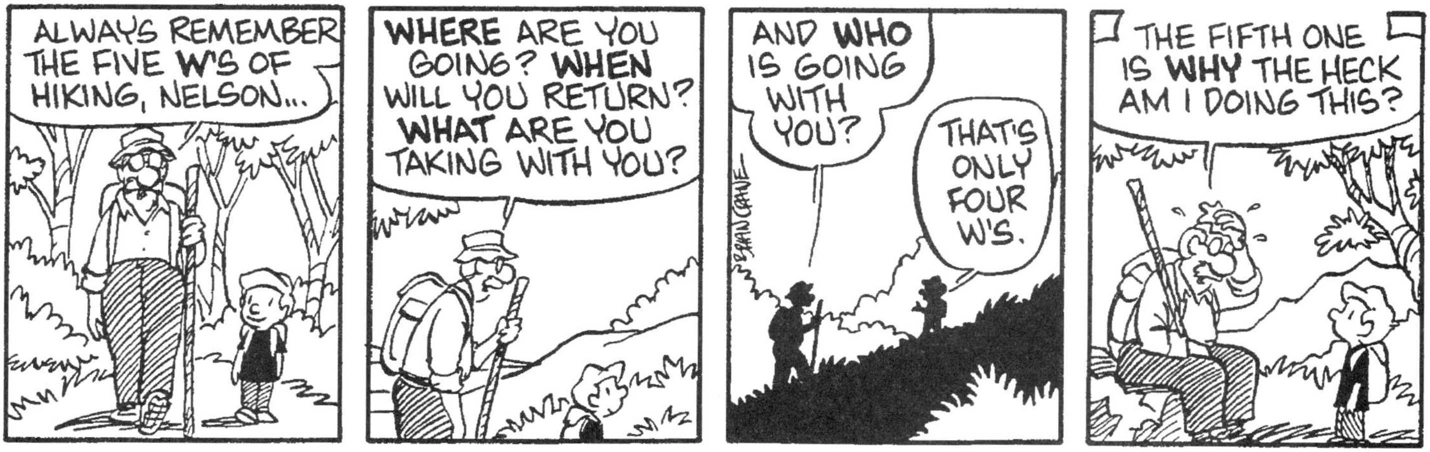
ALWAYS REMEMBER THE FIVE **W**'S OF HIKING, NELSON...
WHERE ARE YOU GOING? **WHEN** WILL YOU RETURN? **WHAT** ARE YOU TAKING WITH YOU?
AND **WHO** IS GOING WITH YOU?
BRIAN CRANE
THAT'S ONLY FOUR W'S.
THE FIFTH ONE IS **WHY** THE HECK AM I DOING THIS?

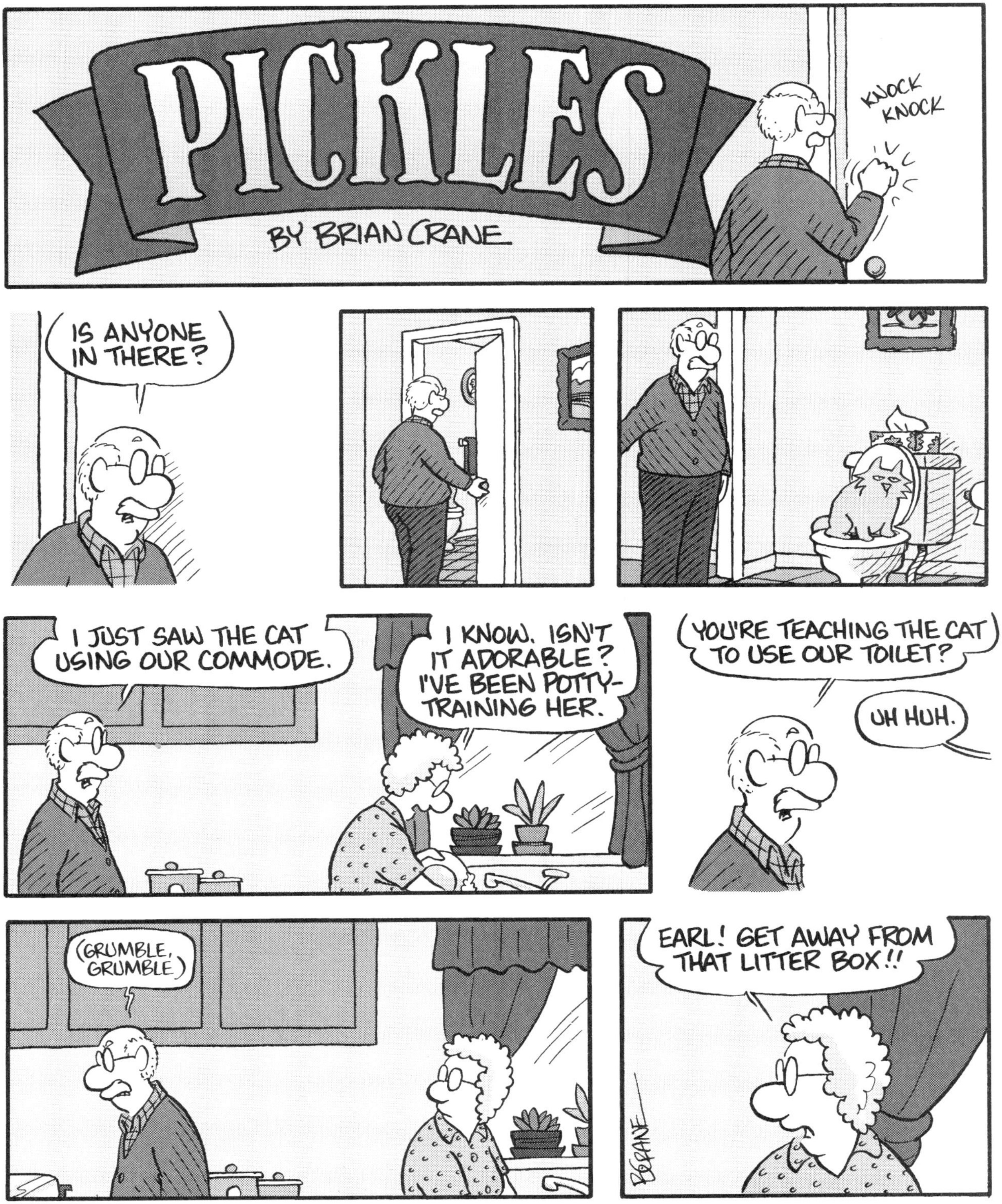
PICKLES
BY BRIAN CRANE
KNOCK KNOCK
IS ANYONE IN THERE?
I JUST SAW THE CAT USING OUR COMMODE.
I KNOW. ISN'T IT ADORABLE? I'VE BEEN POTTY-TRAINING HER.
YOU'RE TEACHING THE CAT TO USE OUR TOILET?
UH HUH.
(GRUMBLE, GRUMBLE)
EARL! GET AWAY FROM THAT LITTER BOX!!
B. CRANE

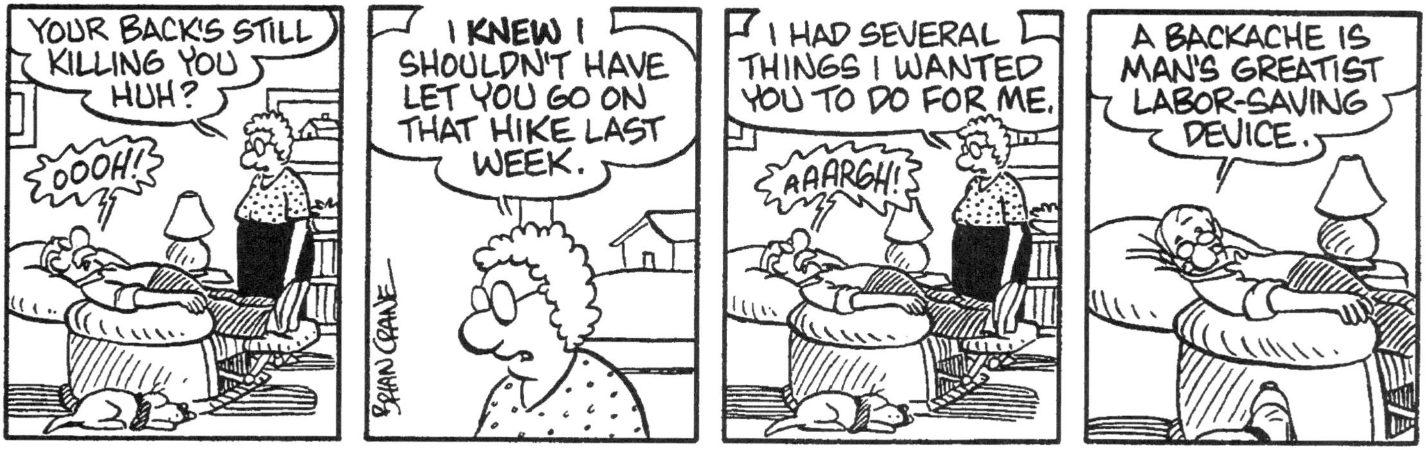
YOUR BACK'S STILL KILLING YOU HUH?
OOOH!
I **KNEW** I SHOULDN'T HAVE LET YOU GO ON THAT HIKE LAST WEEK.
BRIAN CRANE
I HAD SEVERAL THINGS I WANTED YOU TO DO FOR ME.
AAARGH!
A BACKACHE IS MAN'S GREATEST LABOR-SAVING DEVICE.

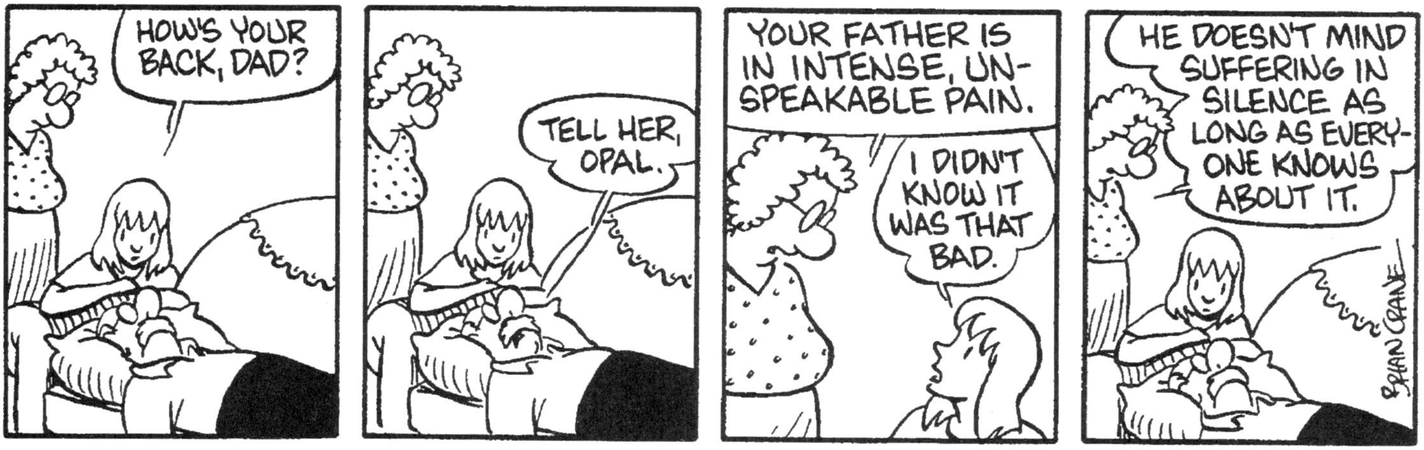
HOW'S YOUR BACK, DAD?
TELL HER, OPAL.
YOUR FATHER IS IN INTENSE, UN-SPEAKABLE PAIN.
I DIDN'T KNOW IT WAS THAT BAD.
HE DOESN'T MIND SUFFERING IN SILENCE AS LONG AS EVERY-ONE KNOWS ABOUT IT.
BRIAN CRANE

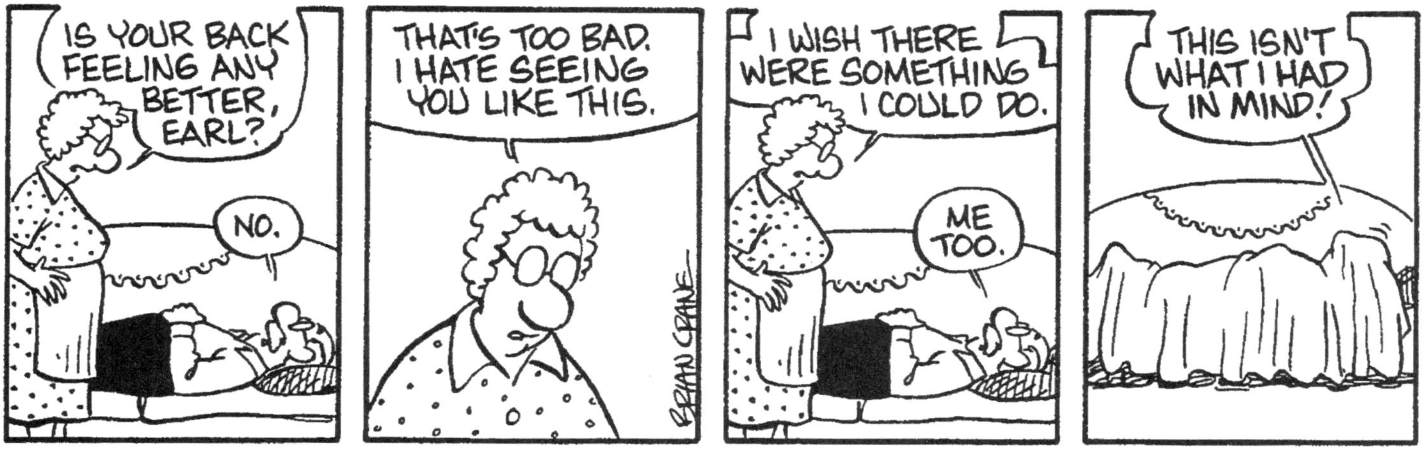
IS YOUR BACK FEELING ANY BETTER, EARL?
NO.
THAT'S TOO BAD. I HATE SEEING YOU LIKE THIS.
BRIAN CRANE
I WISH THERE WERE SOMETHING I COULD DO.
ME TOO.
THIS ISN'T WHAT I HAD IN MIND!

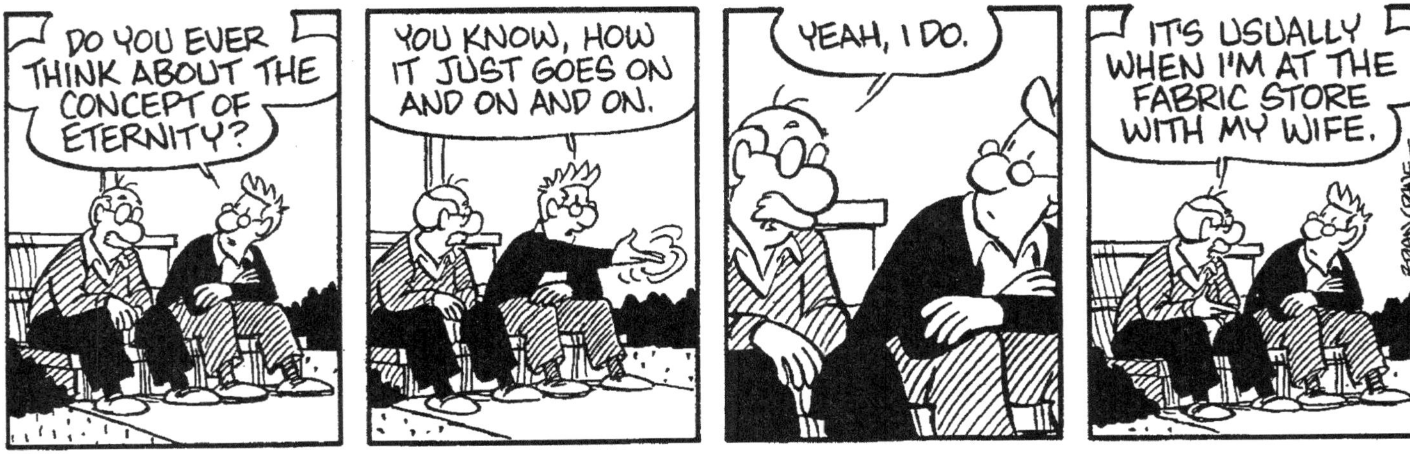
DO YOU EVER THINK ABOUT THE CONCEPT OF ETERNITY?
YOU KNOW, HOW IT JUST GOES ON AND ON AND ON.
YEAH, I DO.
IT'S USUALLY WHEN I'M AT THE FABRIC STORE WITH MY WIFE.

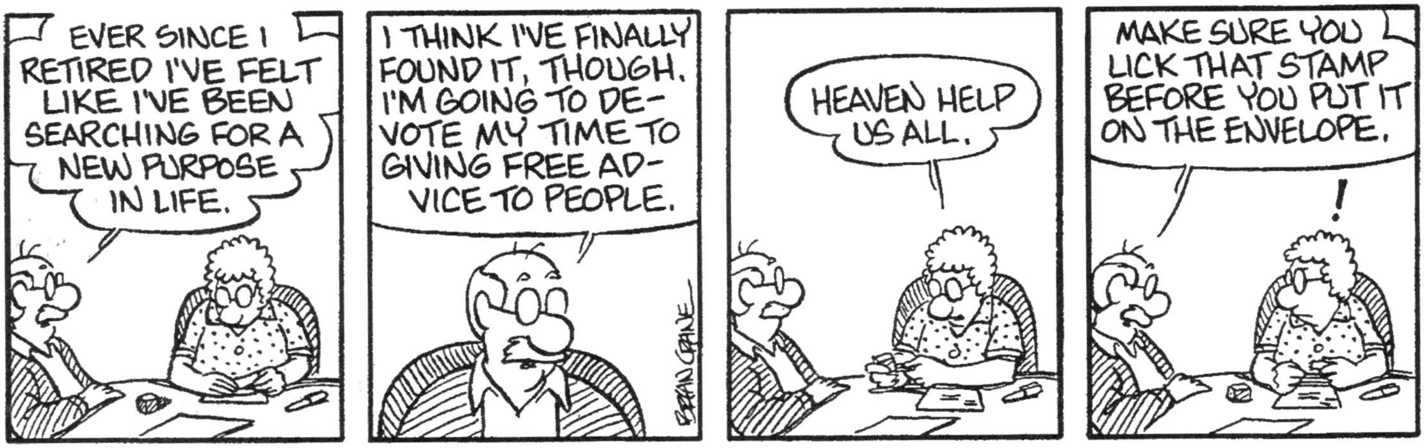
EVER SINCE I RETIRED I'VE FELT LIKE I'VE BEEN SEARCHING FOR A NEW PURPOSE IN LIFE.
I THINK I'VE FINALLY FOUND IT, THOUGH. I'M GOING TO DEVOTE MY TIME TO GIVING FREE ADVICE TO PEOPLE.
HEAVEN HELP US ALL.
MAKE SURE YOU LICK THAT STAMP BEFORE YOU PUT IT ON THE ENVELOPE.
!

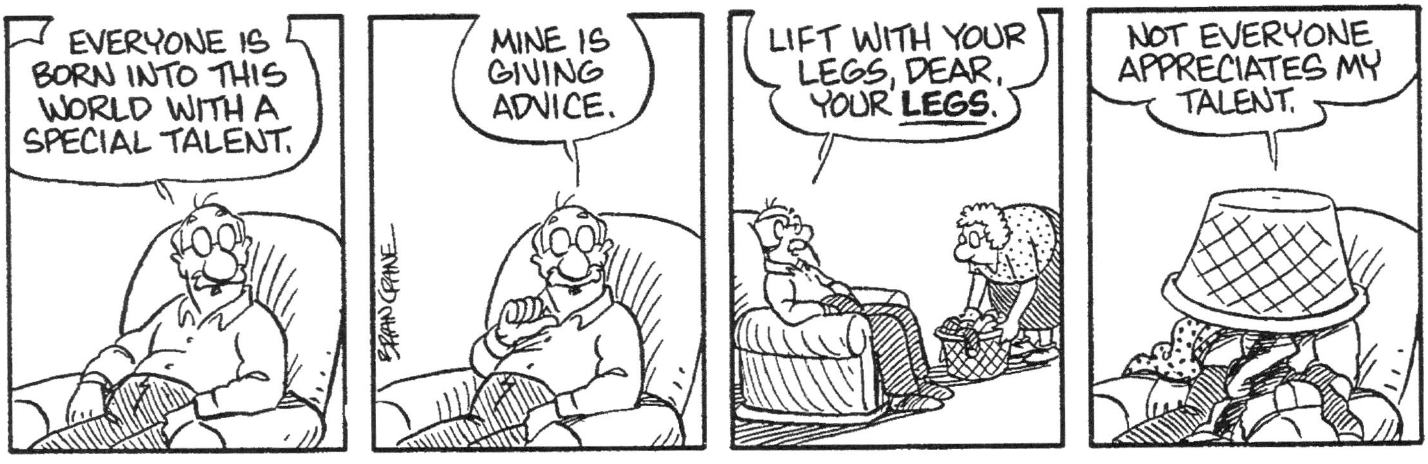
EVERYONE IS BORN INTO THIS WORLD WITH A SPECIAL TALENT.
MINE IS GIVING ADVICE.
LIFT WITH YOUR LEGS, DEAR, YOUR **LEGS**.
NOT EVERYONE APPRECIATES MY TALENT.

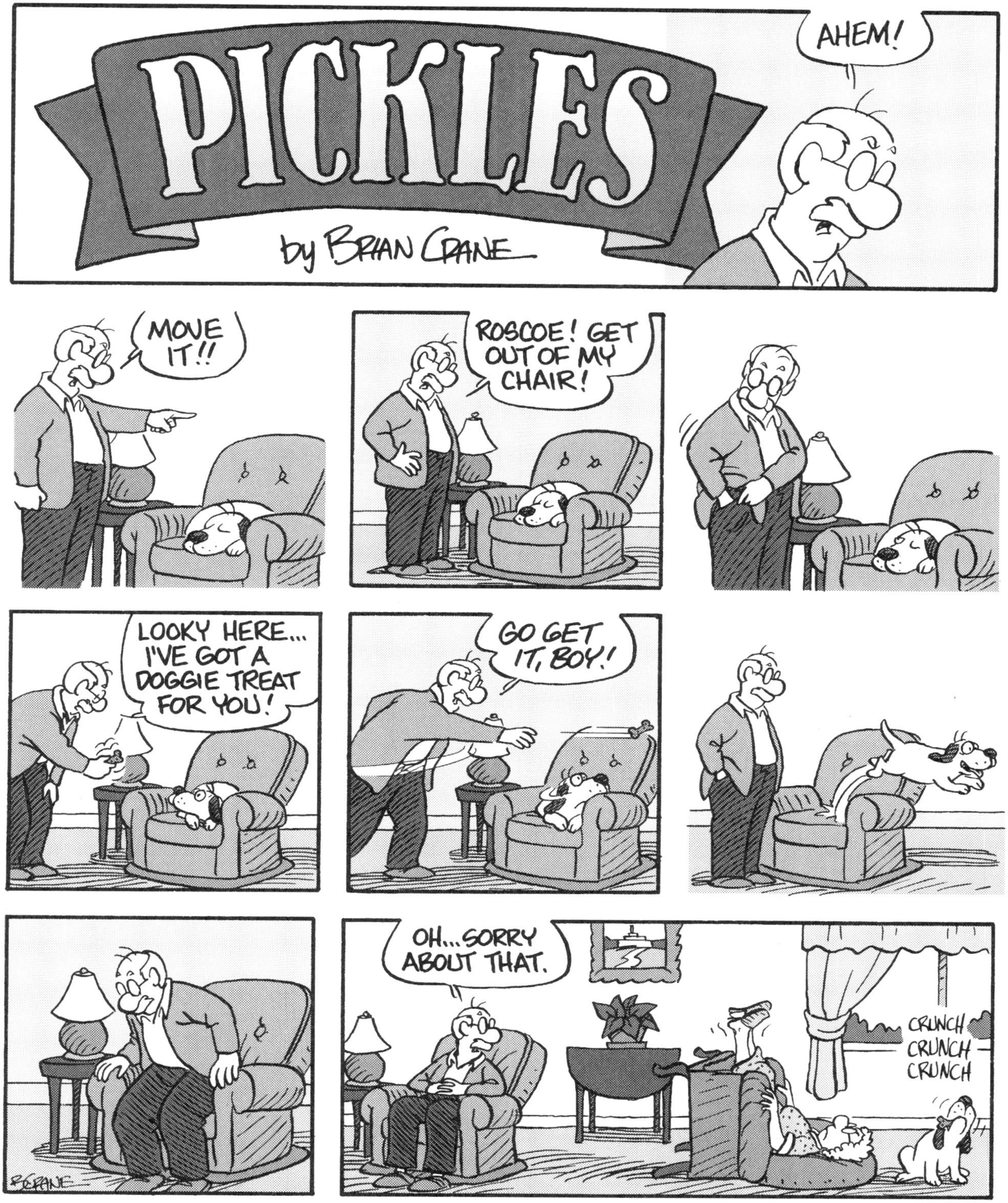

PICKLES
by BRIAN CRANE
AHEM!
MOVE IT!!
ROSCOE! GET OUT OF MY CHAIR!
LOOKY HERE... I'VE GOT A DOGGIE TREAT FOR YOU!
GO GET IT, BOY!
B. CRANE
OH... SORRY ABOUT THAT.
CRUNCH
CRUNCH
CRUNCH

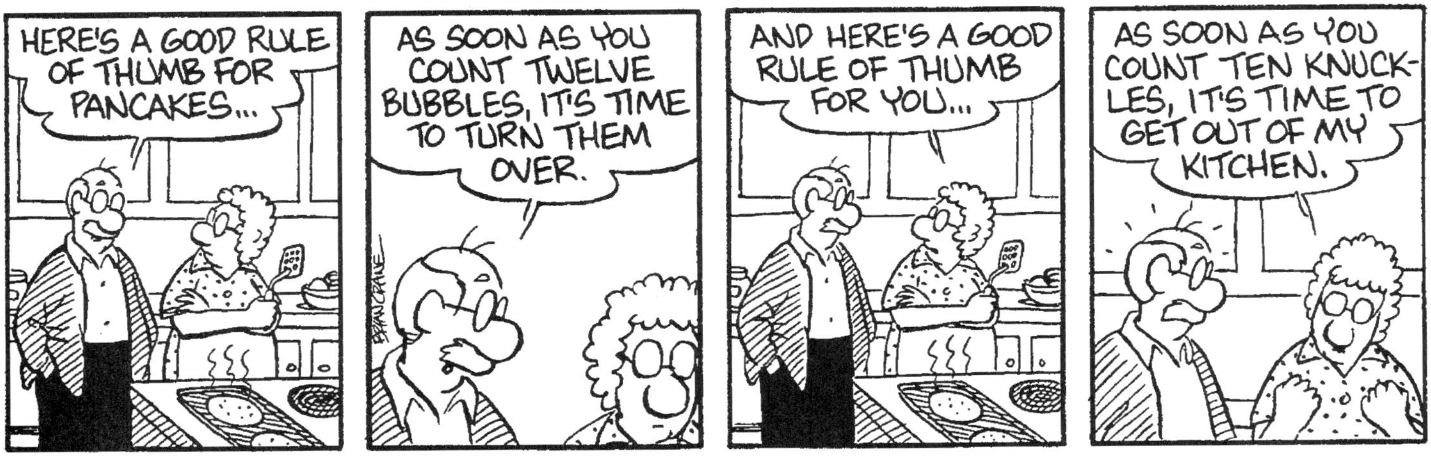
HERE'S A GOOD RULE OF THUMB FOR PANCAKES...
AS SOON AS YOU COUNT TWELVE BUBBLES, IT'S TIME TO TURN THEM OVER.
AND HERE'S A GOOD RULE OF THUMB FOR YOU...
AS SOON AS YOU COUNT TEN KNUCK-LES, IT'S TIME TO GET OUT OF MY KITCHEN.

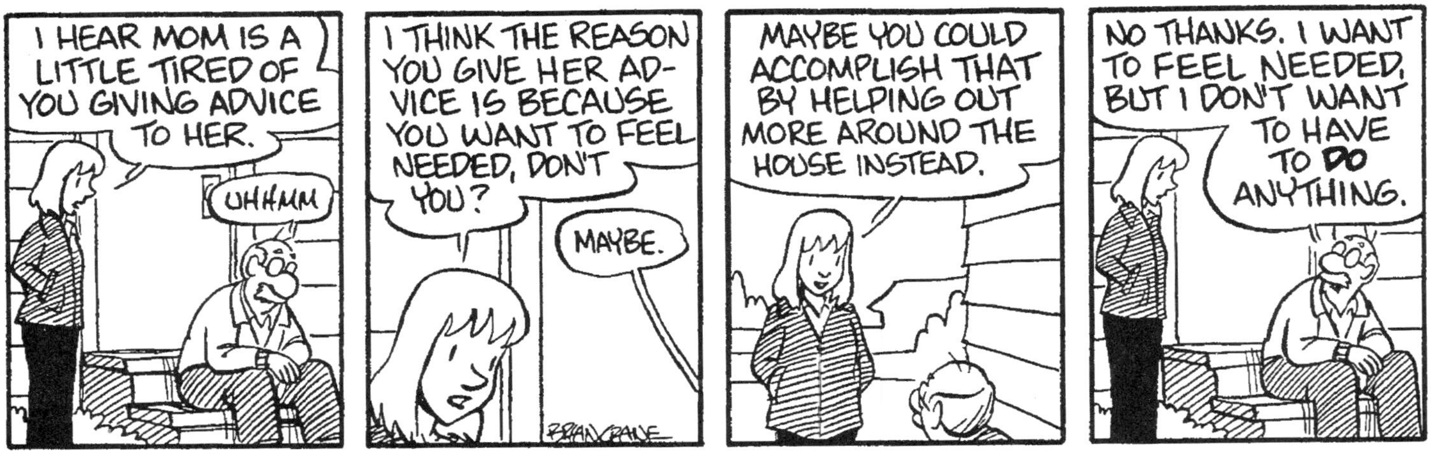
I HEAR MOM IS A LITTLE TIRED OF YOU GIVING ADVICE TO HER.
UHHMM
I THINK THE REASON YOU GIVE HER AD-VICE IS BECAUSE YOU WANT TO FEEL NEEDED, DON'T YOU?
MAYBE.
MAYBE YOU COULD ACCOMPLISH THAT BY HELPING OUT MORE AROUND THE HOUSE INSTEAD.
NO THANKS. I WANT TO FEEL NEEDED, BUT I DON'T WANT TO HAVE TO **DO** ANYTHING.

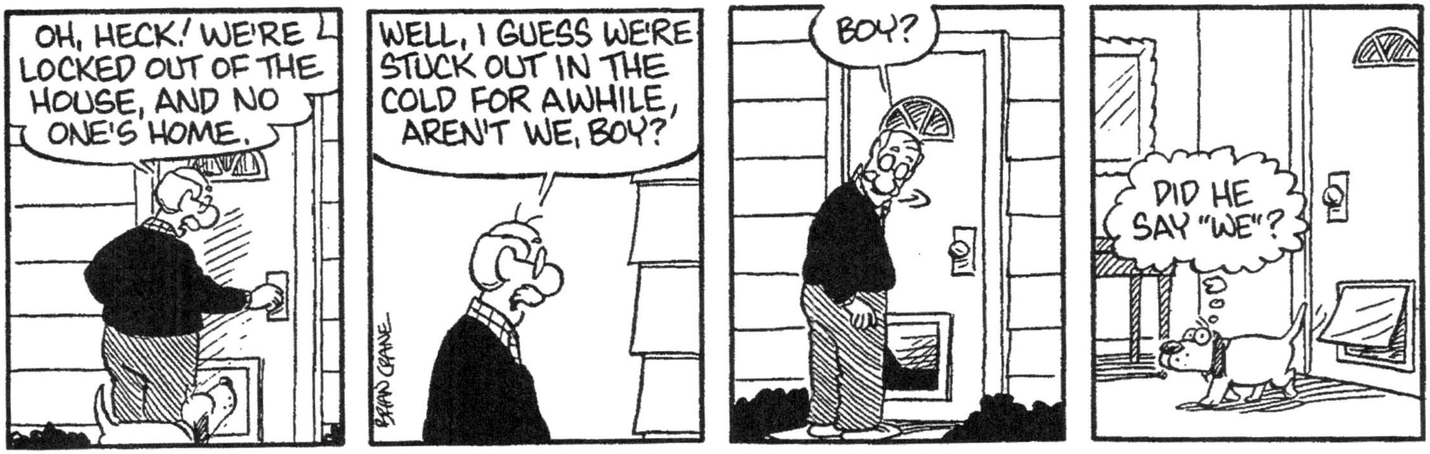
OH, HECK! WE'RE LOCKED OUT OF THE HOUSE, AND NO ONE'S HOME.
WELL, I GUESS WE'RE STUCK OUT IN THE COLD FOR AWHILE, AREN'T WE, BOY?
BOY?
DID HE SAY "WE"?

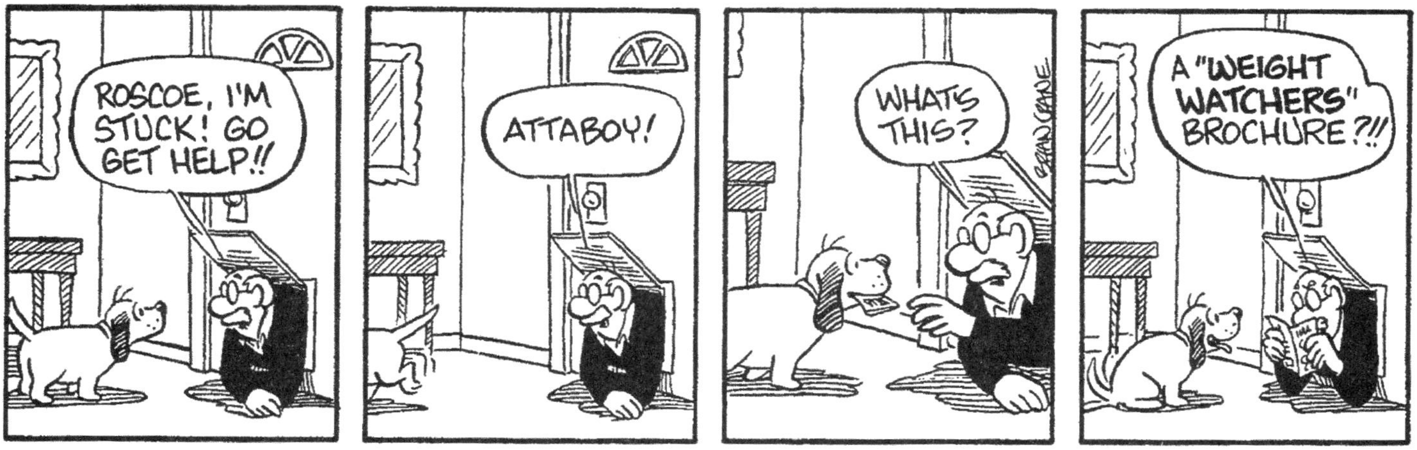
ROSCOE, I'M STUCK! GO GET HELP!!
ATTABOY!
WHAT'S THIS?
A "**WEIGHT WATCHERS**" BROCHURE?!!

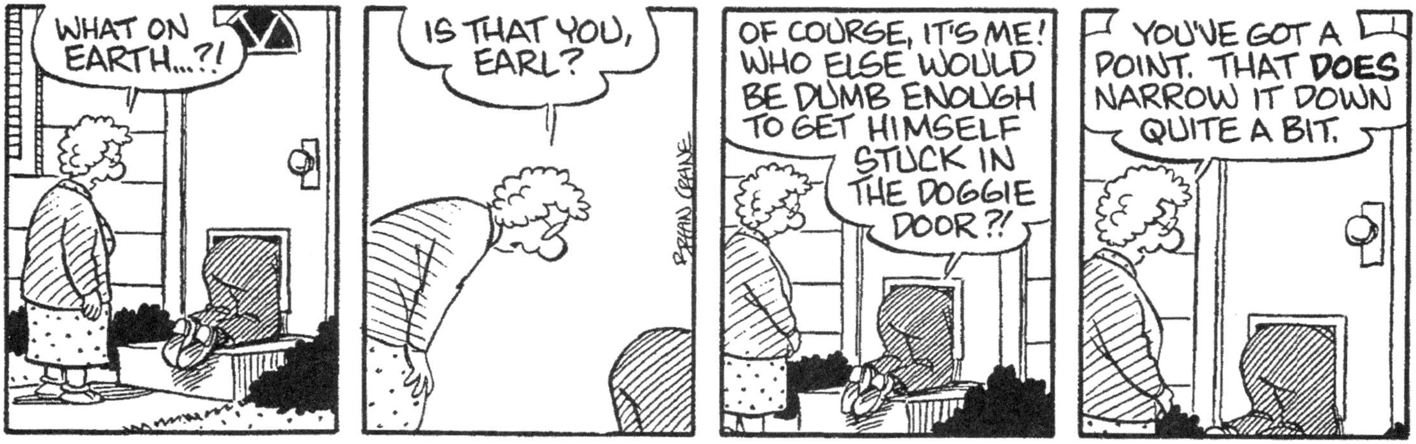
WHAT ON EARTH...?!
IS THAT YOU, EARL?
OF COURSE, IT'S ME! WHO ELSE WOULD BE DUMB ENOUGH TO GET HIMSELF STUCK IN THE DOGGIE DOOR?!
YOU'VE GOT A POINT. THAT **DOES** NARROW IT DOWN QUITE A BIT.

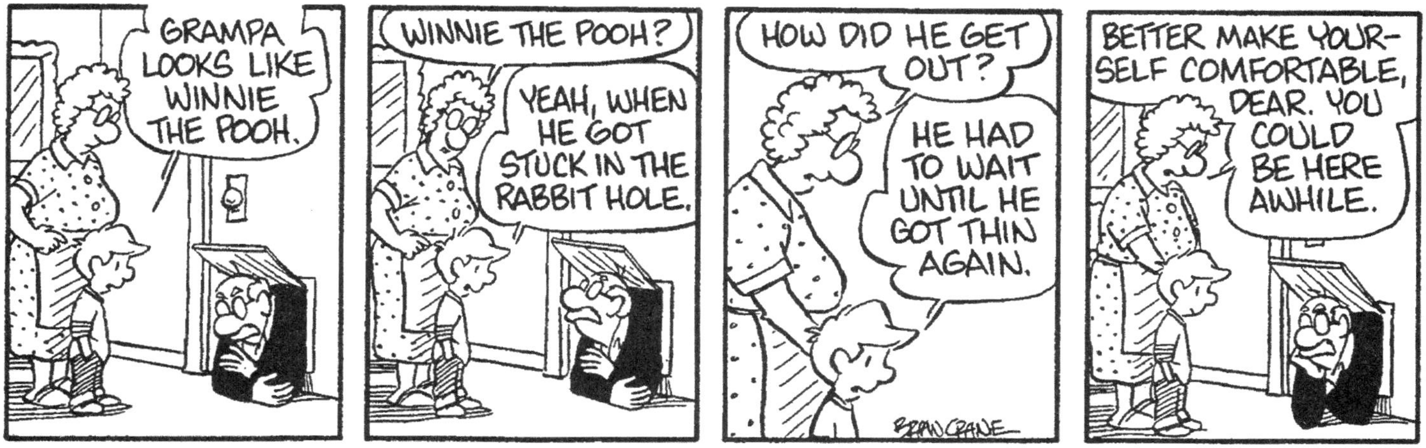
GRAMPA LOOKS LIKE WINNIE THE POOH.
WINNIE THE POOH?
YEAH, WHEN HE GOT STUCK IN THE RABBIT HOLE.
HOW DID HE GET OUT?
HE HAD TO WAIT UNTIL HE GOT THIN AGAIN.
BETTER MAKE YOURSELF COMFORTABLE, DEAR. YOU COULD BE HERE AWHILE.

PICKLES by Brian Crane

WHAT DO YOU THINK YOU'RE DOING UP THERE?

YOU'RE BEING VERY CHILDISH.

COME DOWN FROM THERE!

OKAY, FINE! STAY THERE. SEE IF I CARE.

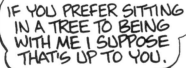

IF YOU PREFER SITTING IN A TREE TO BEING WITH ME I SUPPOSE THAT'S UP TO YOU.

I WORK MY FINGERS TO THE BONE FOR YOU AND THIS IS THE THANKS I GET!

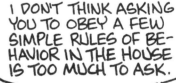

I DON'T THINK ASKING YOU TO OBEY A FEW SIMPLE RULES OF BEHAVIOR IN THE HOUSE IS TOO MUCH TO ASK.

AND THAT'S ALL I'M GOING TO SAY ABOUT IT.

LET ME KNOW IF YOU CHANGE YOUR MIND AND DECIDE TO COME DOWN.

AND IF YOU DO, BRING THE CAT WITH YOU.

74

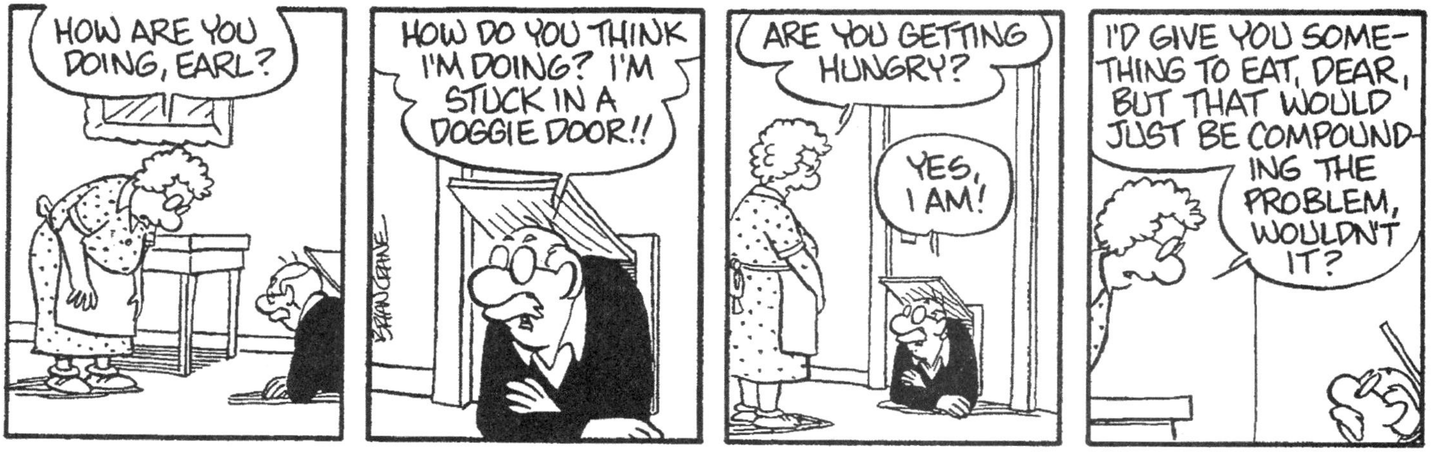
HOW ARE YOU DOING, EARL?
HOW DO YOU THINK I'M DOING? I'M STUCK IN A DOGGIE DOOR!!
BRIAN CRANE
ARE YOU GETTING HUNGRY?
YES, I AM!
I'D GIVE YOU SOMETHING TO EAT, DEAR, BUT THAT WOULD JUST BE COMPOUNDING THE PROBLEM, WOULDN'T IT?

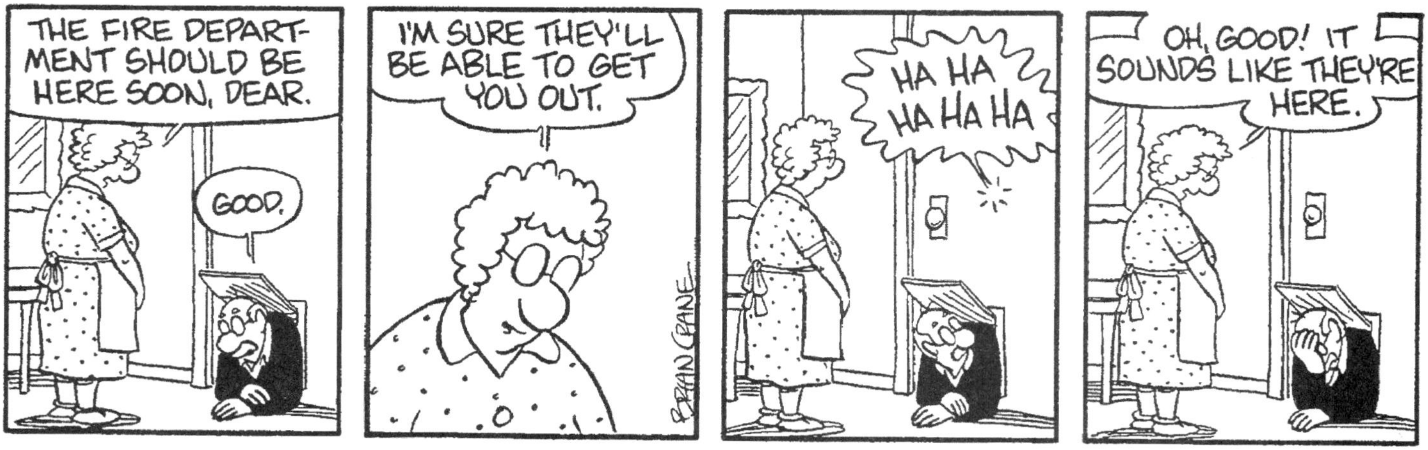
THE FIRE DEPARTMENT SHOULD BE HERE SOON, DEAR.
GOOD.
I'M SURE THEY'LL BE ABLE TO GET YOU OUT.
BRIAN CRANE
HA HA HA HA HA
OH, GOOD! IT SOUNDS LIKE THEY'RE HERE.

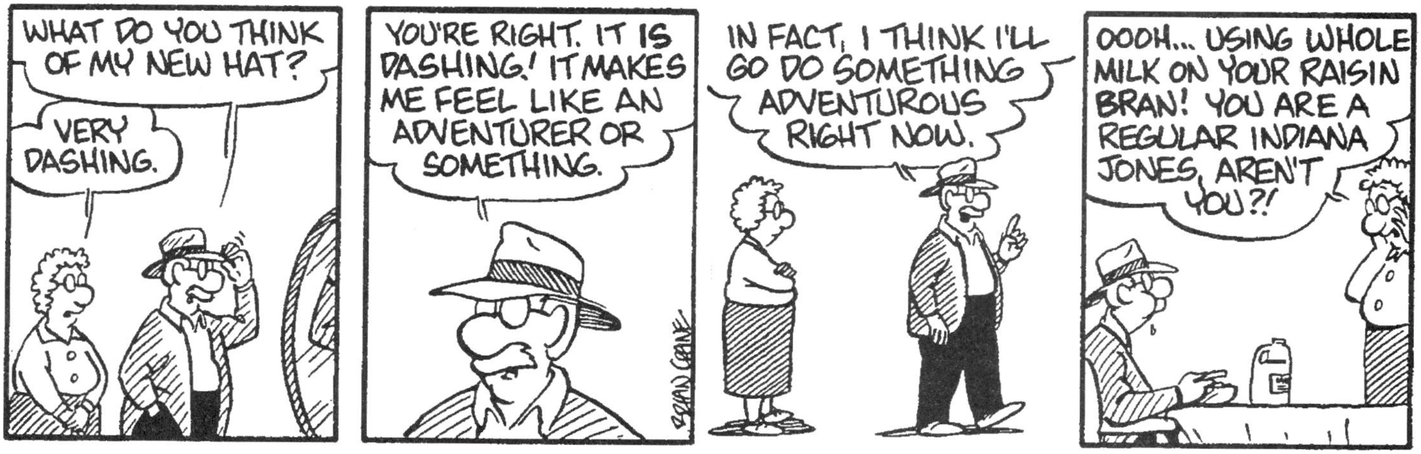
WHAT DO YOU THINK OF MY NEW HAT?
VERY DASHING.
YOU'RE RIGHT. IT IS DASHING! IT MAKES ME FEEL LIKE AN ADVENTURER OR SOMETHING.
BRIAN CRANE
IN FACT, I THINK I'LL GO DO SOMETHING ADVENTUROUS RIGHT NOW.
OOOH... USING WHOLE MILK ON YOUR RAISIN BRAN! YOU ARE A REGULAR INDIANA JONES, AREN'T YOU?!

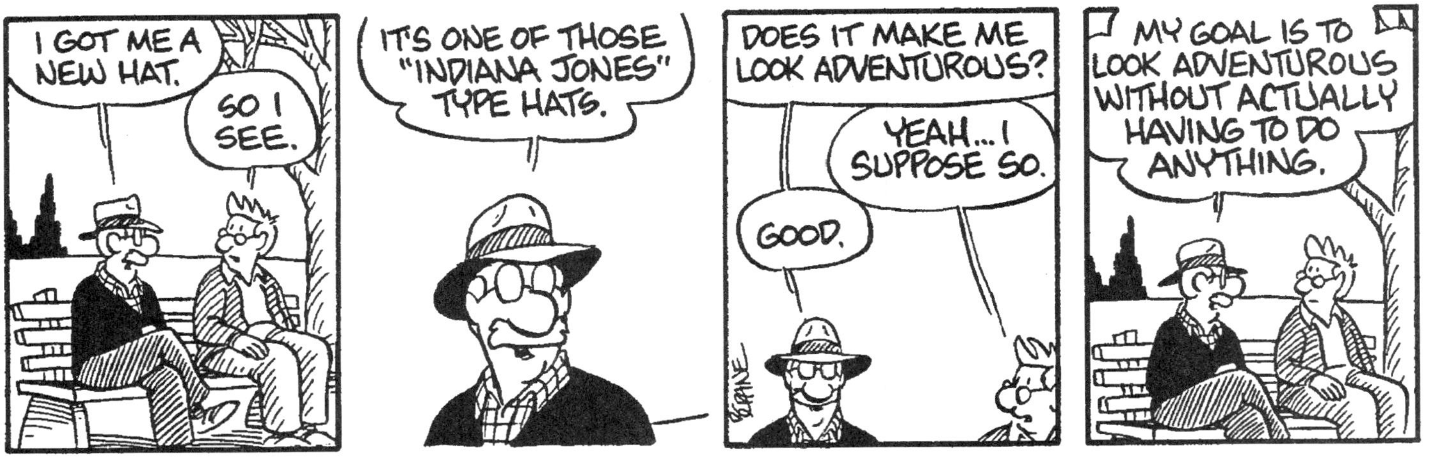
I GOT ME A NEW HAT.
SO I SEE.
IT'S ONE OF THOSE "INDIANA JONES" TYPE HATS.
DOES IT MAKE ME LOOK ADVENTUROUS?
YEAH... I SUPPOSE SO.
GOOD.
MY GOAL IS TO LOOK ADVENTUROUS WITHOUT ACTUALLY HAVING TO DO ANYTHING.

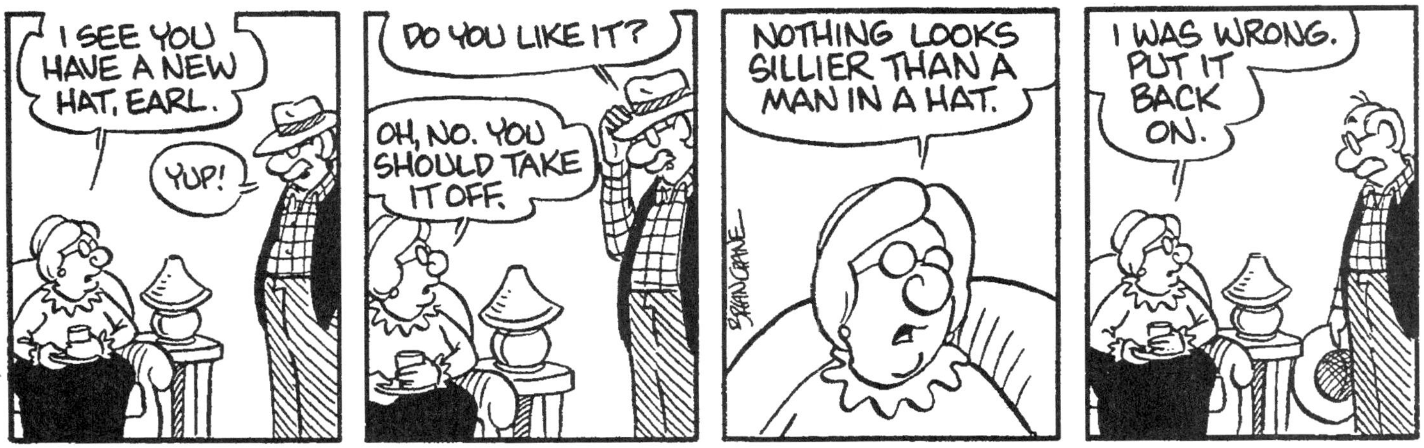
I SEE YOU HAVE A NEW HAT, EARL.
YUP!
DO YOU LIKE IT?
OH, NO. YOU SHOULD TAKE IT OFF.
NOTHING LOOKS SILLIER THAN A MAN IN A HAT.
I WAS WRONG. PUT IT BACK ON.

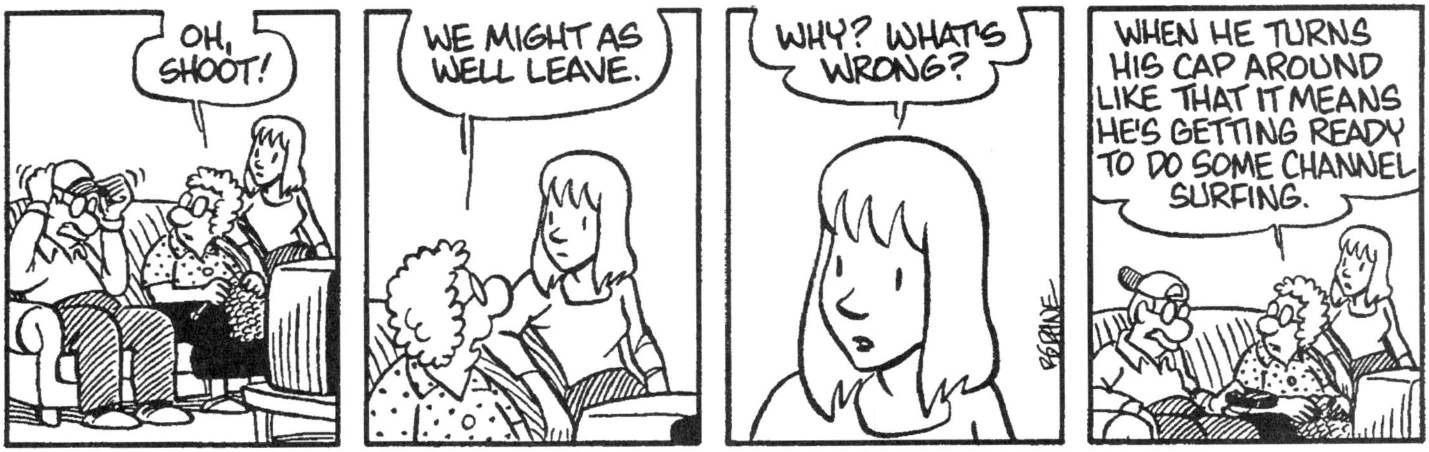
OH, SHOOT!
WE MIGHT AS WELL LEAVE.
WHY? WHAT'S WRONG?
WHEN HE TURNS HIS CAP AROUND LIKE THAT IT MEANS HE'S GETTING READY TO DO SOME CHANNEL SURFING.

PICKLES

by Brian Crane

SHHH... QUIET!

I HEAR SOMETHING.

LISTEN! DO YOU HEAR THAT?

NO. WHAT IS IT?

IT'S THE CALL OF THE OPEN ROAD!

AGAIN?

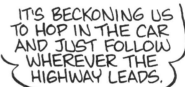

IT'S BECKONING US TO HOP IN THE CAR AND JUST FOLLOW WHEREVER THE HIGHWAY LEADS.

OVER HILL AND DALE, HITHER AND YON, LIKE WANDERING NOMADS...

HOW COME THE OPEN ROAD ALWAYS TAKES US TO THE ICE CREAM PARLOR?

IT'S A MYSTERY.

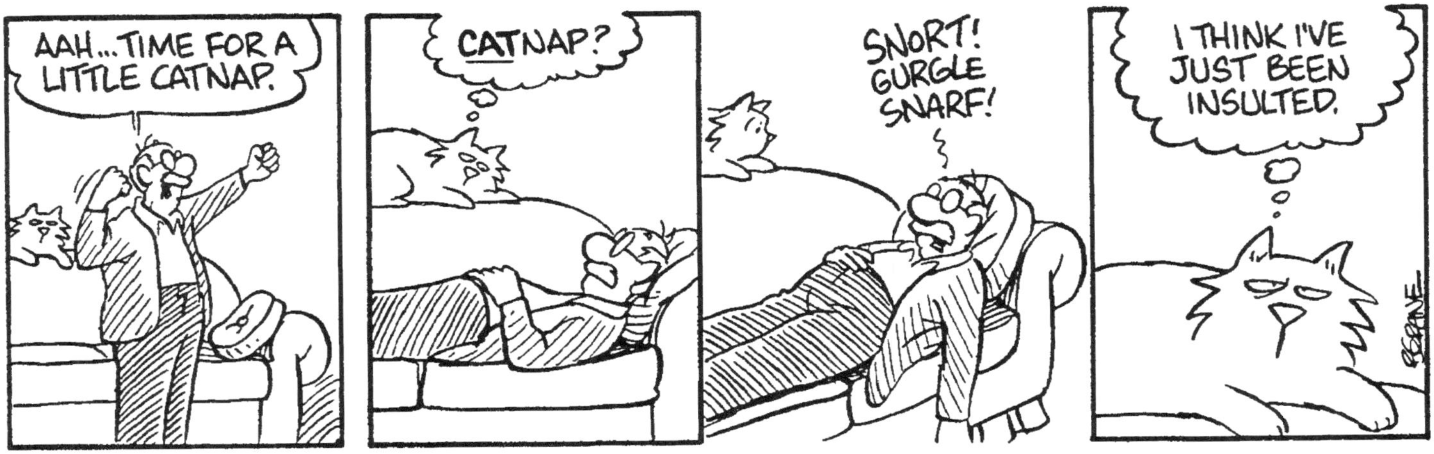
AAH...TIME FOR A LITTLE CATNAP.
CATNAP?
SNORT! GURGLE SNARF!
I THINK I'VE JUST BEEN INSULTED.

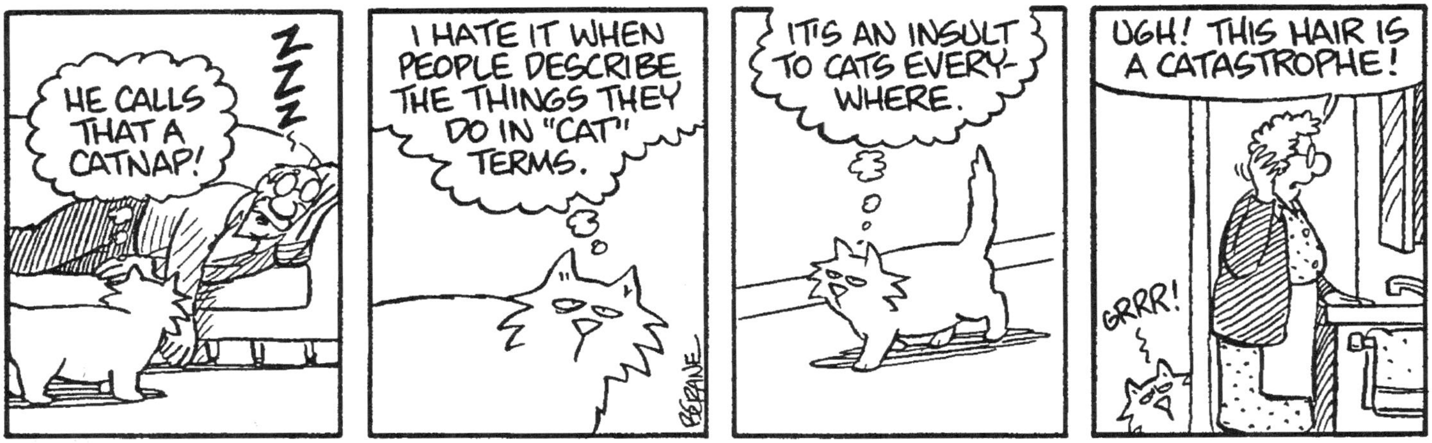
HE CALLS THAT A CATNAP!
ZZZ
I HATE IT WHEN PEOPLE DESCRIBE THE THINGS THEY DO IN "CAT" TERMS.
IT'S AN INSULT TO CATS EVERY-WHERE.
UGH! THIS HAIR IS A CATASTROPHE!
GRRR!

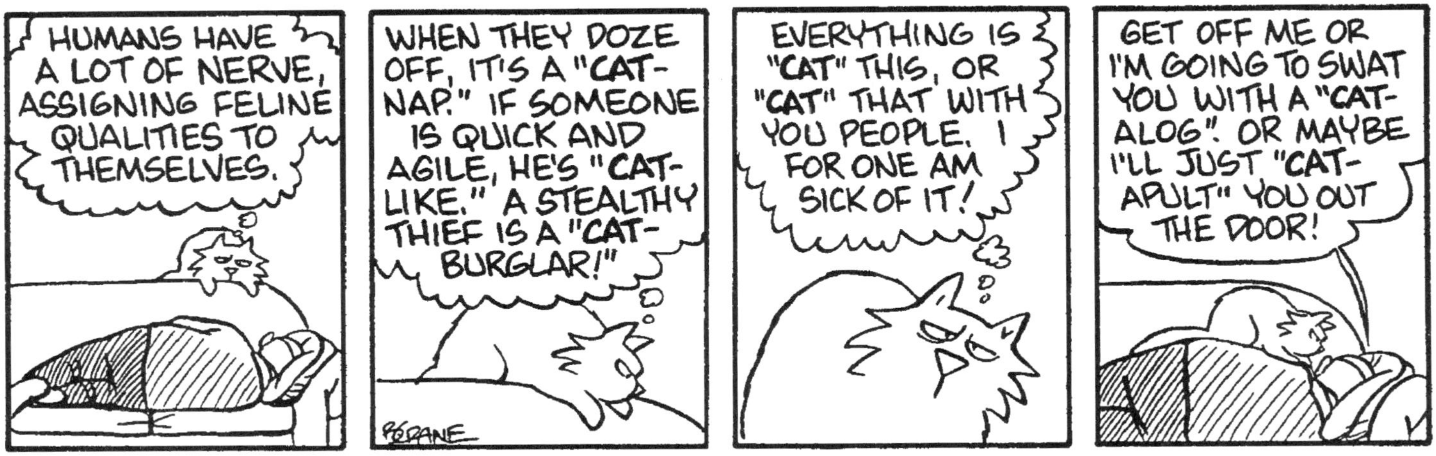
HUMANS HAVE A LOT OF NERVE, ASSIGNING FELINE QUALITIES TO THEMSELVES.
WHEN THEY DOZE OFF, IT'S A "CAT-NAP." IF SOMEONE IS QUICK AND AGILE, HE'S "CAT-LIKE." A STEALTHY THIEF IS A "CAT-BURGLAR!"
EVERYTHING IS "CAT" THIS, OR "CAT" THAT WITH YOU PEOPLE. I FOR ONE AM SICK OF IT!
GET OFF ME OR I'M GOING TO SWAT YOU WITH A "CAT-ALOG". OR MAYBE I'LL JUST "CAT-APULT" YOU OUT THE DOOR!

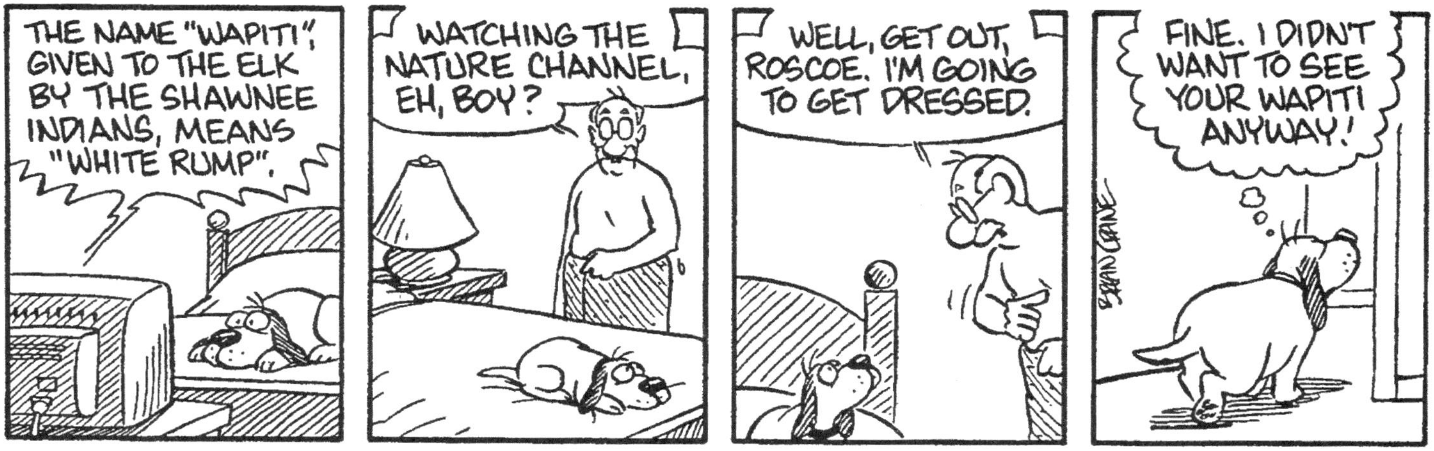
THE NAME "WAPITI", GIVEN TO THE ELK BY THE SHAWNEE INDIANS, MEANS "WHITE RUMP".
WATCHING THE NATURE CHANNEL, EH, BOY?
WELL, GET OUT, ROSCOE. I'M GOING TO GET DRESSED.
FINE. I DIDN'T WANT TO SEE YOUR WAPITI ANYWAY!

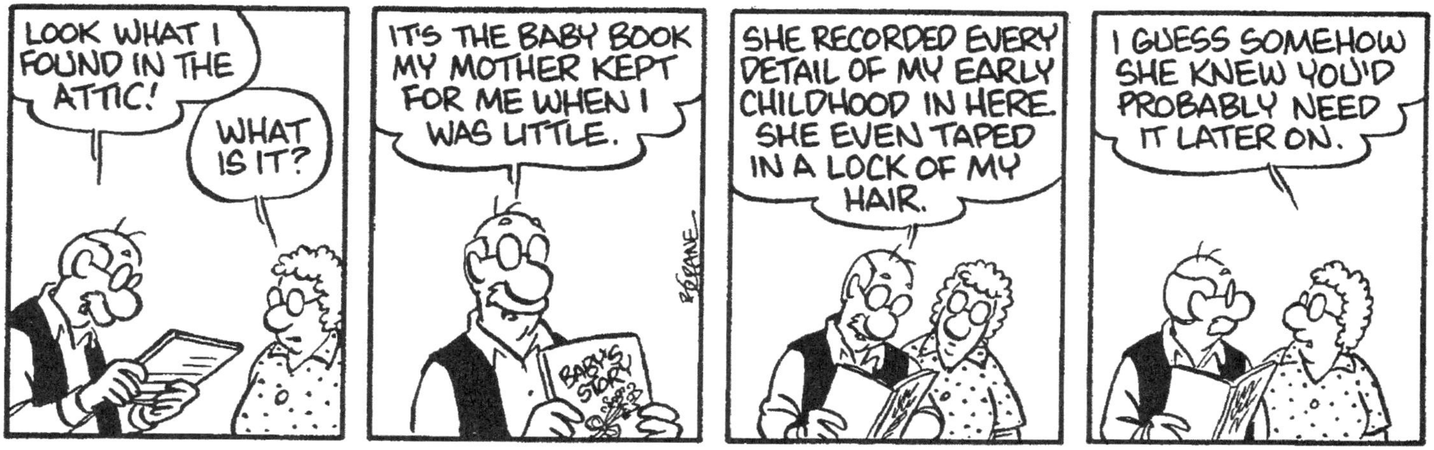
LOOK WHAT I FOUND IN THE ATTIC!
WHAT IS IT?
IT'S THE BABY BOOK MY MOTHER KEPT FOR ME WHEN I WAS LITTLE.
BABY'S STORY
SHE RECORDED EVERY DETAIL OF MY EARLY CHILDHOOD IN HERE. SHE EVEN TAPED IN A LOCK OF MY HAIR.
I GUESS SOMEHOW SHE KNEW YOU'D PROBABLY NEED IT LATER ON.

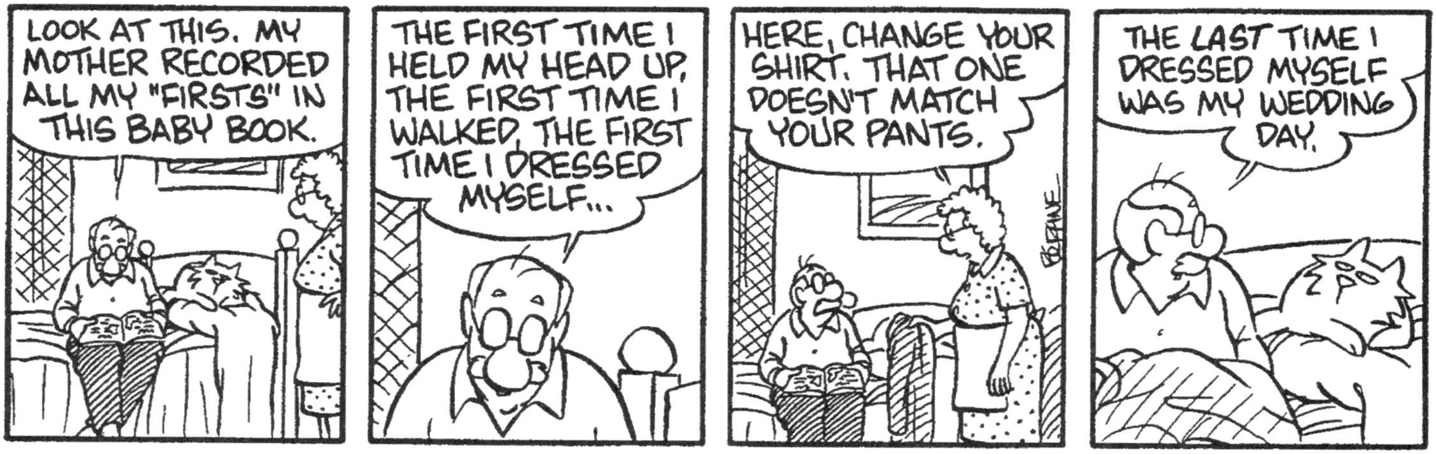
LOOK AT THIS. MY MOTHER RECORDED ALL MY "FIRSTS" IN THIS BABY BOOK.
THE FIRST TIME I HELD MY HEAD UP, THE FIRST TIME I WALKED, THE FIRST TIME I DRESSED MYSELF...
HERE, CHANGE YOUR SHIRT. THAT ONE DOESN'T MATCH YOUR PANTS.
THE LAST TIME I DRESSED MYSELF WAS MY WEDDING DAY.

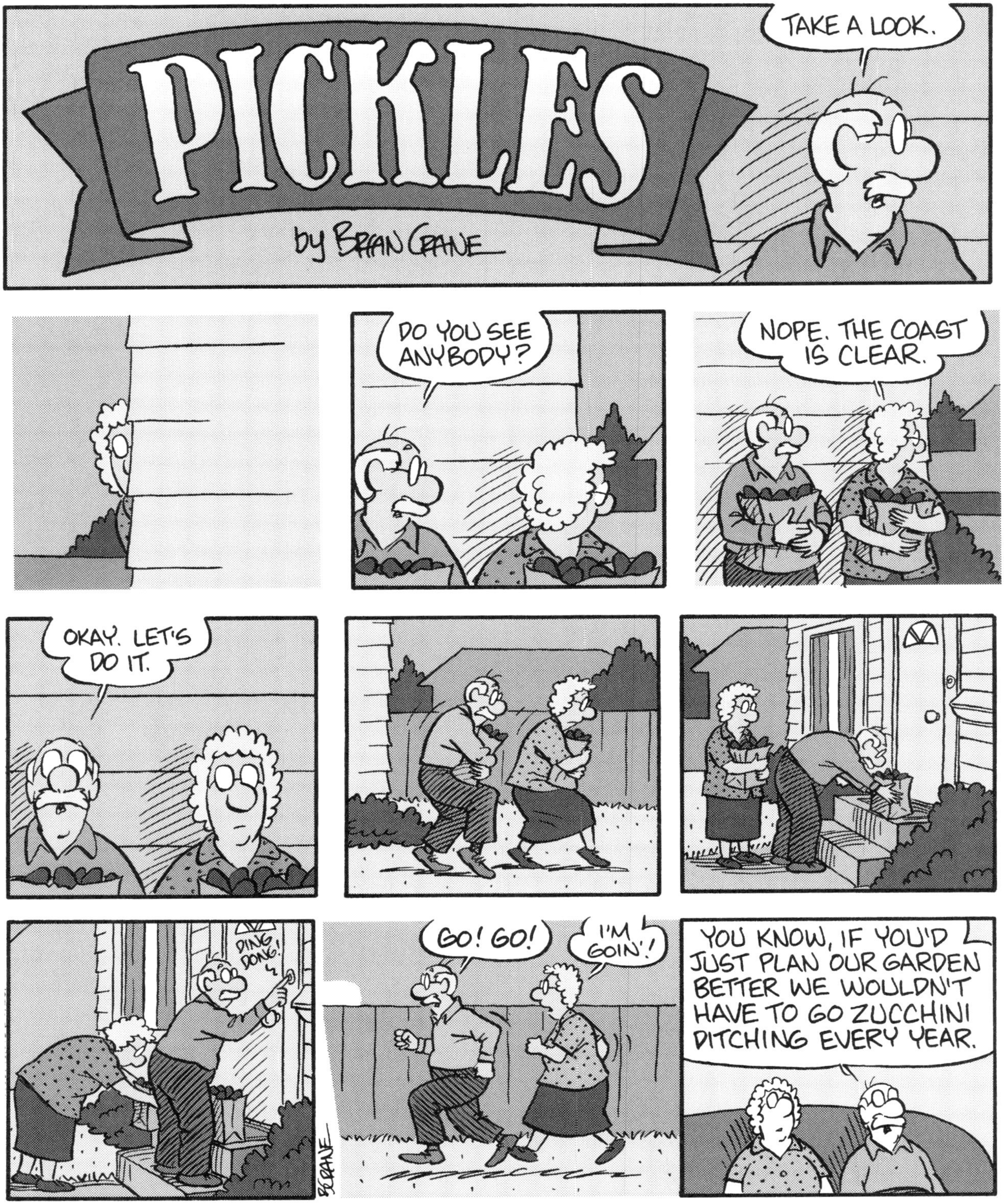
PICKLES
by BRIAN CRANE
TAKE A LOOK.
DO YOU SEE ANYBODY?
NOPE. THE COAST IS CLEAR.
OKAY. LET'S DO IT.
DING DONG!
GO! GO!
I'M GOIN'!
YOU KNOW, IF YOU'D JUST PLAN OUR GARDEN BETTER WE WOULDN'T HAVE TO GO ZUCCHINI DITCHING EVERY YEAR.
B. CRANE

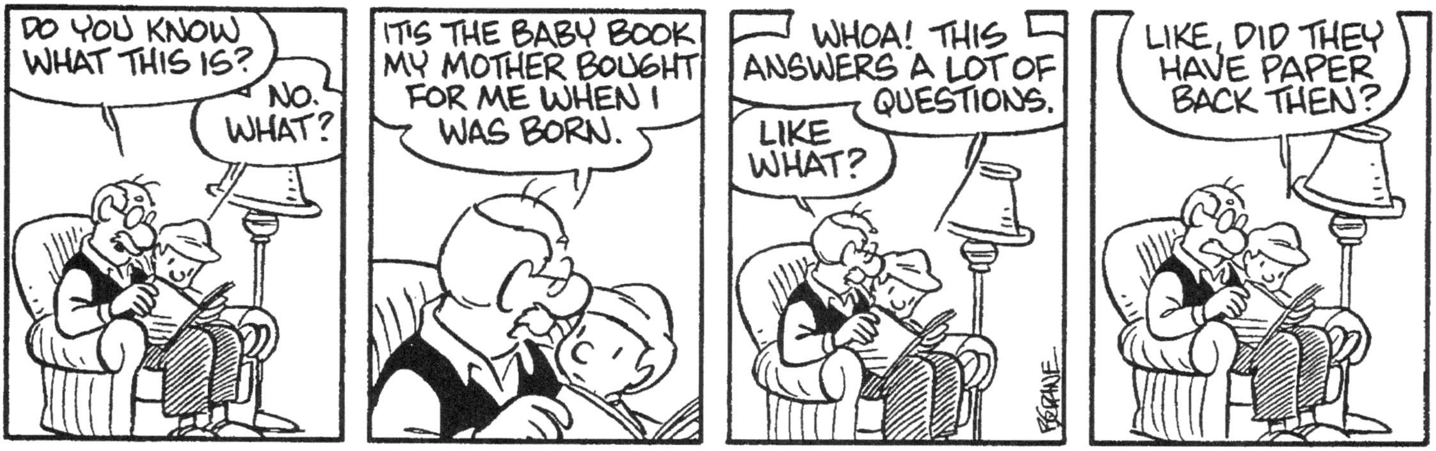
DO YOU KNOW WHAT THIS IS?
NO. WHAT?
IT'S THE BABY BOOK MY MOTHER BOUGHT FOR ME WHEN I WAS BORN.
WHOA! THIS ANSWERS A LOT OF QUESTIONS.
LIKE WHAT?
LIKE, DID THEY HAVE PAPER BACK THEN?

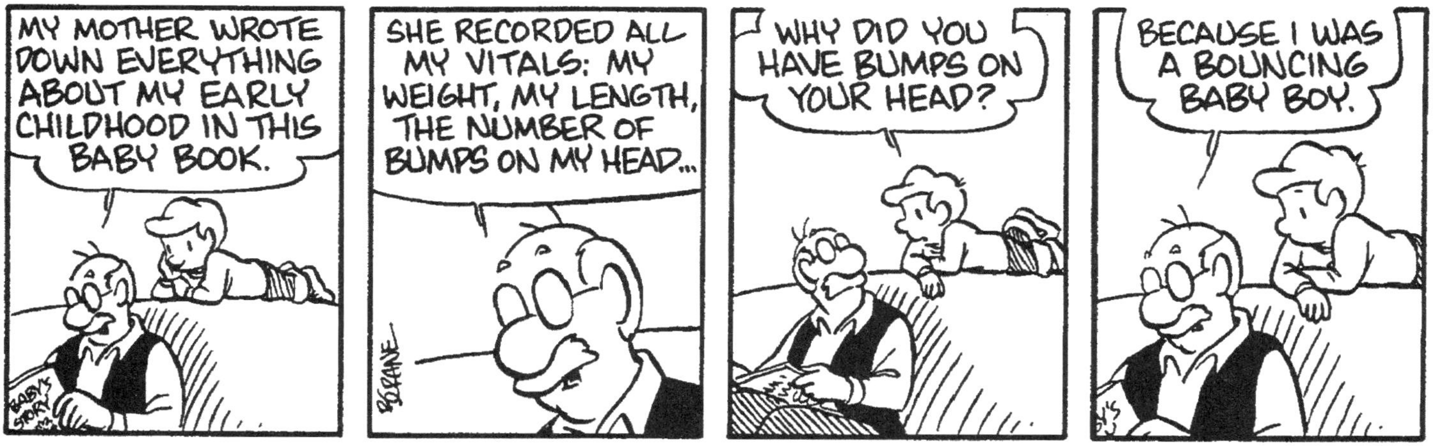
MY MOTHER WROTE DOWN EVERYTHING ABOUT MY EARLY CHILDHOOD IN THIS BABY BOOK.
BABY'S STORY
SHE RECORDED ALL MY VITALS: MY WEIGHT, MY LENGTH, THE NUMBER OF BUMPS ON MY HEAD...
WHY DID YOU HAVE BUMPS ON YOUR HEAD?
BECAUSE I WAS A BOUNCING BABY BOY.

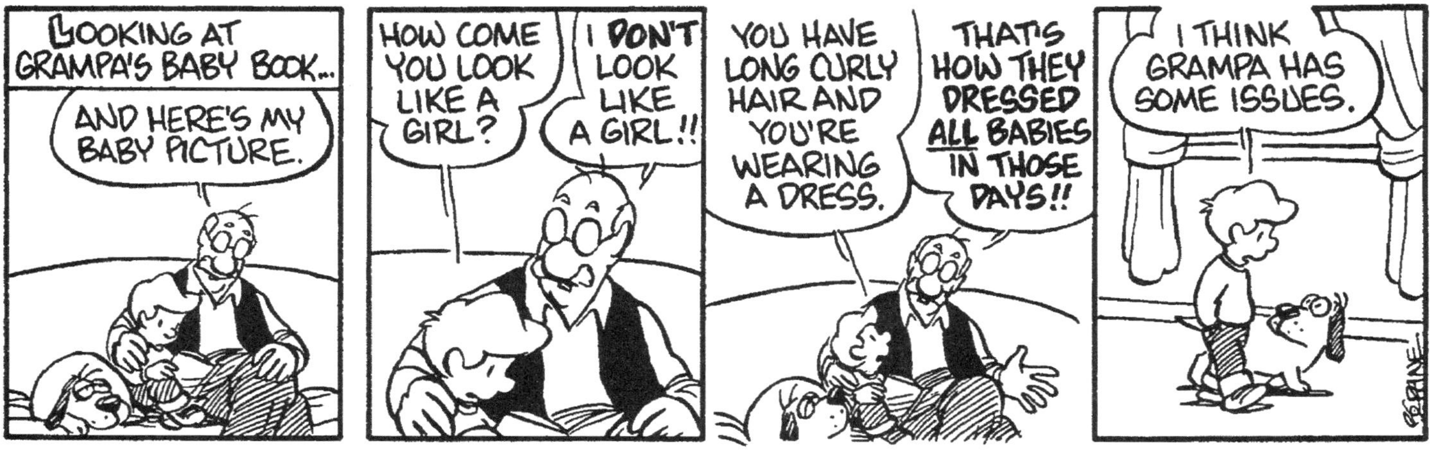
LOOKING AT GRAMPA'S BABY BOOK...
AND HERE'S MY BABY PICTURE.
HOW COME YOU LOOK LIKE A GIRL?
I **DON'T** LOOK LIKE A GIRL!!
YOU HAVE LONG CURLY HAIR AND YOU'RE WEARING A DRESS.
THAT'S **HOW THEY DRESSED <u>ALL</u> BABIES IN THOSE DAYS!!**
I THINK GRAMPA HAS SOME ISSUES.

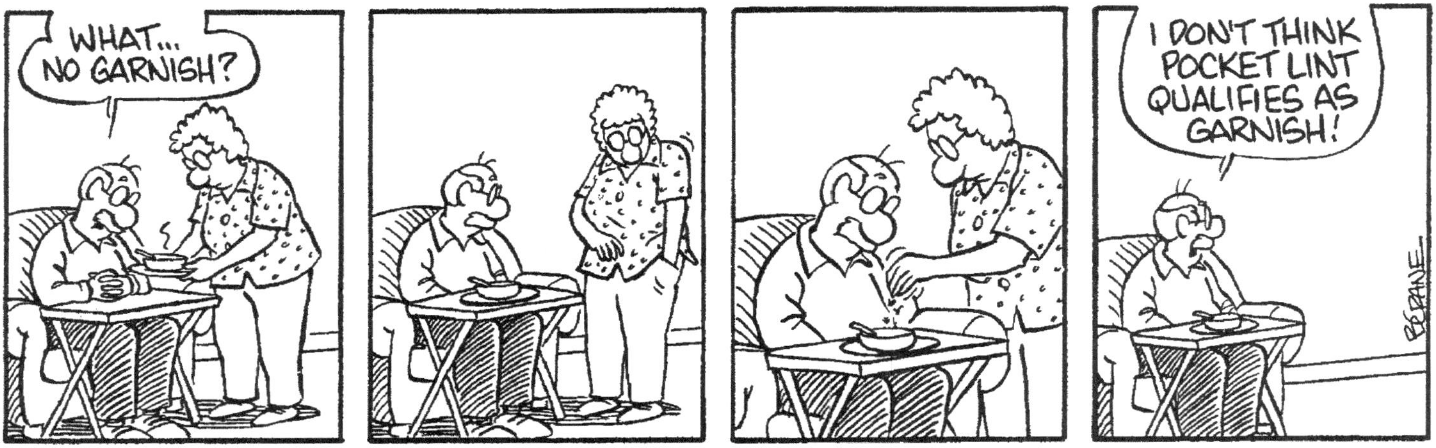
WHAT... NO GARNISH?
I DON'T THINK POCKET LINT QUALIFIES AS GARNISH!

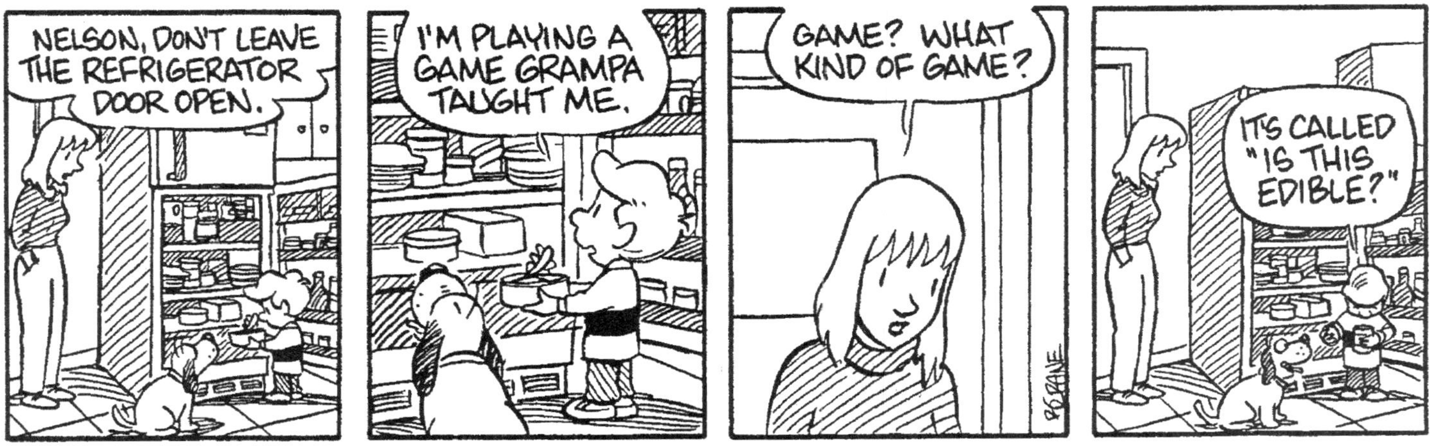
NELSON, DON'T LEAVE THE REFRIGERATOR DOOR OPEN.
I'M PLAYING A GAME GRAMPA TAUGHT ME.
GAME? WHAT KIND OF GAME?
IT'S CALLED "IS THIS EDIBLE?"

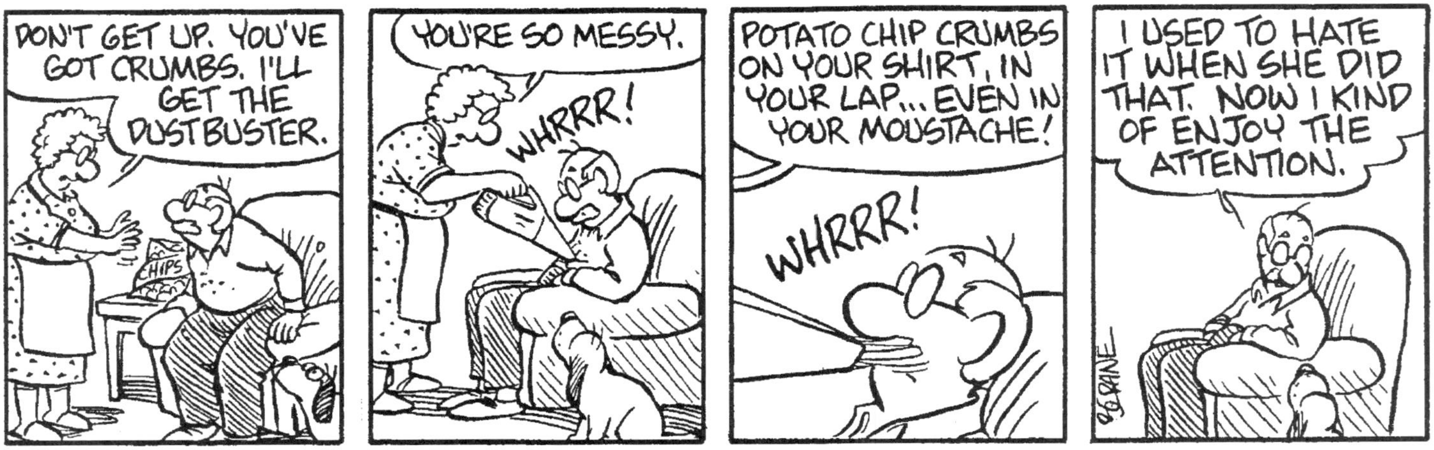
DON'T GET UP. YOU'VE GOT CRUMBS. I'LL GET THE DUSTBUSTER.
CHIPS
YOU'RE SO MESSY.
WHRRR!
POTATO CHIP CRUMBS ON YOUR SHIRT, IN YOUR LAP... EVEN IN YOUR MOUSTACHE!
WHRRR!
I USED TO HATE IT WHEN SHE DID THAT. NOW I KIND OF ENJOY THE ATTENTION.

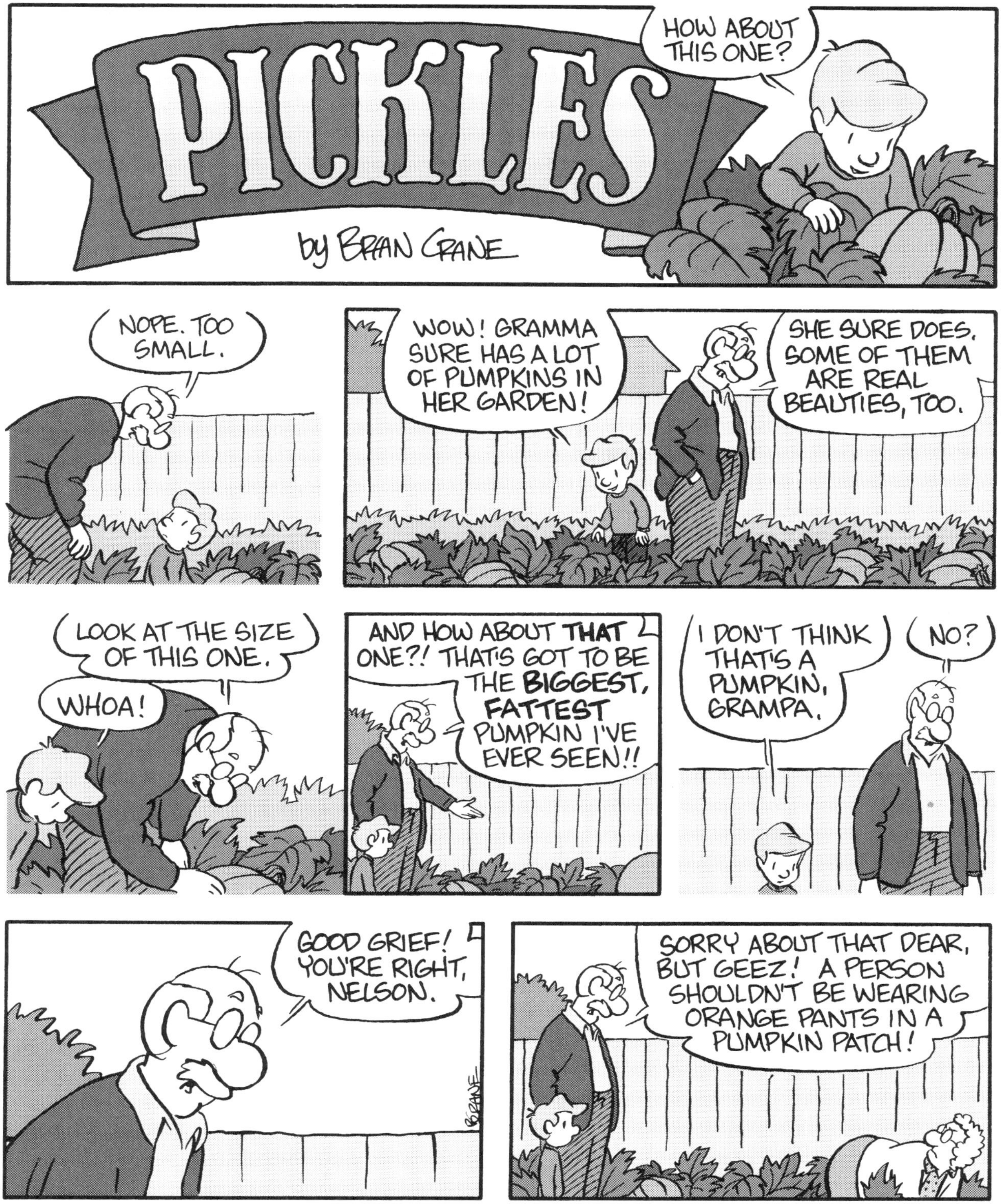
PICKLES
by BRIAN CRANE
HOW ABOUT THIS ONE?
NOPE. TOO SMALL.
WOW! GRAMMA SURE HAS A LOT OF PUMPKINS IN HER GARDEN!
SHE SURE DOES. SOME OF THEM ARE REAL BEAUTIES, TOO.
LOOK AT THE SIZE OF THIS ONE.
WHOA!
AND HOW ABOUT THAT ONE?! THAT'S GOT TO BE THE BIGGEST, FATTEST PUMPKIN I'VE EVER SEEN!!
I DON'T THINK THAT'S A PUMPKIN, GRAMPA.
NO?
GOOD GRIEF! YOU'RE RIGHT, NELSON.
SORRY ABOUT THAT DEAR, BUT GEEZ! A PERSON SHOULDN'T BE WEARING ORANGE PANTS IN A PUMPKIN PATCH!

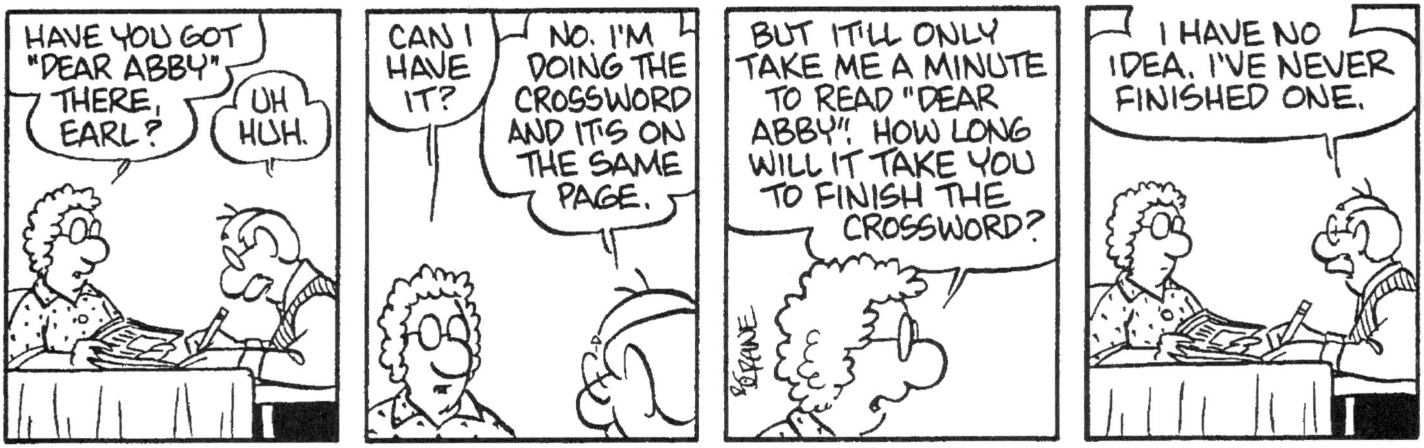
HAVE YOU GOT "DEAR ABBY" THERE, EARL?
UH HUH.
CAN I HAVE IT?
NO. I'M DOING THE CROSSWORD AND IT'S ON THE SAME PAGE.
BUT IT'LL ONLY TAKE ME A MINUTE TO READ "DEAR ABBY". HOW LONG WILL IT TAKE YOU TO FINISH THE CROSSWORD?
I HAVE NO IDEA. I'VE NEVER FINISHED ONE.

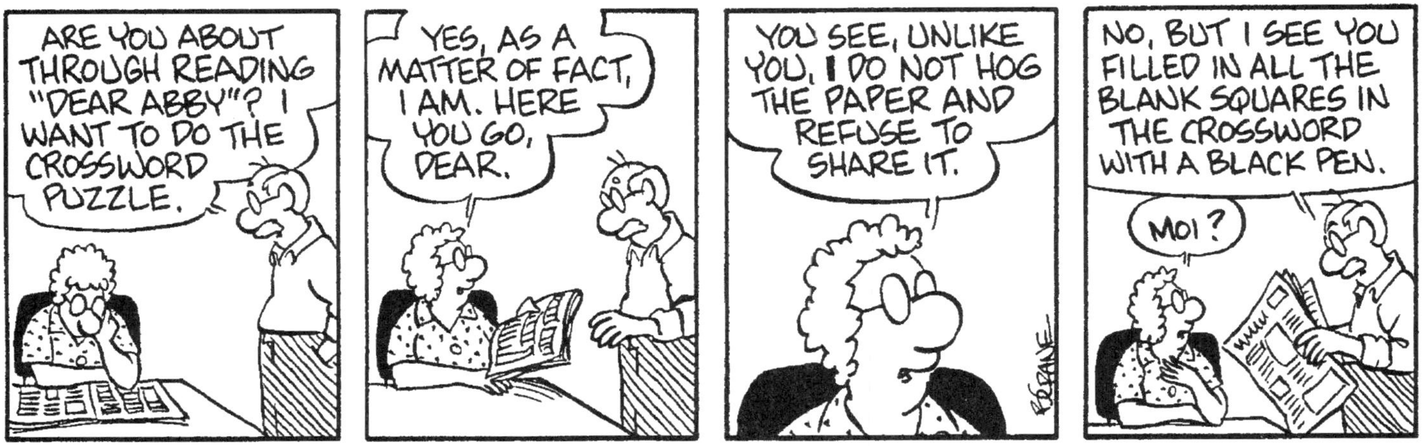
ARE YOU ABOUT THROUGH READING "DEAR ABBY"? I WANT TO DO THE CROSSWORD PUZZLE.
YES, AS A MATTER OF FACT, I AM. HERE YOU GO, DEAR.
YOU SEE, UNLIKE YOU, I DO NOT HOG THE PAPER AND REFUSE TO SHARE IT.
NO, BUT I SEE YOU FILLED IN ALL THE BLANK SQUARES IN THE CROSSWORD WITH A BLACK PEN.
MOI?

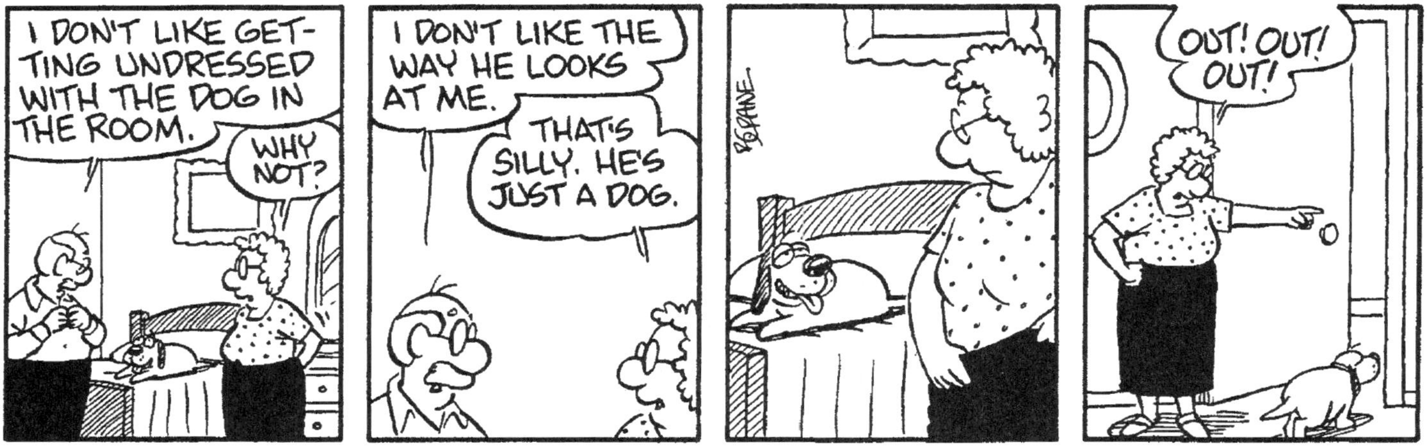
I DON'T LIKE GETTING UNDRESSED WITH THE DOG IN THE ROOM.
WHY NOT?
I DON'T LIKE THE WAY HE LOOKS AT ME.
THAT'S SILLY. HE'S JUST A DOG.
OUT! OUT! OUT!

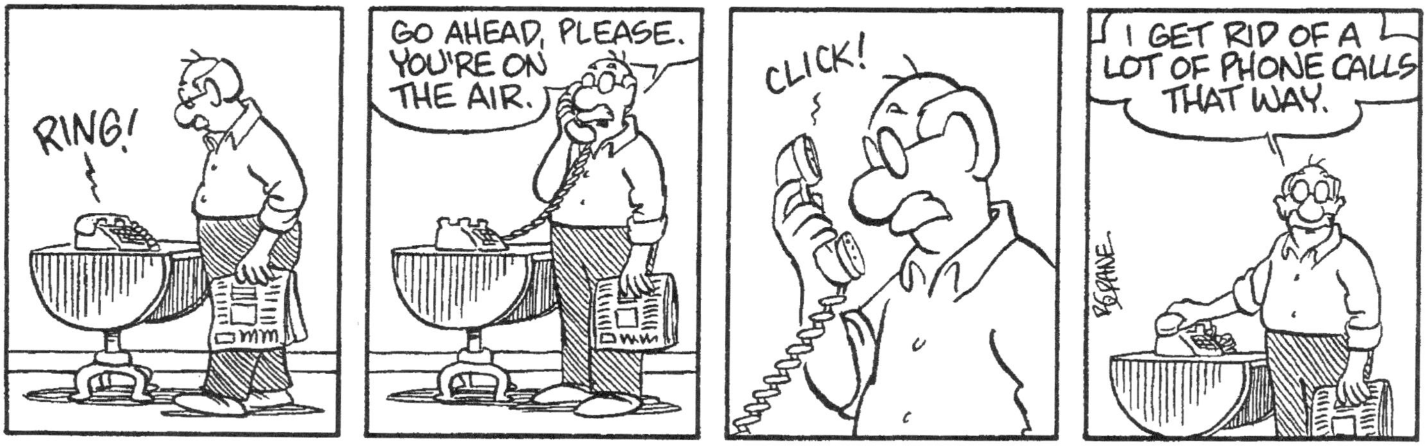
RING!
GO AHEAD, PLEASE. YOU'RE ON THE AIR.
CLICK!
I GET RID OF A LOT OF PHONE CALLS THAT WAY.

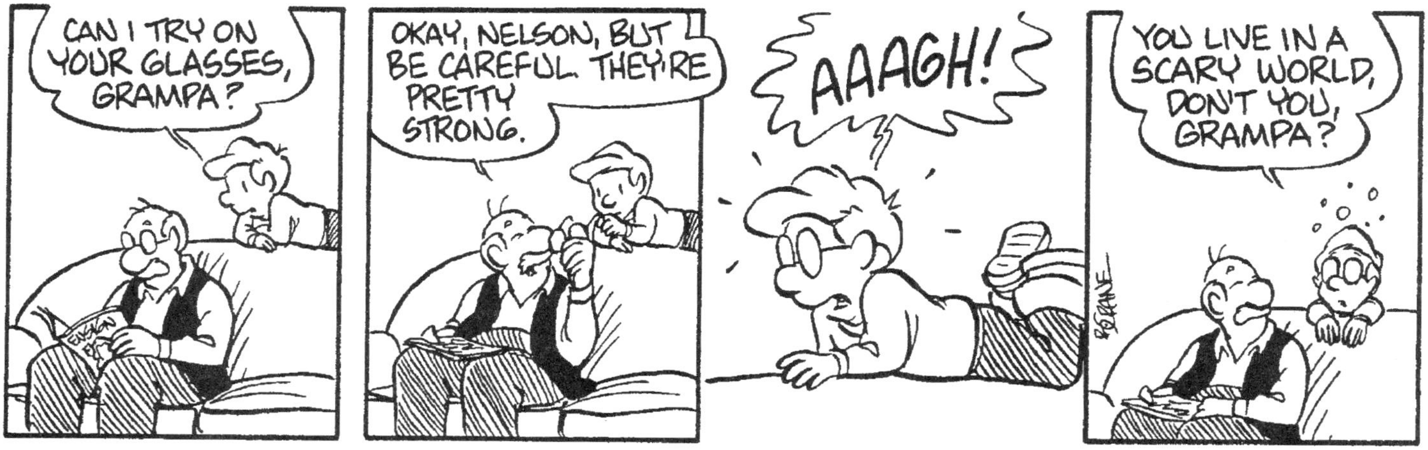
CAN I TRY ON YOUR GLASSES, GRAMPA?
OKAY, NELSON, BUT BE CAREFUL. THEY'RE PRETTY STRONG.
AAAGH!
YOU LIVE IN A SCARY WORLD, DON'T YOU, GRAMPA?

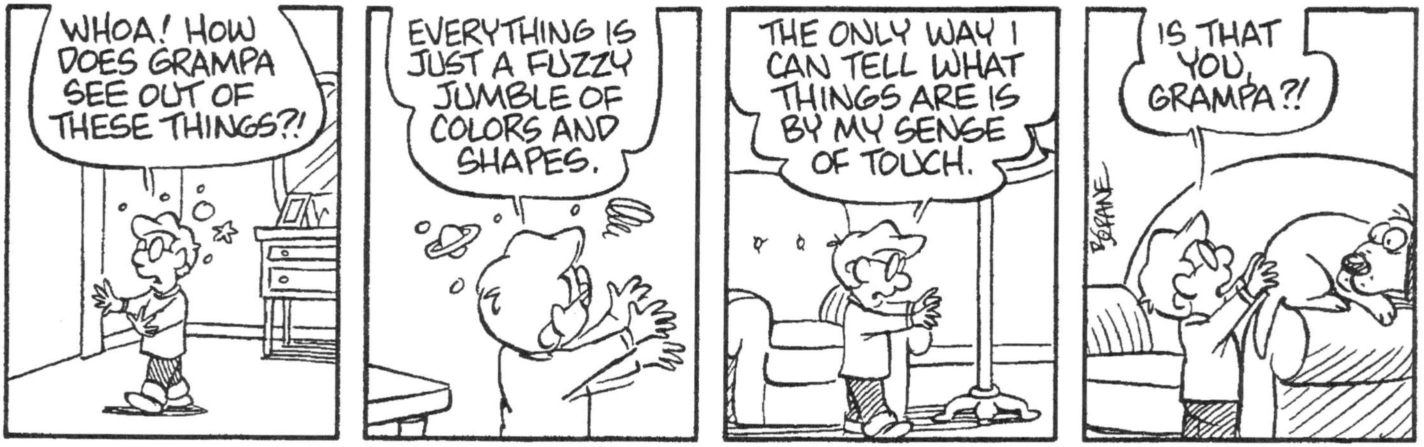
WHOA! HOW DOES GRAMPA SEE OUT OF THESE THINGS?!
EVERYTHING IS JUST A FUZZY JUMBLE OF COLORS AND SHAPES.
THE ONLY WAY I CAN TELL WHAT THINGS ARE IS BY MY SENSE OF TOUCH.
IS THAT YOU, GRAMPA?!

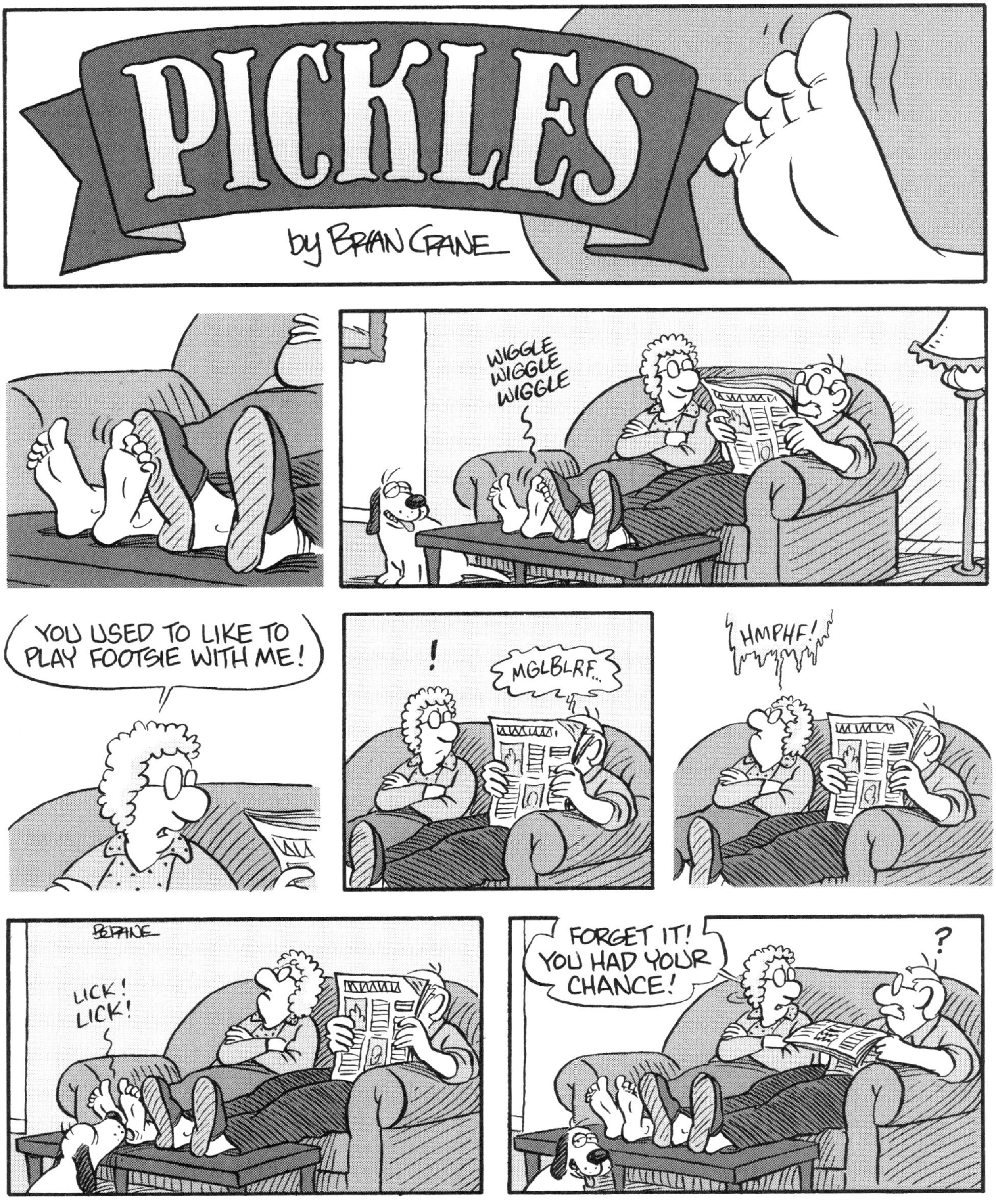
PICKLES
by BRIAN CRANE
WIGGLE WIGGLE WIGGLE
YOU USED TO LIKE TO PLAY FOOTSIE WITH ME!
!
MGLBLRF...
HMPHF!
B.CRANE
LICK! LICK!
FORGET IT! YOU HAD YOUR CHANCE!
?

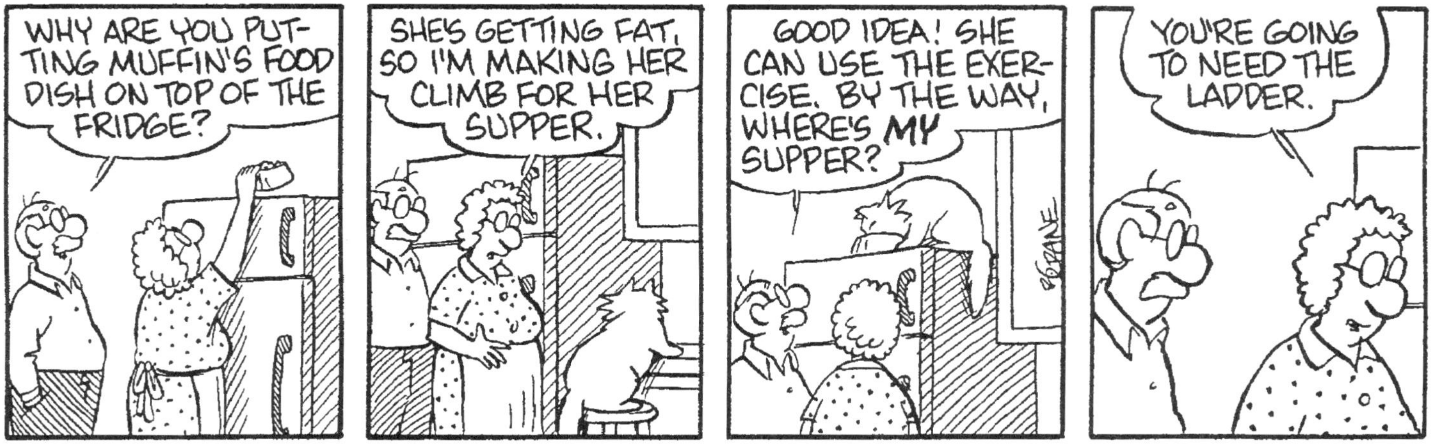
WHY ARE YOU PUTTING MUFFIN'S FOOD DISH ON TOP OF THE FRIDGE?
SHE'S GETTING FAT, SO I'M MAKING HER CLIMB FOR HER SUPPER.
GOOD IDEA! SHE CAN USE THE EXERCISE. BY THE WAY, WHERE'S **MY** SUPPER?
YOU'RE GOING TO NEED THE LADDER.

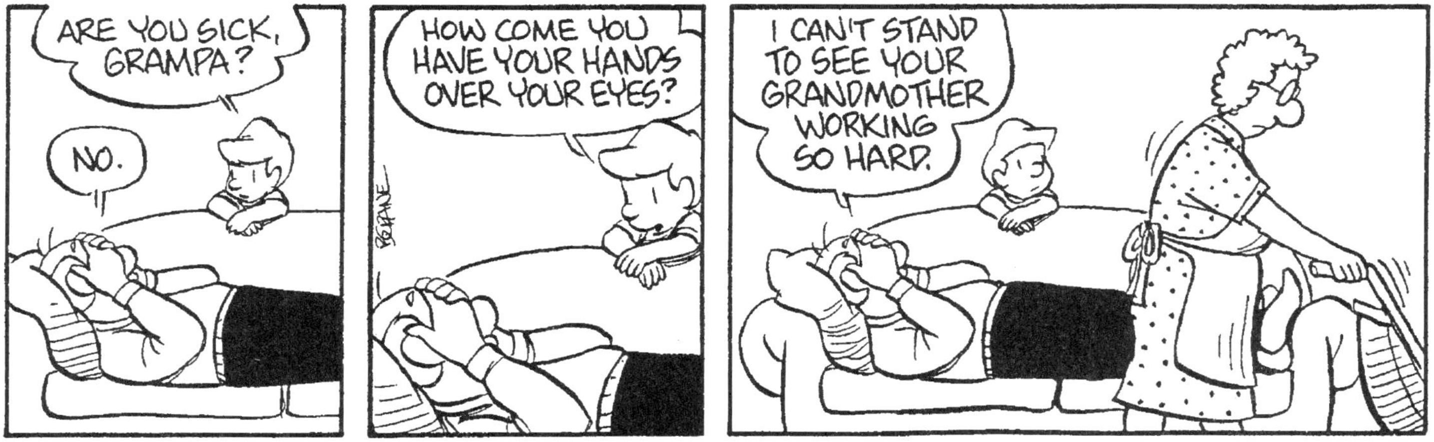
ARE YOU SICK, GRAMPA?
NO.
HOW COME YOU HAVE YOUR HANDS OVER YOUR EYES?
I CAN'T STAND TO SEE YOUR GRANDMOTHER WORKING SO HARD.

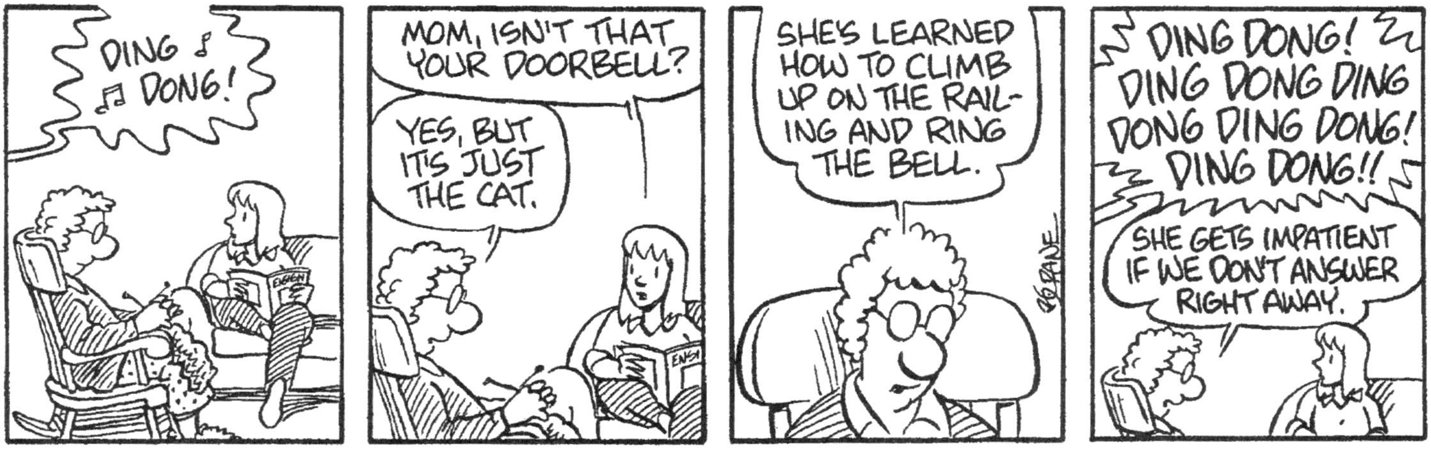
DING ♪ ♫ DONG!
MOM, ISN'T THAT YOUR DOORBELL?
YES, BUT IT'S JUST THE CAT.
SHE'S LEARNED HOW TO CLIMB UP ON THE RAILING AND RING THE BELL.
DING DONG! DING DONG DING DONG DING DONG! DING DONG!!
SHE GETS IMPATIENT IF WE DON'T ANSWER RIGHT AWAY.

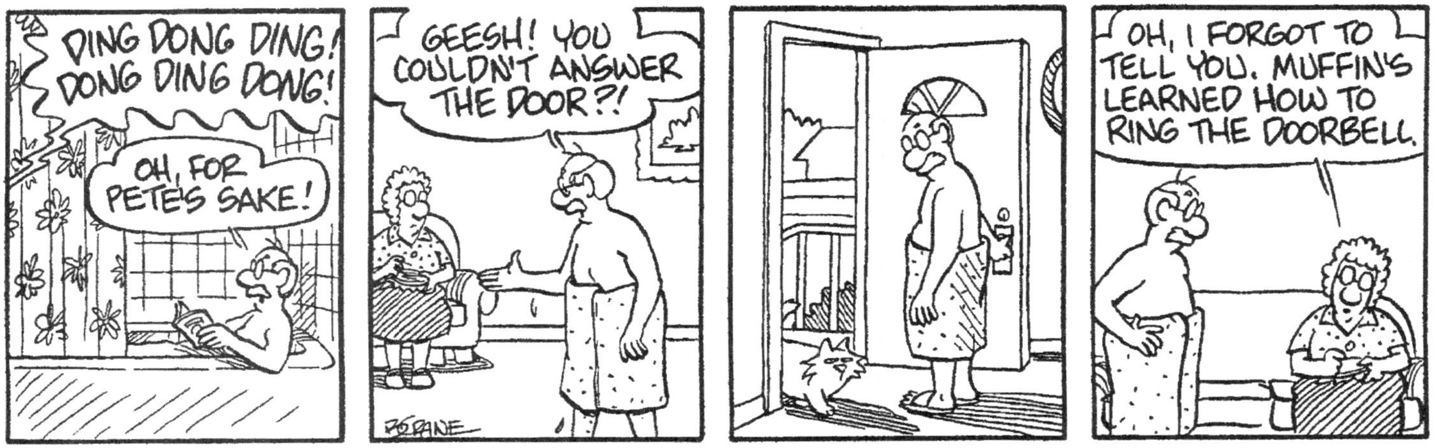
DING DONG DING! DONG DING DONG!
OH, FOR PETE'S SAKE!
GEESH! YOU COULDN'T ANSWER THE DOOR?!
OH, I FORGOT TO TELL YOU. MUFFIN'S LEARNED HOW TO RING THE DOORBELL.

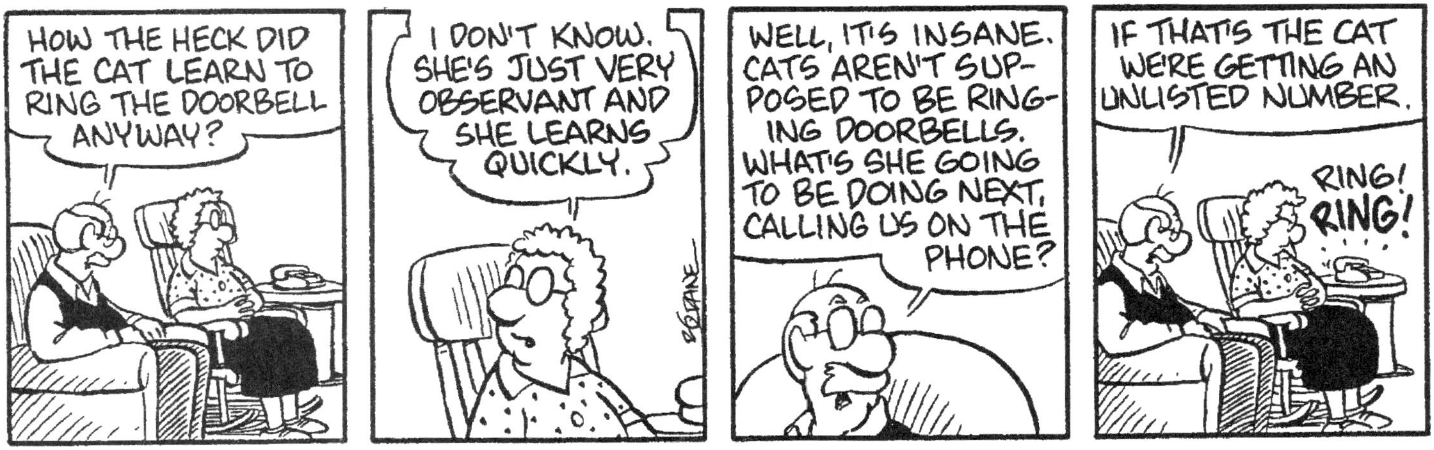
HOW THE HECK DID THE CAT LEARN TO RING THE DOORBELL ANYWAY?
I DON'T KNOW. SHE'S JUST VERY OBSERVANT AND SHE LEARNS QUICKLY.
WELL, IT'S INSANE. CATS AREN'T SUPPOSED TO BE RINGING DOORBELLS. WHAT'S SHE GOING TO BE DOING NEXT, CALLING US ON THE PHONE?
IF THAT'S THE CAT WE'RE GETTING AN UNLISTED NUMBER.
RING! RING!

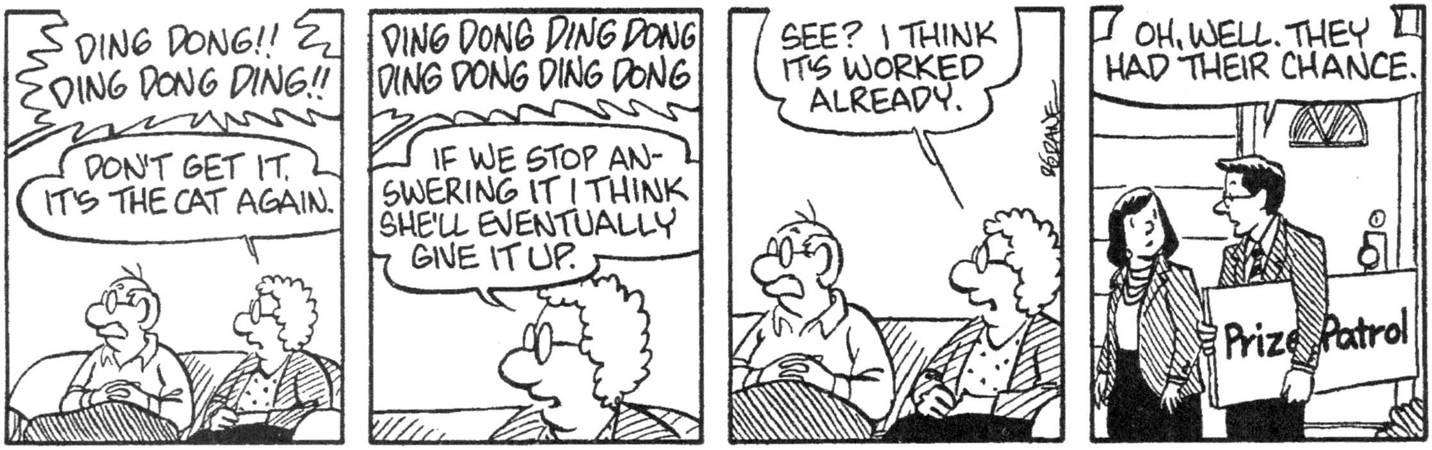
DING DONG!! DING DONG DING!!
DON'T GET IT. IT'S THE CAT AGAIN.
DING DONG DING DONG DING DONG DING DONG
IF WE STOP ANSWERING IT I THINK SHE'LL EVENTUALLY GIVE IT UP.
SEE? I THINK IT'S WORKED ALREADY.
OH, WELL. THEY HAD THEIR CHANCE.
Prize Patrol

PICKLES

by BRIAN CRANE

I WANT YOU TO TAKE DOWN THE CHRISTMAS LIGHTS TODAY.

WHAT? IT'S APRIL ALREADY?

WHATCHA DOIN', GRAMPA?

I'M GETTING READY TO TAKE DOWN THE CHRISTMAS LIGHTS.

DON'T YOU NEED A LADDER?

NOPE. YOU SEE, SON, THERE'S A *HARD* WAY AND AN *EASY* WAY TO DO EVERYTHING.

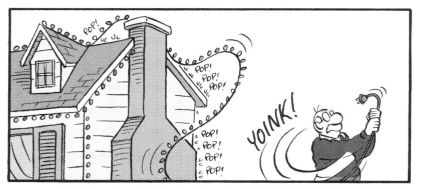

POP! POP! POP! POP! POP! POP! POP! POP! POP!

YOINK!

WHICH WAY WAS THAT?

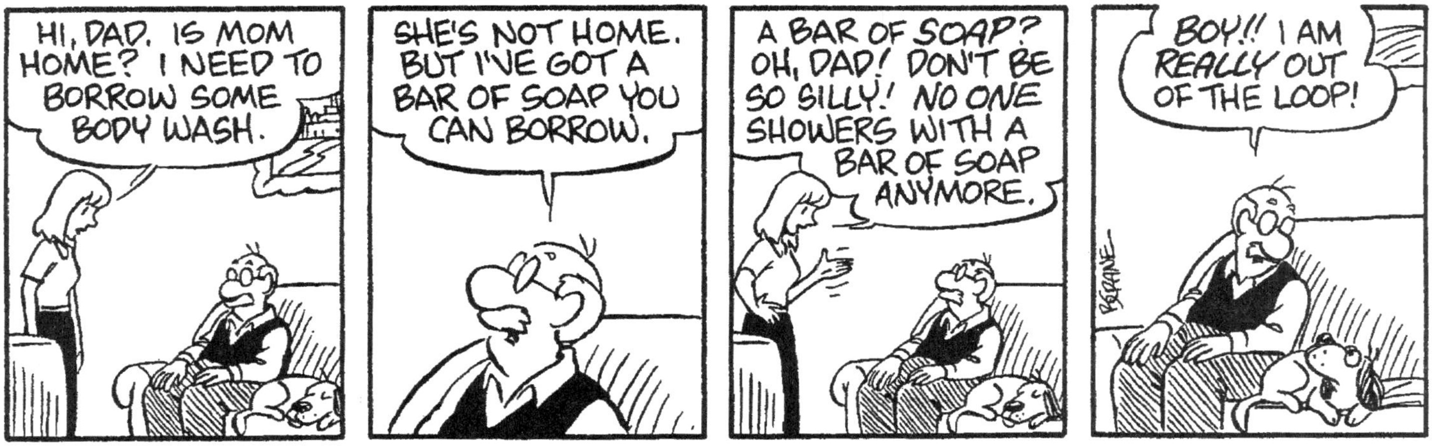
HI, DAD. IS MOM HOME? I NEED TO BORROW SOME BODY WASH.
SHE'S NOT HOME. BUT I'VE GOT A BAR OF SOAP YOU CAN BORROW.
A BAR OF SOAP? OH, DAD! DON'T BE SO SILLY! NO ONE SHOWERS WITH A BAR OF SOAP ANYMORE.
BOY!! I AM REALLY OUT OF THE LOOP!

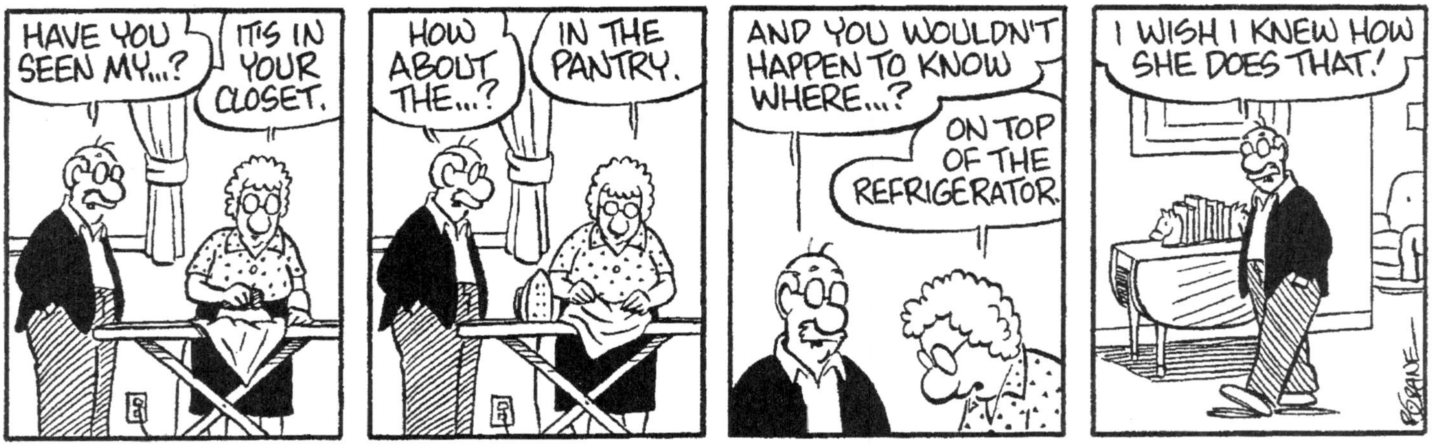
HAVE YOU SEEN MY...?
IT'S IN YOUR CLOSET.
HOW ABOUT THE...?
IN THE PANTRY.
AND YOU WOULDN'T HAPPEN TO KNOW WHERE...?
ON TOP OF THE REFRIGERATOR.
I WISH I KNEW HOW SHE DOES THAT!

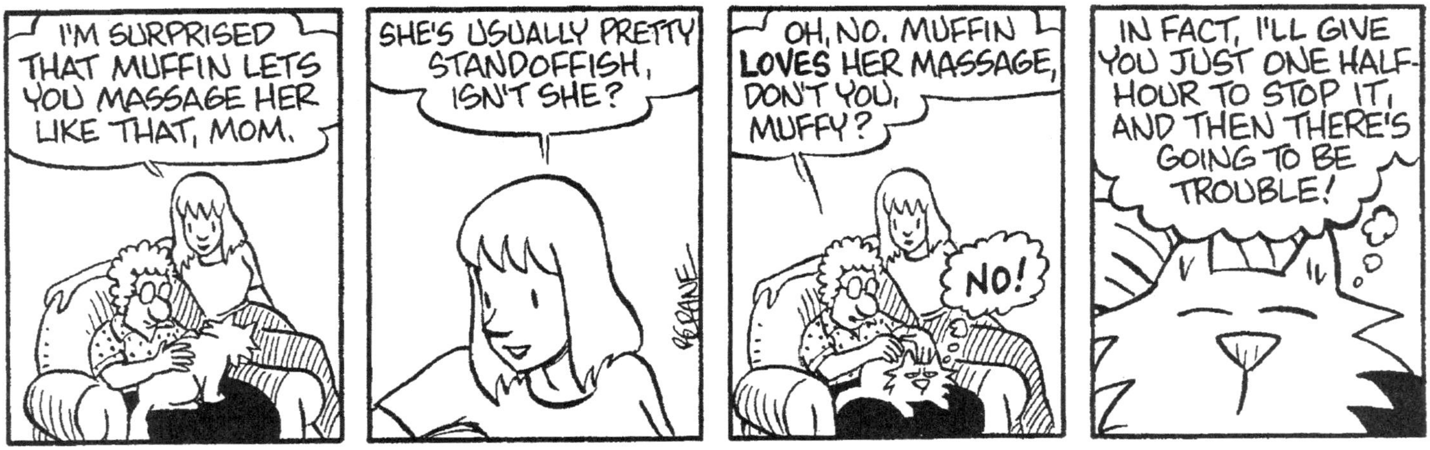
I'M SURPRISED THAT MUFFIN LETS YOU MASSAGE HER LIKE THAT, MOM.
SHE'S USUALLY PRETTY STANDOFFISH, ISN'T SHE?
OH, NO. MUFFIN LOVES HER MASSAGE, DON'T YOU, MUFFY?
NO!
IN FACT, I'LL GIVE YOU JUST ONE HALF-HOUR TO STOP IT, AND THEN THERE'S GOING TO BE TROUBLE!

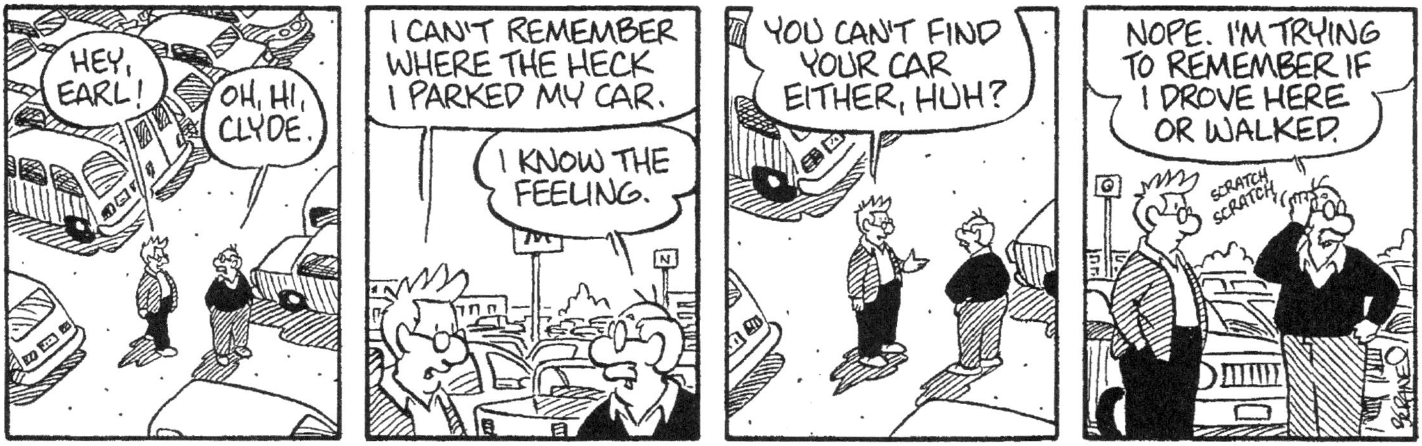
HEY, EARL!
OH, HI, CLYDE.
I CAN'T REMEMBER WHERE THE HECK I PARKED MY CAR.
I KNOW THE FEELING.
YOU CAN'T FIND YOUR CAR EITHER, HUH?
NOPE. I'M TRYING TO REMEMBER IF I DROVE HERE OR WALKED.
SCRATCH SCRATCH

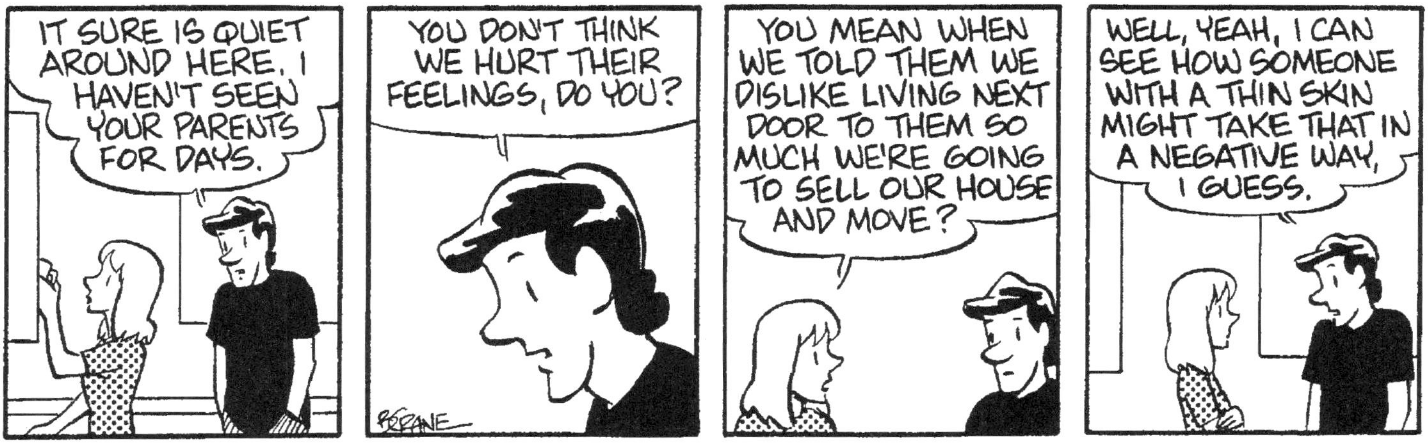
IT SURE IS QUIET AROUND HERE. I HAVEN'T SEEN YOUR PARENTS FOR DAYS.
YOU DON'T THINK WE HURT THEIR FEELINGS, DO YOU?
YOU MEAN WHEN WE TOLD THEM WE DISLIKE LIVING NEXT DOOR TO THEM SO MUCH WE'RE GOING TO SELL OUR HOUSE AND MOVE?
WELL, YEAH, I CAN SEE HOW SOMEONE WITH A THIN SKIN MIGHT TAKE THAT IN A NEGATIVE WAY, I GUESS.

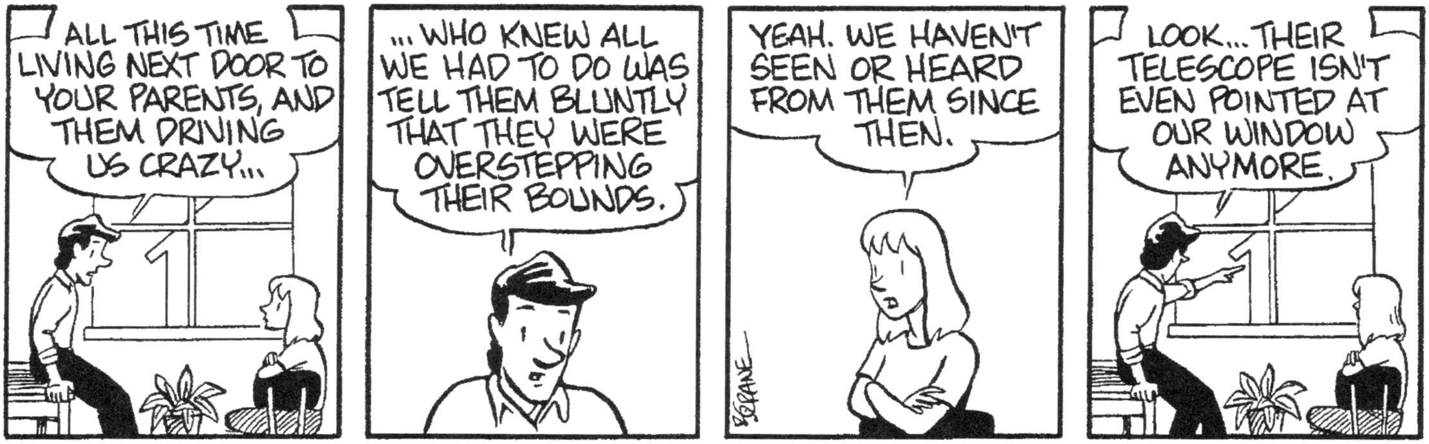
ALL THIS TIME LIVING NEXT DOOR TO YOUR PARENTS, AND THEM DRIVING US CRAZY...
...WHO KNEW ALL WE HAD TO DO WAS TELL THEM BLUNTLY THAT THEY WERE OVERSTEPPING THEIR BOUNDS.
YEAH. WE HAVEN'T SEEN OR HEARD FROM THEM SINCE THEN.
LOOK... THEIR TELESCOPE ISN'T EVEN POINTED AT OUR WINDOW ANYMORE.

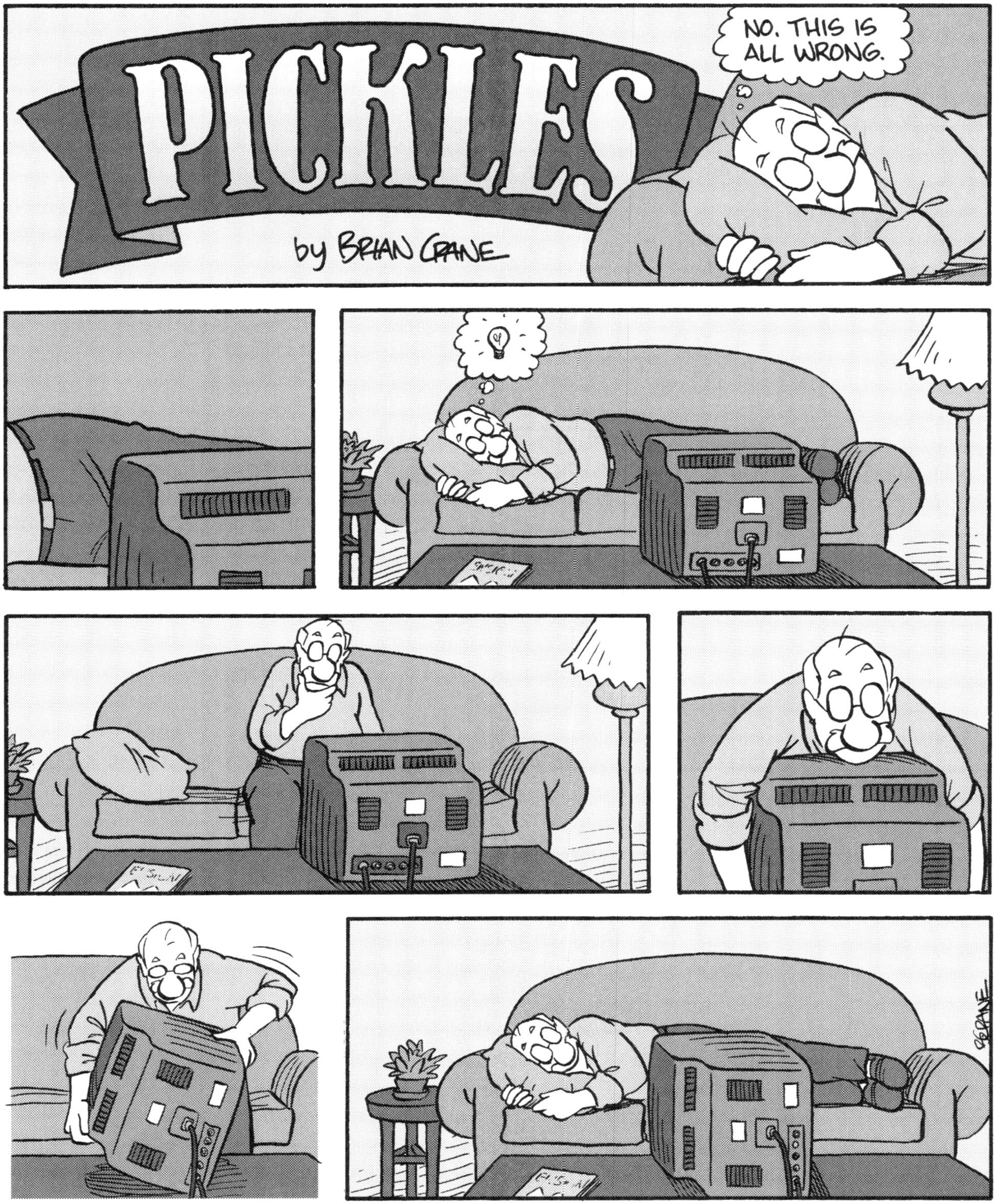
PICKLES
by BRIAN CRANE
NO. THIS IS ALL WRONG.

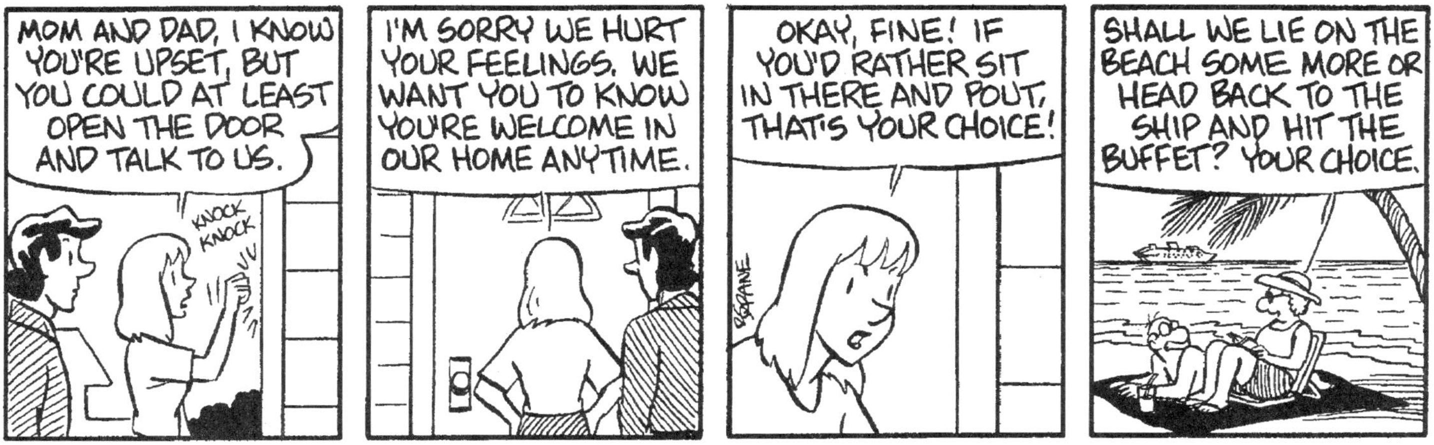
MOM AND DAD, I KNOW YOU'RE UPSET, BUT YOU COULD AT LEAST OPEN THE DOOR AND TALK TO US.
KNOCK KNOCK
I'M SORRY WE HURT YOUR FEELINGS. WE WANT YOU TO KNOW YOU'RE WELCOME IN OUR HOME ANYTIME.
OKAY, FINE! IF YOU'D RATHER SIT IN THERE AND POUT, THAT'S YOUR CHOICE!
SHALL WE LIE ON THE BEACH SOME MORE OR HEAD BACK TO THE SHIP AND HIT THE BUFFET? YOUR CHOICE.

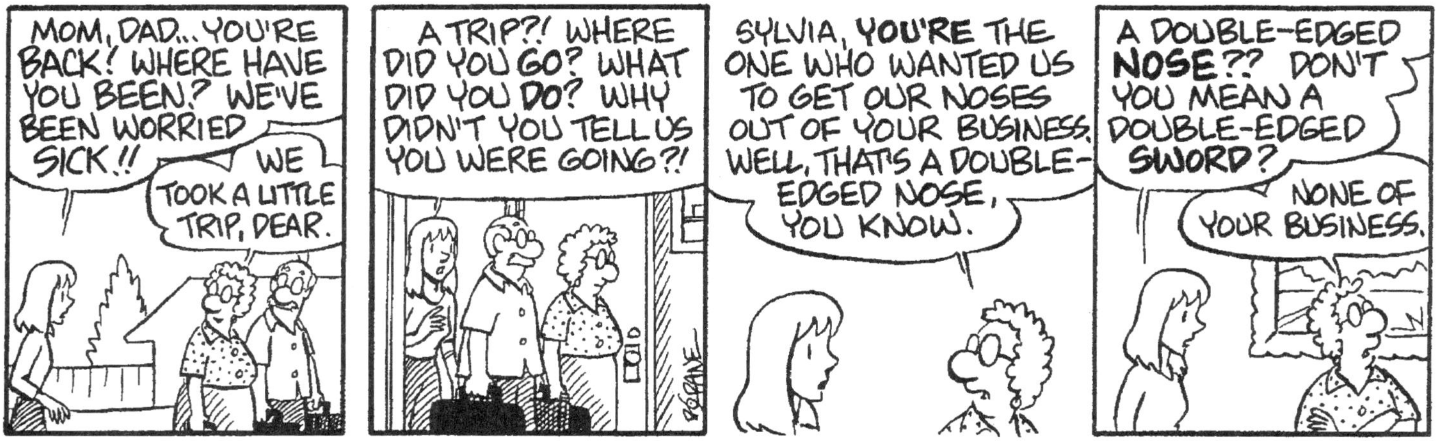
MOM, DAD... YOU'RE BACK! WHERE HAVE YOU BEEN? WE'VE BEEN WORRIED SICK!!
WE TOOK A LITTLE TRIP, DEAR.
A TRIP?! WHERE DID YOU **GO**? WHAT DID YOU **DO**? WHY DIDN'T YOU TELL US YOU WERE GOING?!
SYLVIA, **YOU'RE** THE ONE WHO WANTED US TO GET OUR NOSES OUT OF YOUR BUSINESS. WELL, THAT'S A DOUBLE-EDGED NOSE, YOU KNOW.
A DOUBLE-EDGED **NOSE**?? DON'T YOU MEAN A DOUBLE-EDGED **SWORD**?
NONE OF YOUR BUSINESS.

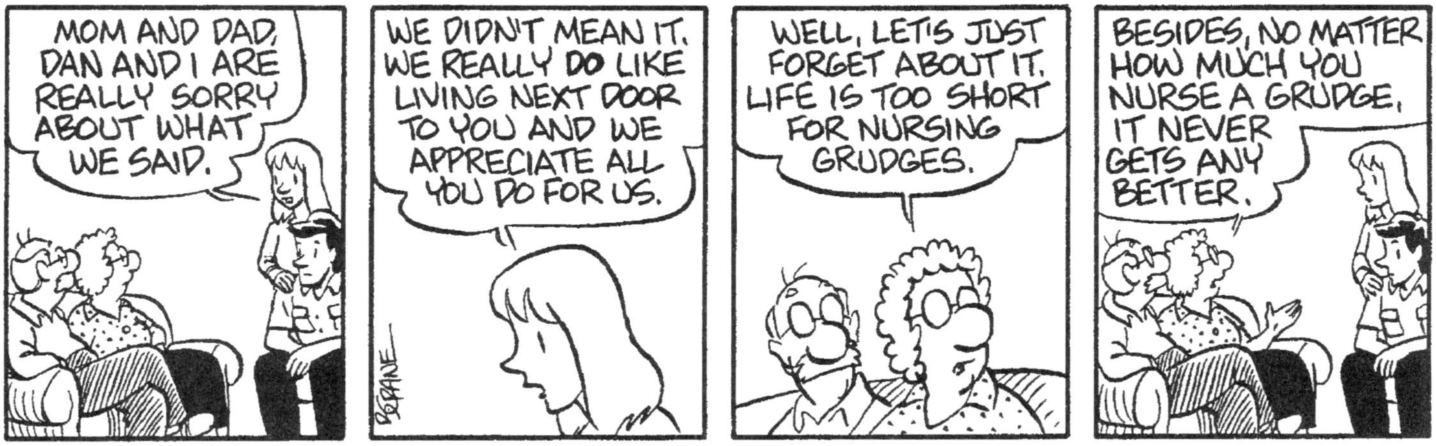
MOM AND DAD, DAN AND I ARE REALLY SORRY ABOUT WHAT WE SAID.
WE DIDN'T MEAN IT. WE REALLY **DO** LIKE LIVING NEXT DOOR TO YOU AND WE APPRECIATE ALL YOU DO FOR US.
WELL, LET'S JUST FORGET ABOUT IT. LIFE IS TOO SHORT FOR NURSING GRUDGES.
BESIDES, NO MATTER HOW MUCH YOU NURSE A GRUDGE, IT NEVER GETS ANY BETTER.

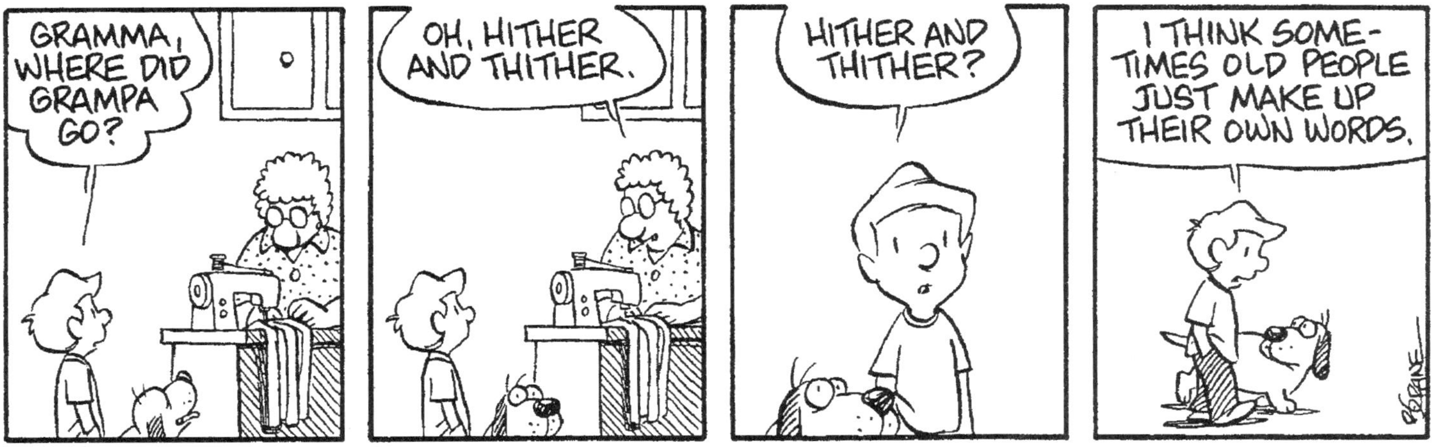
GRAMMA, WHERE DID GRAMPA GO?
OH, HITHER AND THITHER.
HITHER AND THITHER?
I THINK SOMETIMES OLD PEOPLE JUST MAKE UP THEIR OWN WORDS.

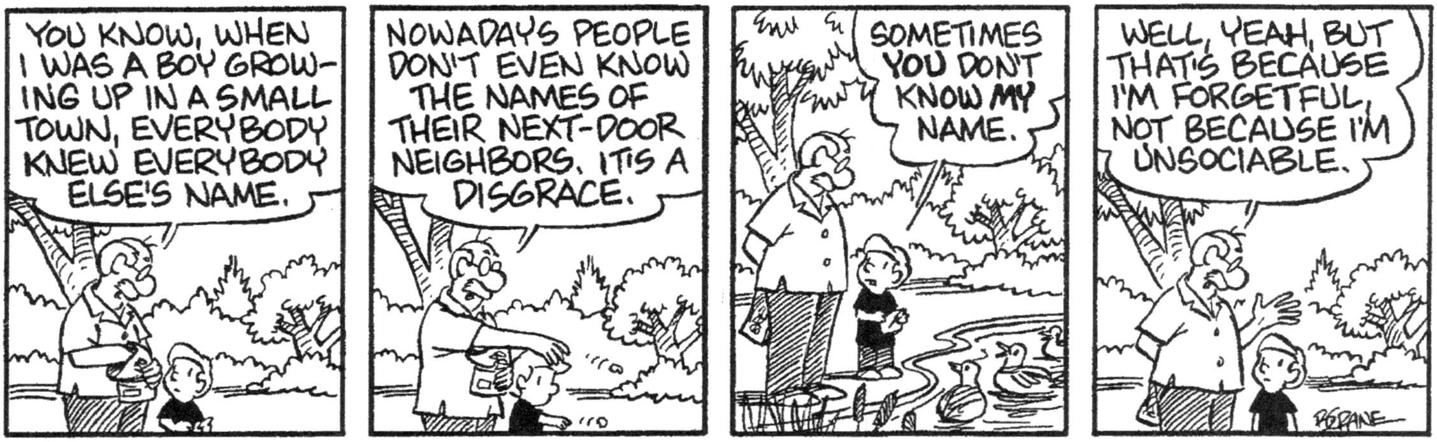
YOU KNOW, WHEN I WAS A BOY GROWING UP IN A SMALL TOWN, EVERYBODY KNEW EVERYBODY ELSE'S NAME.
NOWADAYS PEOPLE DON'T EVEN KNOW THE NAMES OF THEIR NEXT-DOOR NEIGHBORS. IT'S A DISGRACE.
SOMETIMES **YOU** DON'T KNOW **MY** NAME.
WELL, YEAH, BUT THAT'S BECAUSE I'M FORGETFUL, NOT BECAUSE I'M UNSOCIABLE.

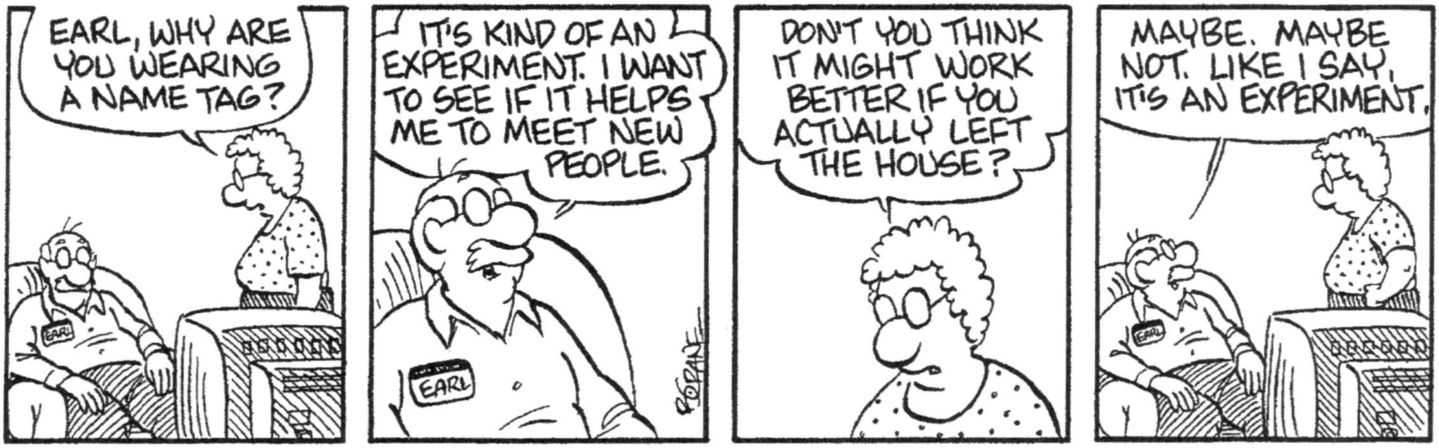
EARL, WHY ARE YOU WEARING A NAME TAG?
EARL
IT'S KIND OF AN EXPERIMENT. I WANT TO SEE IF IT HELPS ME TO MEET NEW PEOPLE.
DON'T YOU THINK IT MIGHT WORK BETTER IF YOU ACTUALLY LEFT THE HOUSE?
MAYBE. MAYBE NOT. LIKE I SAY, IT'S AN EXPERIMENT.

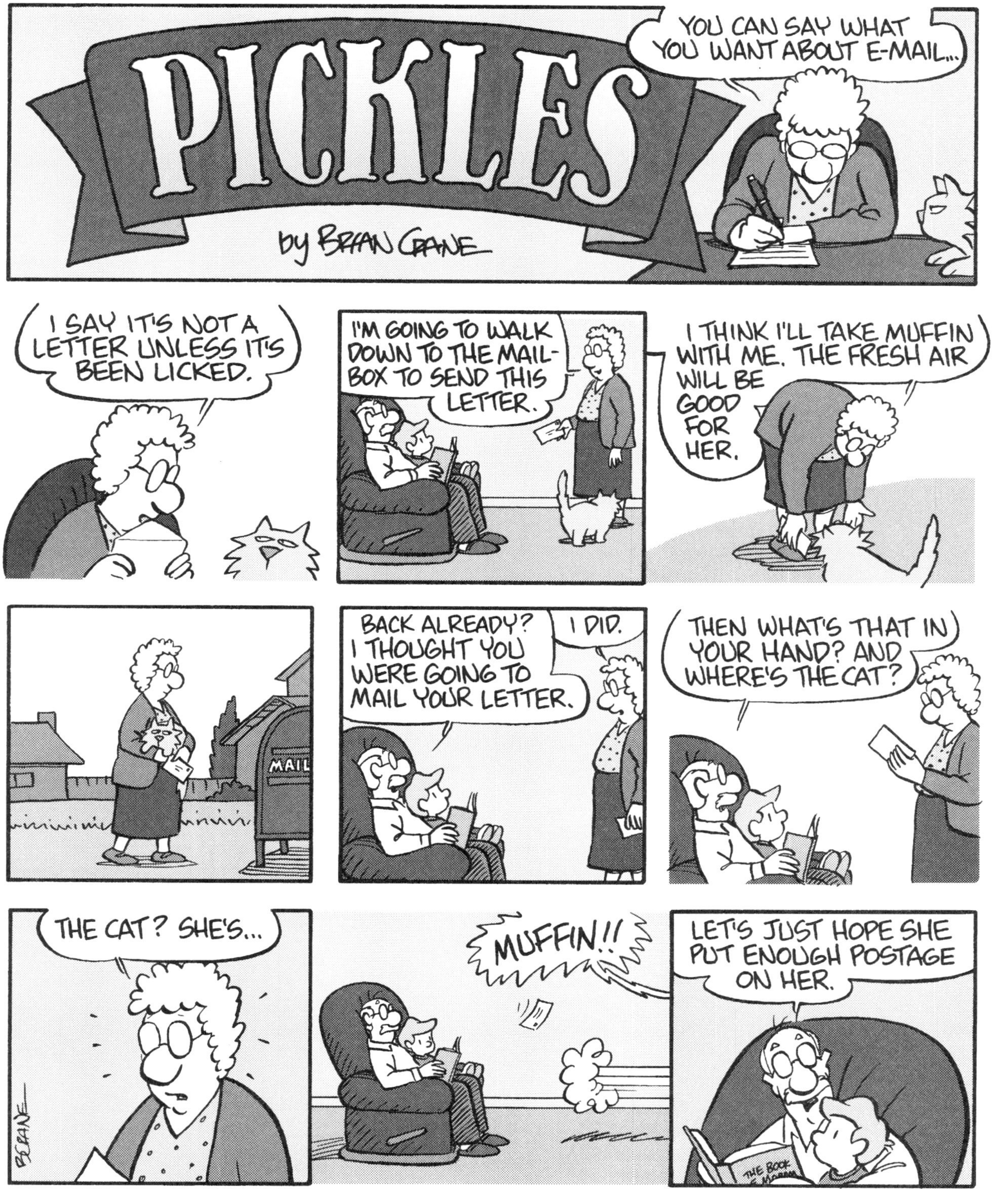
PICKLES
by BRIAN CRANE
YOU CAN SAY WHAT YOU WANT ABOUT E-MAIL...
I SAY IT'S NOT A LETTER UNLESS IT'S BEEN LICKED.
I'M GOING TO WALK DOWN TO THE MAILBOX TO SEND THIS LETTER.
I THINK I'LL TAKE MUFFIN WITH ME. THE FRESH AIR WILL BE GOOD FOR HER.
MAIL
BACK ALREADY? I THOUGHT YOU WERE GOING TO MAIL YOUR LETTER.
I DID.
THEN WHAT'S THAT IN YOUR HAND? AND WHERE'S THE CAT?
THE CAT? SHE'S...
MUFFIN!!
LET'S JUST HOPE SHE PUT ENOUGH POSTAGE ON HER.
BCRANE

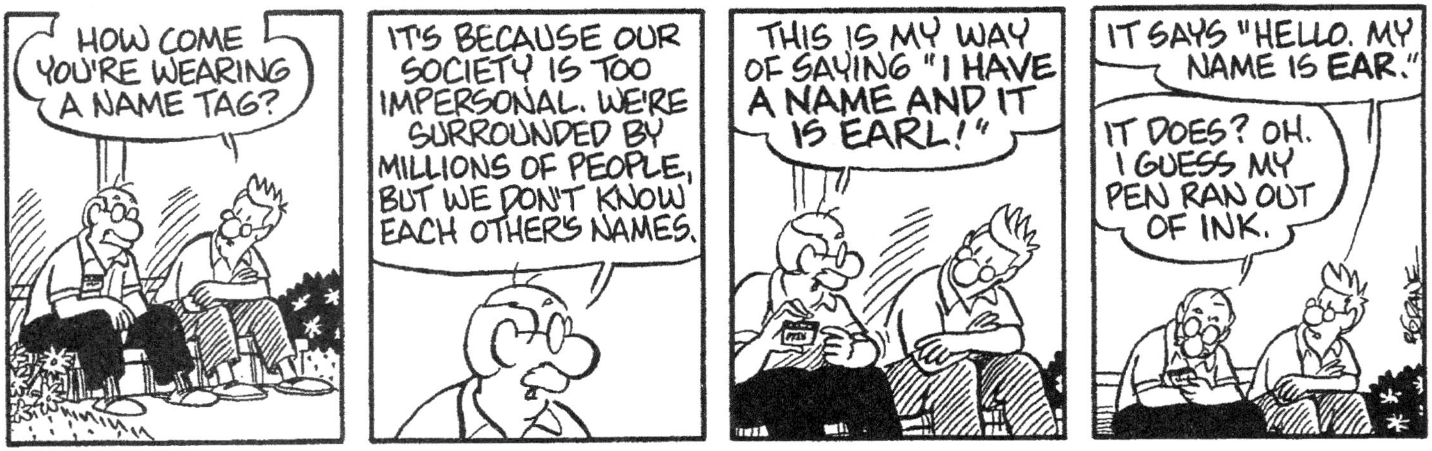
HOW COME YOU'RE WEARING A NAME TAG?
IT'S BECAUSE OUR SOCIETY IS TOO IMPERSONAL. WE'RE SURROUNDED BY MILLIONS OF PEOPLE, BUT WE DON'T KNOW EACH OTHER'S NAMES.
THIS IS MY WAY OF SAYING "I HAVE A NAME AND IT IS EARL!"
IT SAYS "HELLO. MY NAME IS EAR."
IT DOES? OH. I GUESS MY PEN RAN OUT OF INK.

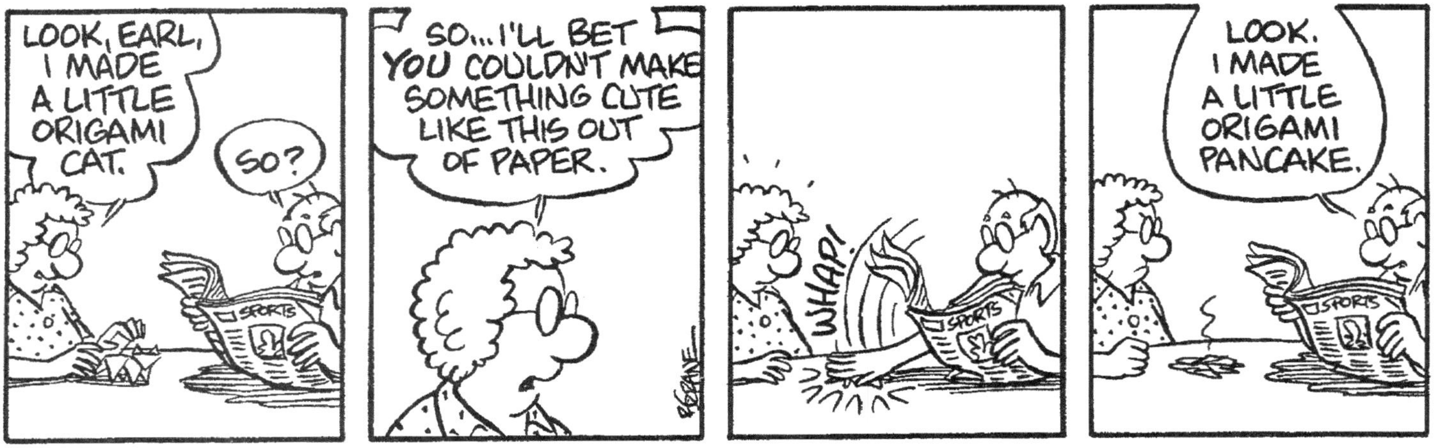
LOOK, EARL, I MADE A LITTLE ORIGAMI CAT.
SO?
SPORTS
SO... I'LL BET YOU COULDN'T MAKE SOMETHING CUTE LIKE THIS OUT OF PAPER.
WHAP!
SPORTS
LOOK. I MADE A LITTLE ORIGAMI PANCAKE.
SPORTS

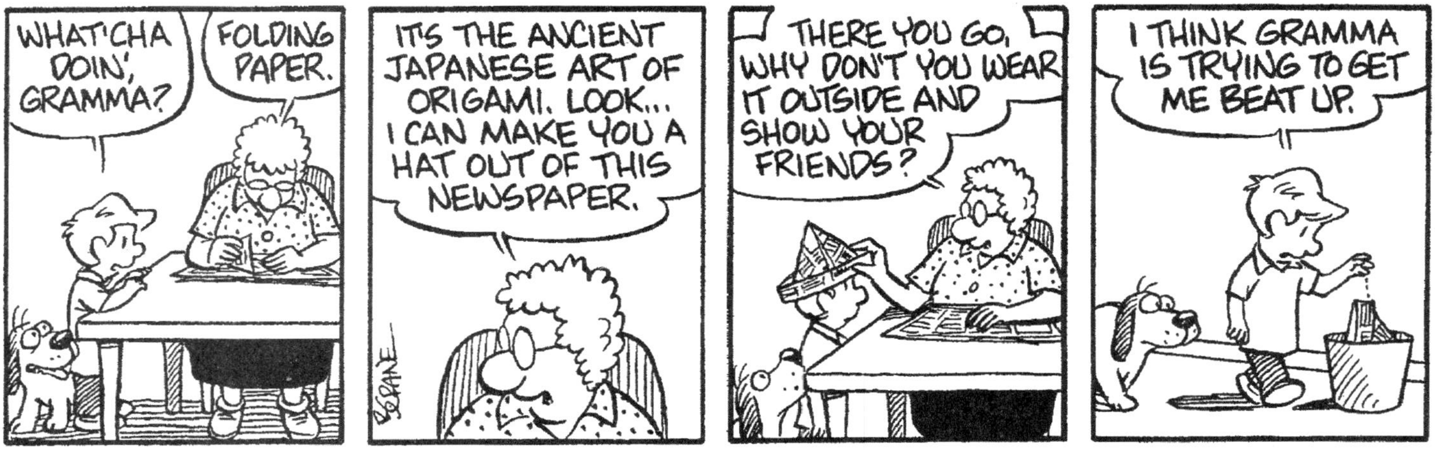
WHAT'CHA DOIN', GRAMMA?
FOLDING PAPER.
IT'S THE ANCIENT JAPANESE ART OF ORIGAMI. LOOK... I CAN MAKE YOU A HAT OUT OF THIS NEWSPAPER.
THERE YOU GO. WHY DON'T YOU WEAR IT OUTSIDE AND SHOW YOUR FRIENDS?
I THINK GRAMMA IS TRYING TO GET ME BEAT UP.

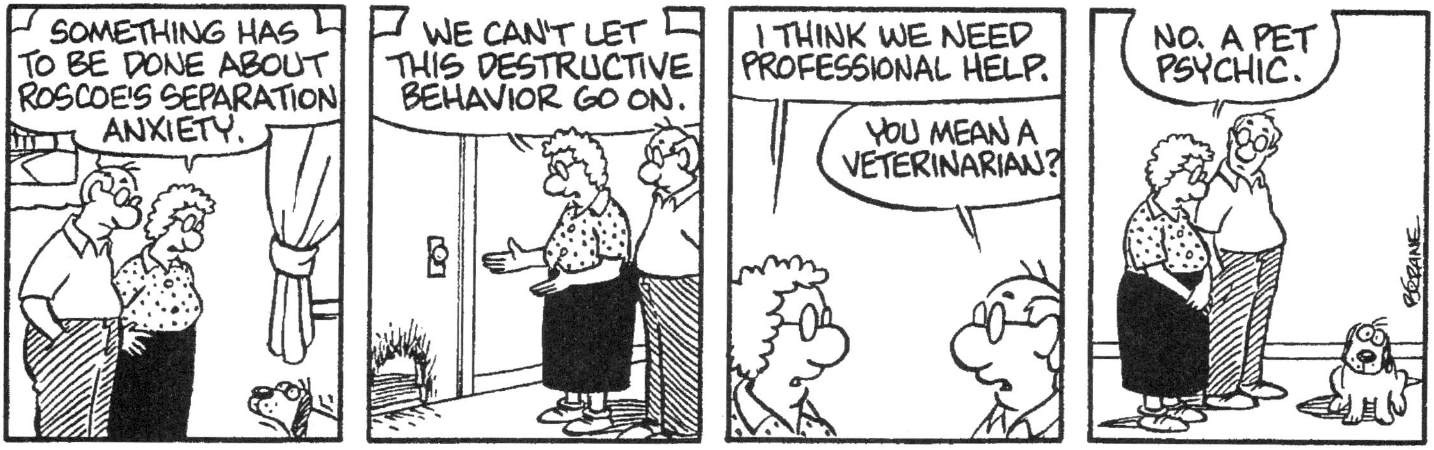
SOMETHING HAS TO BE DONE ABOUT ROSCOE'S SEPARATION ANXIETY.
WE CAN'T LET THIS DESTRUCTIVE BEHAVIOR GO ON.
I THINK WE NEED PROFESSIONAL HELP.
YOU MEAN A VETERINARIAN?
NO. A PET PSYCHIC.

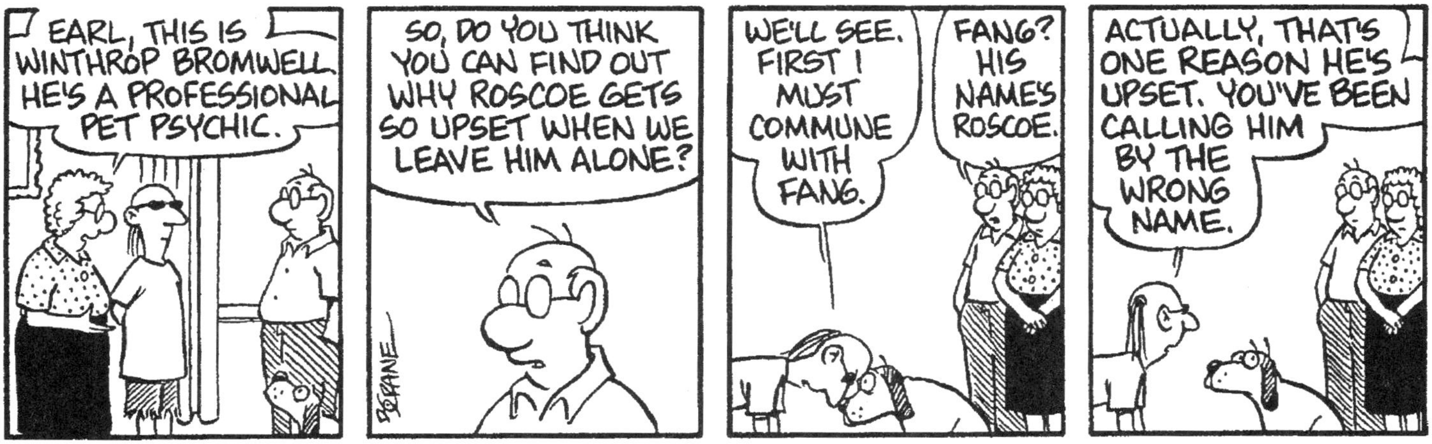
EARL, THIS IS WINTHROP BROMWELL. HE'S A PROFESSIONAL PET PSYCHIC.
SO, DO YOU THINK YOU CAN FIND OUT WHY ROSCOE GETS SO UPSET WHEN WE LEAVE HIM ALONE?
WE'LL SEE. FIRST I MUST COMMUNE WITH FANG.
FANG? HIS NAME'S ROSCOE.
ACTUALLY, THAT'S ONE REASON HE'S UPSET. YOU'VE BEEN CALLING HIM BY THE WRONG NAME.

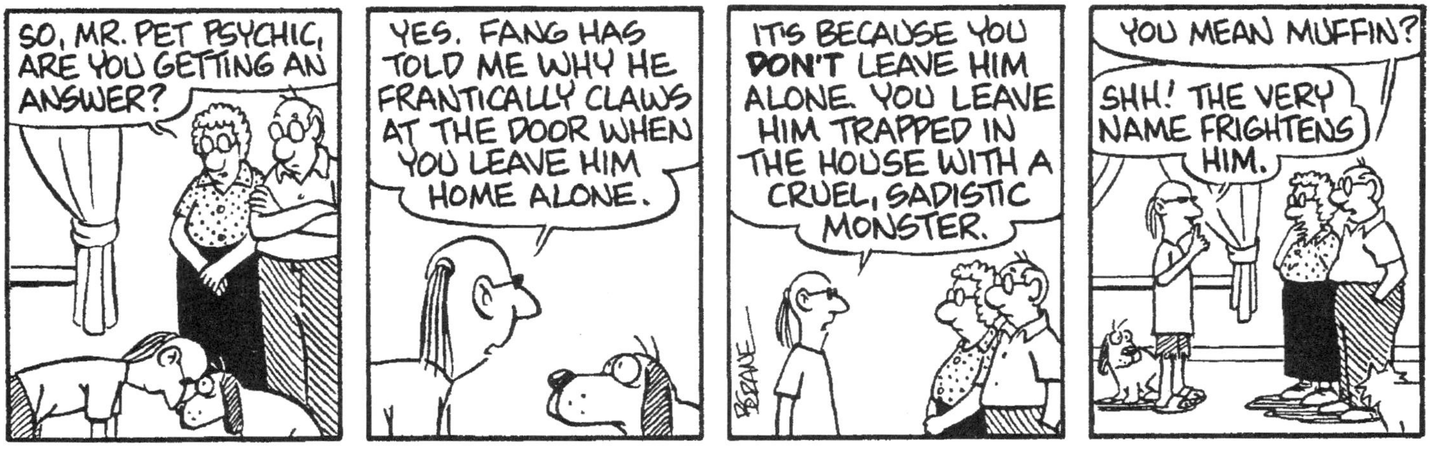
SO, MR. PET PSYCHIC, ARE YOU GETTING AN ANSWER?
YES. FANG HAS TOLD ME WHY HE FRANTICALLY CLAWS AT THE DOOR WHEN YOU LEAVE HIM HOME ALONE.
IT'S BECAUSE YOU **DON'T** LEAVE HIM ALONE. YOU LEAVE HIM TRAPPED IN THE HOUSE WITH A CRUEL, SADISTIC MONSTER.
YOU MEAN MUFFIN?
SHH! THE VERY NAME FRIGHTENS HIM.

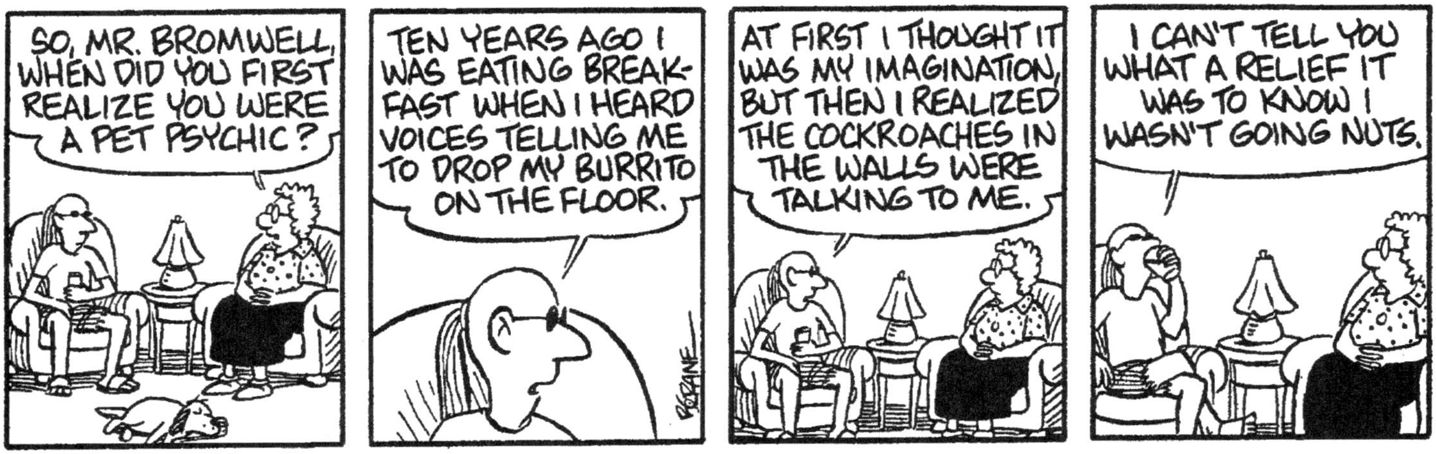
SO, MR. BROMWELL, WHEN DID YOU FIRST REALIZE YOU WERE A PET PSYCHIC?
TEN YEARS AGO I WAS EATING BREAK-FAST WHEN I HEARD VOICES TELLING ME TO DROP MY BURRITO ON THE FLOOR.
AT FIRST I THOUGHT IT WAS MY IMAGINATION, BUT THEN I REALIZED THE COCKROACHES IN THE WALLS WERE TALKING TO ME.
I CAN'T TELL YOU WHAT A RELIEF IT WAS TO KNOW I WASN'T GOING NUTS.

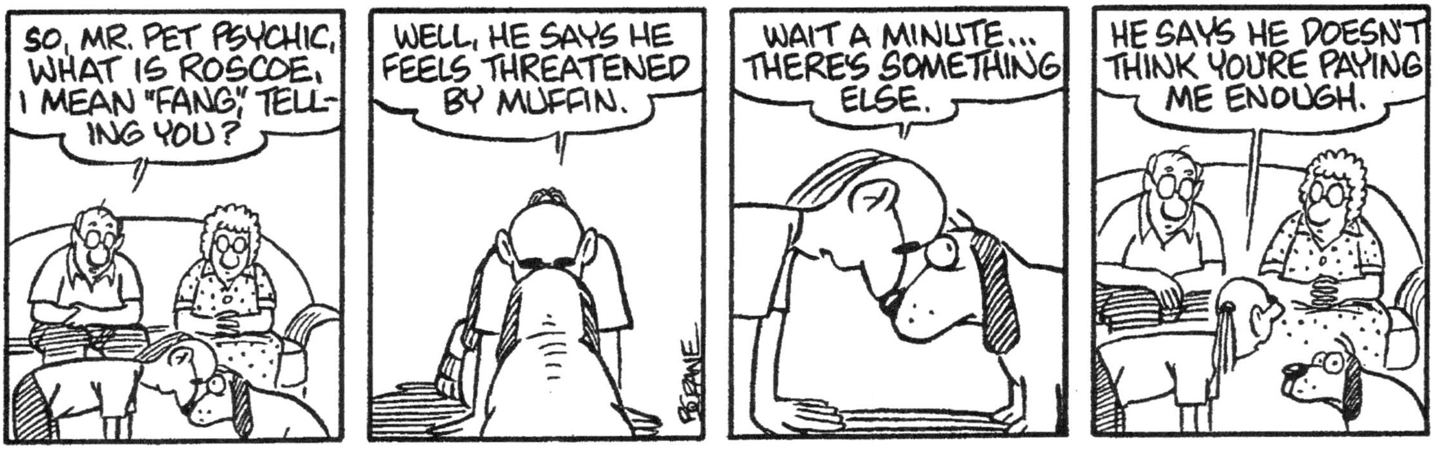
SO, MR. PET PSYCHIC, WHAT IS ROSCOE, I MEAN "FANG," TELL-ING YOU?
WELL, HE SAYS HE FEELS THREATENED BY MUFFIN.
WAIT A MINUTE... THERE'S SOMETHING ELSE.
HE SAYS HE DOESN'T THINK YOU'RE PAYING ME ENOUGH.

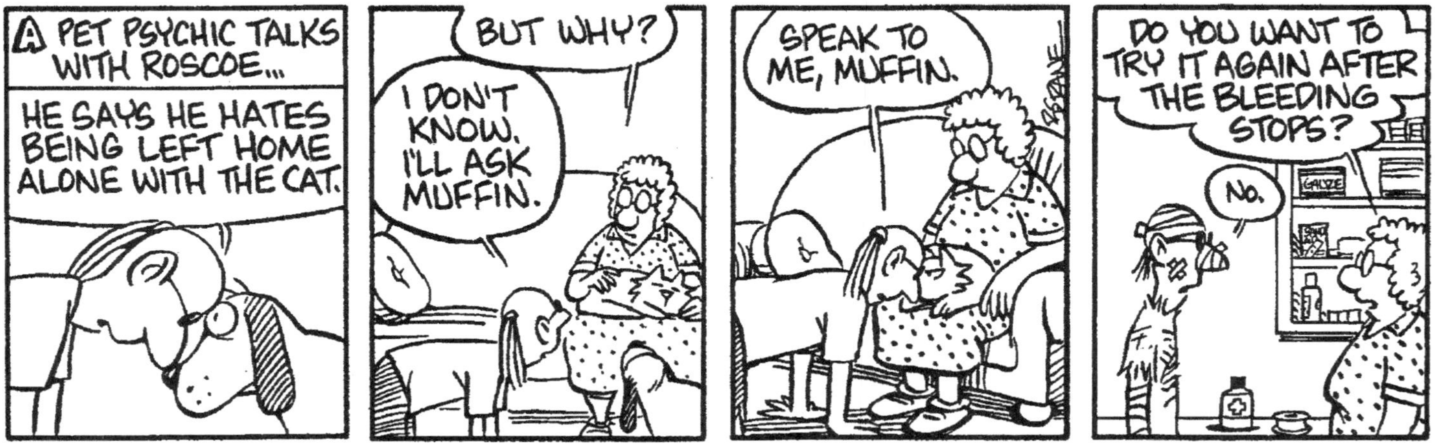
A PET PSYCHIC TALKS WITH ROSCOE...
HE SAYS HE HATES BEING LEFT HOME ALONE WITH THE CAT.
BUT WHY?
I DON'T KNOW. I'LL ASK MUFFIN.
SPEAK TO ME, MUFFIN.
DO YOU WANT TO TRY IT AGAIN AFTER THE BLEEDING STOPS?
No.
GAUZE

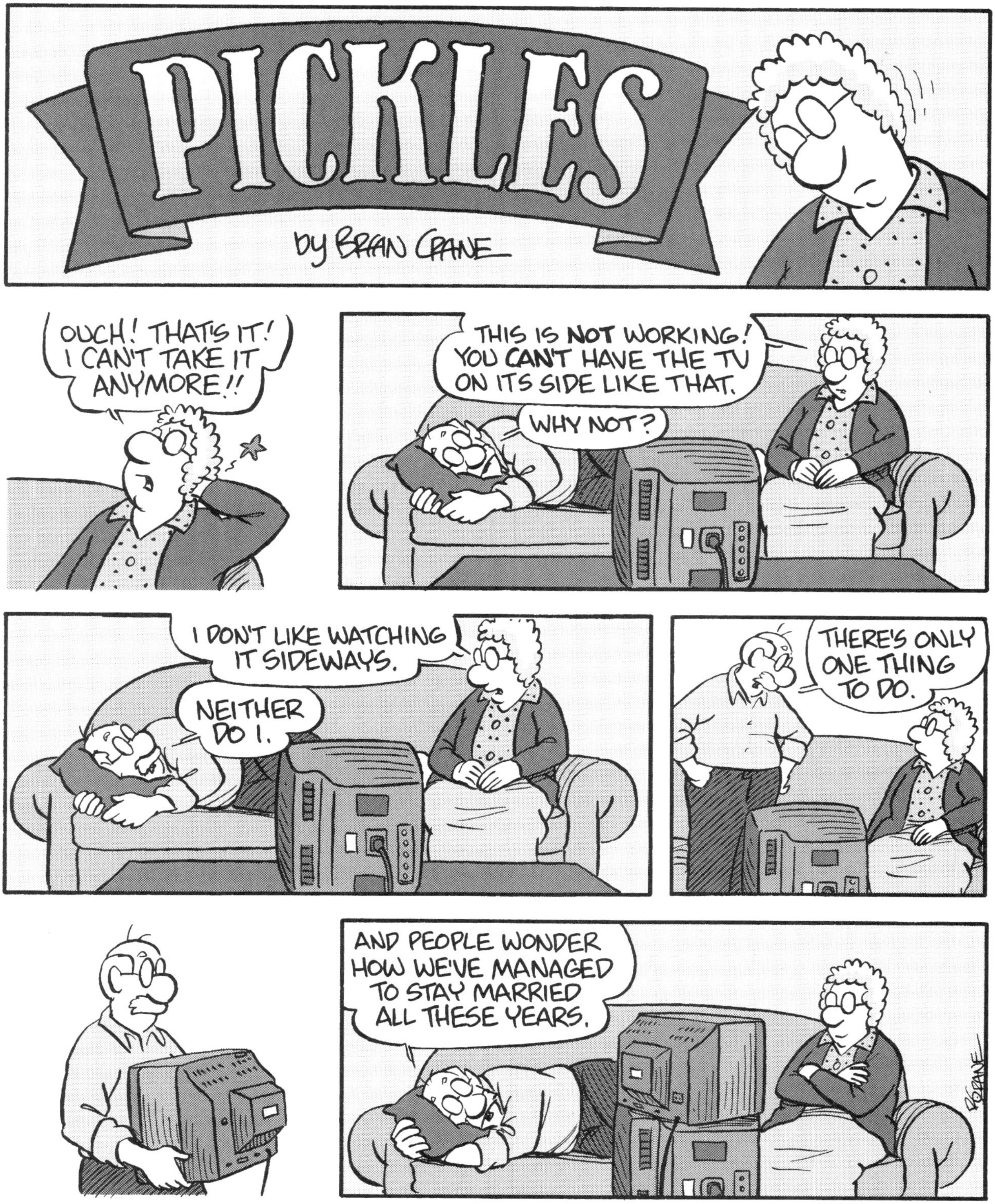
PICKLES
by BRIAN CRANE
OUCH! THAT'S IT! I CAN'T TAKE IT ANYMORE!!
THIS IS NOT WORKING! YOU CAN'T HAVE THE TV ON ITS SIDE LIKE THAT.
WHY NOT?
I DON'T LIKE WATCHING IT SIDEWAYS.
NEITHER DO I.
THERE'S ONLY ONE THING TO DO.
AND PEOPLE WONDER HOW WE'VE MANAGED TO STAY MARRIED ALL THESE YEARS.

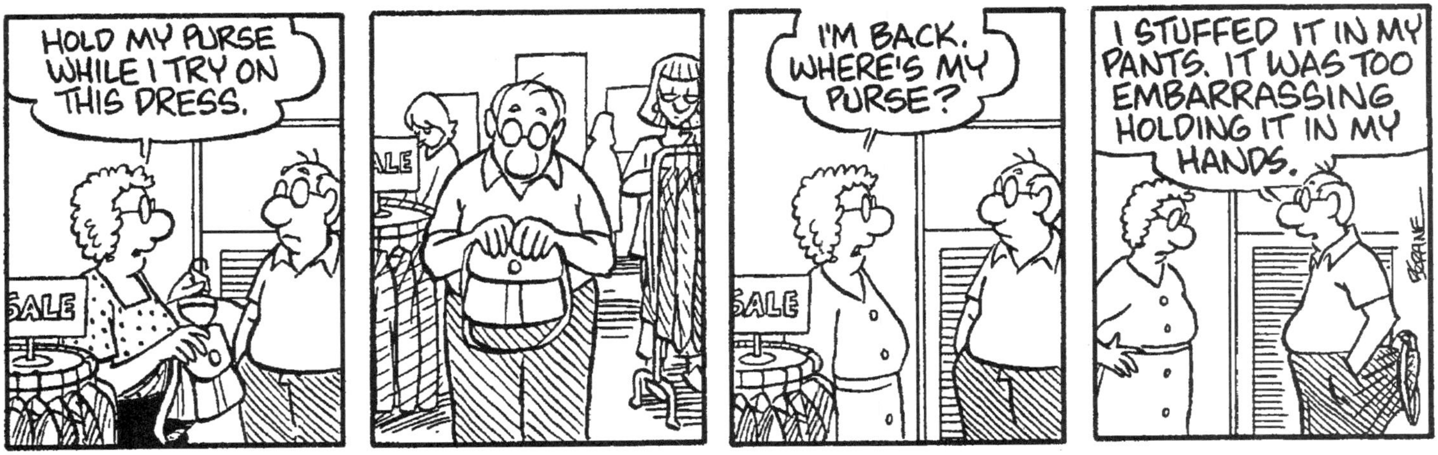
HOLD MY PURSE WHILE I TRY ON THIS DRESS.
SALE
I'M BACK. WHERE'S MY PURSE?
I STUFFED IT IN MY PANTS. IT WAS TOO EMBARRASSING HOLDING IT IN MY HANDS.

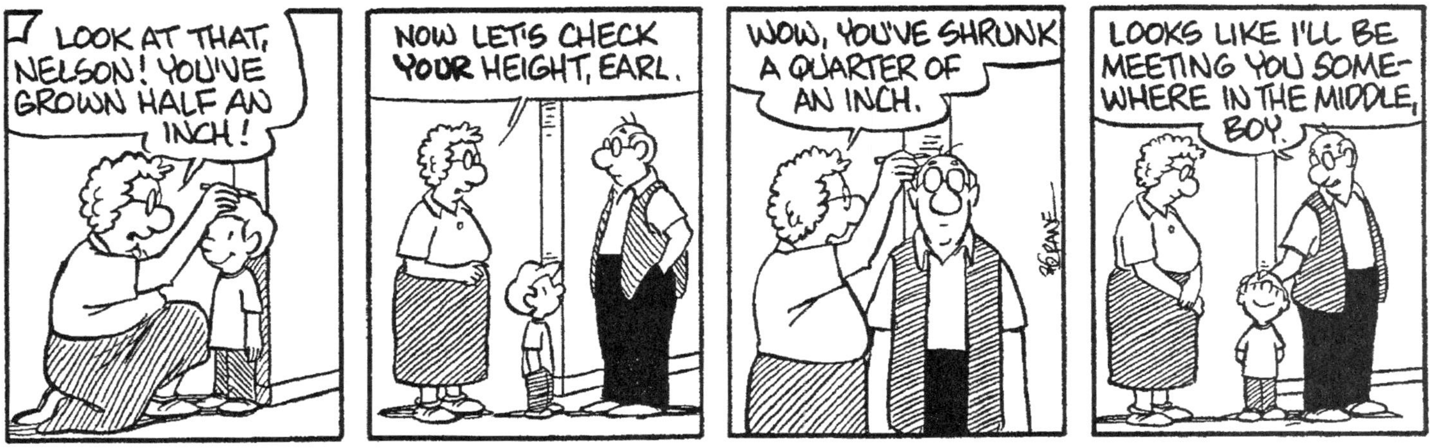
LOOK AT THAT, NELSON! YOU'VE GROWN HALF AN INCH!
NOW LET'S CHECK **YOUR** HEIGHT, EARL.
WOW, YOU'VE SHRUNK A QUARTER OF AN INCH.
LOOKS LIKE I'LL BE MEETING YOU SOME-WHERE IN THE MIDDLE, BOY.

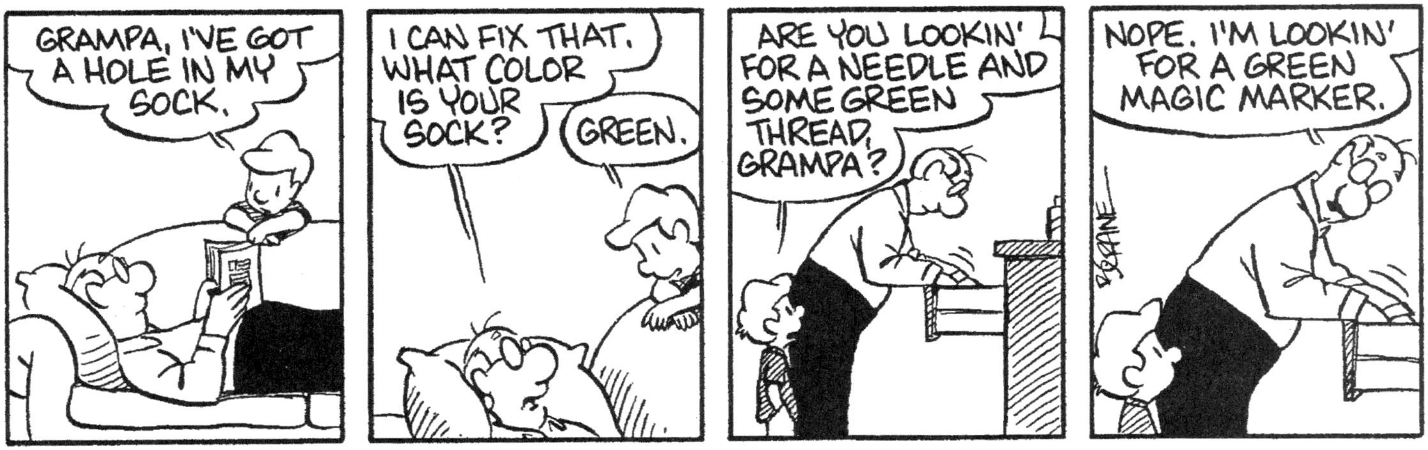
GRAMPA, I'VE GOT A HOLE IN MY SOCK.
I CAN FIX THAT. WHAT COLOR IS YOUR SOCK?
GREEN.
ARE YOU LOOKIN' FOR A NEEDLE AND SOME GREEN THREAD, GRAMPA?
NOPE. I'M LOOKIN' FOR A GREEN MAGIC MARKER.

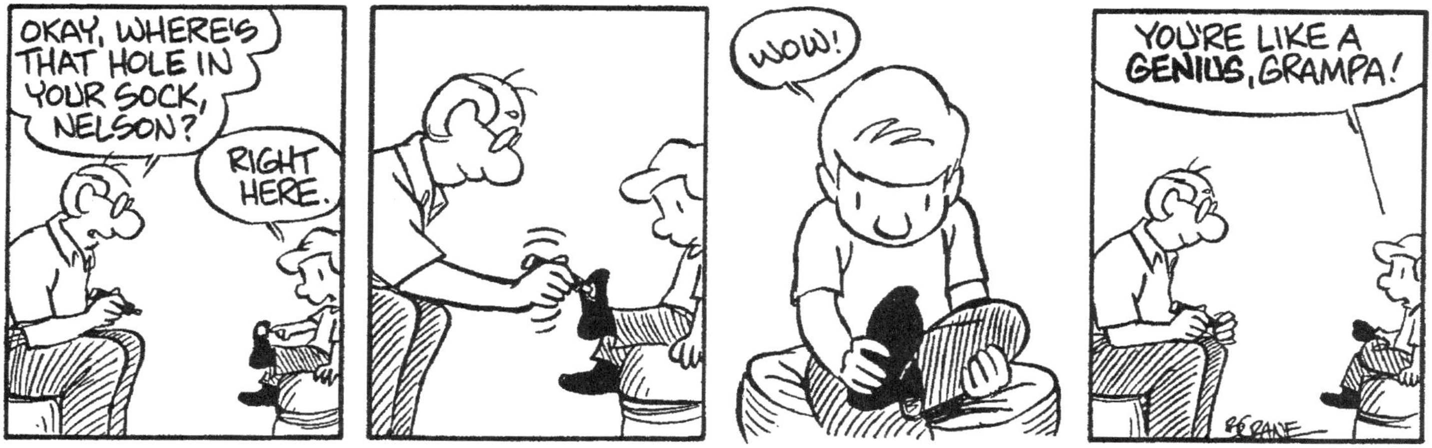
OKAY, WHERE'S THAT HOLE IN YOUR SOCK, NELSON?
RIGHT HERE.
WOW!
YOU'RE LIKE A **GENIUS**, GRAMPA!

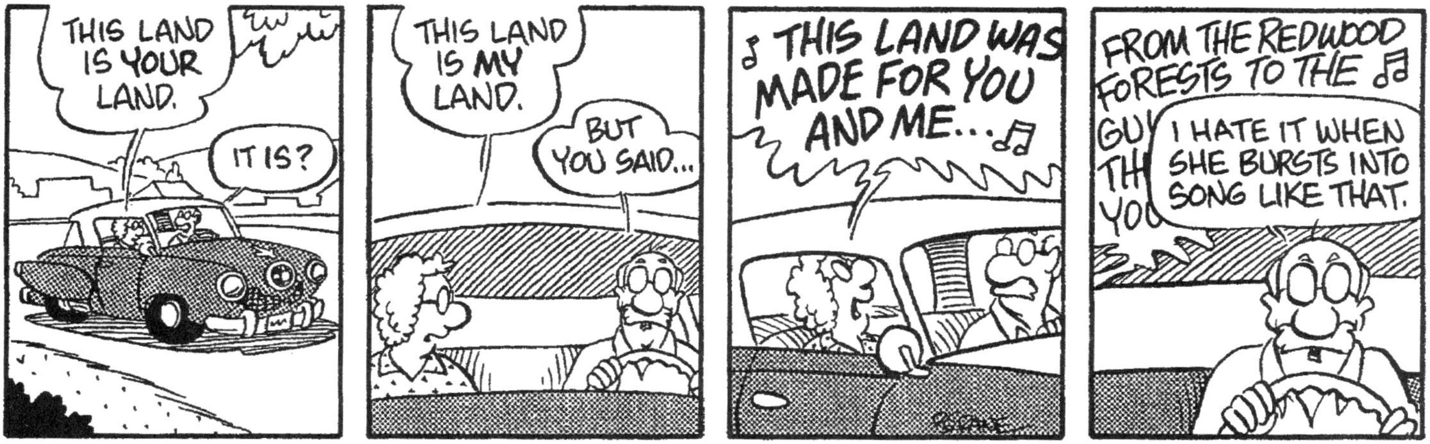
THIS LAND IS **YOUR** LAND.
IT IS?
THIS LAND IS **MY** LAND.
BUT YOU SAID...
THIS LAND WAS MADE FOR YOU AND ME...
FROM THE REDWOOD FORESTS TO THE
I HATE IT WHEN SHE BURSTS INTO SONG LIKE THAT.

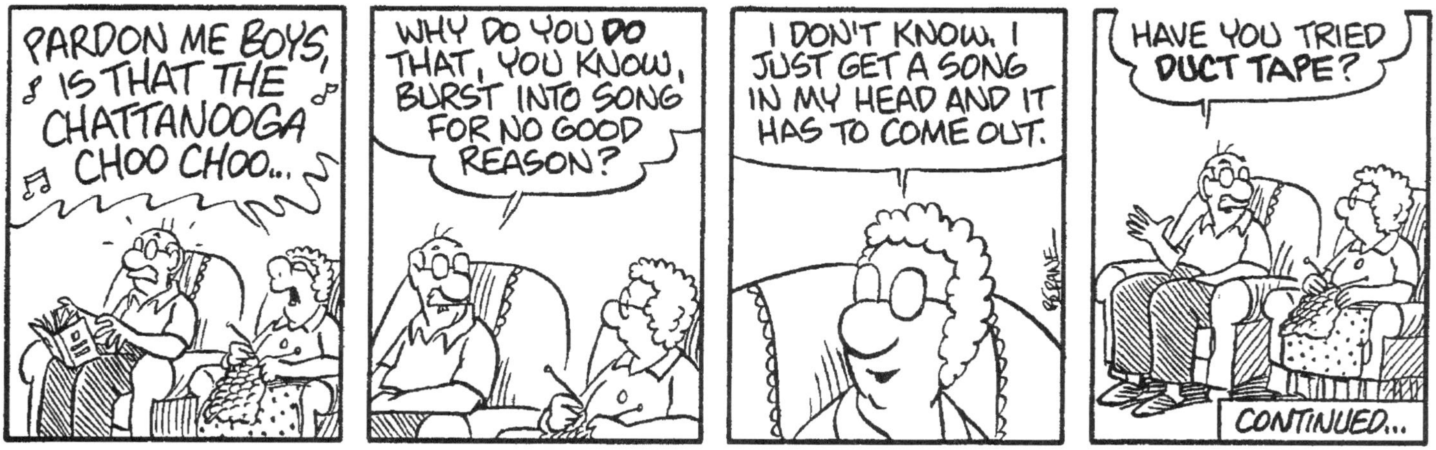
PARDON ME BOYS, IS THAT THE CHATTANOOGA CHOO CHOO...
WHY DO YOU **DO** THAT, YOU KNOW, BURST INTO SONG FOR NO GOOD REASON?
I DON'T KNOW. I JUST GET A SONG IN MY HEAD AND IT HAS TO COME OUT.
HAVE YOU TRIED **DUCT TAPE**?
CONTINUED...

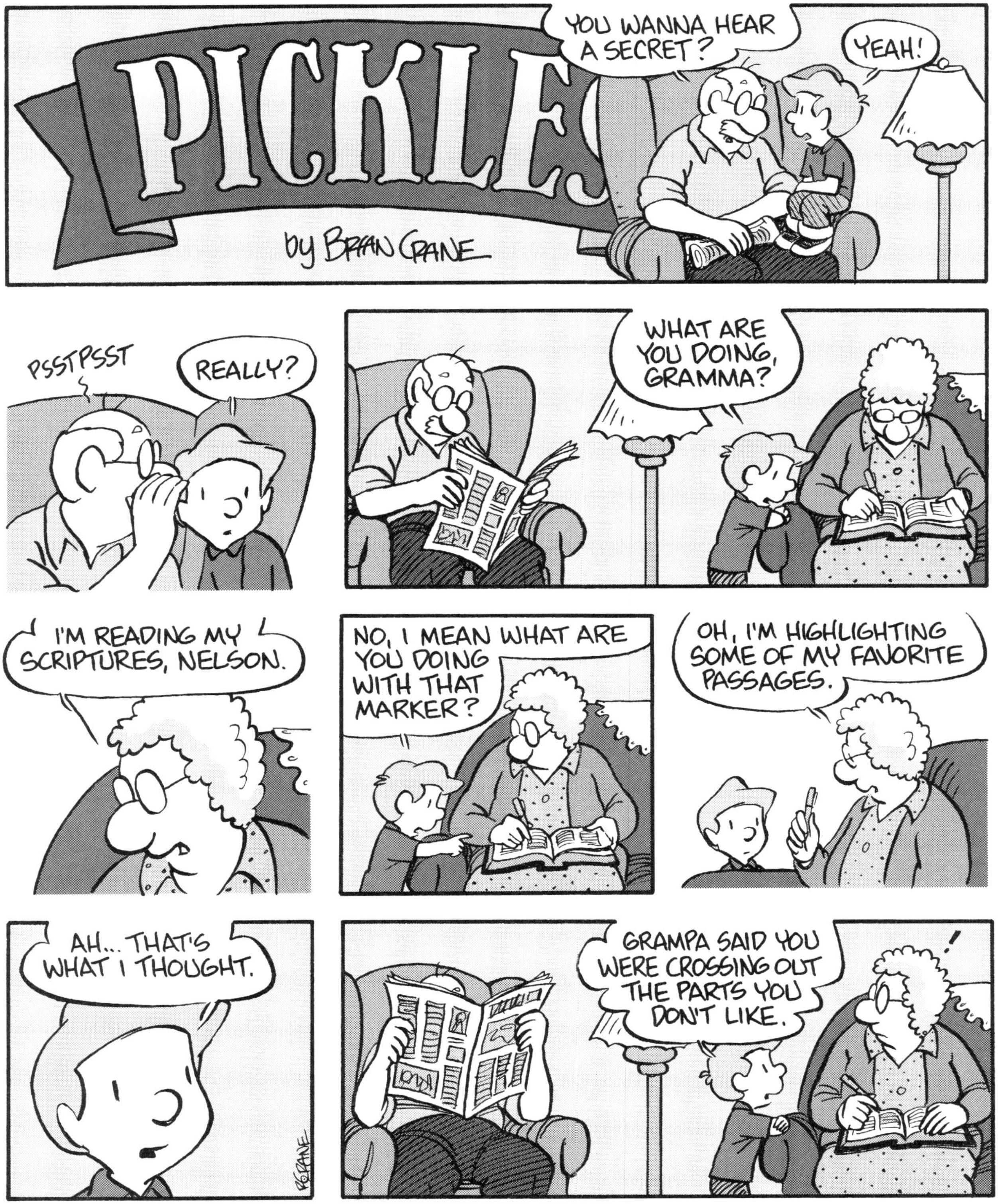
PICKLES
by BRIAN CRANE
YOU WANNA HEAR A SECRET?
YEAH!
PSSTPSST
REALLY?
WHAT ARE YOU DOING, GRAMMA?
I'M READING MY SCRIPTURES, NELSON.
NO, I MEAN WHAT ARE YOU DOING WITH THAT MARKER?
OH, I'M HIGHLIGHTING SOME OF MY FAVORITE PASSAGES.
AH... THAT'S WHAT I THOUGHT.
GRAMPA SAID YOU WERE CROSSING OUT THE PARTS YOU DON'T LIKE.
!

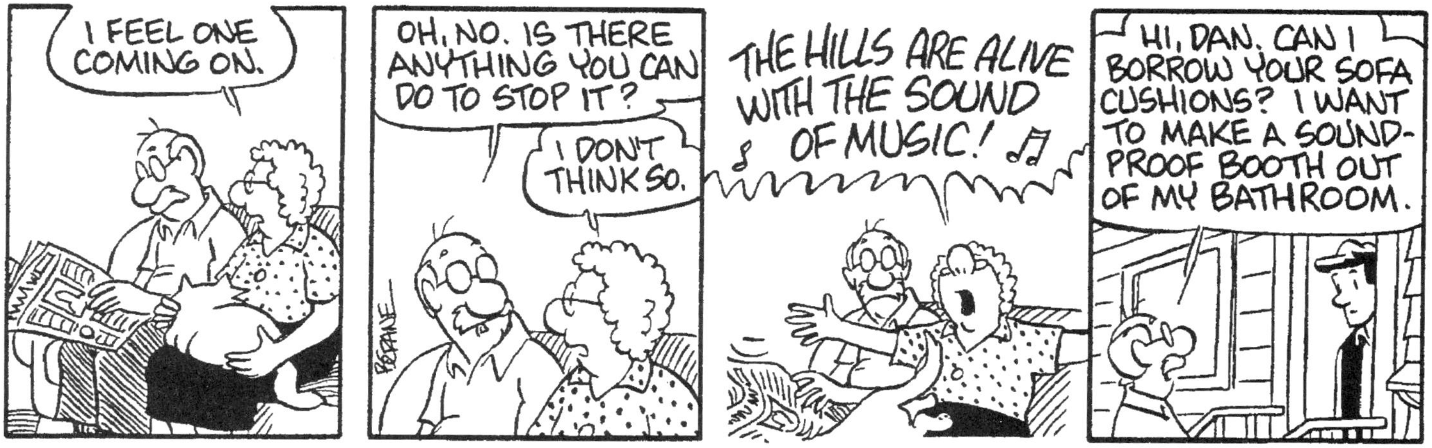
I FEEL ONE COMING ON.
OH, NO. IS THERE ANYTHING YOU CAN DO TO STOP IT?
I DON'T THINK SO.
THE HILLS ARE ALIVE WITH THE SOUND OF MUSIC!
HI, DAN. CAN I BORROW YOUR SOFA CUSHIONS? I WANT TO MAKE A SOUND-PROOF BOOTH OUT OF MY BATHROOM.

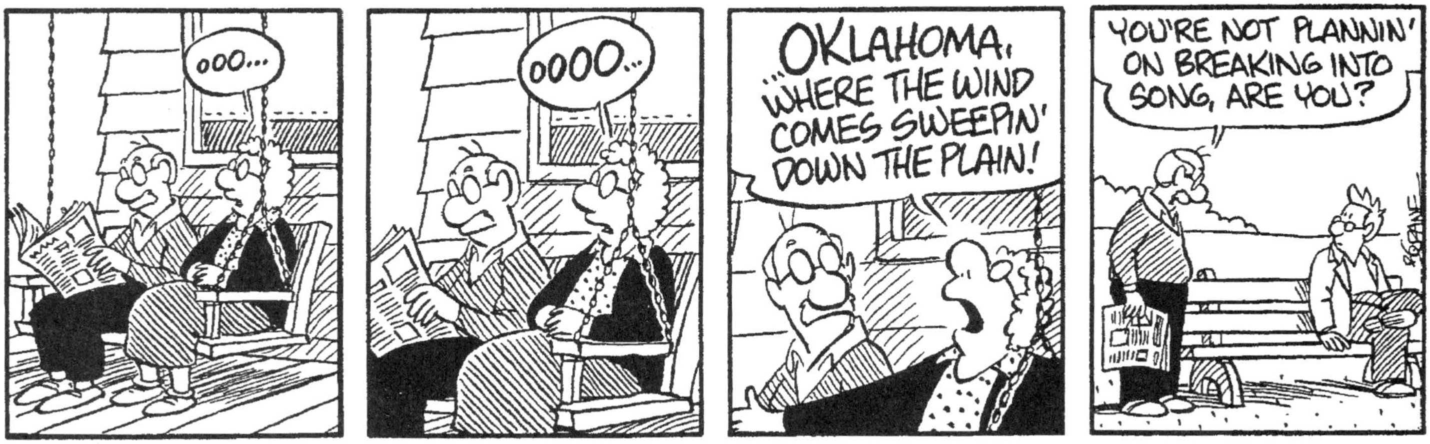
OOO...
OOOO...
OKLAHOMA, WHERE THE WIND COMES SWEEPIN' DOWN THE PLAIN!
YOU'RE NOT PLANNIN' ON BREAKING INTO SONG, ARE YOU?

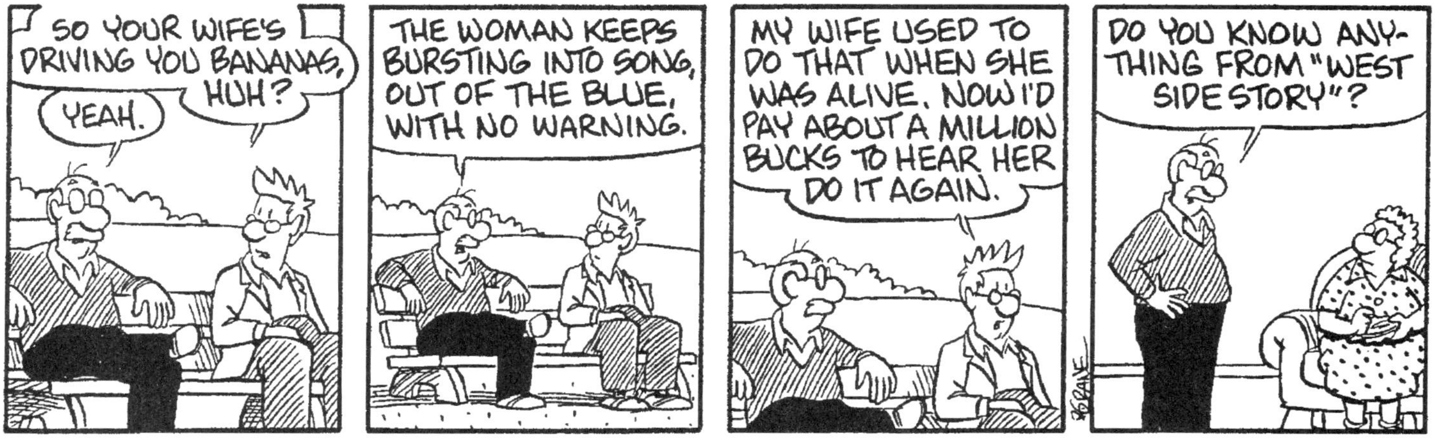
SO YOUR WIFE'S DRIVING YOU BANANAS, HUH?
YEAH.
THE WOMAN KEEPS BURSTING INTO SONG, OUT OF THE BLUE, WITH NO WARNING.
MY WIFE USED TO DO THAT WHEN SHE WAS ALIVE. NOW I'D PAY ABOUT A MILLION BUCKS TO HEAR HER DO IT AGAIN.
DO YOU KNOW ANYTHING FROM "WEST SIDE STORY"?

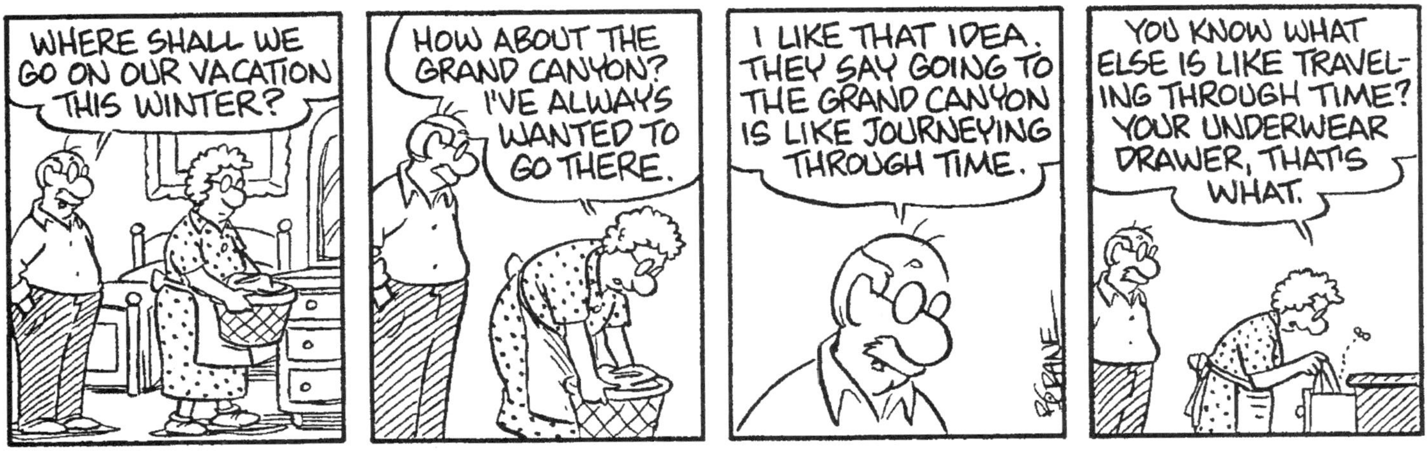
WHERE SHALL WE GO ON OUR VACATION THIS WINTER?
HOW ABOUT THE GRAND CANYON? I'VE ALWAYS WANTED TO GO THERE.
I LIKE THAT IDEA. THEY SAY GOING TO THE GRAND CANYON IS LIKE JOURNEYING THROUGH TIME.
YOU KNOW WHAT ELSE IS LIKE TRAVELING THROUGH TIME? YOUR UNDERWEAR DRAWER, THAT'S WHAT.

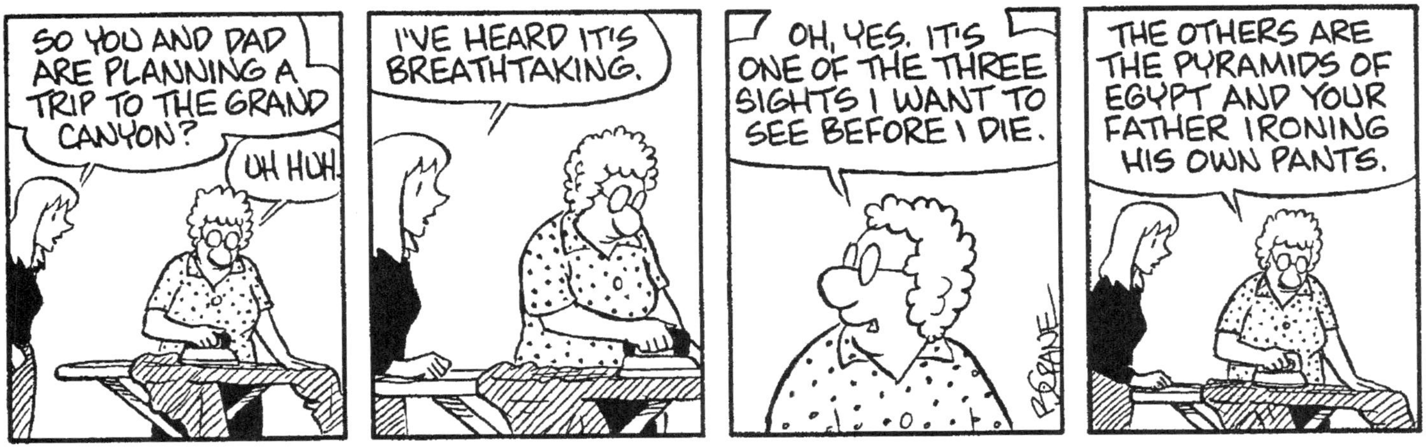
SO YOU AND DAD ARE PLANNING A TRIP TO THE GRAND CANYON?
UH HUH.
I'VE HEARD IT'S BREATHTAKING.
OH, YES. IT'S ONE OF THE THREE SIGHTS I WANT TO SEE BEFORE I DIE.
THE OTHERS ARE THE PYRAMIDS OF EGYPT AND YOUR FATHER IRONING HIS OWN PANTS.

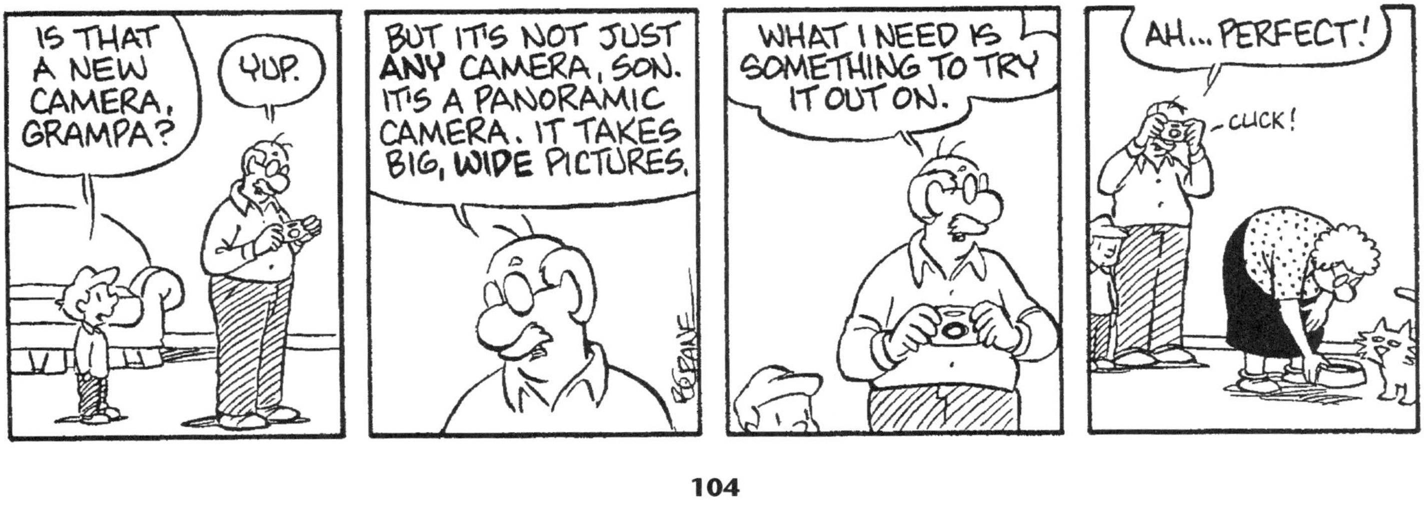
IS THAT A NEW CAMERA, GRAMPA?
YUP.
BUT IT'S NOT JUST **ANY** CAMERA, SON. IT'S A PANORAMIC CAMERA. IT TAKES BIG, **WIDE** PICTURES.
WHAT I NEED IS SOMETHING TO TRY IT OUT ON.
AH... PERFECT!
CLICK!

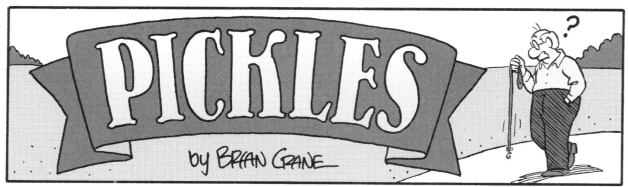

WELL THAT'S ODD!

HEY, EARL!

OH, HI, CLYDE.

WHY ARE YOU HOLDING THAT DOG LEASH?

GOOD QUESTION. I WAS JUST TRYING TO FIGURE THAT OUT MYSELF.

I MUST BE HAVING A SENIOR MOMENT...

I CAN'T REMEMBER IF I **FOUND** A LEASH OR **LOST** A DOG.

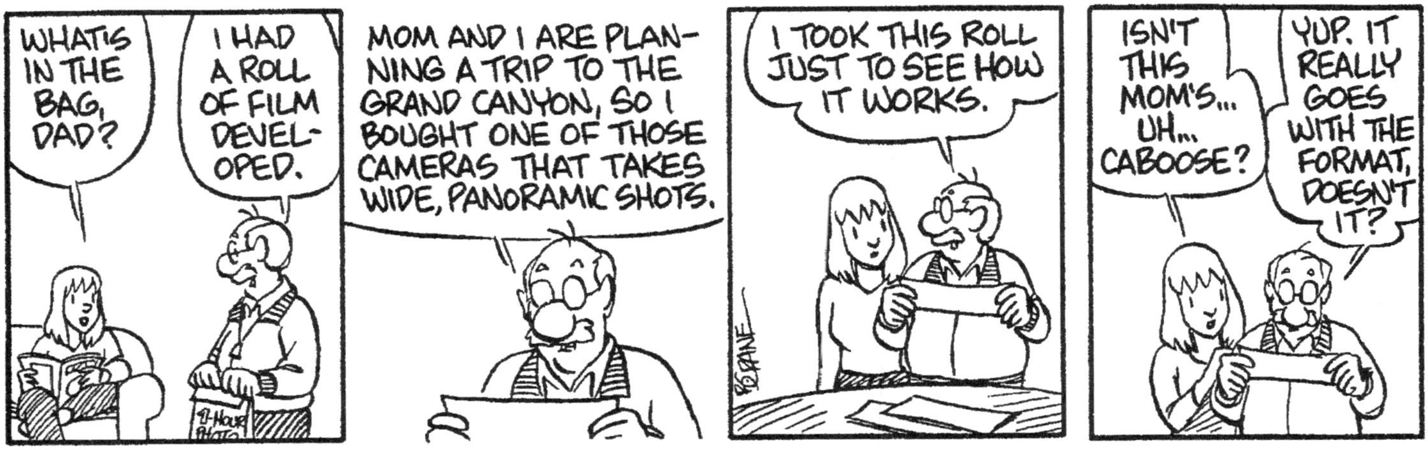
WHAT IS IN THE BAG, DAD?
I HAD A ROLL OF FILM DEVEL-OPED.
MOM AND I ARE PLAN-NING A TRIP TO THE GRAND CANYON, SO I BOUGHT ONE OF THOSE CAMERAS THAT TAKES WIDE, PANORAMIC SHOTS.
I TOOK THIS ROLL JUST TO SEE HOW IT WORKS.
ISN'T THIS MOM'S... UH... CABOOSE?
YUP. IT REALLY GOES WITH THE FORMAT, DOESN'T IT?

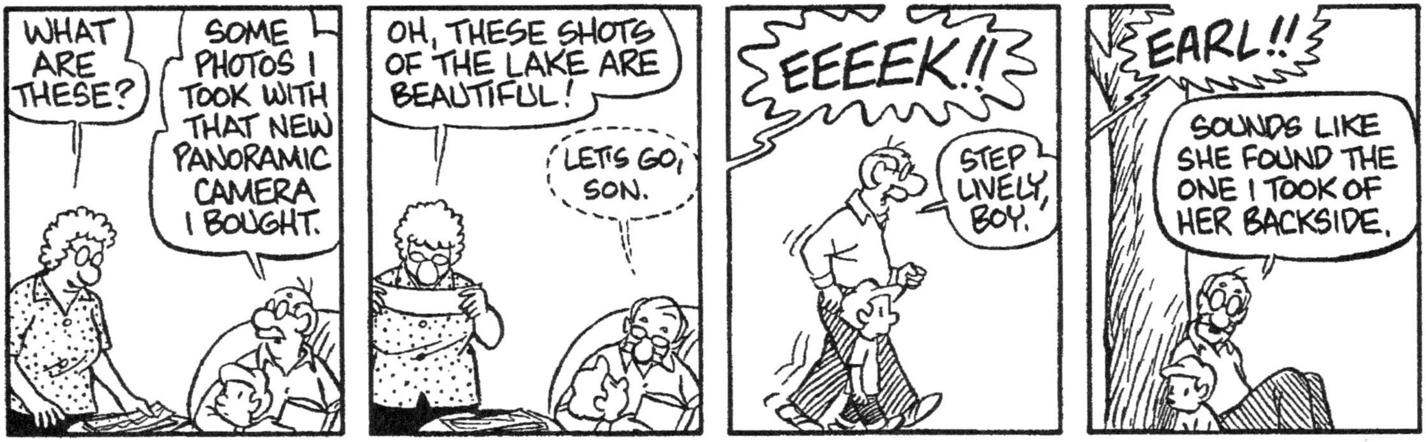
WHAT ARE THESE?
SOME PHOTOS I TOOK WITH THAT NEW PANORAMIC CAMERA I BOUGHT.
OH, THESE SHOTS OF THE LAKE ARE BEAUTIFUL!
LET'S GO, SON.
EEEEK!!
STEP LIVELY, BOY.
EARL!!
SOUNDS LIKE SHE FOUND THE ONE I TOOK OF HER BACKSIDE.

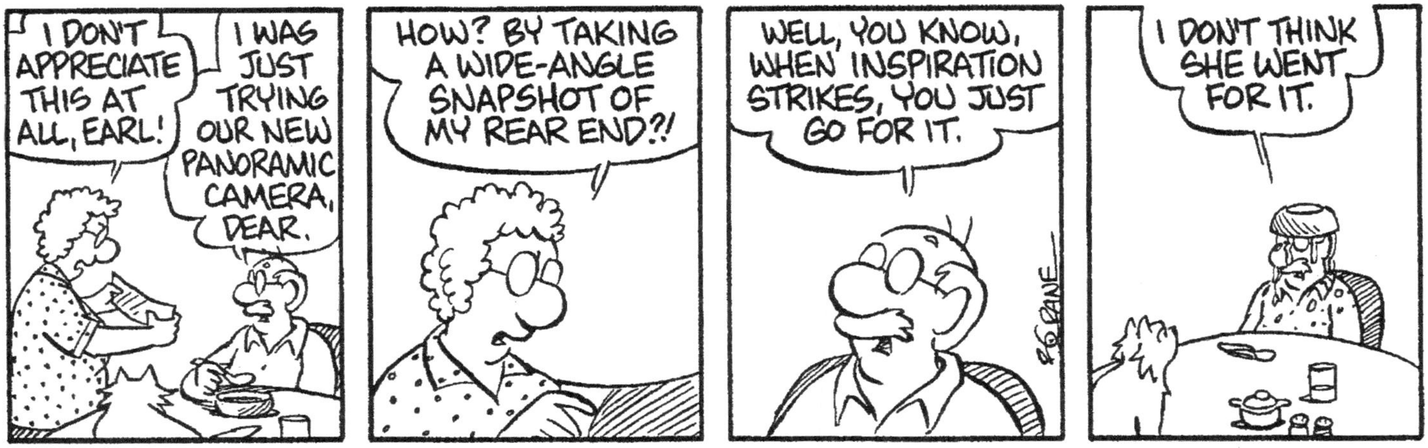
I DON'T APPRECIATE THIS AT ALL, EARL!
I WAS JUST TRYING OUR NEW PANORAMIC CAMERA, DEAR.
HOW? BY TAKING A WIDE-ANGLE SNAPSHOT OF MY REAR END?!
WELL, YOU KNOW, WHEN INSPIRATION STRIKES, YOU JUST GO FOR IT.
I DON'T THINK SHE WENT FOR IT.

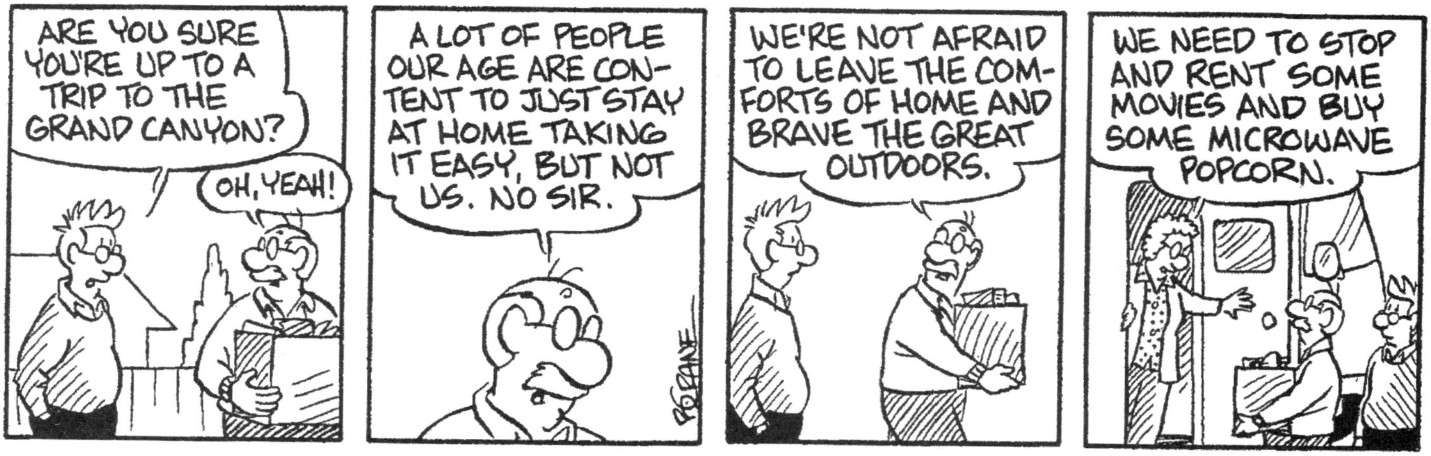
ARE YOU SURE YOU'RE UP TO A TRIP TO THE GRAND CANYON?
OH, YEAH!
A LOT OF PEOPLE OUR AGE ARE CONTENT TO JUST STAY AT HOME TAKING IT EASY, BUT NOT US. NO SIR.
WE'RE NOT AFRAID TO LEAVE THE COMFORTS OF HOME AND BRAVE THE GREAT OUTDOORS.
WE NEED TO STOP AND RENT SOME MOVIES AND BUY SOME MICROWAVE POPCORN.

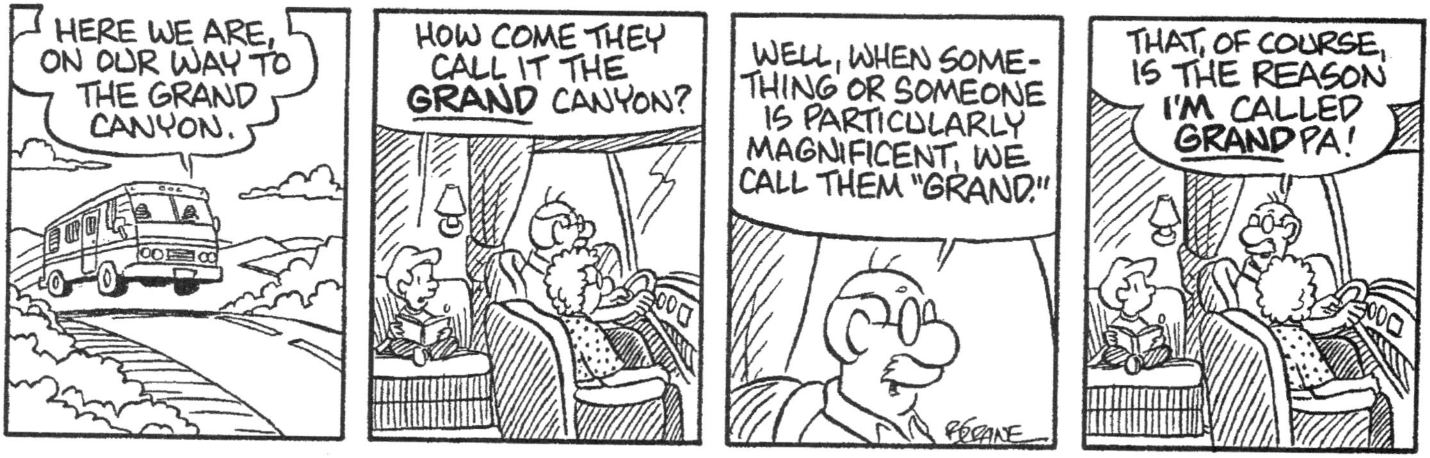
HERE WE ARE, ON OUR WAY TO THE GRAND CANYON.
HOW COME THEY CALL IT THE GRAND CANYON?
WELL, WHEN SOMETHING OR SOMEONE IS PARTICULARLY MAGNIFICENT, WE CALL THEM "GRAND."
THAT, OF COURSE, IS THE REASON I'M CALLED GRANDPA!

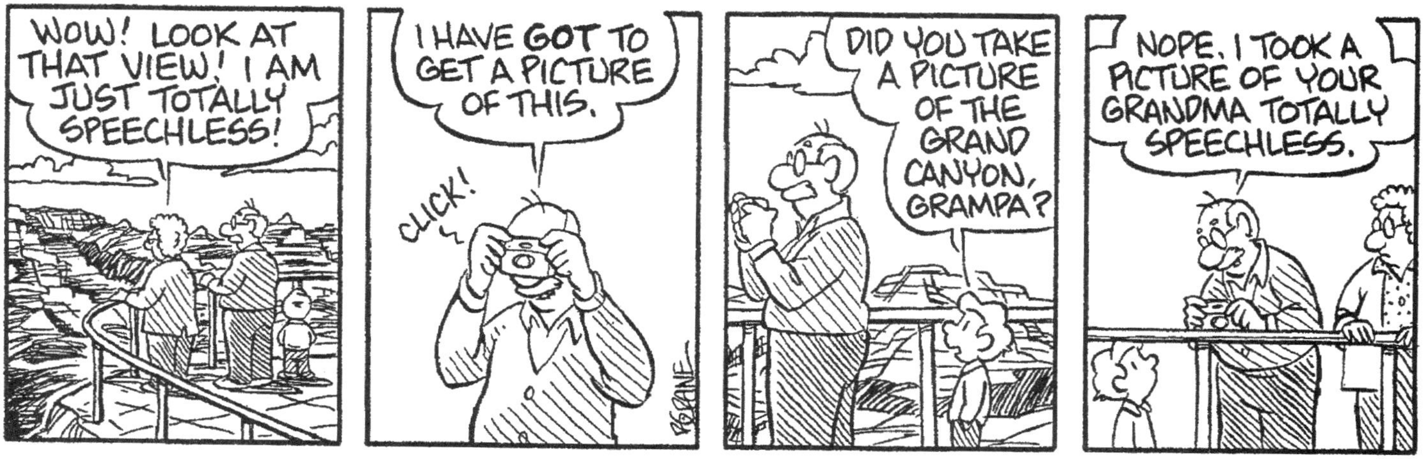
WOW! LOOK AT THAT VIEW! I AM JUST TOTALLY SPEECHLESS!
I HAVE GOT TO GET A PICTURE OF THIS.
CLICK!
DID YOU TAKE A PICTURE OF THE GRAND CANYON, GRAMPA?
NOPE. I TOOK A PICTURE OF YOUR GRANDMA TOTALLY SPEECHLESS.

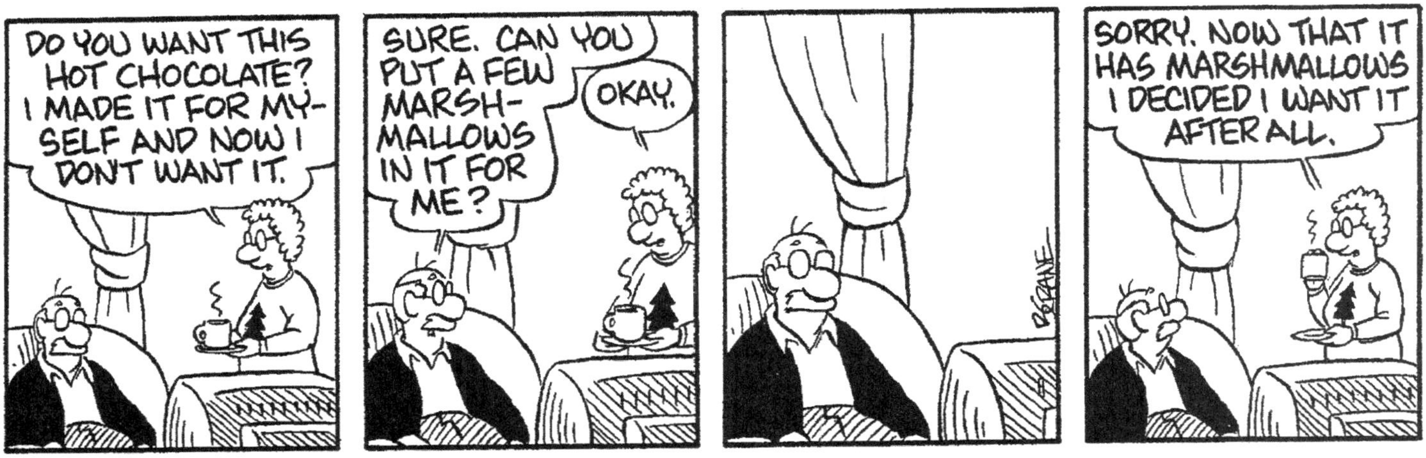
DO YOU WANT THIS HOT CHOCOLATE? I MADE IT FOR MY-SELF AND NOW I DON'T WANT IT.
SURE. CAN YOU PUT A FEW MARSH-MALLOWS IN IT FOR ME?
OKAY.
SORRY. NOW THAT IT HAS MARSHMALLOWS I DECIDED I WANT IT AFTER ALL.

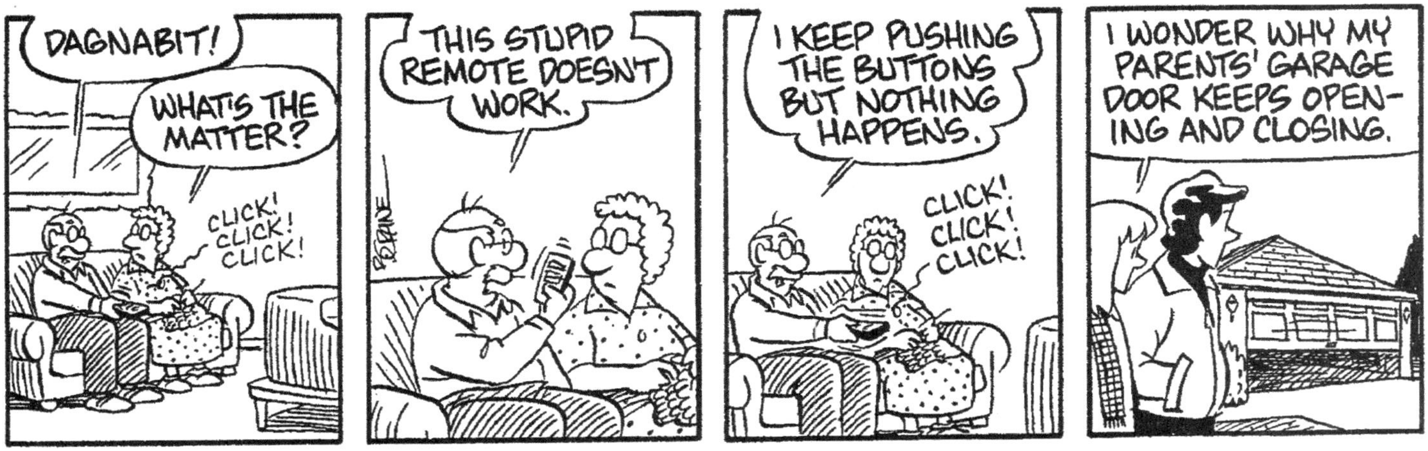
DAGNABIT!
WHAT'S THE MATTER?
CLICK! CLICK! CLICK!
THIS STUPID REMOTE DOESN'T WORK.
I KEEP PUSHING THE BUTTONS BUT NOTHING HAPPENS.
CLICK! CLICK! CLICK!
I WONDER WHY MY PARENTS' GARAGE DOOR KEEPS OPEN-ING AND CLOSING.

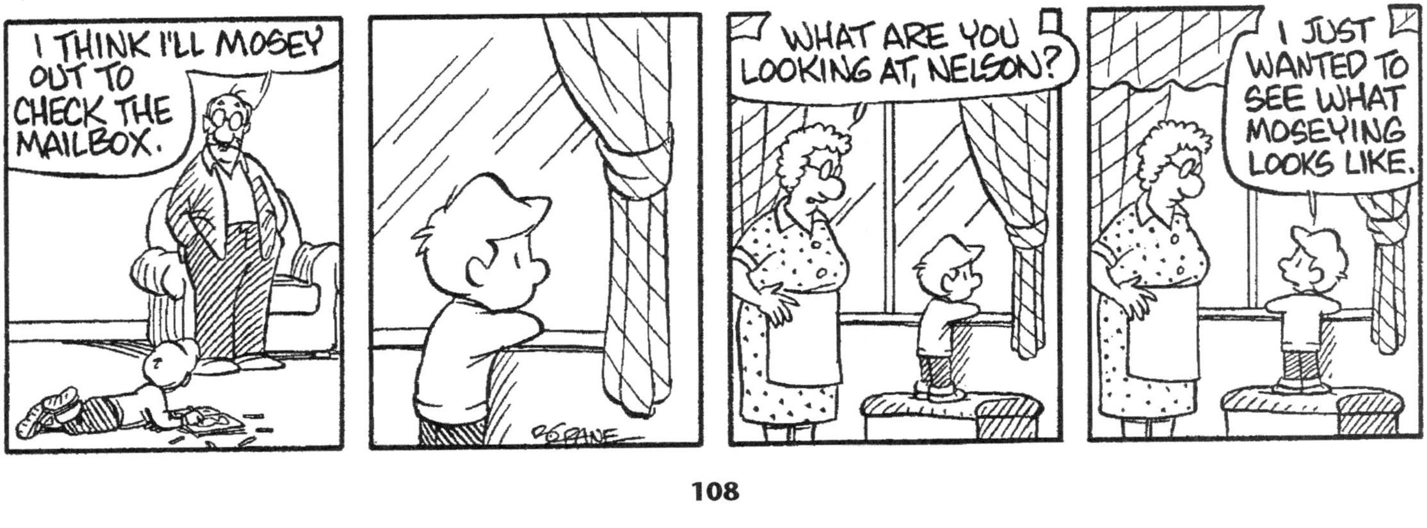
I THINK I'LL MOSEY OUT TO CHECK THE MAILBOX.
WHAT ARE YOU LOOKING AT, NELSON?
I JUST WANTED TO SEE WHAT MOSEYING LOOKS LIKE.

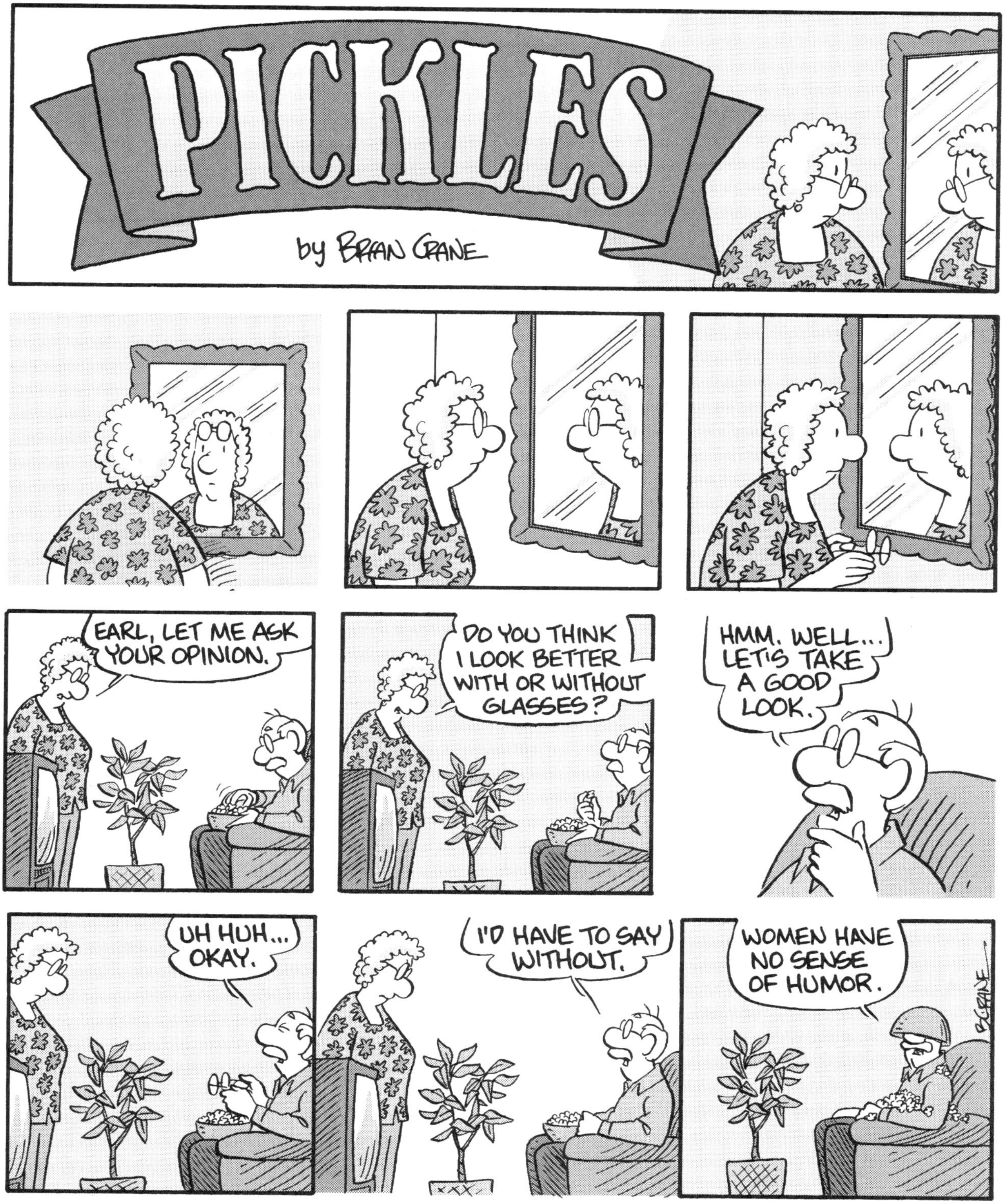
PICKLES
by BRIAN CRANE
EARL, LET ME ASK YOUR OPINION.
DO YOU THINK I LOOK BETTER WITH OR WITHOUT GLASSES?
HMM. WELL... LET'S TAKE A GOOD LOOK.
UH HUH... OKAY.
I'D HAVE TO SAY WITHOUT.
WOMEN HAVE NO SENSE OF HUMOR.
B. CRANE

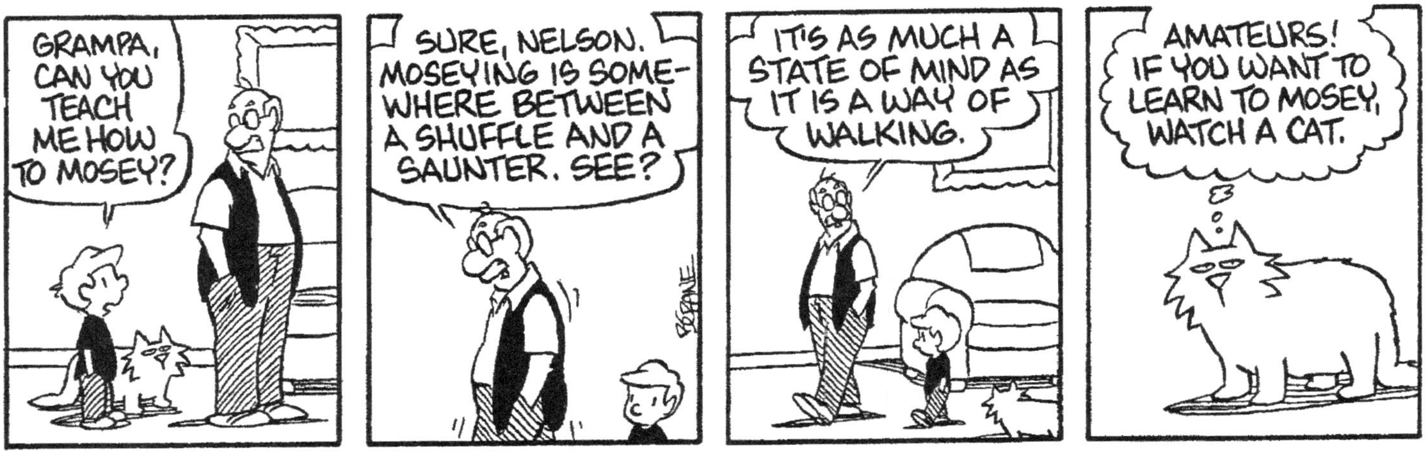
GRAMPA, CAN YOU TEACH ME HOW TO MOSEY?
SURE, NELSON. MOSEYING IS SOMEWHERE BETWEEN A SHUFFLE AND A SAUNTER. SEE?
IT'S AS MUCH A STATE OF MIND AS IT IS A WAY OF WALKING.
AMATEURS! IF YOU WANT TO LEARN TO MOSEY, WATCH A CAT.

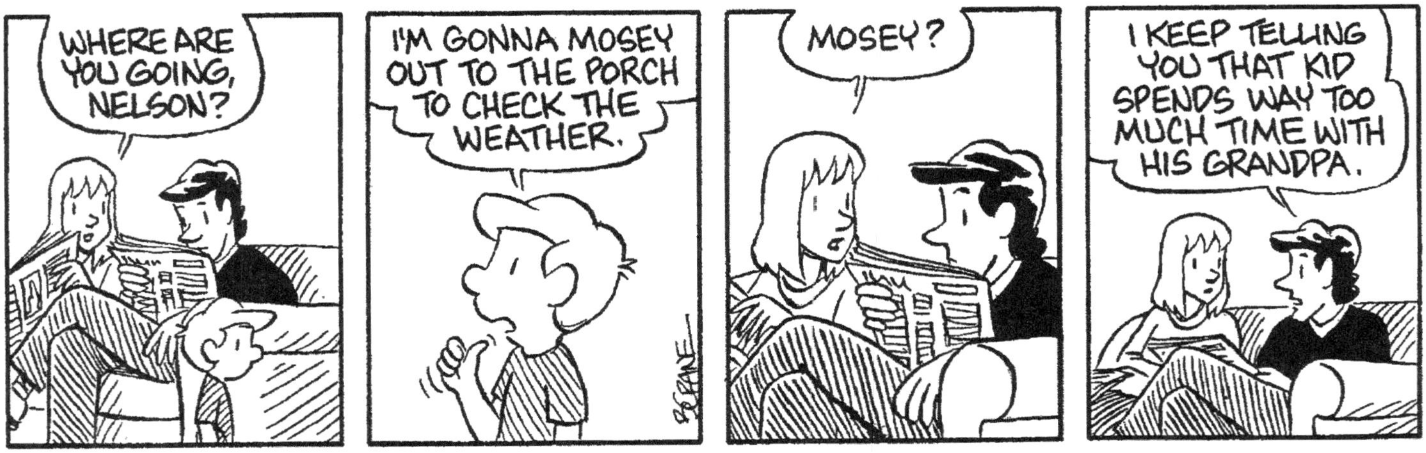
WHERE ARE YOU GOING, NELSON?
I'M GONNA MOSEY OUT TO THE PORCH TO CHECK THE WEATHER.
MOSEY?
I KEEP TELLING YOU THAT KID SPENDS WAY TOO MUCH TIME WITH HIS GRANDPA.

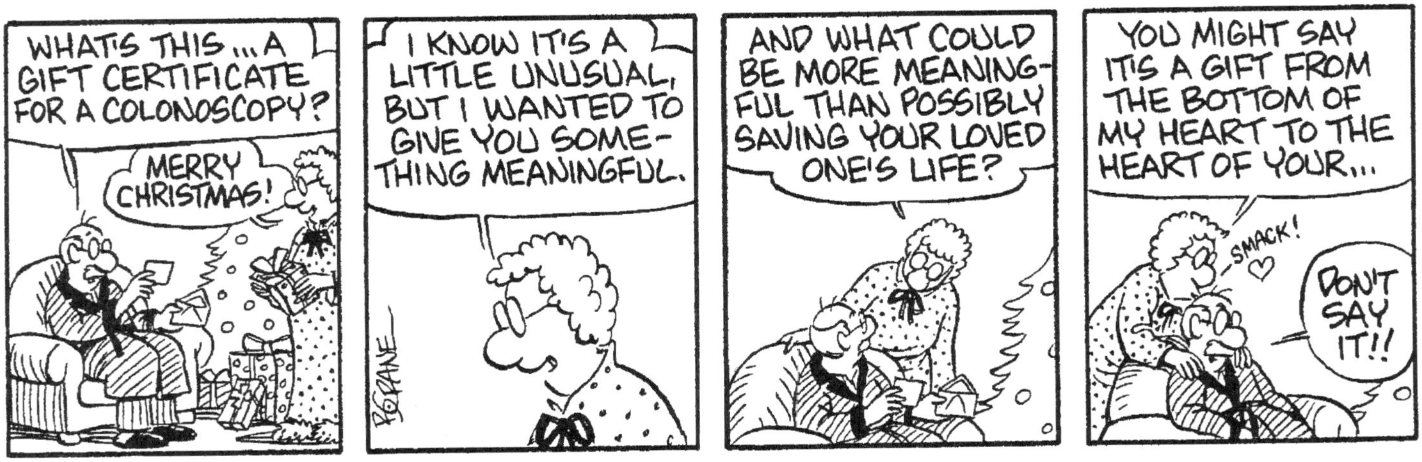
WHAT'S THIS ... A GIFT CERTIFICATE FOR A COLONOSCOPY?
MERRY CHRISTMAS!
I KNOW IT'S A LITTLE UNUSUAL, BUT I WANTED TO GIVE YOU SOMETHING MEANINGFUL.
AND WHAT COULD BE MORE MEANINGFUL THAN POSSIBLY SAVING YOUR LOVED ONE'S LIFE?
YOU MIGHT SAY IT'S A GIFT FROM THE BOTTOM OF MY HEART TO THE HEART OF YOUR...
SMACK!
DON'T SAY IT!!

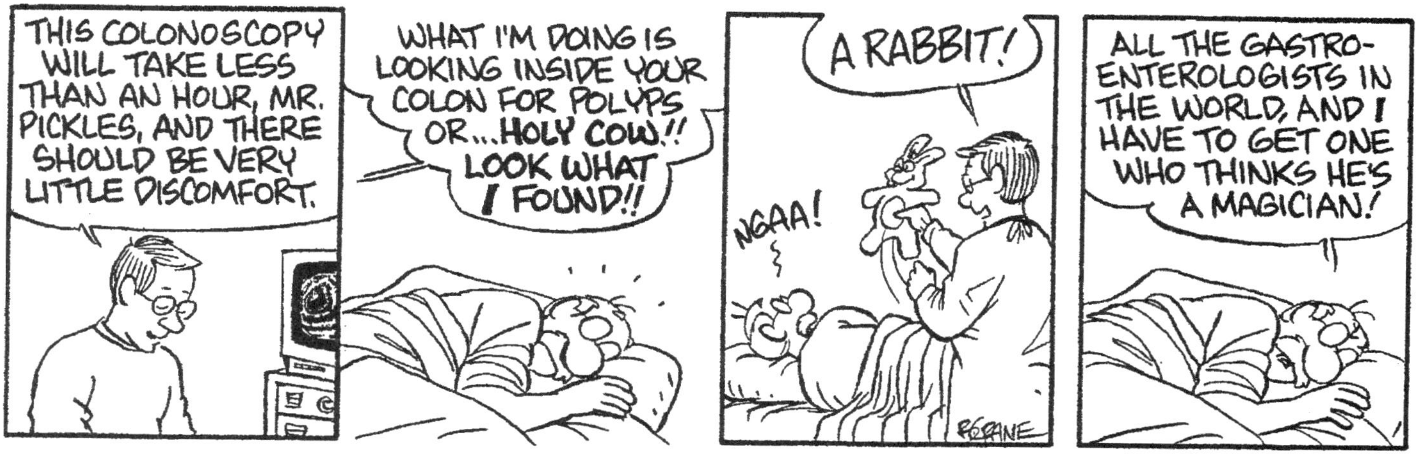
THIS COLONOSCOPY WILL TAKE LESS THAN AN HOUR, MR. PICKLES, AND THERE SHOULD BE VERY LITTLE DISCOMFORT.
WHAT I'M DOING IS LOOKING INSIDE YOUR COLON FOR POLYPS OR...**HOLY COW!!** **LOOK WHAT *I* FOUND!!**
A RABBIT!
NGAA!
ALL THE GASTRO-ENTEROLOGISTS IN THE WORLD, AND **I** HAVE TO GET ONE WHO THINKS HE'S A MAGICIAN!

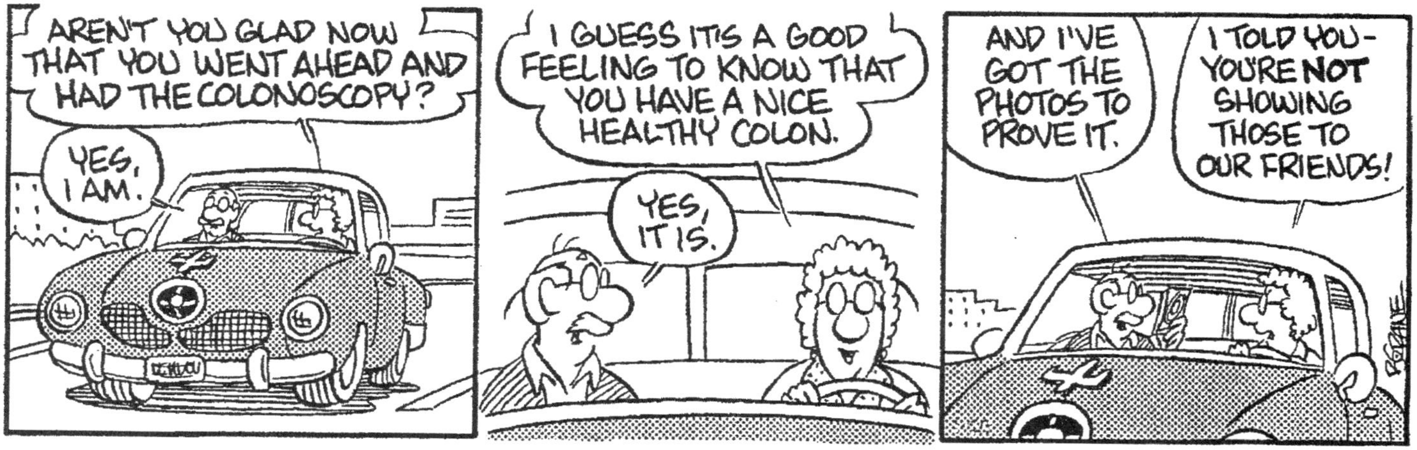
AREN'T YOU GLAD NOW THAT YOU WENT AHEAD AND HAD THE COLONOSCOPY?
YES, I AM.
I GUESS IT'S A GOOD FEELING TO KNOW THAT YOU HAVE A NICE HEALTHY COLON.
YES, IT IS.
AND I'VE GOT THE PHOTOS TO PROVE IT.
I TOLD YOU- YOU'RE **NOT** SHOWING THOSE TO OUR FRIENDS!

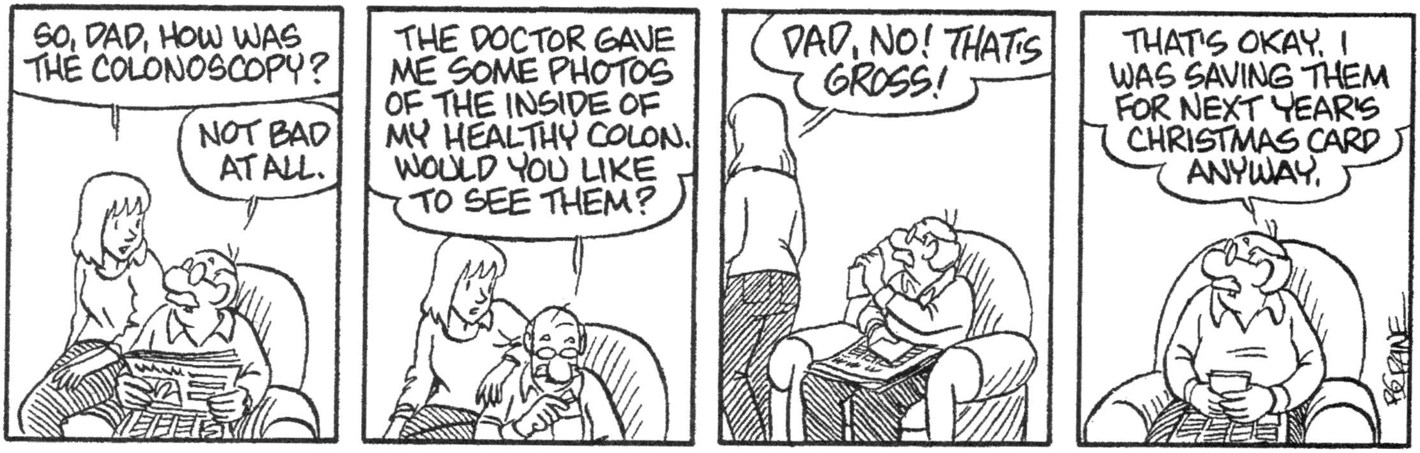
SO, DAD, HOW WAS THE COLONOSCOPY?
NOT BAD AT ALL.
THE DOCTOR GAVE ME SOME PHOTOS OF THE INSIDE OF MY HEALTHY COLON. WOULD YOU LIKE TO SEE THEM?
DAD, NO! THAT'S GROSS!
THAT'S OKAY. I WAS SAVING THEM FOR NEXT YEAR'S CHRISTMAS CARD ANYWAY.

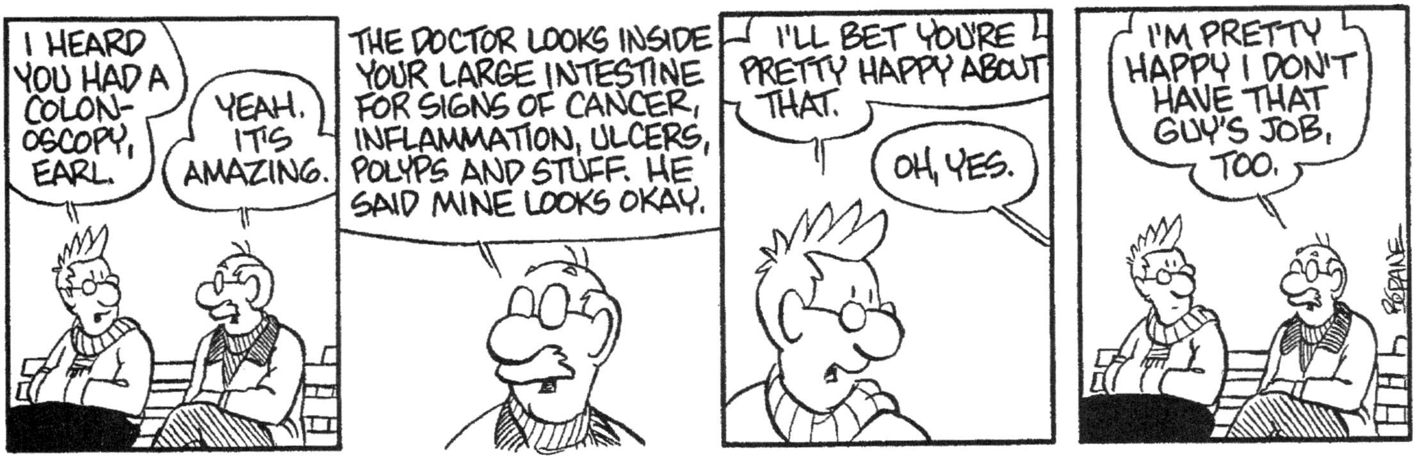
I HEARD YOU HAD A COLON-OSCOPY, EARL.
YEAH. IT'S AMAZING.
THE DOCTOR LOOKS INSIDE YOUR LARGE INTESTINE FOR SIGNS OF CANCER, INFLAMMATION, ULCERS, POLYPS AND STUFF. HE SAID MINE LOOKS OKAY.
I'LL BET YOU'RE PRETTY HAPPY ABOUT THAT.
OH, YES.
I'M PRETTY HAPPY I DON'T HAVE THAT GUY'S JOB, TOO.

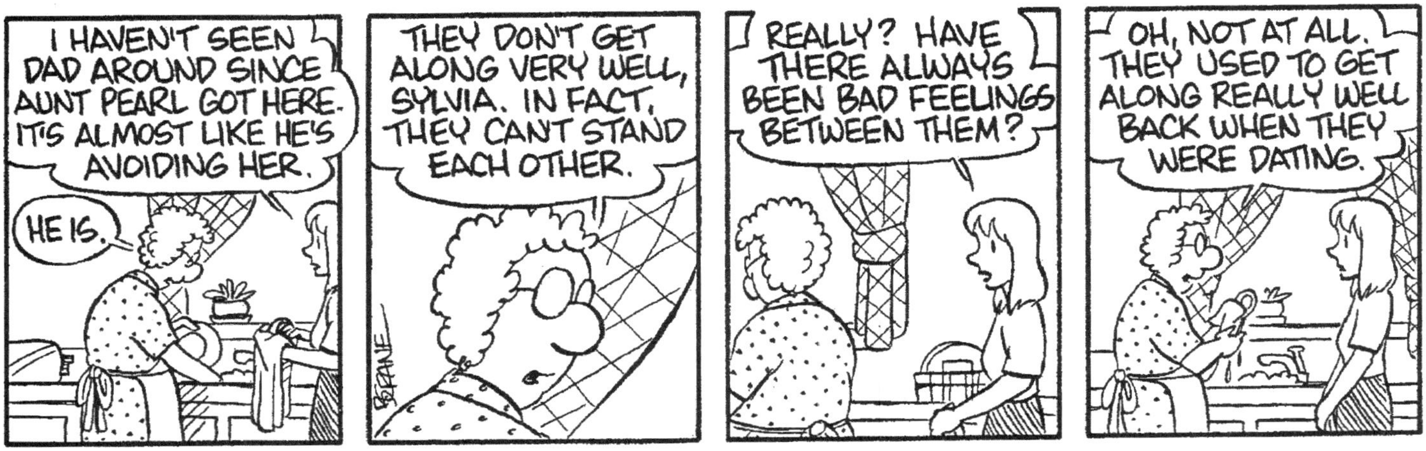
I HAVEN'T SEEN DAD AROUND SINCE AUNT PEARL GOT HERE. IT'S ALMOST LIKE HE'S AVOIDING HER.
HE IS.
THEY DON'T GET ALONG VERY WELL, SYLVIA. IN FACT, THEY CAN'T STAND EACH OTHER.
REALLY? HAVE THERE ALWAYS BEEN BAD FEELINGS BETWEEN THEM?
OH, NOT AT ALL. THEY USED TO GET ALONG REALLY WELL BACK WHEN THEY WERE DATING.

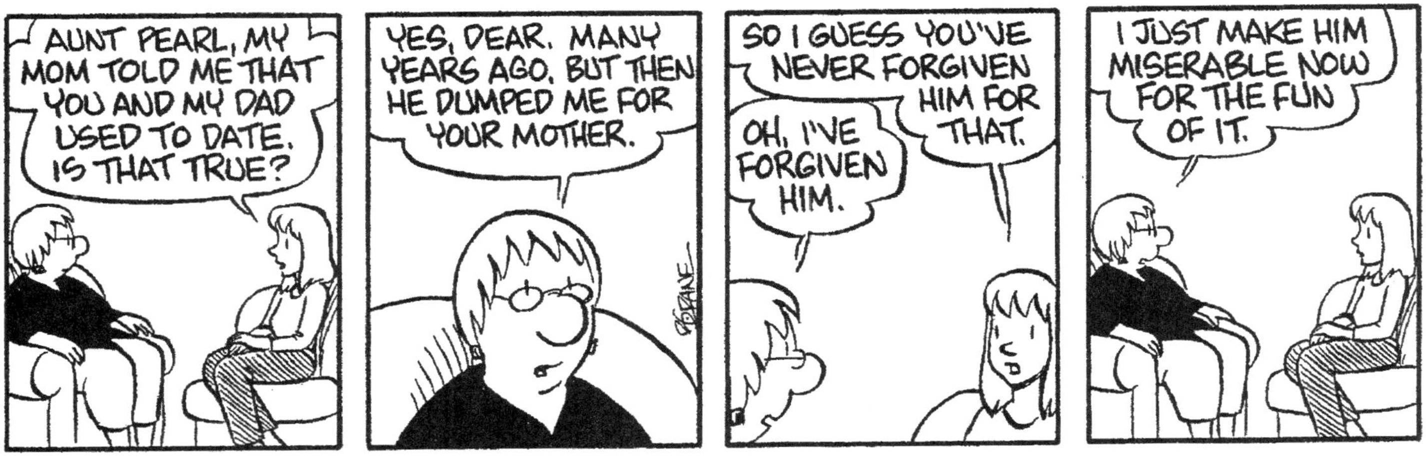
AUNT PEARL, MY MOM TOLD ME THAT YOU AND MY DAD USED TO DATE. IS THAT TRUE?
YES, DEAR. MANY YEARS AGO. BUT THEN HE DUMPED ME FOR YOUR MOTHER.
SO I GUESS YOU'VE NEVER FORGIVEN HIM FOR THAT.
OH, I'VE FORGIVEN HIM.
I JUST MAKE HIM MISERABLE NOW FOR THE FUN OF IT.

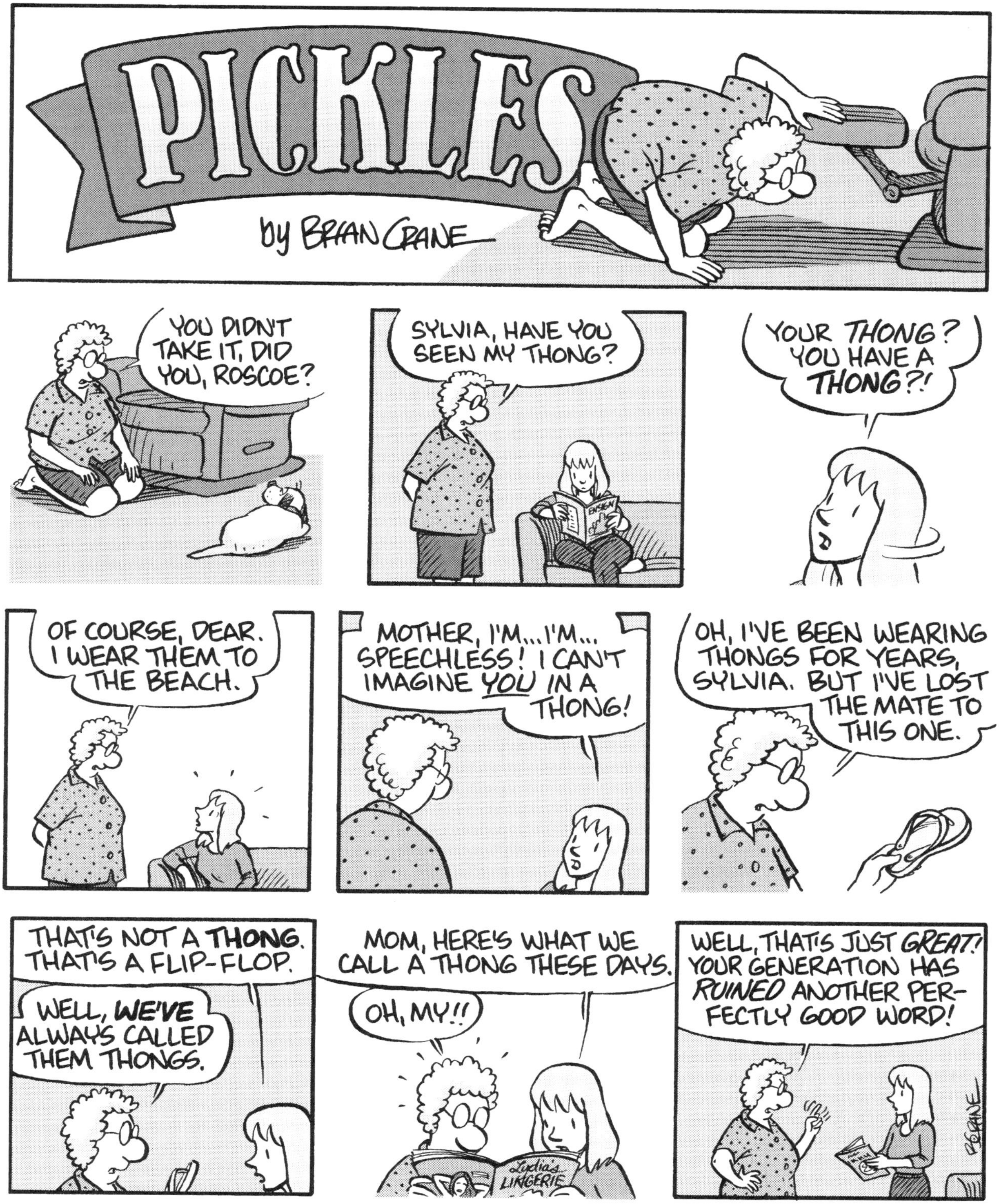
PICKLES
by BRIAN CRANE
YOU DIDN'T TAKE IT, DID YOU, ROSCOE?
SYLVIA, HAVE YOU SEEN MY THONG?
YOUR THONG? YOU HAVE A **THONG**?!
OF COURSE, DEAR. I WEAR THEM TO THE BEACH.
MOTHER, I'M...I'M... SPEECHLESS! I CAN'T IMAGINE YOU IN A THONG!
OH, I'VE BEEN WEARING THONGS FOR YEARS, SYLVIA. BUT I'VE LOST THE MATE TO THIS ONE.
THAT'S NOT A **THONG**. THAT'S A FLIP-FLOP.
WELL, **WE'VE** ALWAYS CALLED THEM THONGS.
MOM, HERE'S WHAT WE CALL A THONG THESE DAYS.
OH, MY!!
Lydia's LINGERIE
WELL, THAT'S JUST *GREAT*! YOUR GENERATION HAS *RUINED* ANOTHER PERFECTLY GOOD WORD!
CRANE

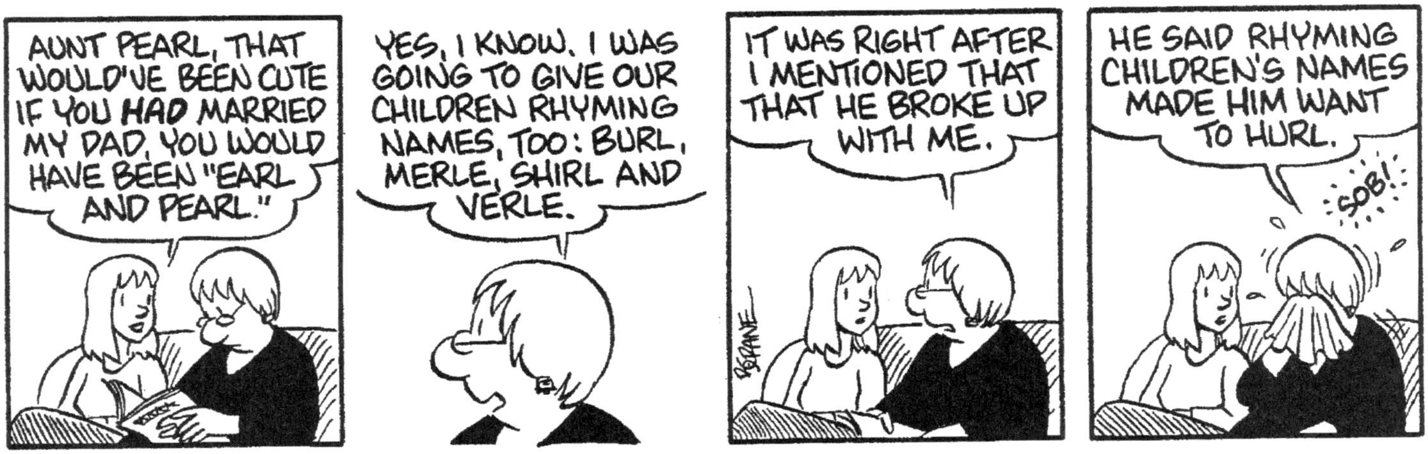
AUNT PEARL, THAT WOULD'VE BEEN CUTE IF YOU **HAD** MARRIED MY DAD. YOU WOULD HAVE BEEN "EARL AND PEARL."
YES, I KNOW. I WAS GOING TO GIVE OUR CHILDREN RHYMING NAMES, TOO: BURL, MERLE, SHIRL AND VERLE.
IT WAS RIGHT AFTER I MENTIONED THAT THAT HE BROKE UP WITH ME.
HE SAID RHYMING CHILDREN'S NAMES MADE HIM WANT TO HURL.
SOB!

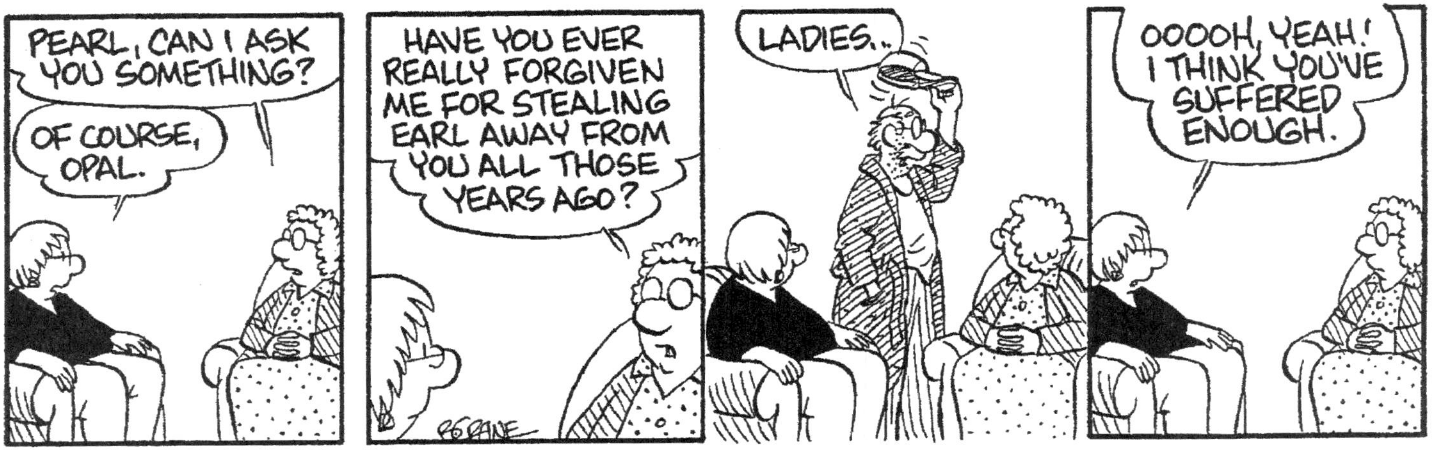
PEARL, CAN I ASK YOU SOMETHING?
OF COURSE, OPAL.
HAVE YOU EVER REALLY FORGIVEN ME FOR STEALING EARL AWAY FROM YOU ALL THOSE YEARS AGO?
LADIES..
OOOOH, YEAH! I THINK YOU'VE SUFFERED ENOUGH.

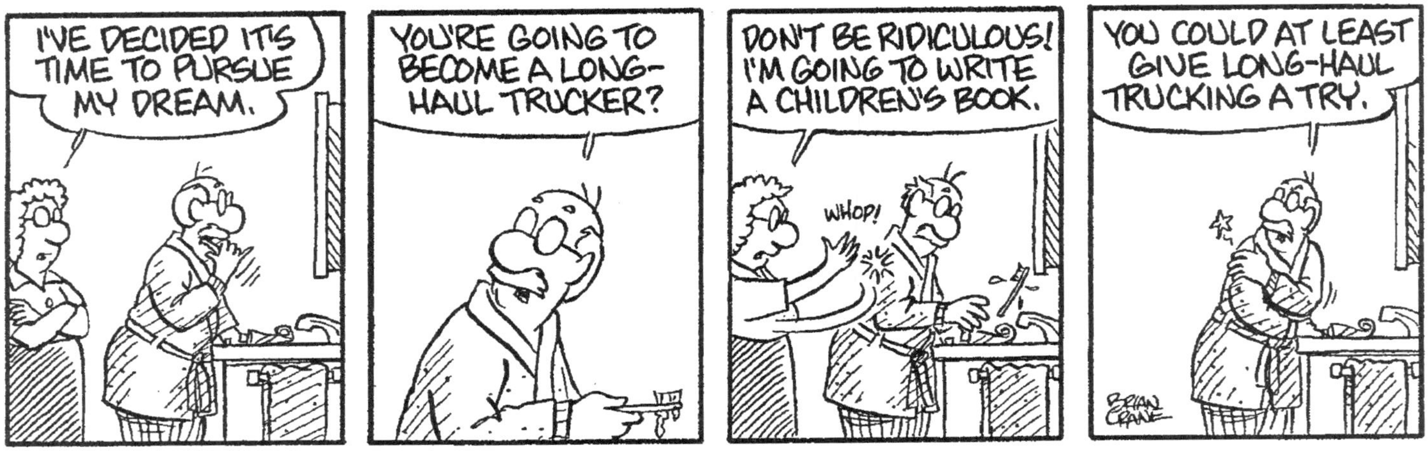
I'VE DECIDED IT'S TIME TO PURSUE MY DREAM.
YOU'RE GOING TO BECOME A LONG-HAUL TRUCKER?
DON'T BE RIDICULOUS! I'M GOING TO WRITE A CHILDREN'S BOOK.
WHOP!
YOU COULD AT LEAST GIVE LONG-HAUL TRUCKING A TRY.
BRIAN CRANE

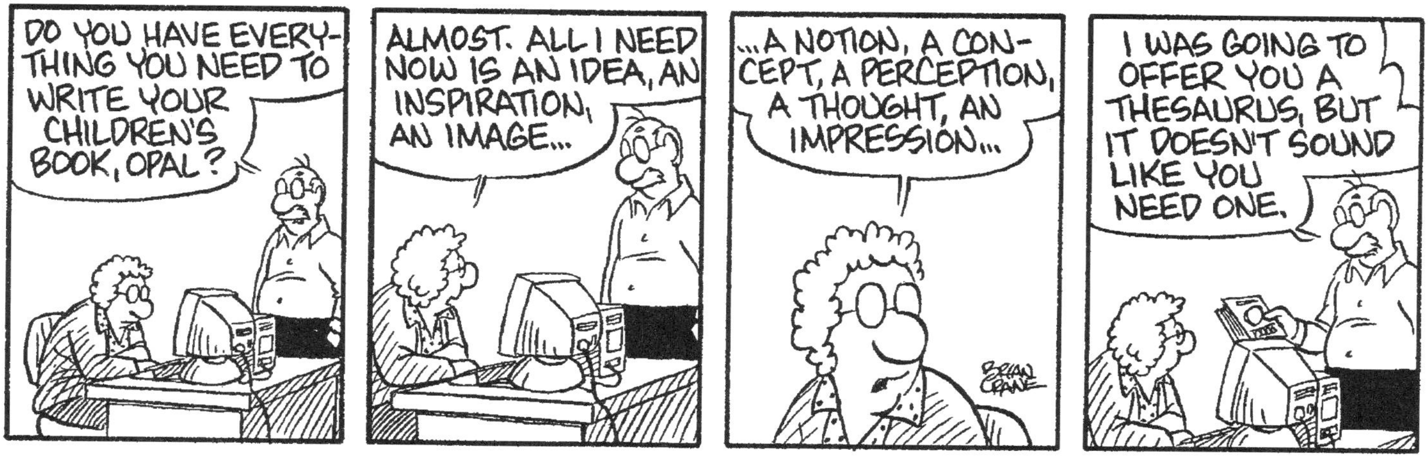
DO YOU HAVE EVERYTHING YOU NEED TO WRITE YOUR CHILDREN'S BOOK, OPAL?
ALMOST. ALL I NEED NOW IS AN IDEA, AN INSPIRATION, AN IMAGE...
...A NOTION, A CONCEPT, A PERCEPTION, A THOUGHT, AN IMPRESSION...
BRIAN CRANE
I WAS GOING TO OFFER YOU A THESAURUS, BUT IT DOESN'T SOUND LIKE YOU NEED ONE.

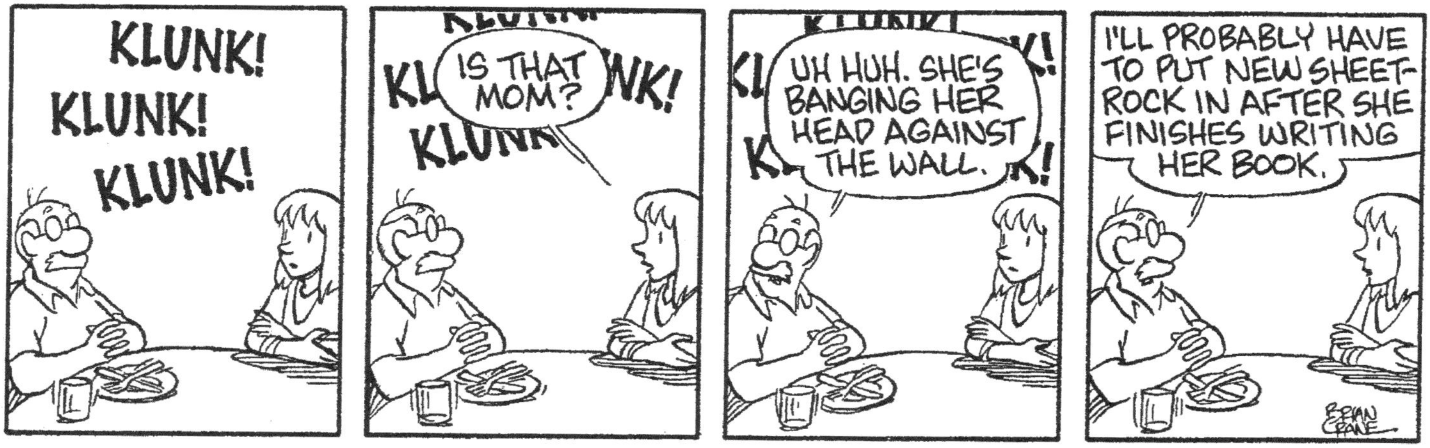
KLUNK!
KLUNK!
KLUNK!
IS THAT MOM?
UH HUH. SHE'S BANGING HER HEAD AGAINST THE WALL.
I'LL PROBABLY HAVE TO PUT NEW SHEET-ROCK IN AFTER SHE FINISHES WRITING HER BOOK.
BRIAN CRANE

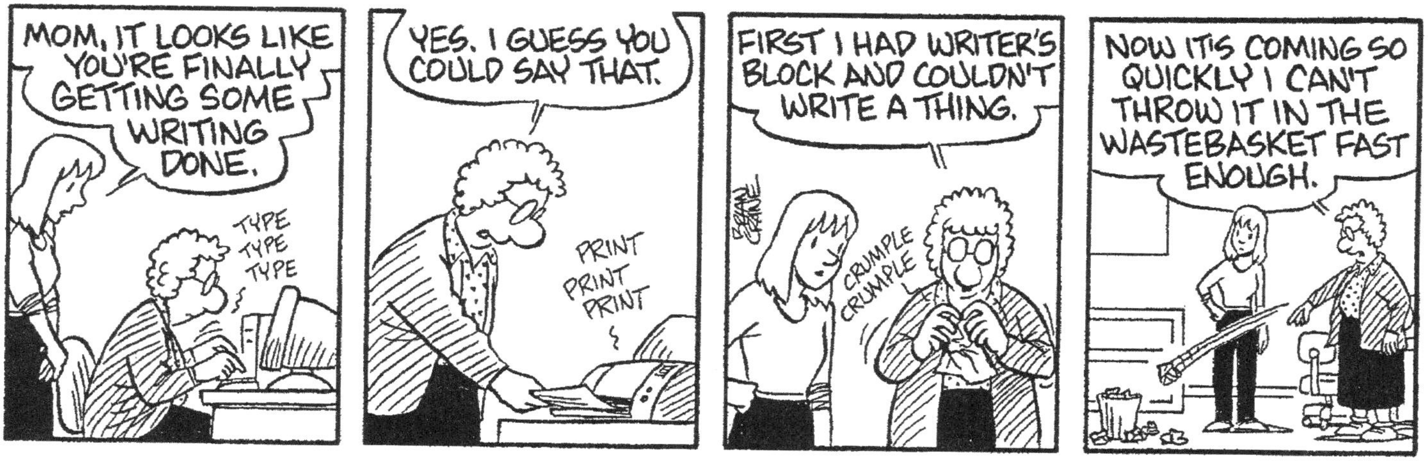
MOM, IT LOOKS LIKE YOU'RE FINALLY GETTING SOME WRITING DONE.
TYPE TYPE TYPE
YES. I GUESS YOU COULD SAY THAT.
PRINT PRINT PRINT
FIRST I HAD WRITER'S BLOCK AND COULDN'T WRITE A THING.
CRUMPLE CRUMPLE
NOW IT'S COMING SO QUICKLY I CAN'T THROW IT IN THE WASTEBASKET FAST ENOUGH.

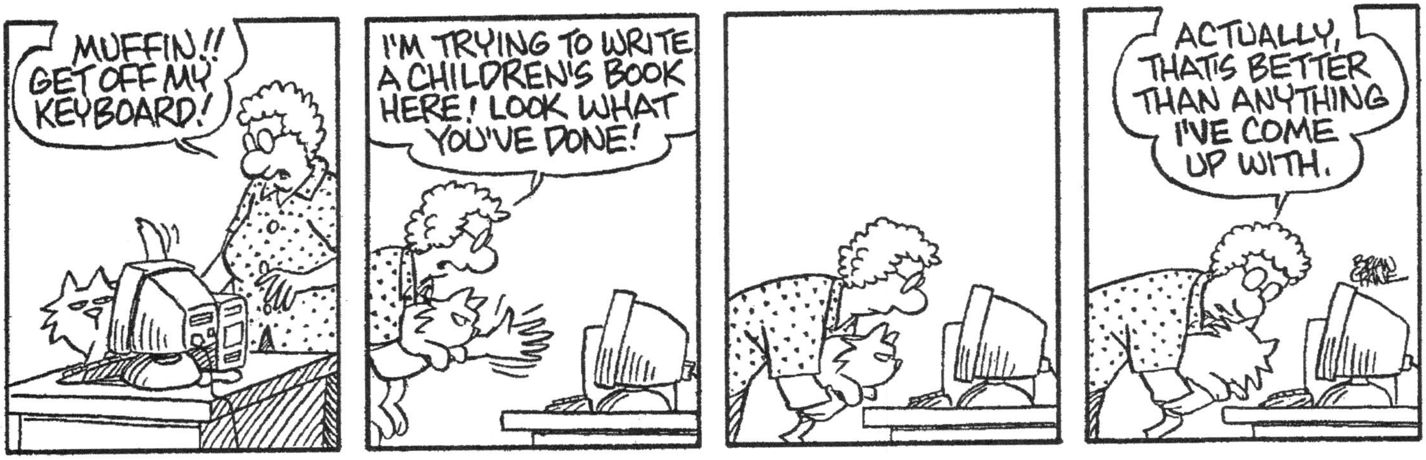
MUFFIN!! GET OFF MY KEYBOARD!
I'M TRYING TO WRITE A CHILDREN'S BOOK HERE! LOOK WHAT YOU'VE DONE!
ACTUALLY, THAT'S BETTER THAN ANYTHING I'VE COME UP WITH.

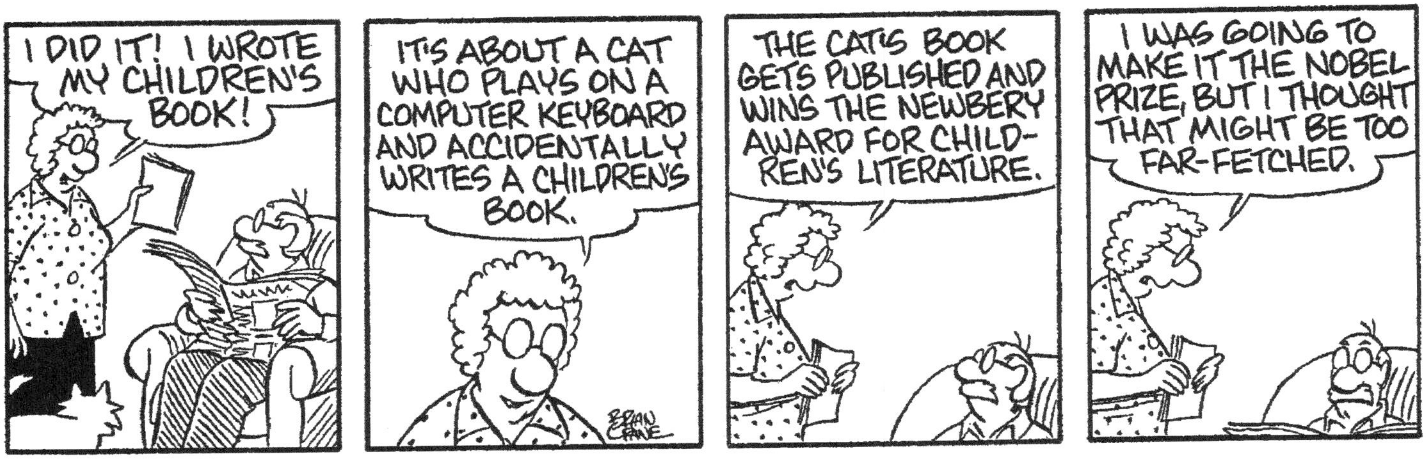
I DID IT! I WROTE MY CHILDREN'S BOOK!
IT'S ABOUT A CAT WHO PLAYS ON A COMPUTER KEYBOARD AND ACCIDENTALLY WRITES A CHILDREN'S BOOK.
THE CAT'S BOOK GETS PUBLISHED AND WINS THE NEWBERY AWARD FOR CHILD-REN'S LITERATURE.
I WAS GOING TO MAKE IT THE NOBEL PRIZE, BUT I THOUGHT THAT MIGHT BE TOO FAR-FETCHED.

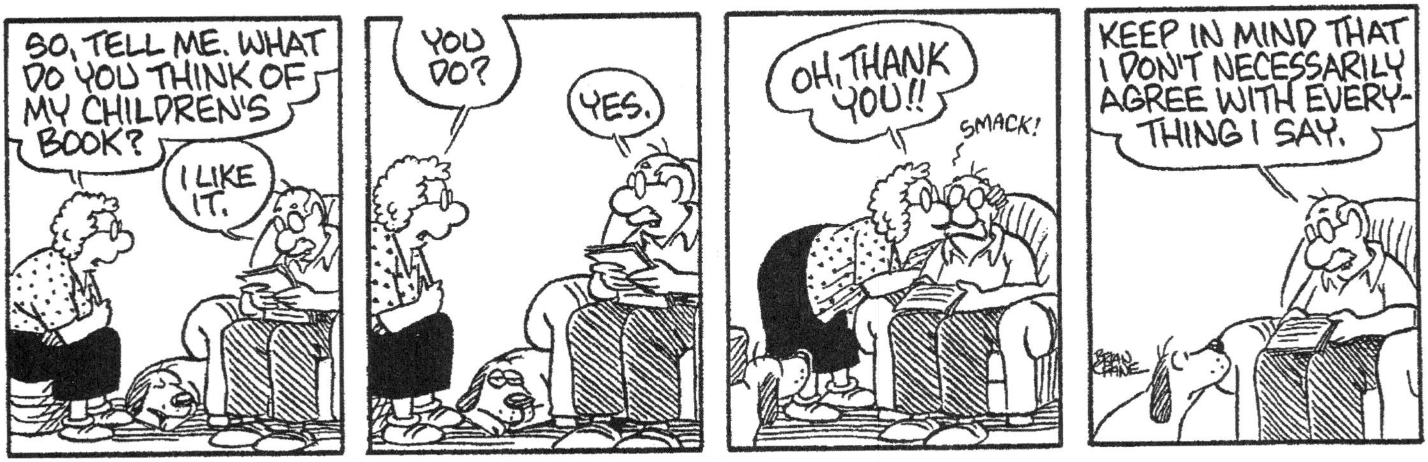
SO, TELL ME. WHAT DO YOU THINK OF MY CHILDREN'S BOOK?
I LIKE IT.
YOU DO?
YES.
OH, THANK YOU!!
SMACK!
KEEP IN MIND THAT I DON'T NECESSARILY AGREE WITH EVERY-THING I SAY.

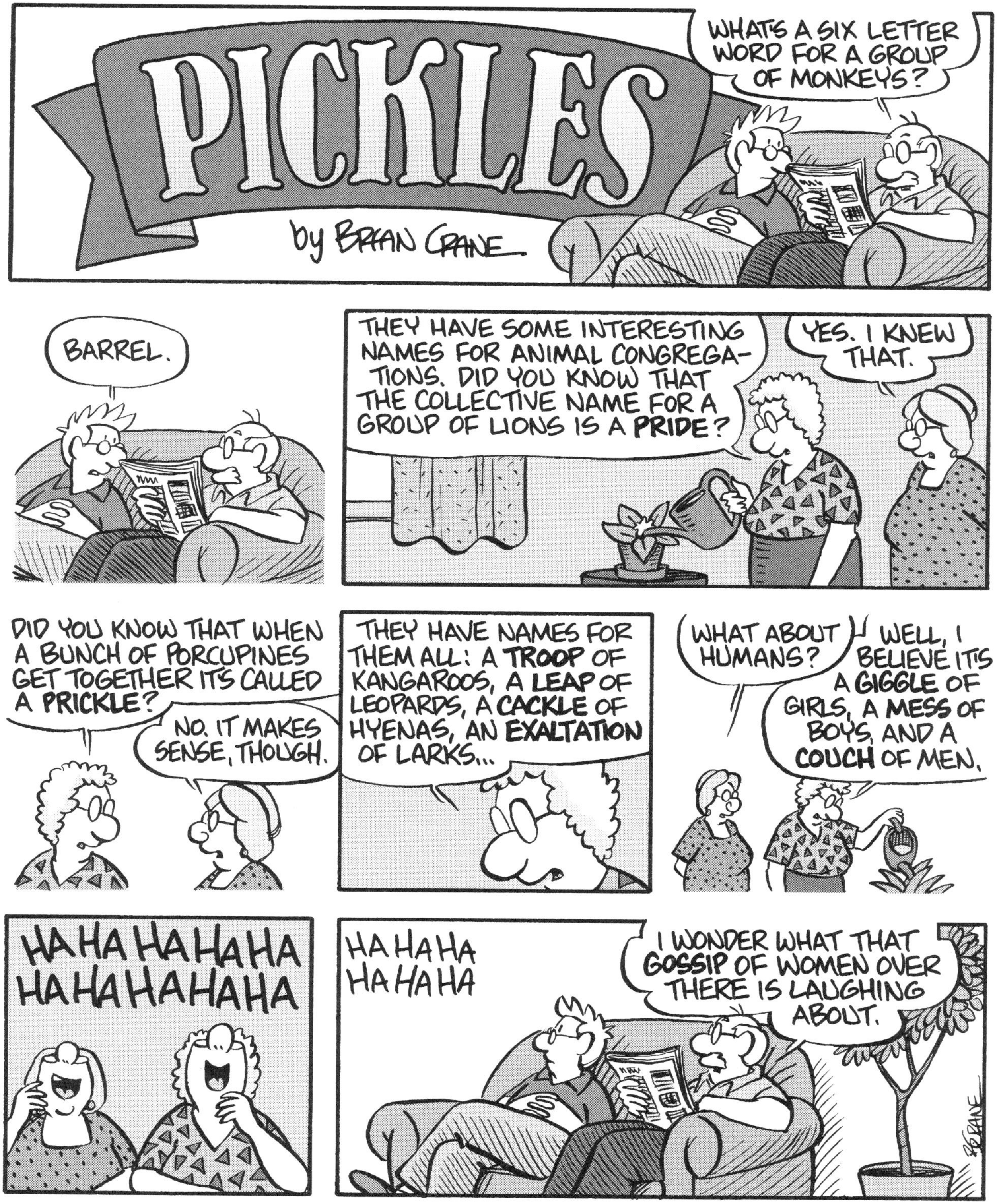
PICKLES
by BRIAN CRANE
WHAT'S A SIX LETTER WORD FOR A GROUP OF MONKEYS?
BARREL.
THEY HAVE SOME INTERESTING NAMES FOR ANIMAL CONGREGATIONS. DID YOU KNOW THAT THE COLLECTIVE NAME FOR A GROUP OF LIONS IS A PRIDE?
YES. I KNEW THAT.
DID YOU KNOW THAT WHEN A BUNCH OF PORCUPINES GET TOGETHER IT'S CALLED A PRICKLE?
NO. IT MAKES SENSE, THOUGH.
THEY HAVE NAMES FOR THEM ALL: A TROOP OF KANGAROOS, A LEAP OF LEOPARDS, A CACKLE OF HYENAS, AN EXALTATION OF LARKS...
WHAT ABOUT HUMANS?
WELL, I BELIEVE IT'S A GIGGLE OF GIRLS, A MESS OF BOYS, AND A COUCH OF MEN.
HA HA HA HA HA HA HA HA HA HA HA HA HA
HA HA HA HA HA HA HA
I WONDER WHAT THAT GOSSIP OF WOMEN OVER THERE IS LAUGHING ABOUT.
BCRANE

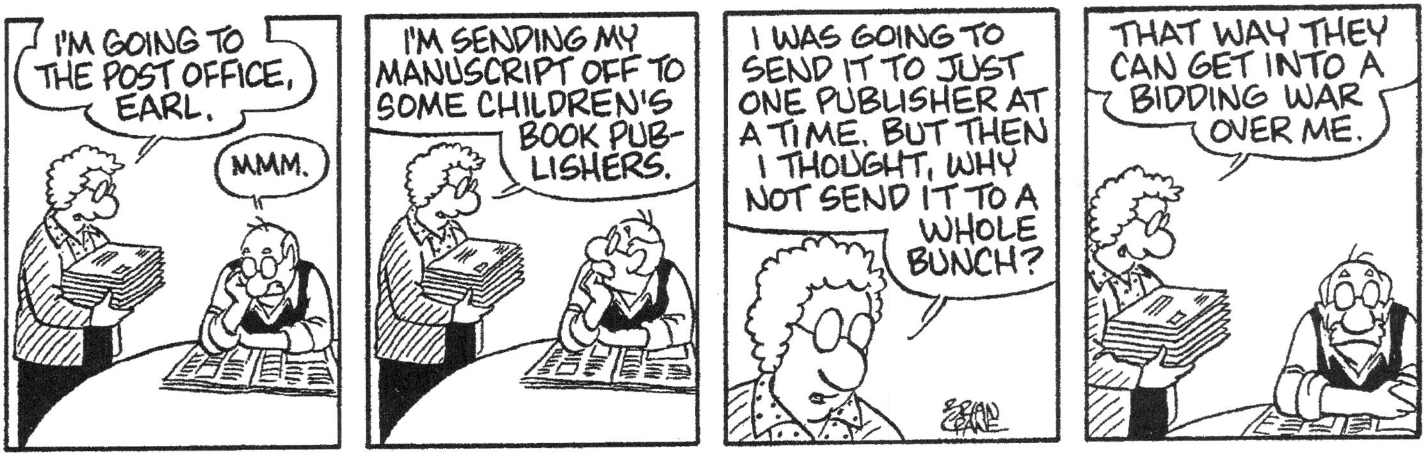
I'M GOING TO THE POST OFFICE, EARL.
MMM.
I'M SENDING MY MANUSCRIPT OFF TO SOME CHILDREN'S BOOK PUBLISHERS.
I WAS GOING TO SEND IT TO JUST ONE PUBLISHER AT A TIME. BUT THEN I THOUGHT, WHY NOT SEND IT TO A WHOLE BUNCH?
BRIAN CRANE
THAT WAY THEY CAN GET INTO A BIDDING WAR OVER ME.

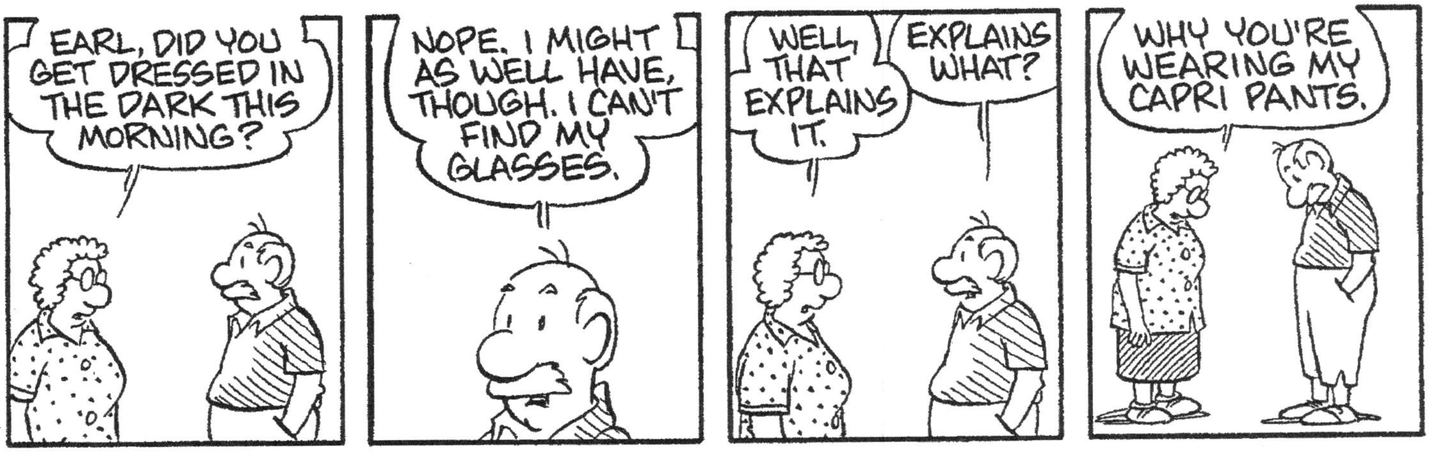
EARL, DID YOU GET DRESSED IN THE DARK THIS MORNING?
NOPE. I MIGHT AS WELL HAVE, THOUGH. I CAN'T FIND MY GLASSES.
WELL, THAT EXPLAINS IT.
EXPLAINS WHAT?
WHY YOU'RE WEARING MY CAPRI PANTS.

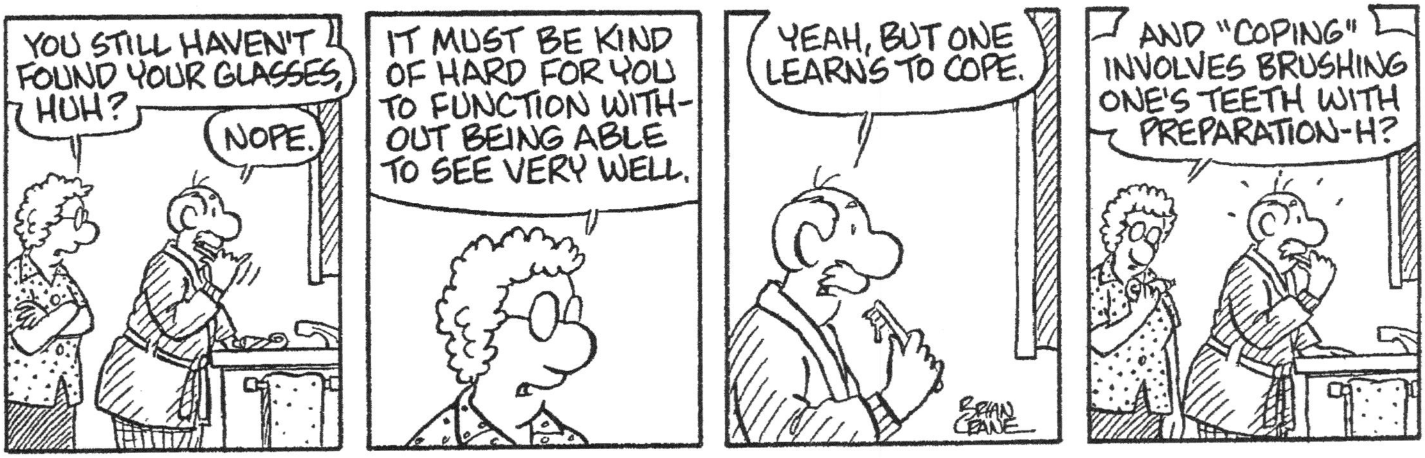
YOU STILL HAVEN'T FOUND YOUR GLASSES, HUH?
NOPE.
IT MUST BE KIND OF HARD FOR YOU TO FUNCTION WITHOUT BEING ABLE TO SEE VERY WELL.
YEAH, BUT ONE LEARNS TO COPE.
BRIAN CRANE
AND "COPING" INVOLVES BRUSHING ONE'S TEETH WITH PREPARATION-H?

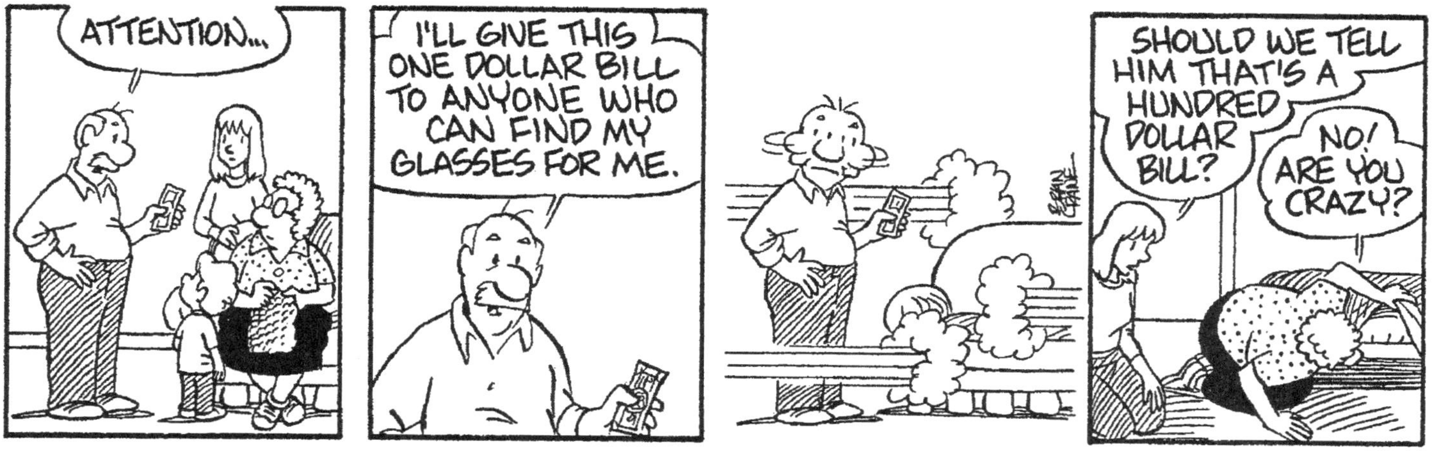
ATTENTION...
I'LL GIVE THIS ONE DOLLAR BILL TO ANYONE WHO CAN FIND MY GLASSES FOR ME.
SHOULD WE TELL HIM THAT'S A HUNDRED DOLLAR BILL?
NO! ARE YOU CRAZY?

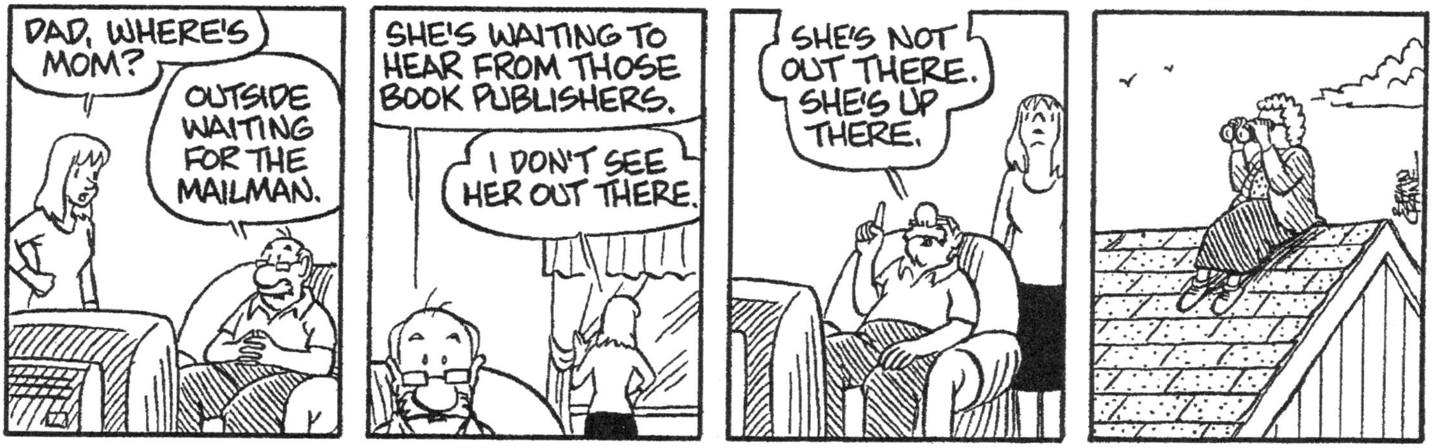
DAD, WHERE'S MOM?
OUTSIDE WAITING FOR THE MAILMAN.
SHE'S WAITING TO HEAR FROM THOSE BOOK PUBLISHERS.
I DON'T SEE HER OUT THERE.
SHE'S NOT OUT THERE. SHE'S UP THERE.

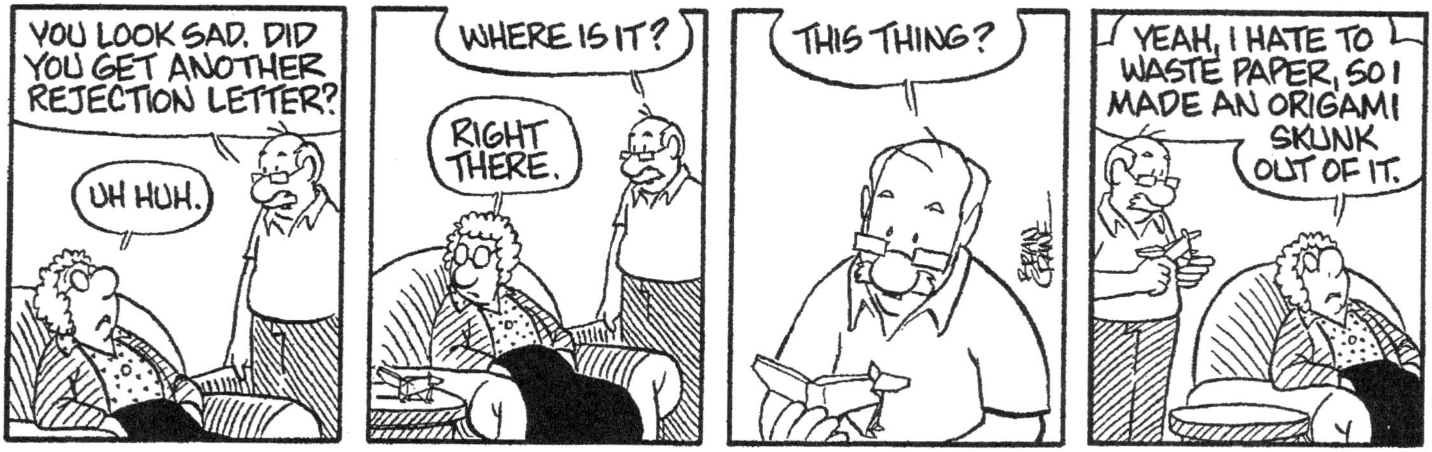
YOU LOOK SAD. DID YOU GET ANOTHER REJECTION LETTER?
UH HUH.
WHERE IS IT?
RIGHT THERE.
THIS THING?
YEAH, I HATE TO WASTE PAPER, SO I MADE AN ORIGAMI SKUNK OUT OF IT.

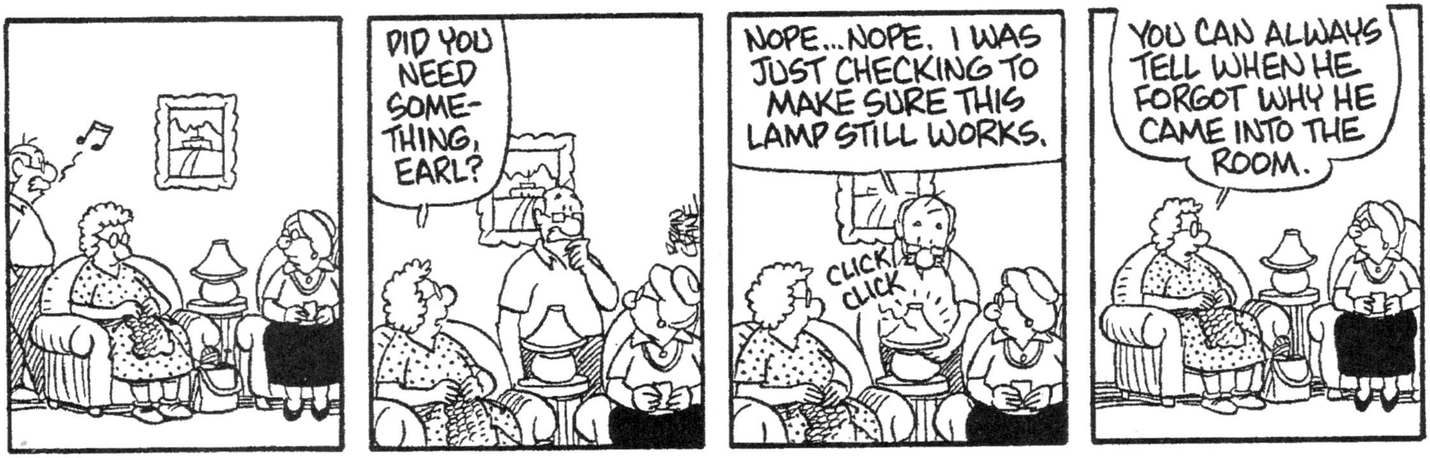
DID YOU NEED SOME-THING, EARL?
NOPE...NOPE. I WAS JUST CHECKING TO MAKE SURE THIS LAMP STILL WORKS.
CLICK CLICK
YOU CAN ALWAYS TELL WHEN HE FORGOT WHY HE CAME INTO THE ROOM.

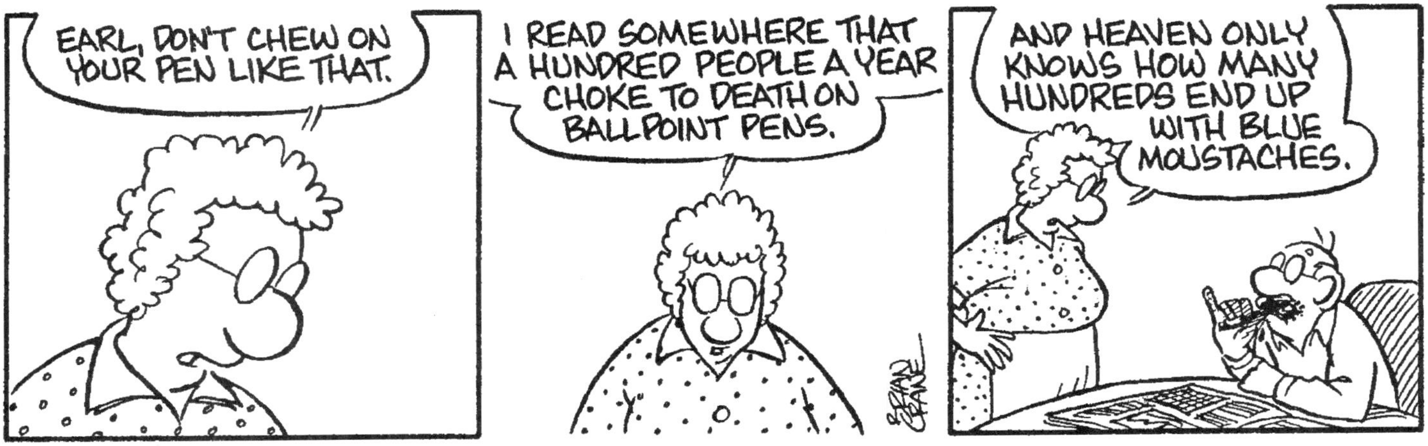
EARL, DON'T CHEW ON YOUR PEN LIKE THAT.
I READ SOMEWHERE THAT A HUNDRED PEOPLE A YEAR CHOKE TO DEATH ON BALLPOINT PENS.
AND HEAVEN ONLY KNOWS HOW MANY HUNDREDS END UP WITH BLUE MOUSTACHES.

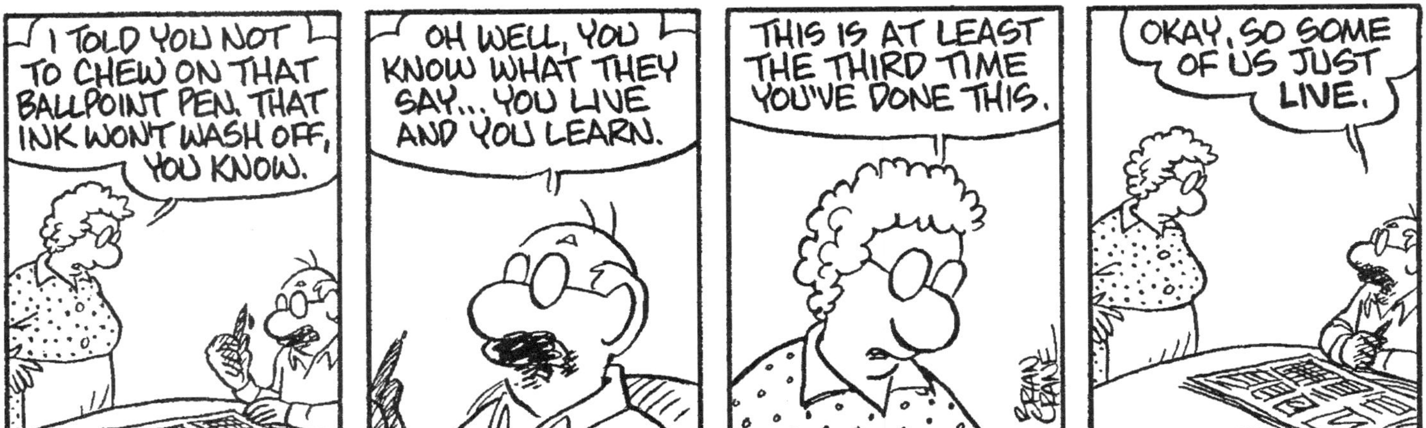
I TOLD YOU NOT TO CHEW ON THAT BALLPOINT PEN. THAT INK WON'T WASH OFF, YOU KNOW.
OH WELL, YOU KNOW WHAT THEY SAY... YOU LIVE AND YOU LEARN.
THIS IS AT LEAST THE THIRD TIME YOU'VE DONE THIS.
OKAY, SO SOME OF US JUST LIVE.

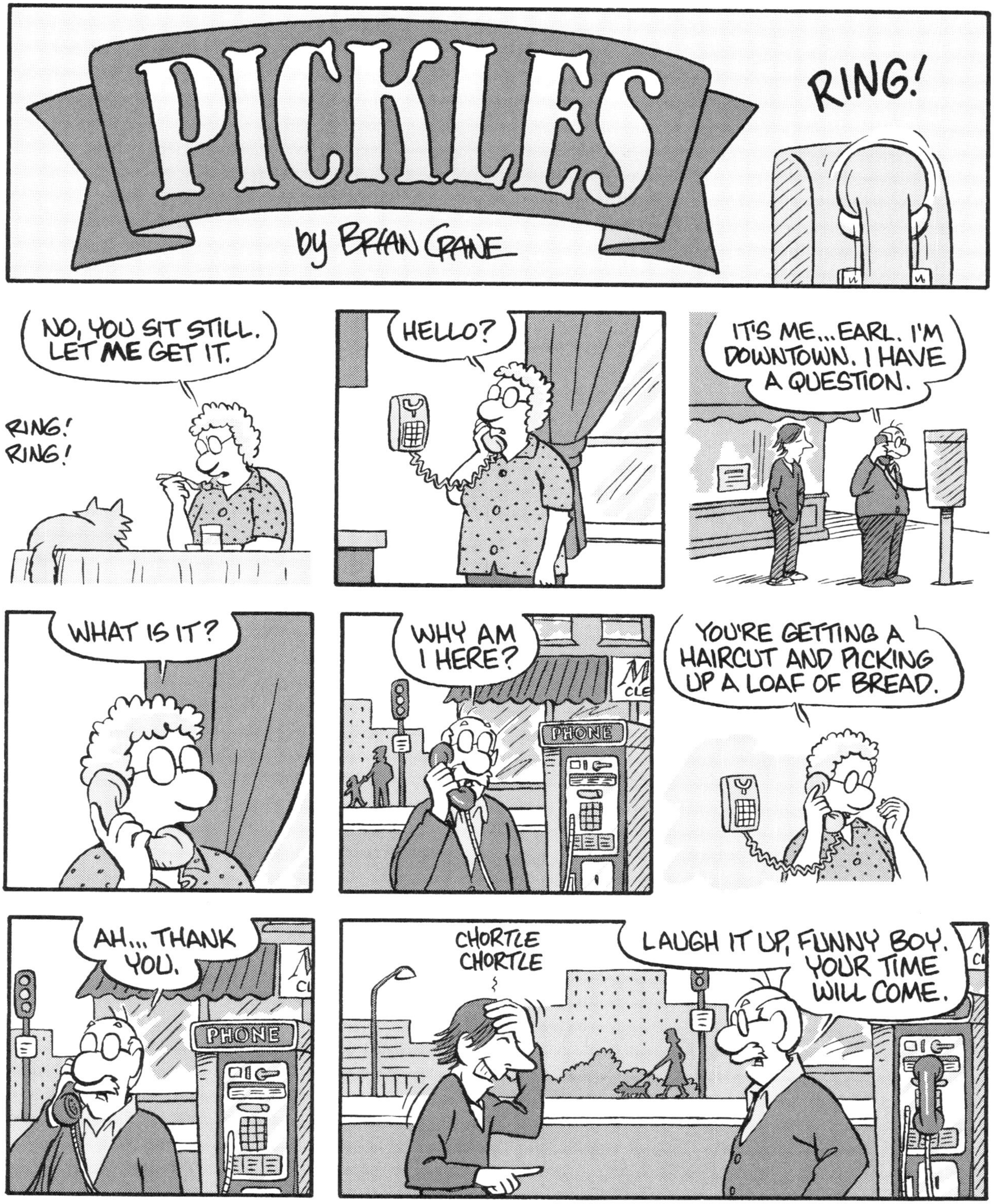
PICKLES
by BRIAN CRANE
RING!
NO, YOU SIT STILL. LET ME GET IT.
RING! RING!
HELLO?
IT'S ME...EARL. I'M DOWNTOWN. I HAVE A QUESTION.
WHAT IS IT?
WHY AM I HERE?
PHONE
YOU'RE GETTING A HAIRCUT AND PICKING UP A LOAF OF BREAD.
AH... THANK YOU.
PHONE
CHORTLE CHORTLE
LAUGH IT UP, FUNNY BOY. YOUR TIME WILL COME.

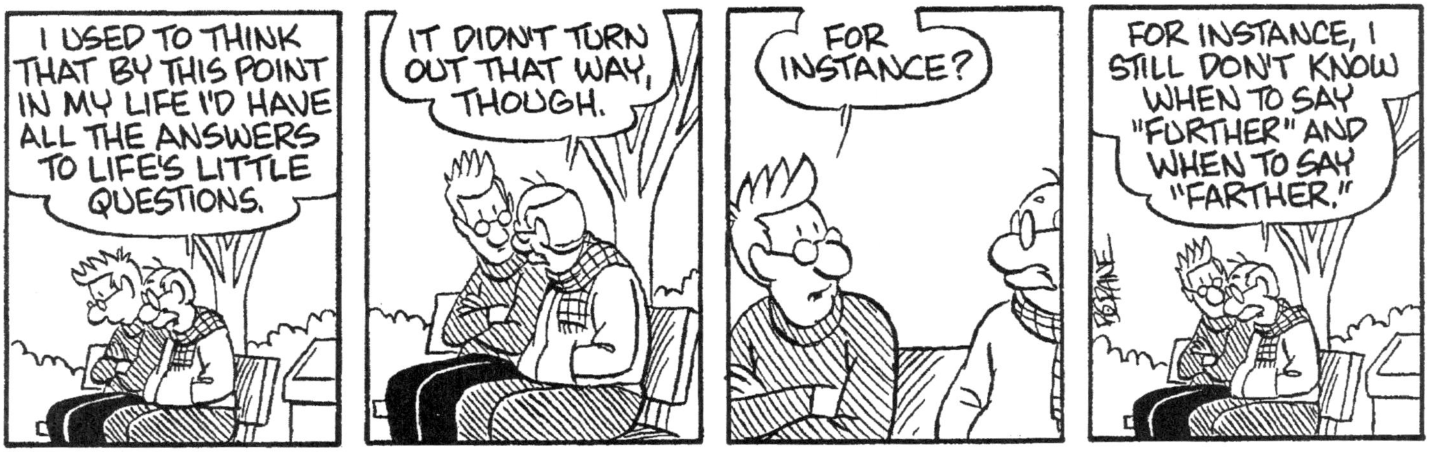
I USED TO THINK THAT BY THIS POINT IN MY LIFE I'D HAVE ALL THE ANSWERS TO LIFE'S LITTLE QUESTIONS.
IT DIDN'T TURN OUT THAT WAY, THOUGH.
FOR INSTANCE?
FOR INSTANCE, I STILL DON'T KNOW WHEN TO SAY "FURTHER" AND WHEN TO SAY "FARTHER."

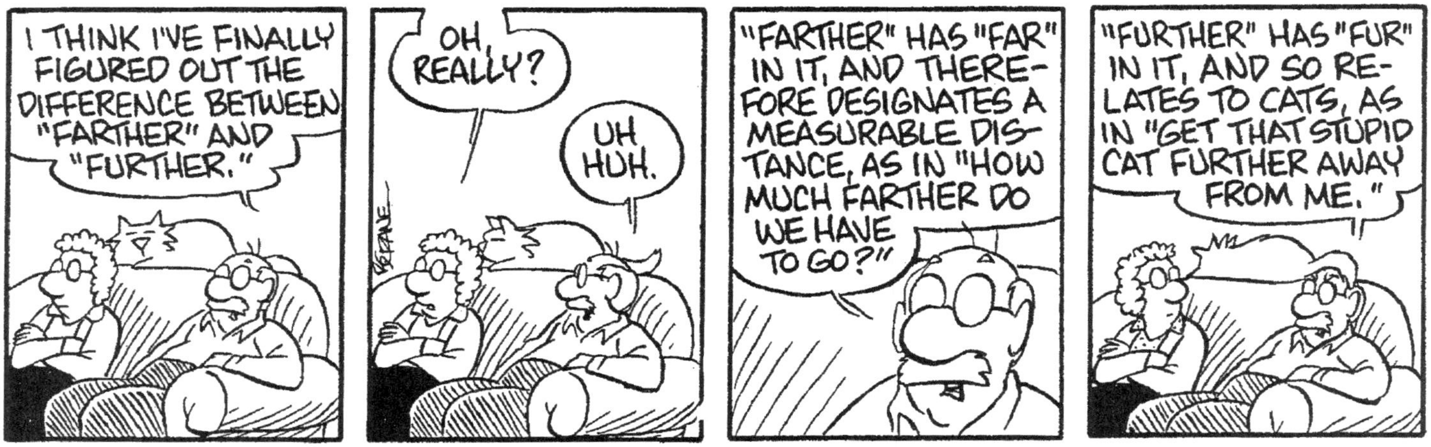
I THINK I'VE FINALLY FIGURED OUT THE DIFFERENCE BETWEEN "FARTHER" AND "FURTHER."
OH, REALLY?
UH HUH.
"FARTHER" HAS "FAR" IN IT, AND THERE-FORE DESIGNATES A MEASURABLE DIS-TANCE, AS IN "HOW MUCH FARTHER DO WE HAVE TO GO?"
"FURTHER" HAS "FUR" IN IT, AND SO RE-LATES TO CATS, AS IN "GET THAT STUPID CAT FURTHER AWAY FROM ME."

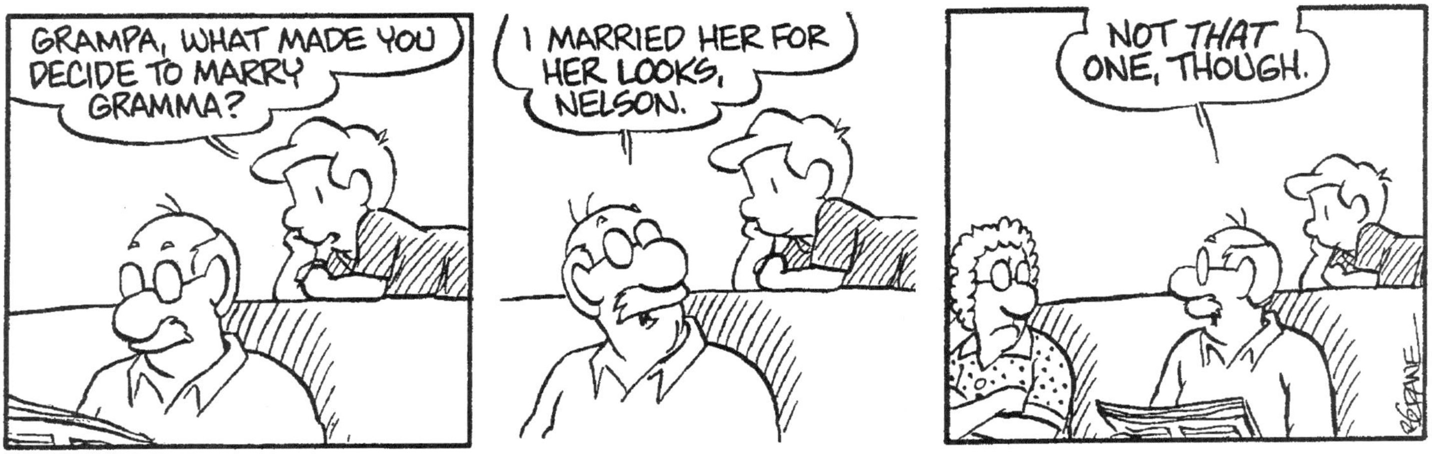
GRAMPA, WHAT MADE YOU DECIDE TO MARRY GRAMMA?
I MARRIED HER FOR HER LOOKS, NELSON.
NOT *THAT* ONE, THOUGH.

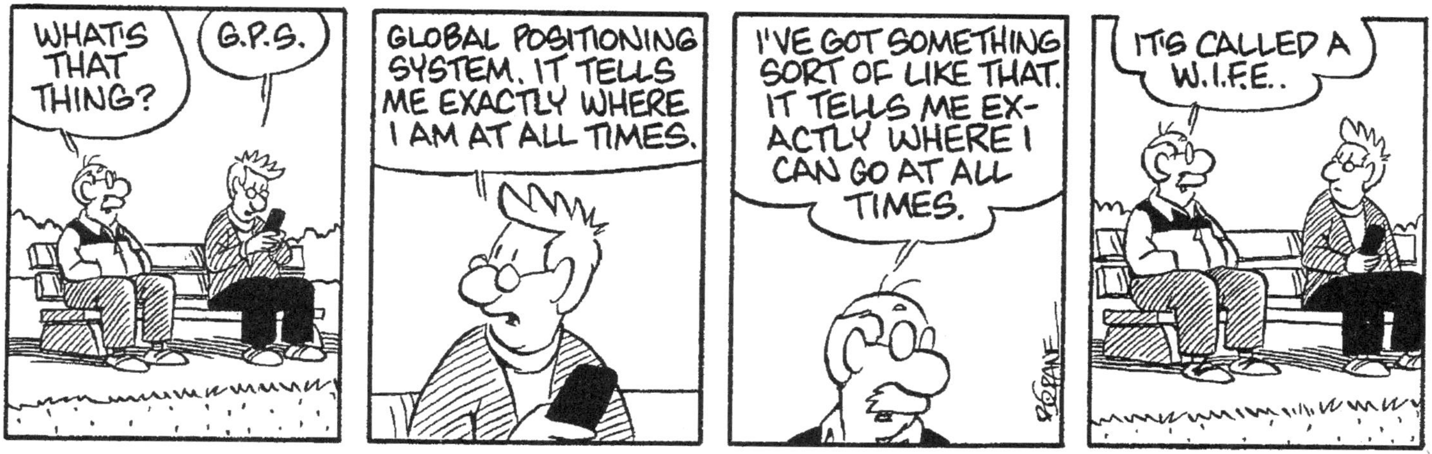
WHAT'S THAT THING?
G.P.S.
GLOBAL POSITIONING SYSTEM. IT TELLS ME EXACTLY WHERE I AM AT ALL TIMES.
I'VE GOT SOMETHING SORT OF LIKE THAT. IT TELLS ME EXACTLY WHERE I CAN GO AT ALL TIMES.
IT'S CALLED A W.I.F.E..

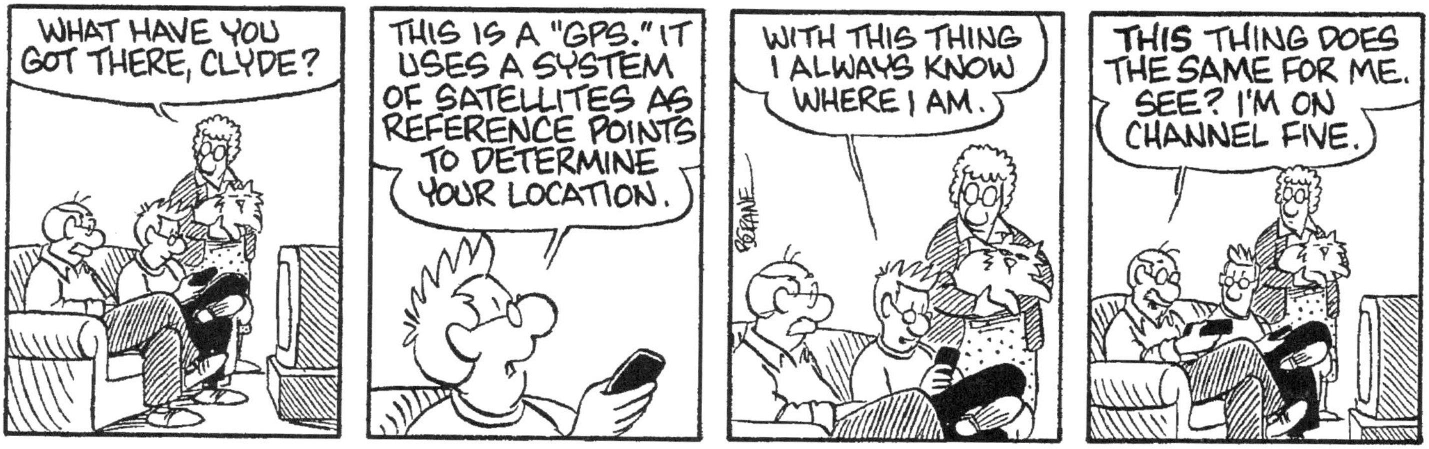
WHAT HAVE YOU GOT THERE, CLYDE?
THIS IS A "GPS." IT USES A SYSTEM OF SATELLITES AS REFERENCE POINTS TO DETERMINE YOUR LOCATION.
WITH THIS THING I ALWAYS KNOW WHERE I AM.
THIS THING DOES THE SAME FOR ME. SEE? I'M ON CHANNEL FIVE.

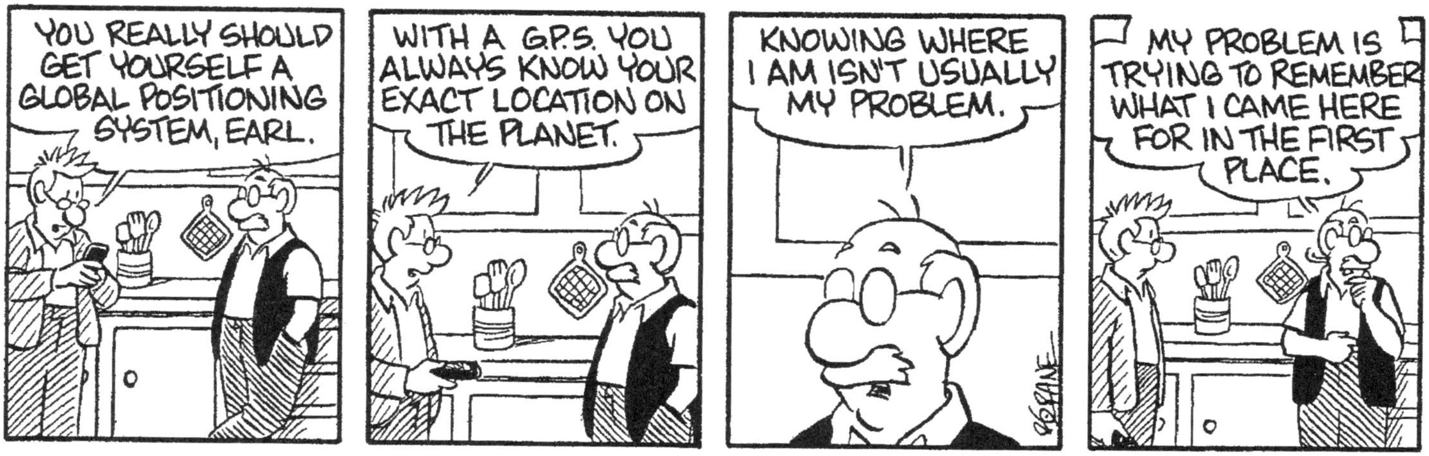
YOU REALLY SHOULD GET YOURSELF A GLOBAL POSITIONING SYSTEM, EARL.
WITH A G.P.S. YOU ALWAYS KNOW YOUR EXACT LOCATION ON THE PLANET.
KNOWING WHERE I AM ISN'T USUALLY MY PROBLEM.
MY PROBLEM IS TRYING TO REMEMBER WHAT I CAME HERE FOR IN THE FIRST PLACE.

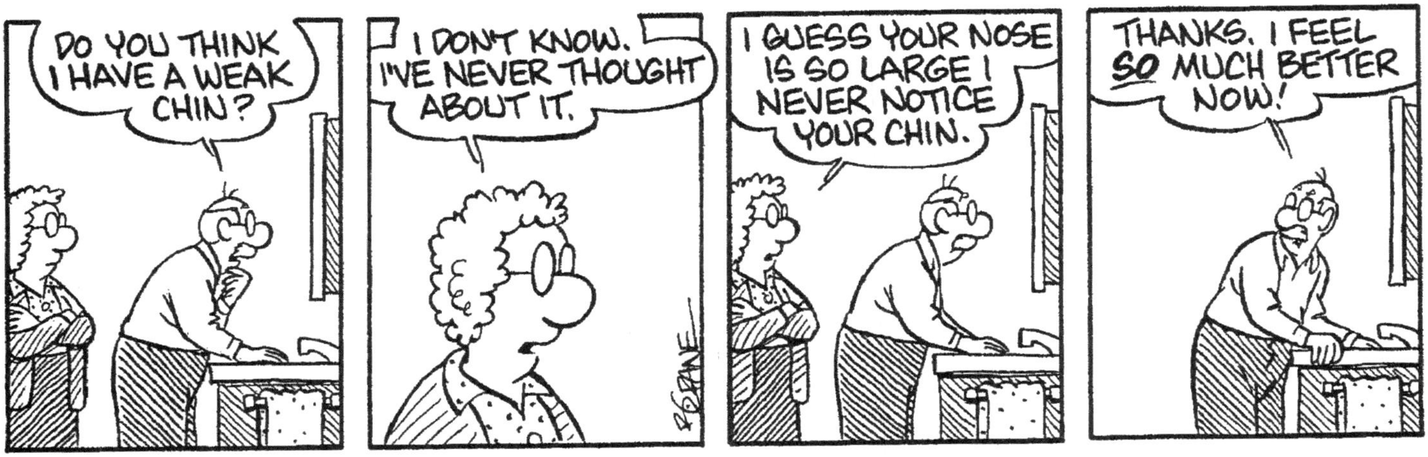
DO YOU THINK I HAVE A WEAK CHIN?
I DON'T KNOW. I'VE NEVER THOUGHT ABOUT IT.
I GUESS YOUR NOSE IS SO LARGE I NEVER NOTICE YOUR CHIN.
THANKS. I FEEL SO MUCH BETTER NOW!

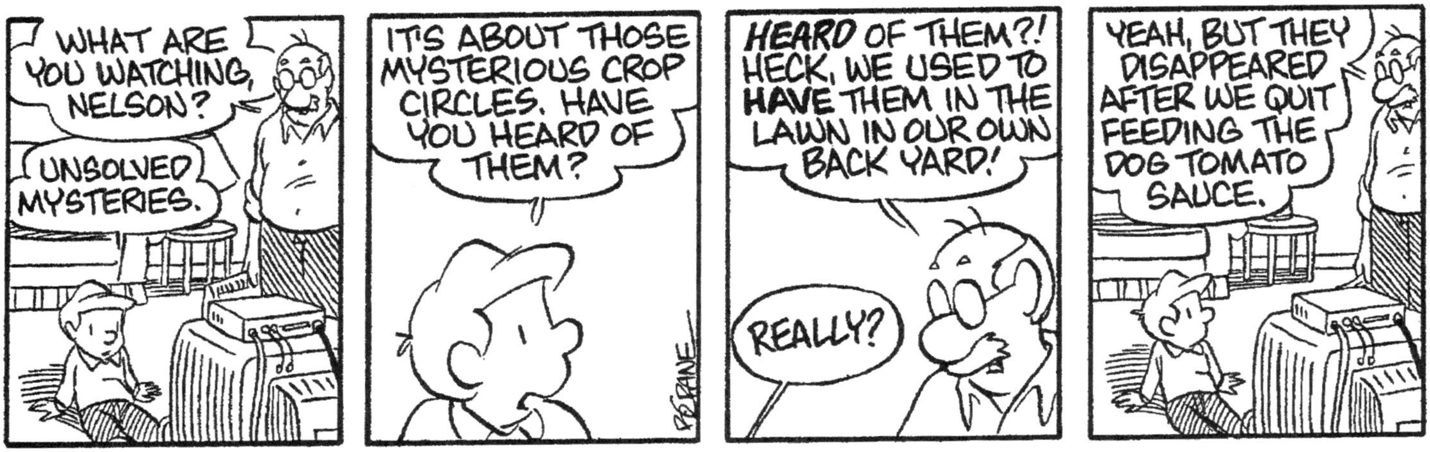
WHAT ARE YOU WATCHING, NELSON?
UNSOLVED MYSTERIES.
IT'S ABOUT THOSE MYSTERIOUS CROP CIRCLES. HAVE YOU HEARD OF THEM?
HEARD OF THEM?! HECK, WE USED TO HAVE THEM IN THE LAWN IN OUR OWN BACK YARD!
REALLY?
YEAH, BUT THEY DISAPPEARED AFTER WE QUIT FEEDING THE DOG TOMATO SAUCE.

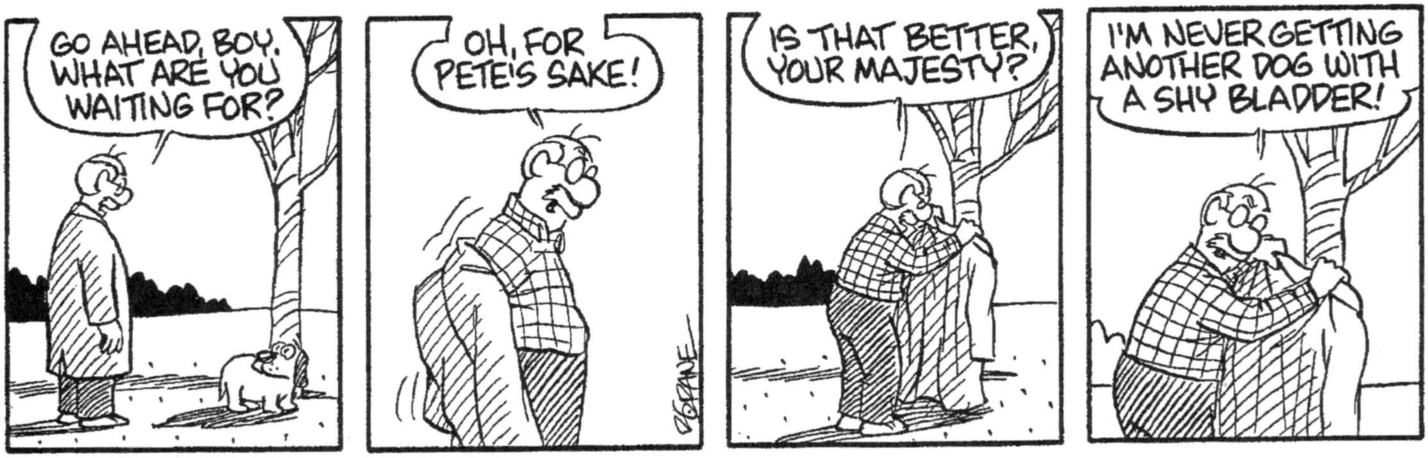
GO AHEAD, BOY. WHAT ARE YOU WAITING FOR?
OH, FOR PETE'S SAKE!
IS THAT BETTER, YOUR MAJESTY?
I'M NEVER GETTING ANOTHER DOG WITH A SHY BLADDER!

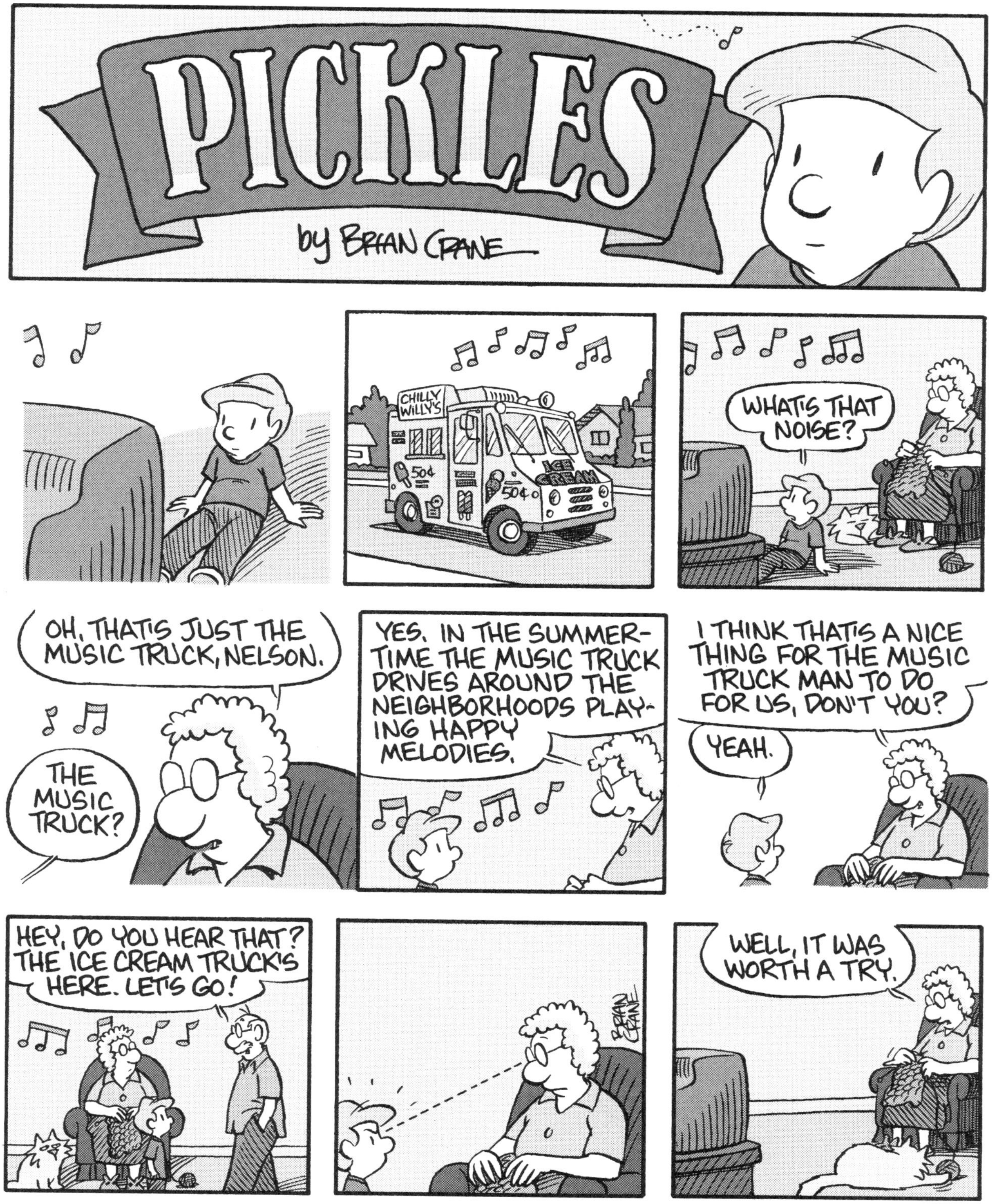
PICKLES
by BRIAN CRANE
CHILLY WILLY'S
50¢
ICE CREAM
50¢
WHAT'S THAT NOISE?
OH, THAT'S JUST THE MUSIC TRUCK, NELSON.
THE MUSIC TRUCK?
YES. IN THE SUMMER-TIME THE MUSIC TRUCK DRIVES AROUND THE NEIGHBORHOODS PLAY-ING HAPPY MELODIES.
I THINK THAT'S A NICE THING FOR THE MUSIC TRUCK MAN TO DO FOR US, DON'T YOU?
YEAH.
HEY, DO YOU HEAR THAT? THE ICE CREAM TRUCK'S HERE. LET'S GO!
BRIAN CRANE
WELL, IT WAS WORTH A TRY.

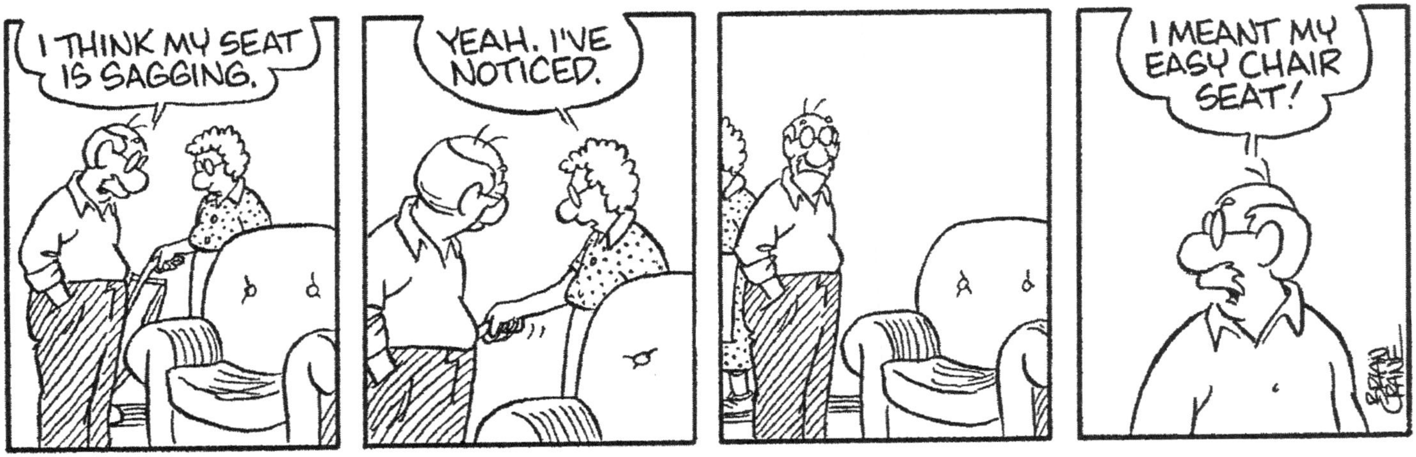
I THINK MY SEAT IS SAGGING.
YEAH. I'VE NOTICED.
I MEANT MY EASY CHAIR SEAT!

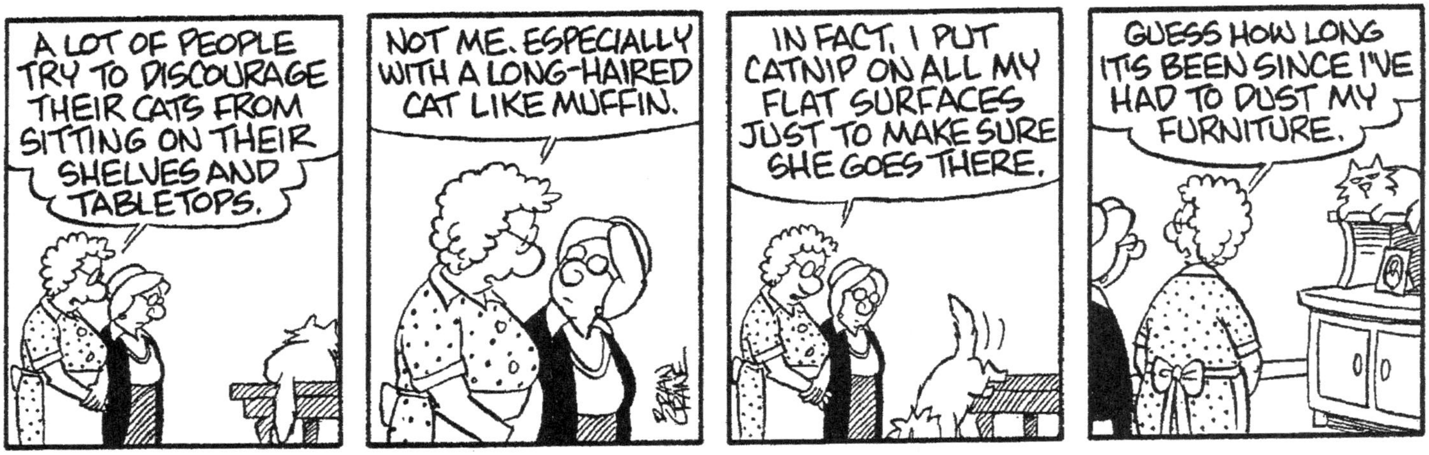
A LOT OF PEOPLE TRY TO DISCOURAGE THEIR CATS FROM SITTING ON THEIR SHELVES AND TABLETOPS.
NOT ME. ESPECIALLY WITH A LONG-HAIRED CAT LIKE MUFFIN.
IN FACT, I PUT CATNIP ON ALL MY FLAT SURFACES JUST TO MAKE SURE SHE GOES THERE.
GUESS HOW LONG IT'S BEEN SINCE I'VE HAD TO DUST MY FURNITURE.

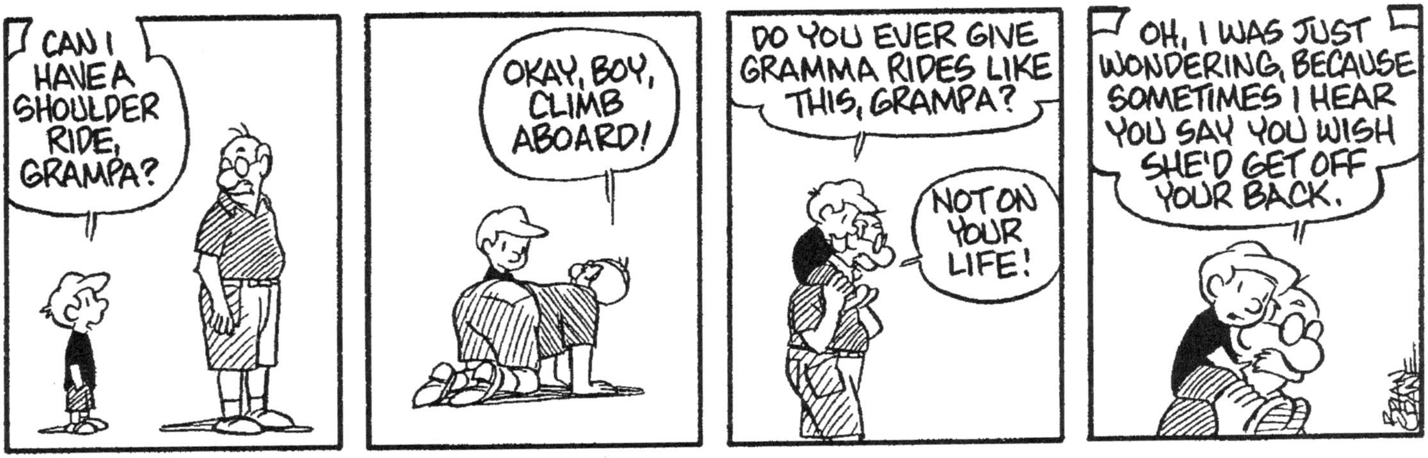
CAN I HAVE A SHOULDER RIDE, GRAMPA?
OKAY, BOY, CLIMB ABOARD!
DO YOU EVER GIVE GRAMMA RIDES LIKE THIS, GRAMPA?
NOT ON YOUR LIFE!
OH, I WAS JUST WONDERING, BECAUSE SOMETIMES I HEAR YOU SAY YOU WISH SHE'D GET OFF YOUR BACK.

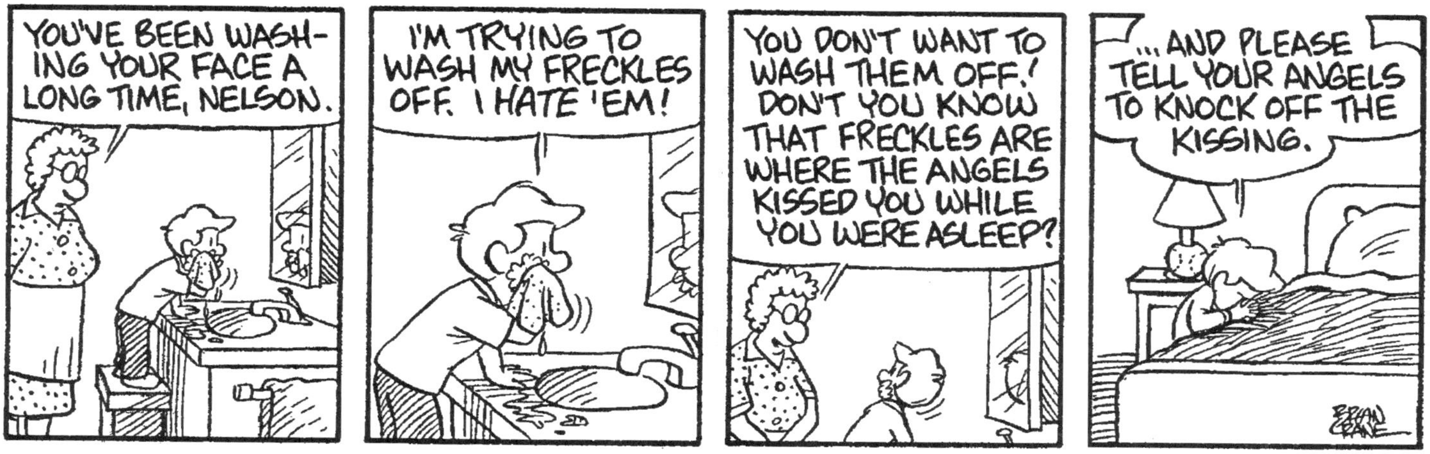
YOU'VE BEEN WASH-ING YOUR FACE A LONG TIME, NELSON.
I'M TRYING TO WASH MY FRECKLES OFF. I HATE 'EM!
YOU DON'T WANT TO WASH THEM OFF! DON'T YOU KNOW THAT FRECKLES ARE WHERE THE ANGELS KISSED YOU WHILE YOU WERE ASLEEP?
...AND PLEASE TELL YOUR ANGELS TO KNOCK OFF THE KISSING.

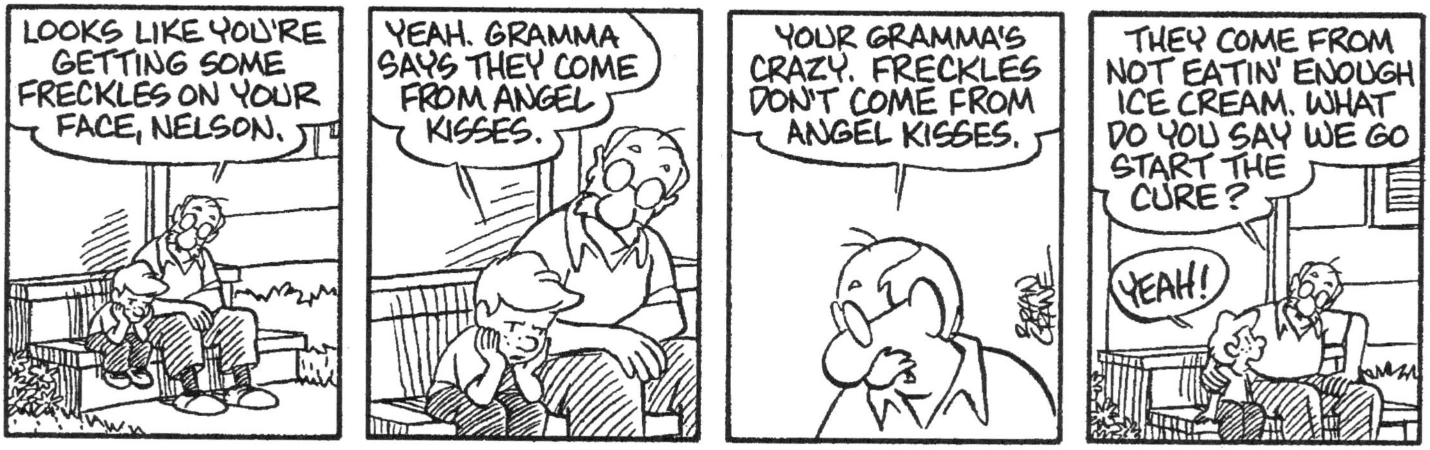
LOOKS LIKE YOU'RE GETTING SOME FRECKLES ON YOUR FACE, NELSON.
YEAH. GRAMMA SAYS THEY COME FROM ANGEL KISSES.
YOUR GRAMMA'S CRAZY. FRECKLES DON'T COME FROM ANGEL KISSES.
THEY COME FROM NOT EATIN' ENOUGH ICE CREAM. WHAT DO YOU SAY WE GO START THE CURE?
YEAH!

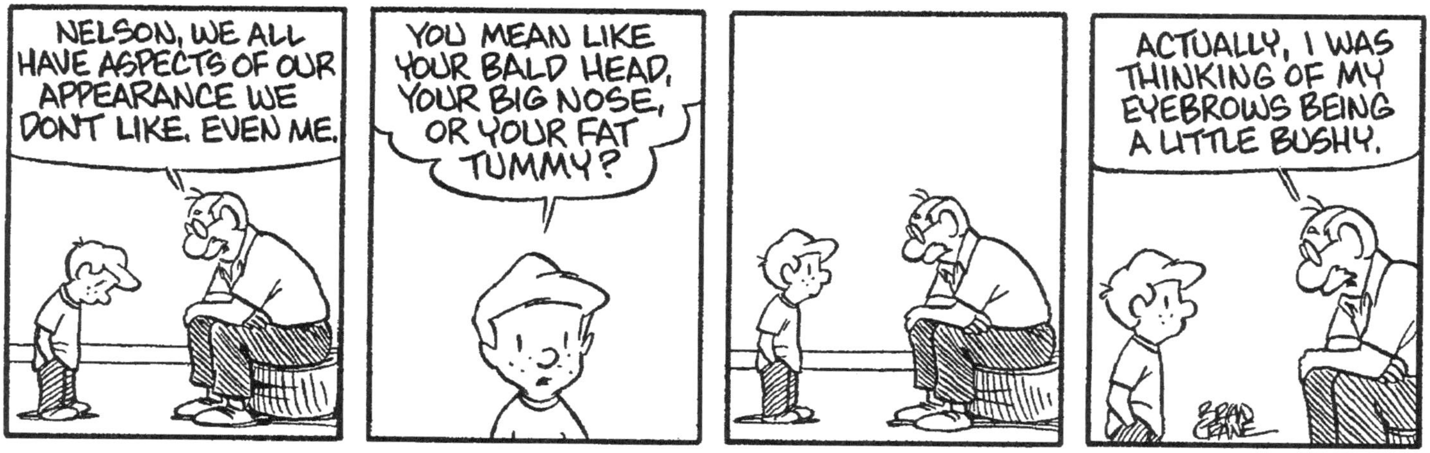
NELSON, WE ALL HAVE ASPECTS OF OUR APPEARANCE WE DON'T LIKE. EVEN ME.
YOU MEAN LIKE YOUR BALD HEAD, YOUR BIG NOSE, OR YOUR FAT TUMMY?
ACTUALLY, I WAS THINKING OF MY EYEBROWS BEING A LITTLE BUSHY.

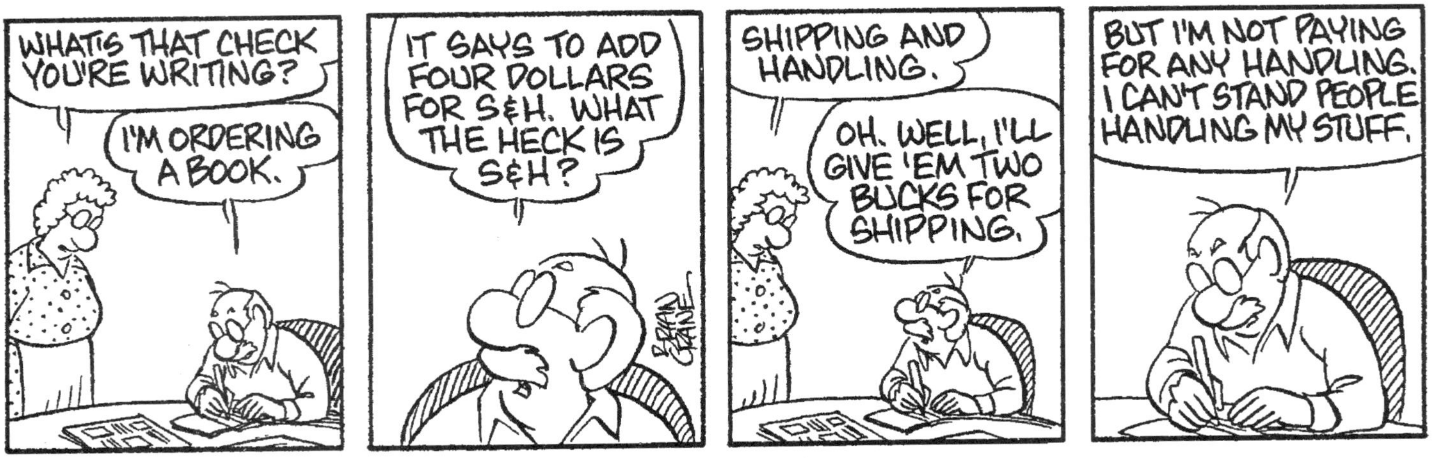
WHAT'S THAT CHECK YOU'RE WRITING?
I'M ORDERING A BOOK.
IT SAYS TO ADD FOUR DOLLARS FOR S&H. WHAT THE HECK IS S&H?
SHIPPING AND HANDLING.
OH. WELL, I'LL GIVE 'EM TWO BUCKS FOR SHIPPING.
BUT I'M NOT PAYING FOR ANY HANDLING. I CAN'T STAND PEOPLE HANDLING MY STUFF.

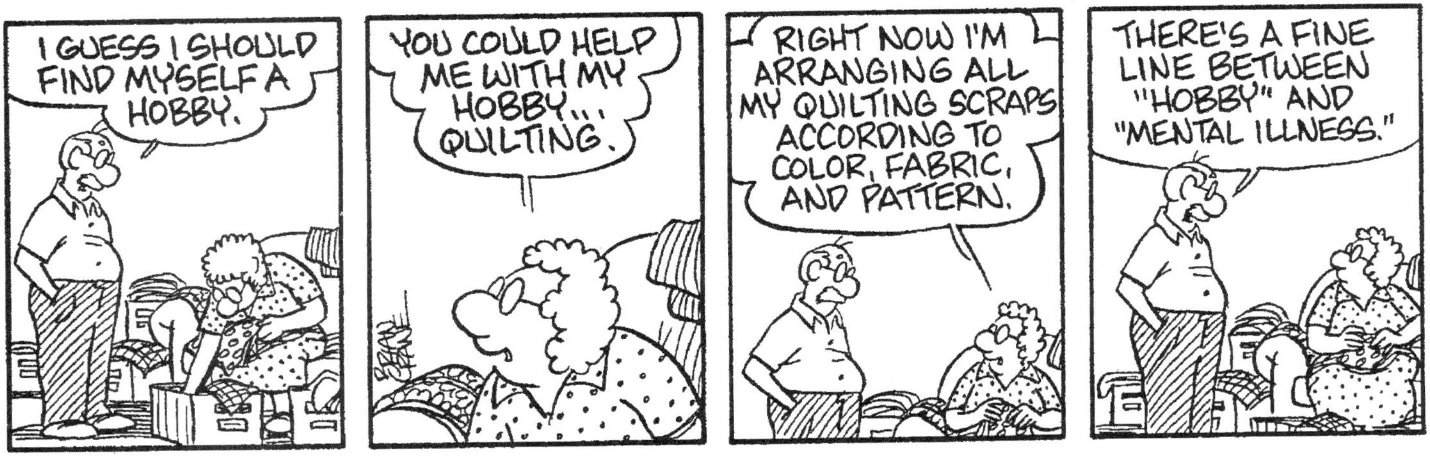
I GUESS I SHOULD FIND MYSELF A HOBBY.
YOU COULD HELP ME WITH MY HOBBY... QUILTING.
RIGHT NOW I'M ARRANGING ALL MY QUILTING SCRAPS ACCORDING TO COLOR, FABRIC, AND PATTERN.
THERE'S A FINE LINE BETWEEN "HOBBY" AND "MENTAL ILLNESS."

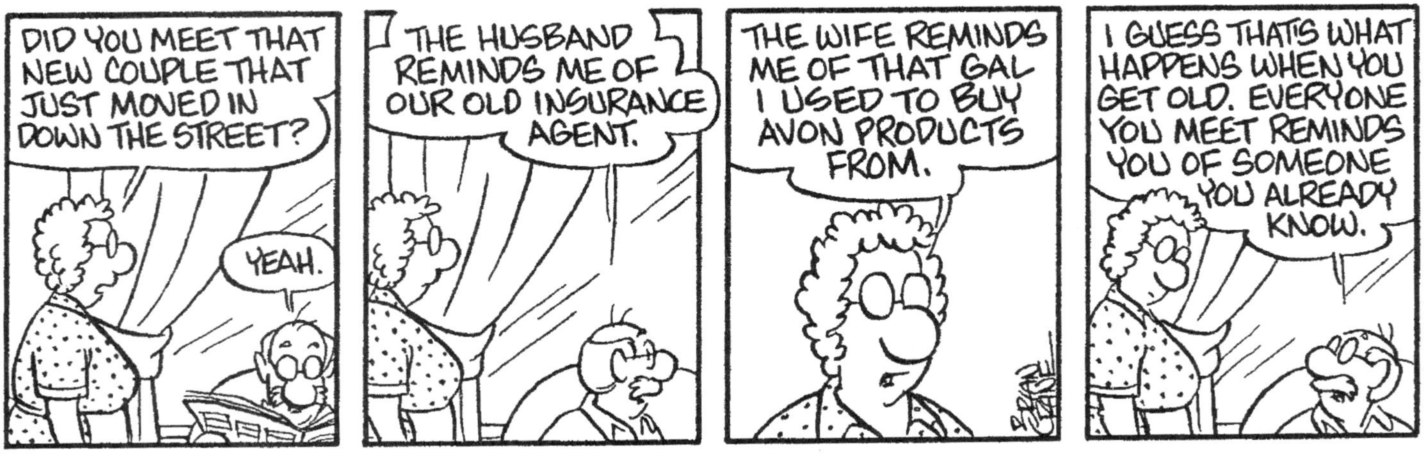
DID YOU MEET THAT NEW COUPLE THAT JUST MOVED IN DOWN THE STREET?
YEAH.
THE HUSBAND REMINDS ME OF OUR OLD INSURANCE AGENT.
THE WIFE REMINDS ME OF THAT GAL I USED TO BUY AVON PRODUCTS FROM.
I GUESS THAT'S WHAT HAPPENS WHEN YOU GET OLD. EVERYONE YOU MEET REMINDS YOU OF SOMEONE YOU ALREADY KNOW.